# TERRORISM

## CONCEPTS IN COMMUNICATION INFORMATICS & LIBRARIANSHIP (CICIL)

General Editor: **S.P. AGRAWAL**

| | | |
|---|---|---|
| CICIL-1 | Development of Library Services in India: Social Science Information **S.P. Agrawal** | Rs. 150 $ 30 |
| CICIL-2 | Development of Documentation in India: Social Science Information **S.P. Agrawal** | Rs. 250 $ 50 |
| CICIL-3 | UNESCO and Social Sciences: Retrospect and Prospect **S.P. Agrawal and J.C. Aggarwal** | Rs. 200 $ 40 |
| CICIL-4 | INDIANA: A Bibliography of Bibliographical Sources **M.K. Jain** | Rs. 200 $ 40 |
| CICIL-5 | Dimensions of Library and Information Science: Papers contributed in honour of the 61st birthday celebrations of Prof. P.N. Kaula **V. Venkatappaiah** (Ed.) | (in press) |
| CICIL-6 | Book Numbers: Some Indian Methods **M.P. Satija and S.P. Agrawal** | (in press) |
| CICIL-7 | National Policy for University Libraries in India: Problems and Perspectives **N.B. Inamdar and L.S. Ramaiah** | Rs. 250 $ 50 |
| CICIL-8 | Media Utilisation for the Development of Women and Children **B.S. Thakur** and **Binod C. Agrawal** | Rs. 150 $ 30 |
| CICIL-9 | Terrorism: An Annotated Bibliography **Susheela Bhan** | Rs. 275 $ 55 |
| CICIL-10 | Transnational Library Relations: The Indo-American Experience **M.B. Konnur** | (in press) |
| CICIL-11 | Geography of Marketing and Commercial Activities in India (Documentation on Research Information) **R.S. Dixit** | (in press) |
| CICIL-12 | Information India 1988: Global View **S.P. Agrawal and J.C. Aggarwal** | Rs. 200 $ 40 |

*ncepts in Communication*
*ormatics & Librarianship-9*

*neral Editor:* **S.P. Agrawal**

# TERRORISM

## An Annotated Bibliography

*Research Team*

**Susheela Bhan**

**Ramanand Malaviya** **Chand Mohan**

**Sudhir Mattoo** **C. Rajyalakshmi**

**CONCEPT PUBLISHING COMPANY, NEW DELHI-110059**

ISBN 81-7022-256-7

First Published 1989



*Published by*
Ashok Kumar Mittal
Concept Publishing Company
A/15-16, Commercial Block, Mohan Garden
NEW DELHI - 110059 (India)

*Lasertypeset by*
Microtech Advance Printing Systems (Pvt.) Ltd.
H-13, Bali Nagar
NEW DELHI - 110015 (India)

*Printed by*
A.P. Offset
1/11787, Panchsheel Garden
Naveen Shahadra
DELHI-110032

## General Editors Introduction

Various volumes in the series *Concepts In Communication, Informatics and Librarianship*, placed in the hands of the reader, have been received well. The response has been a matter of deep satisfaction to me personally. In all humility, we have assumed that the series have filled a long felt need.

The significance of the present volume, however, is much greater for reasons which do not merit reiteration here. Violence has plagued mankind since the times of Abel and Cains and it is difficult to visualize an age ever without it. Over centuries, it has extended in dimensions of men and means, space and time, form and intensity; and violence indulged in for ill-conceived objectives or perceived sometimes as 'noble' goals leads to terrorism. Terrorism, however, symbolizes an unparalled hold of the *shadripu* (the six enemies) over its perpetrators. Having emerged as one of the most effective and brutal forms of violence, easy availability of sophisticated gadgets and lethal weaponary has rendered it more gruesome than ever. The point to note is that in respect of terrorism it is not a mere question of control but that of total elimination.

What is it that will help us to understand the complex issues the terrorist and the victim of the terrorist is faced with? What resources and what communication and educational processes in particular need to be pressed into service to fight terrorism? The pages that follow constitute a guide to world literature on terrorism. The survey should indicate the trends, the gaps and the possibilities. It should lead to a more concerted search and research into issues that are as relevant as they are crucial to the contemporary situation.

**– S.P. AGRAWAL**

# CONTENTS

# Preface

The idea of preparing a bibliography on Terrorism emerged in pursuance of the decision taken by IPRA to take up a research project on the Impact of Ethnic Conflict on Children and Youth. One of the requirements for planning the study was a quick survey of research available in the area. As we went about conducting such a survey we found that this exercise could be anything but a quick one because the involvement of youth in various forms of violence and conflict was far greater than we had imagined. Terrorism, among others, we found, was a phenomenon of the youth. We, therefore, decided to begin with a comprehensive bibliography on the subject.

This bibliography has been prepared in two parts. The first part contains around 800 titles. Abstracts already available have been taken from different secondary sources and these are mentioned in the abbreviated form at the end of each abstract. We prepared abstracts for only those titles which were not available from any source. The abbreviations of the secondary sources used in the bibliography are as follows:

1. BRD - Book Review Digest
2. CIS - Congressional Information Service
3. IPSA - International Political Science Abstract
4. N & G - Norton, Augustus R. and Greenberg, Martin H. – International Terrorism: - An Annotated Bibliography and Research Guide. Westview, 1979.
5. PAISB - Public Affairs Information Service Bulletin

6. PRAJ:PRID - Peace Research Abstracts Journal Dundas, Ontario, Canada.
7. PSA - Police Science Abstracts.
8. RW - Robert Woito - To End War – A New Approach to International Conflict. New York, Pilgrim Press, 1982.
9. SAJ - Sociological Abstracts Journal.
10. T - Terrorism: An International Journal

Abstracts which do not carry any mention of the source have been prepared by the IPRA team.

The second part of the bibliography contains 31 titles which were prepared belatedly and included in the volume as an addenda to the first part. Part III which contains 1932 titles gives references only. The titles were not available in any of the libraries in Delhi and we could not therefore prepare abstracts for these. Part four of the bibliography lists forthcoming publications numbering thirty three.

Arrangement in the bibliography is alphabetical by the surname of the author. Entries relate to Books, Journals, Newspapers, Dissertations and other Documents. Certain minimum changes were made in the format of the titles of the book entries to bring about uniformity. However, such uniformity became impractical in case of Journals and Newspaper entries for reasons beyond our control. We hope the readers will bear with us for this and many other limitations of which we are painfully aware.

We visited numerous libraries to compile this work. It is difficult to name all these. However, we would like to acknowledge the assistance rendered by the staff of the libraries at Indian Council of Social Science Research, Delhi University, Jawaharlal Nehru University, Sapru House, American Centre, Indian Institute of Public Administration, Parliament, India International Centre and the Indian Society for International Law. We are specially indebted to Mr. S.P. Agrawal and Miss N. Ruprail of NASSDOC, ICSSR and Miss Heera Kapasi of the American Centre Library for going out of their way to help our research team.

Considering the unprecedented growth in terrorist activities all

over and in our own country in particular, the present volume could be of immense value to scholars who are trying to understand the menace of terrorism and to find ways of fighting it. Hopefully, the volume will also indicate the gaps in research that need to be filled up on a priority basis.

*Ist February 1989* SUSHEELA BHAN

# PART — I

# ABSTRACTS

0001 Adam, Sunil. How not to Tackle Terrorists. *Hindustan Times,* (Delhi), 7 December 1986.

The author advises the Central Government, the Punjab Government and the Hindus not to overreact to the 'Khuda Carnage'. Playing into the hands of the extremists will result in the alienation of minorities and polarisation of population. Author denounces the behaviour of political elite, especially opposition parties and warns the Government that if it does not provide the necessary support to Barnala Government, moderate elements may use militant postures.

0002 Aggarwala, Narinder; Fenello, Michael J. and Fitzgerald, General F. Air Hijacking, An International Perspective. *International Conciliation*, Number 585, November 1971, pp.7-27.

Includes treatments of political aspects of hijacking, and technical prevention and legal suppression of hijacking. An appendix listing the ratification states of the Tokyo, Hague, and Montreal Conventions is now some-what dated; however, the overview of attempts to control hijacking through treaty making is useful still.

(N&G)

0003 Alexander, Yonah and Freedom, Lawrance Zelic. (Eds.). *Perspectives on Terrorism*. Delhi, Hindustan Publishing Corporation, 1985.

This work contains a collection of papers on a diverse range of terrorist activities ranging from Skyjackings of the 1960's and 1970's to hostage taking, to bombings and assaults and to the implied and explicit dangers in the future technology and nuclear weapons.

0004 Alexander, Yonah and Cline, Ray S. *Terrorism the Soviet Connection.* New York, Crane Russak, 1984.

This book examines the involvement of USSR in much of world's contemporary terrorism. An appendix with selected PLO documents found in Lebanon in June 1982, has been included to provide evidence of USSR involvement with PLO

0005 Alexander, Yonah. (Ed.). *International Terrorism : National, Regional and Global Perspectives*. New York, Praeger Publishers, 1976.

A useful collection of regionally oriented contributions. A 40 page bibliography has been provided, but it has been superseded by the more current bibliography in Alexander and Finger (1977).

(N&G)

0006 Alexander, Yonah. (Ed.). *International Terrorism*. New York, Praeger, 1976.

A collection of 11 essays intended as an overview of the topic. Individual essays deal with Canadian, U.S., British and Soviet perspectives on and policy toward, terrorists; experience with terrorism in Latin America, Northern Ireland and Palestine; prospects for terrorism in southern Africa. The final essay, entitled "International Terrorism and the United Nations", also discusses actions of the OAS and the International Civil Aviation Organization, and concludes with an ominous warning concerning prevention of nuclear blackmail.

(PRAJ: PRID)

0007 Alexander, Yonah and Gleason, J.M. *Behavioral and Quantitative Perspectives on Terrorism*. New York, Pergamon Press, 1981.

This compilation of original research integrates for the first time psychological and statistical analyses of terrorism. By examining such aspects as the psychodynamics of terrorist organizations, psychological profiles of individual actors, and the diffusion of international terrorist incidents, the authors succeed in outlining the future directions of research into the scope and causes of the terrorist threat. The authors draw conclusions from case studies that include Northern Ireland and the Third World, and conclude with an assessment of future terrorist activities.

(PRAJ: PRID)

0008 Alexander, Yonah; Carlton, David and Wilkinson, Paul. *Terrorism: Theory and Practice*. Boulder, Colo, Westview Press, 1979.

Includes contributions by a number of specialists treating terrorist movements in general, Northern Ireland, the media and terrorism, hostage negotiations, counter—terror options, the sanctioning of terrorism, and a prospectus on the future of "Political substate violence." The contributors are well-known in the field and include Robert A. Friedlander, Abraham Miller et. al., in addition to the editors.

(N&G)

0009 Alexander, Yonah and Finger, Seymour M. (Eds.) *Terrorism : Interdisciplinary Perspectives*. New York, The John Jay Press, 1977.

Clearly, one of the very best edited works on the subject. Terrorism is treated from historical, political, strategic, legal, communications and psychological perspectives.

The work is enhanced by a 50 page bibliography which includes both scholarly and journalistic references. Many of the articles were first presented at a conference sponsored by the Ralph Bunche Institute of the United Nations in June 1976.

(N&G)

0010 Alexander, Yonah and O'Day, Alan. *Terrorism in Ireland*. New York, St. Martin's Press, 1984.

The volume contains thirteen essays. The essays attempt to look at certain selected aspects of Irish terrorism.

The first three essays assess some of the broader and international dimensions of Irish terrorism. The four case studies in the second part of the volume deal with some specific aspects of terrorist problems; the role of women, the psychological make-up of terrorists, political assassination, and a historical consideration of the attitudes of Catholic Church.

The third section looks at the problem of political communication and terrorism.

The final section deals with the future of terrorism in Northern Ireland. The general observation is that IRA terrorism will continue in the foreseeable future.

0011 Alexander Yonah and Ebinger, Charles K. (Eds.). *Political Terrorism and Energy: The Threat and Response*. New York, Praeger, 1982.

The contributors to this volume have discussed the extreme vulnerability to sabotage of U.S.A.'s basic industrial infrastructures by terrorists using highly sophisticated conventional technology and/or the threatened use of the ultimate weapon: nuclear terrorism, resulting in crippling of the domestic economy. Contributors have also suggested and recommended what policy U.S. should adopt on terrorism.

0012 Alexander, Yonah and Myers, Kenneth A (Eds.). *Terrorism in Europe*. London, Croomhelm Ltd, 1982.

Contributors to this volume have examined terrorist and anarchist movements of late nineteenth century Europe from historical perspectives along with the political and legal aspects of modern terrorism with selected case studies of contemporary terrorist movements.

0013 Alexander, Yonah; Brousse, Marjorie Ann and Naves, Allan S. (Eds). *Control of Terrorism: International Documents*. New York, Crane, Russak and Company, 1979.

This volume deals with the acts of violence employed by subnational groups - ethnic, religious and national.

The documents in this volume include major treaties from early twentieth century on terrorism, the international and regional treaties currently in force and resolutions of two major international governmental organisations.

0014 Alexander, Yonah and Kilmarx, Robert A. (Eds.). *Political Terrorism and Business : The Threat and Response*. New York, Praeger, 1979.

This book is a collection of twenty essays which examine terrorist movements in the United States and worldwide; the threat these pose to businesses and to their executives; response to the threat by governments and judiciaries, including international cooperations, inside and outside the United Nations; the response by corporations; the medical and psychological problems facing a hostage; police techniques, including hostage negotiations and rescue; and possible technological developments affecting both the terrorist threat and counter—measures against it.

(BRD)

0015 Alexander, Yonah and Levine, Herbert M. Prepare for the Next Entabbe. *Chitty's Law Journal*, Volume 25, 1977, pp. 240-242.

The authors see a future of yet more explosions, hijackings and assassina-

tions. Unless the imperative for international cooperation against terrorism is met, the governments and people of the world "will be the hostage of global blackmailers forever."

(N&G)

0016 Alexander, Yonah. Some Perspectives on International Terrorism. *International Problems*, Volume 114, Numbers 3-4, 1975, pp. 24-29.

Contemporary terrorism is executed by "sub-national groups" who have contempt for legal and moral norms. Justification for their violent needs rests on the "cause". The magnitude and brutality of modern terrosim has increased due to sanctification of violence, availability of weapons, potential accessibility to nuclear and biological weapons, etc., swift communication, transportation and interconnection among them across national borders. The global situation will menace the "survival of civilization". Responses to terrorism vary from sanctification to very strong counter-forces. It is obvious that society as a whole has not taken maximum concerted action against it. To be most effective, this will have to be enforced with international consensus.

(PRAJ: PRID)

0017 Alexander, Yonah. Terrorism, the Media and the Police. *Journal of International Affairs*, Volume 32, Spring-Summer 1978, pp. 101-113.

Alexander argues that terrorism is violence for effect and that terrorists seek to exploit the symbolism of their act through the attention and recognition available via the mass media. Furthermore, the publicity given to terror violence incites imitation, "the exportation of violent techniques." He is concerned that the symbiotic relationship between terrorist and newsman produces the impression of a sympathetic media and thus encourages terrorism. He calls for further study of this problem and provides worthwhile bibliographic data on the preliminary study of the issue. Finally, he calls for a solution to the problem which will not involve surrendering media prerogatives.

(N&G)

0018 Alexander, Yonah (Suny-Oneonta). Communications Aspects of International Terrorism. *International Studies Association*. Toronto, Ont., February 25-29, 1976.

"This paper deals with the mass media coverage of international terrorism and its consequences, as well as the strategic significance of communications between domestic and foreign terror groups."

The study is based on more than 1000 terrorist incidents as reported in 150 newspapers. Sometimes terrorists' top aim is not to injure anyone, but to draw world attention. The mass media provide this -- and this promotes more terrorism. Examples are Patricia Hearst and the SLA, and even more the PLO. The press tends to romanticise, glorify, even sanctify "the freedom fighter". The techniques publicized are then imitated elsewhere. If the media could stop reporting terrorist incidents, this might break the vicious circle; but what about freedom of the press? Voluntary constraints in the media would be best. There exists now a transnational network of terrorists' collaboration; even diverging ideologies cooperate, at least in maintaining a weapons supply. A resolution by the American Society of Criminology calls for national legislation to prevent and punish terrorism, for barring the use of technology by terrorists, and for cooperation among all states on these matters.

(PRAJ: PRID)

0019 Almond, Harry H., Jr. The Legal Regulation of International Terrorism. *Conflict*, Volume 3, Numbers 2-3, 1981, pp. 143-165.

The legal regulation of international terrorism derives from the shared expectations of states about the permissible uses of violence for attaining legitimate "Political" aims. Effective regulation depends upon the identification that characterizes when violence is permissible, i.e., - "Criminal" or "illegal" - and is enforceable when there are shared commitments to ensure that those who conduct impermissibe violence will be prosecuted, and granted no asylum, or extradited. Because justification of terrorism is actualized in asylum, the identification of what acts constitute impermissible violence is primarily a matter in which there must be continuing accommodation among the differing and competing policies of states as to their political goals.

(IPSA)

0020 Al-Rayyes, Riad and Nahas, Dunia. *Guerrillas for Palestine.* New York, St. Martin's Press, 1976.

A balanced and concise primer on the Fedayeen. Of particular note are sections dealing with the political apparatus within the PLO (and especially summaries of each National Assembly session through the 12th of 1974); Fedayeen relations with the Arab states and the USSR and PRC, and profiles of the principal leaders. On the negative side the book lacks any analysis of Fedayeen ideological positioning, or any treatment of terrorism per se.

(N&G)

0021 Amann, Peter H. The Black Legion. *Progressive*, Volume 43, Number 12, December 1979, p. 63.

Seeks information on and the papers of Ben Allen, an investigator for the La Follette Subcommittee in 1936-1937, and left wing researcher on U.S. corporate control, for a study of the Black Legion, a terrorist offshoot of the Ku Klux Klan in the 1930s.

(PRAJ: PRID)

0022 Amos, John W., II; Stolfi, Russel H.S. Controlling International Terrorism: Alternatives Palatable and Unpalatable. *Annals of the American Academy of Political and Social Science*, Volume 463, September 1982, pp. 69-83.

Operating from the premise that the literature on the control of international terrorism is inadequate, the authors systematically develop general alternatives for mastering international terrorism. Using a perspective terrorist incident as the vehicle for considering the general strategies to be followed within the framework of ongoing international terrorism, the authors analyze the incident as a historical event. As such, the event can be set within a given historical context and examined comprehensively from the viewpoint of alternative possible beginnings, strategies to be followed and tactics to be effected within the framework of the incident itself, and systematic consideration of a range of possible outcomes. The authors consider that adequate control must include storages encompassing at least factors of politics, law enforcement, propaganda, armed military force, psychology and time.

(IPSA)

0023 Amos, John W., II. Terrorism in the Middle East: The Diffusion of Violence. bibl *In Middle East Annual*. 1984, pp. 149-62, 85.

Background and changing nature of Near East violence in the past decade.

(PAISB)

0024 Anand, V.K. Lt. Col. (Retd.). *Terrorism and Security*. New Delhi, Deep and Deep Publication, 1984.

This work has been divided mainly in two parts, one dealing with the acts of terrorism and the second with survival techniques. Terrorist targets are not only individuals and property but the very power structure and the entire governing system which they perceive as the fountain head of all ills - real or imaginary. Only individuals and groups capable of playing a constructive role can help combat terrorism.

0025 Anand, V.K. Lt. Col. (Retd.). Tackling the Menace of Booby Traps. *Times of India*, (Delhi), 17 June 1985.

The author explains the design, working and tackling of UXBs (unexploded bombs) for public information.

0026 Anon. Around the World. *Peking Review*, Volume 19, Number 31, July 30, 1976, p. 16.

Chinese U.N. representative Lai Ya-li has condemned both the "adventurist acts of terrorism, such as assassination, kidnaping and hijacking of aircraft" exemplified by the hijacking of the French aircraft to Uganda, and also the Israeli attack on the Entabbe airport which terminated the hijacking by "...armed aggression against a sovereign state".

(PRAJ: PRID)

0027 Anon. International Terrorism. *U.N. Monthly Chronicle*, Volume 9, Number 9, October 1972. (Pages in brackets after name of country)

At the September meeting of the U.N. General Assembly, several countries raised the question of international terrorist in their speeches, some countries took the stand that a complete ban on such terrorism would handicap the various freedom movements who, fighting in legitimate causes, had no other weapon. However, most countries condemned all forms of international terrorism. Countries making comments on the subject were : Brazil (68); USA (71); Dominican Republic (76); Denmark (77); France (82); Haiti (85); Japan (86); U.K. (88); Australia (89); Canada (96); Greece (102); New Zealand (103); Finland (104); South Africa (106) (who protested about the terrorist campaigns waged by Africans); Iran (108); Venezuela (109); Bahrain (111).

(PRAJ: PRID)

0028 Anon. Prevention of International Terrorism. *U.N. Monthly Chronicle*, Volume 9, Number 9, October 1972, pp. 44-50.

The Secretary-General submitted an item on measures to prevent terrorism. Final wording was, "Measures to prevent international terrorism which endangers or takes innocent lives or jeopardizes fundamental freedoms, and study of the underlying causes of those forms of terrorism and acts of violence which lie in misery, frustration, grievance and despair which cause some people to sacrifice human lives, including their own, in an attempt to effect radical changes." This item was accepted as part of the agenda. Lists of countries voting for and against its inclusion on the agenda are given on pages 44 and 45.

(PRAJ: PRID)

0029 Anon. A Pig for Terrorists. *New Scientist*, Volume 68, December 11, 1975, pp. 642.

GKN Sankey has designed an armored vehicle, the AT 105, expressly to combat terrorists, and expects to sell substantial numbers worldwide. Technical details are given. Improvements over its predecessor, the AT 104, resulted directly from experience in Northern Ireland.

(PRAJ: PRID)

0030 Anon. Terrorism. *U.N. Chronicle*, July 1979, p. 74.

The Ad Hoc Committee on International Terrorism called for closer co-operation among States and for incorporation into appropriate bilateral treaties of special clauses providing for the prosecution or extradition of international terrorists. Member States were urged to refrain from organizing, instigating, or assisting in acts of civil strife or terrorist acts in another State or acquiescing in organized activities within its territory directed towards another State.

(PRAJ: PRID)

0031 Anon. Terrorism. *U.N. Monthly Chronicle*, Volume 10, Number 10, November 1972. (Pages as noted after names of countries).

Almost every country participating in the General Debate of the 27th Session of the United Nations General Assembly had a comment to make about terrorism. Countries which were fighting for independence or closely allied to such countries on the whole wanted a definition of terrorism before taking a stand. Acts of violence were the only route open to Palestine and African guerrillas. These were not acts of terrorism, but acts of patriotism. The same acts were denounced by other countries as outright terrorism. Portugal condemned such acts. Niagara (44) and the Syrian Arab Republic (96) defended such acts. Other speakers were: Guatemala (46), Jamaica (47), Barbados (49), Costa Rica (50), Guinea (51), Mexico (55), Chile (55), Liberia (59), China (60), Colombia (64),Yugoslavia (66), Chad (68), Nicaragua (72), Austria (74), Belgium (75), Peru (76), Luxembourg (78), Madagascar (80), Sudan (84), Morocco (85), Niger (86), Phillipines (97), Libyan Arab Republic (103), Afghanistan (104), Fiji (107), Sierra Leone (109), Malta (112), Paraguay (115), Sweden (117), Cuba (120), Ethiopia (122), Somalia (123).

(PRAJ: PRID)

0032 Anon. Technology and Terrorism. *World Issue*, June - July 1977, pp. 15, 17, 18.

Technological advancement has made it possible throughout history for a man or a group to control many others. Once it was the spear. Today it might be the atomic bomb. But this control can be established by disruption, and disruption may occur in transportation, communication, water or energy supplies, etc. The important question, as the power of terrorists increases, is how to provide technical security at politically acceptable levels. Methods used against terrorist groups violate civil liberties. "We can expect an accelerating struggle between those determined to preserve human rights, freedom and dignity and those dedicated to the increasingly difficult task of protecting the public". The roots of terrorism are not all madness and criminality. Nor is it a national problem. Where injustices exist, there will be terrorism. Any move to increase repressive government results in a countermove.

"A hope, if any exists, lies in our ability and resolve not to overreact - and this is difficult - to terrorist threats".

(PRAJ: PRID)

0033 Anon. 35 Member Group Established to Draft Convention Against Taking Hostages. *U.N. Monthly Chronicle*, January 1977, p. 81.

On December 15 the General Assembly decided to establish an Ad Hoc Committee of 35-members to draft at the earliest possible date an international convention against the taking of hostages. The resolution in draft form was submitted by the Federal Republic of Germany. At the same session the Assembly expressed deep concern over increasing acts of international terrorism which "endanger or take innocent human lives or jeopardize fundamental freedoms." The Ad Hoc Committee on International Terrorism is continuing its work.

(PRAJ: PRID)

0034 Anon. Terrorism. *U.N. Monthly Chronicle*, November 1976.

During the General Debate of the U.N. General Assembly in October, there was strong support for the proposal of the Federal Republic of Germany "that the U.N. should draft a convention banning the taking of hostages internationally and making sure that the perpetrators were either extradited or brought before a court in the country in which they had been seized." All speakers agreed on the necessity of international action against terrorists. Delegates represented: Argentina (21), Austria (21), Barbados (24), Bahrain (24), Bhutan (21), Bolivia (27), Canada (22), Chile (34), Colombia (36), Congo (38), Denmark (43), Dominican Republic (43), France (49), Federal Republic of Germany (51), Honduras (57), Iceland (59), Iran (61), Israel (63), Italy (65), Jamaica (65), Mexico (78), Mozambique (79), Netherlands (81), New Zealand (86), Nicaragua (82), Norway (85), Panama (87), Paraguay (88), Philippines (89), Portugal (90), Spain (96), Sweden (100), Uganda (104), United Kingdom (108), U.S.A. (111), Uruguay (111), Zaire (114).

(PRAJ: PRID)

0035 Anon. The World Looks At ... The Hostages. *Atlas World Press Review*, January 1980, p. 15.

The world press showed no support for the Iranian taking Americans hostage, but in most cases showed an understanding of why the Iranians acted as they did. The strongest criticism came from the *Financial Times*, London, which accused Iran of "a combination of paranoia, xenophobia and megalomania". *Le Monde*, Paris, felt that the rancor of the Iranians against the Americans was justified, but not a justification for taking hostages. *Die Welt*, Hamburg, considered it possible that the action might help America to find itself again. *La Stampa*, Turin, feared that local incidents like this could threaten to involve the whole world. *Al-Ahram*, Cairo, saw the hostage incident as a "natural result of the failure of the Iranian Revolution." *Al Thawra*, Baghdad, saw the incident as helping American plans and helping the Iranian policy of enmity among Arab nations. The *Daily Nation*, Nairobi, commented that Islamic nations would consider America right and Iran wrong. *Economic Times*, Bombay, called for international legislation to suppress terrorism. The *South China Morning Post*, Hong Kong, blamed American hospitality to the Shah, and saw it as doing neither the Shah nor the U.S. any good. *Jornal do Brazil*, Rio de Janeiro, was concerned that "Iran's insanity would bring about a tragic end to the Ayatollah's regime". *Globe and Mail*, Toronto, saw the cause of the trouble in Iran as going back to the Middle Ages, but reinforced by recent actions. *Excelsior*, Mexico City, wanted no part of the quarrel.

(PRAJ: PRID)

0036 Anon. The World Looks At ... The Mountbatten Murder. *Atlas*, October 1979, pp. 20-24.

*Star*, Toronto, called the assassination one of history's most outrageous acts. *Economic Times*, Bombay, considered the tragedy that a man who brought independence to a whole subcontinent should have died in an act of terrorism. *Handelsblatt*, Dusseldorf, saw Mountbatten as the symbol of a peaceful dissolution of Britain's colonial heritage. *Hindustan Times*, New Delhi, noted the need for a compromise to end the problem. *Le Figaro*, Paris, saw the murder as being a turning point. *Daily Mirror*, London, saw the murder as uniting the civilized world against the IRA, and *Financial Times*, London, hoped that IRA sympathizers, particularly those in the U.S. would stop to think what they were doing. *Irish Times*, Dublin, called Mountbatten a world figure and felt that his murder was a concern of the whole world. *Irish Independent*, Dublin, wrote "We stand ashamed before the world, ashamed that we should be considered linked to the assassins."

(PRAJ: PRID)

0037 Anon. Entebbe Aftermath. *Atlas*, September 1976, pp. 8-9.

Kenya and South Africa reacted almost identically in praising the daring and efficiency of the Israeli raid at Entebbe to free the hostages. Switzerland (*Neul Zurcher Zeitung*, July 12) took the view that while the PLO has support, unless it detaches itself from terrorism, it will lose this. *Pravda* (Moscow, July 10) calls the raid a 'gangster action' and condemns the raid just as much as it condemns the original hijacking.

(PRAJ: PRID)

0038 Anon. Turning the Terrorist Tide. *World Press Review*, April 1982, p. 56. (From the Economist, London, Feb. 6).

In five countries where terrorist attacks had been common — Italy, Northern Ireland, Spain, West Germany and Turkey - the number of political murders has dropped sharply. Security services are much more successful in arresting terrorists. There is more efficient police work and a greater public readiness to cooperate with the police. West German police have a vast amount of information stored in their computers and coordination among police forces has improved. Most countries have organized anti-terrorist units. In Turkey, the extension of martial law by the army has cut down terrorism significantly. In Spain, people no longer distrust the police as they did in Franco's time, and are more willing to give information. Even in the Basque country, there is more cooperation. In 1981 Ireland had a death toll of 99, which was worse than in 1980, but better than in 1976, when the number reached 297. In Italy, the police success in freeing General Dozier and capturing many of the terrorists gave new impetus to the drive against terrorism. In that country, the Communist Party is strongly anti-terrorist and has provided the police with names of terrorist groups. Cooperation among police forces in Spain has helped considerably. Europe's terrorists appear to be on the defensive these days.

(PRAJ: PRID)

0039 Anon. Early Warning - Gloom Over Uslter. *Atlas*, October 1979, p. 10.

*La Stampa* (Turin) believes that the IRA has changed from being a sprawling coalition of amateurs into a tightly knit "killer Mafia". It may be increasinlgy isolated from the Catholic base, but it is much more efficient, as shown by the assassination of Lord Mountbatten. The danger inherent in this change is that conciliatory political reforms which would have influenced a Catholic-dominated

IRA will have little or no effect on the new IRA. Terrorism may not be eliminated for at least a generation.

(PRAJ: PRID)

0040 Anon. The Tupamaros : Uruguay's Urban Guerrillas. *Survival*, Volume 13, Number 3, March 1971, pp. 100-103.

A brief history of the Tupamaro organization and its activities is given. At present the Tupamaros are having difficulty gaining popular support, as the average Uruguayan is not as impoverished as many people in other South American countries. The Tupamaro movement may be seriously undermined if the coalition of leftist parties does well in the Uruguayan elections. There seems to be conflict in the Tupamaro leadership as to whether or not they should seek to overthrow the government by elections or by violence.

(PRAJ: PRID)

0041 Anon. Mid East Beat. The Mecca Incident. *Atlas World Press Review*, February 1980, p. 16.

The pro-government paper *Al-Riyad* of Saudi Arabia complains about the reporting of the takeover of Mecca's Al-Haram mosque by religious extremists. The editorial charges that the incident was used to provide "a wealth of material for lies and cheap intrigues against Islam and Muslims." In particular, it accused the Soviet paper TASS of seeking to cause confusion by not reporting the international sympathy for Saudi Arabia's suffering.

(PRAJ: PRID)

0042 Anon. World Beat. Terrorism in Soweto. *Atlas World Press Review*, January 1980, p. 10.

Terrorists attacked the Orlando police station in Soweto, South Africa, killing 2 black policemen and wounding another and a civilian. *Citizen*, Johannesburg, called the attack "Callous", and charged that the terrorists wanted to take over the country. *Die Transvaler* of the same city claimed that the terrorists were trying to break the morale of black policemen, and did not believe in democratic procedures or constitutional change. *Sunday Times* commented that the best anti-terrorist strategy was the creation of a just society. *Sunday Post* foresaw more violence if every white South African did not realize the effects on the blacks of the present society.

(PRAJ: PRID)

0043 Anon. Turkey : The Next Train? *Atlas*, June 1979, p. 49. (From Neue Zurcher Zeitung, Zurich, April 8)

Turkey is gripped by terrorism and no one can guess whether the latest murder of a prominent newspaper editor was ordered by the Right or the Left. The only outside link to Turkish terrorists is the Palestinian movement, which trained Turkish youth belonging to the People's Front. The Turkish Communist Party is banned, but survives underground. But it discourages acts of terrorism and calls for infiltration and mass demonstrations. The Turkish Workers' Party is another Leftist bloc, but it also eschews terrorism. Another Leftist party, the Turkish Worker's and Farmer's Party, follows Mao's theories and opposes the Soviet Union who, it charges, is trying to take over the Middle East. There are 2 Right-wing parties : National Action Party and the Party of National Salvation. All of the parties seem to have youth groups, but all claim to be non-violent and unarmed. Premier Ecevit's Republican People's Party, social-democratic in action, has control. Challenging it most is Turkesch's National Action Party. Turkesch advocates raising living standards, a multiparty system, strong ties to

NATO, and has strong support from the young and middle class. Last year, after two warring Moslem sects disturbed the peace, martial law was declared in 13 provinces. 109 people were killed in the clashes and left and right wing agitators were involved. Repression was very severe in Turkey at the time and there was criticism of the role of the Army. But martial law seems relatively mild now. Whenever there is rumor of a demonstration, troops move in to stop it. A few incendiary publications have been banned. Premier Ecevit travels about unguarded and there is little security control despite 900 terrorist victims in the last year.

(PRAJ: PRID)

0044 Anon. The World Looks At... The IRA Bombings. *World Press Review*, September 1982, p. 20.

There was widespread condemnation of the renewed IRA bombings. *The Star*, Toronto, charged that the IRA cared no more for self-determination than for life. *Rand Daily Mail*, Johannesburg, claimed the IRA has lost any sympathy it ever had. *La Republica*, Rome, commented that even the most nationalist recognize that reunification must be gradual. *Le Figaro*, Paris, reported that the IRA had "left a bloody calling card in the center of London". *Daily Express*, London, thought that it was time that Britain recognized the limit to its patience with the Irish Republic, and that this limit had been passed with these bombings. *Financial Times*, London, agreed and pointed out the increasing danger from the IRA as events continue to move against them. *Irish Independent*, Dublin, declared that Ireland did not want the North back through such acts.

(PRAJ: PRID)

0045 Anzovin, Steven (Ed.). *Terrorism*. New York, The H.W. Wilson Company, 1986.

The articles, essays, speeches and discussions reprinted in this volume deal with several aspects of terrorism.

First section deals with the nature of terrorism today (its definition, recent history, its devastating effects on the social fabric of Lebanon) and terrorist links with foreign states that have adopted terrorism as a part of their aggressive foreign policy.

Section II deals with the problems faced by States wanting to control terrorism in the face of other States cooperating with terrorists.

A third section, deals with the ways terrorism should not be fought.

The final section deals with more effective ways of combatting terrorism, domestic and foreign. Most of the contributors believe, that terrorism is likely to be an abiding problem in our world.

0046 Arblaster, Anthony. Terrorism : Myths, Meaning and Methods. *Political Studies*, Volume 24, Number 3, September 1977, pp. 413-424.

A review of ten books treating the question of terrorism and political violence in contemporary politics. With few exceptions these studies are not primarily concerned with terrorism as such, and still less with the several varieties of political violence. They are concerned with terrorism as and when it is used for political ends which they do not endorse, and against states whose legitimacy they accept. Thus their chosen areas of study are confined by political boundaries. This criteria of selection is not made explicit in these works. The implications of this hidden assumption are explored by the author.

(IPSA)

0047 Aston, C.C. *A Contemporary Crisis : Political Hostage taking and the Experience of Western Europe. Westport,* Green Wood Press, 1982.

This book contains an account of the siege at the Munich Oympics in September 1972, when Palestinian terrorists took hostage and killed 11 Israeli athletes. The author has also attempted to provide a typology of 127 cases of hostage-taking that took place in western Europe between 1970 and 1980.

The author's purpose is to analyze political terrorism as a crisis for governments. The intent is to provide policy advice to governments through rigorous examination of hostage - taking situations, including kidnappings and sieges, rather than to offer moral judgements or high level generalizations about the issue.

(BRD)

0048 Aston, Clive C. The United Nations Convention Against the Taking of Hostages : Realistic or Rhetoric? *Terrorism : An International Journal*, Volume 5, Numbers 1-2, 1981-82.

In an effort to circumvent the lack of international agreement on needed measures against political terrorism and impelled by the siege of their embassy in Stockholm in 1975, the West German Government decided to propose a convention banning a more specific manifestation of terrorism : the taking of hostages. The author reviews the central political issues that have pervaded the debates on this item within the United Nations until its final adoption in 1979. The most crucial issue was whether the scope of the proposed convention should include actions undertaken by those movements engaged in a recognized struggle for national liberation. The resulting compromise required to ensure its adoption by the General Assembly has left the Convention with an inherent tautology which will undoubtedly hinder and may prevent its general ratification and subsequent entry into force.

(T)

0049 Assets Protection. Patient Sieges : Dealing with Hostage-Takers. *Idem*. Volume 1, Number 3, 1976, pp. 21-27.

Includes a recounting of cases from the U.S., Britain, Ireland and the Netherlands. Subjects treated include utility of concessions, physical containment, psychological and physical pressures, role of mediators, and the selection, training and techniques of negotiators.

(N&G)

0050 Avery, William P. *Terrorism, Violence and the International Transfer of Conventional Armaments*. A paper presented at the April 1978 meeting of the Midwest Political Science Association, Chicago, Illinois.

An attempt to explore the relationship between terrorist political violence and the international transfer of arms. Among the findings of this preliminary study was the fact that riots and guerrilla warfare were found only marginally important for armament decisions, while armed attacks were found to be practically the sole type of political violence exerting important influence for such decisions. The study is less important for what it proves, than it is as a suggestion of an additional research direction.

(N&G)

0051 Ayers, Russell W. Policing Plutonium : The Civil Liberties Fallout. *Harvard Civil Rights / Civil Liberties Law Review*, Volume 10, Spring 1975, pp. 369-443.

The legal impact of measures which may be needed to prevent thefts of plutonium.

(N&G)

0052 Barnett, R.W. The U.S. Navy's Role in Countering Maritime Terrorism. *Terrorism : An International Journal*, Volume 6, Number 3, 1982-83.

There have been few spectacular acts of maritime terrorism. About ninety-five percent of all incidents of what would be classified as transnational maritime terrorism involved bombings hijackings, and "other" attacks. Nearly all of these took place when ships were in Port, and the victims were predominantly merchant ships. Only a small number of terrorist attacks have been reported against men-of-war; none against U.S. Navy ships. Bombing, including various forms of mining, comprises the major threat to merchant ships, while the dangers of U.S. Navy ships would be aggravated by the presence of nuclear weapons of nuclear propulsion plants.

Counter terrorism as carried out by the U.S. Navy involves actions to deter or defeat direct terrorist activity (against the ship itself) and indirect activity (against other U.S. interests). U.S. Navy ships are especially well organized, constructed, and equipped to deal with the former, but they would be virtually powerless to assist U.S. merchant ships against the most probable threats (bombing, hijacking and attacks) in the most probable location (overseas ports).

(T)

0053 Bassiouni M. Cherif (Ed.). *International Terrorism and Political Crimes*. Charles C Thomas, Illinois, 1973.

This volume contains papers presented at the III International Symposium sponsored by the International Institute for Advanced Criminal Sciences (Siracuse-Italy) from June 4 to June 16, 1972.

The papers provide different aspects and issues related to terrorism like wars of national liberation, hijacking, kidnapping, jurisdiction and extradition, and international control of terrorism. Also the conclusions and recommendations of the conference which were drafted into a 'Final Document' are included in this volume.

(BRD)

0054 Bauer, Gitta; Saxton, Brian and Wolff, George. Coping with Terrorism. *Atlas*, September 1976, pp. 11-14.

This discussion of terrorism was conducted by *Atlas* editors, Alfred Balk and Marion K. Sanders, with Gitta Bauer of Springer News Services, Brian Saxton, U.N. Correspondent for the BBC, and George Wolff, UN Correspondent for Agence France-Presse. On the question of whether the terrorism today is something new, Bauer and Saxton consider it different from anything in the past, particularly because today it has the support of legitimate governments and because of technological advances. Wolff sees terrorism as a part of war and notes its effectiveness in war. The only way to handle it is to have trained sections of the police specifically for this. There is the problem of preserving society's basic freedoms, but in Wolff's opinion, the military approach is the only workable way to stop terrorism. Bauer pointed out that proper and efficient security measures could prevent hijackings taking place, and Wolff agrees that

prevention is very important. To the question of the use of boycotts, there was agreement that these are not likely to work on a worldwide scale. There might be an effective one involving certain nations, but not the Third World. Yet all agree that terrorism is so dangerous because it is on an international scale with international planning and it is only through strong international action that it can be contained.

(PRAJ: PRID)

0055 Baumann, Carol Edler. *The Diplomatic Kidnapping - A Revolutionary Tactic of Urban Terrorism.* The Hague, Martinus Nijhoff, 1973.

This work analyses diplomatic kidnappings particularly those in Latin America and Canada within the context of Urban guerrilla terrorism, international legal names, and world diplomatic practice. Also an attempt has been made to provide various policy alternatives to control, if not to totally prevent the diplonapping spree.

0056 Baumann, Michael. *Terror or Love ? Bommi Baumann's own Story of his Life as a West German Urban Guerrila.* New York, Grove Press, Inc., 1979. (Reprint of 1977 edition published by the Pulp Press, Inc.).

Translation of *Wie alles anfing* which was banned in the Federal Republic. One of the rare first-person accounts by a German terrorist. Baumann was an early member of the June 2nd Movement, and the Wieland Commune. Unfortunately his rambling -- even incoherent -- account sheds little light on the broader questions raised by the left's resort to terrorism in Germany. If anything, the book seems to be prototypical of the confusion and alienation that describes many of those associated with the violence of the Left. A useful chronology.

(N&G)

0057 BDM Corporation. *Analysis of the Terrorist Threat to the Commercial Nuclear Industry.* Report submitted to the Special Safeguards Study, Nuclear Regulatory Commission of the U.S. Government. Virginia, McLean, September 30, 1975.

This very extensive study examines the skills, objectives, motivations and disincentives for nuclear terrorists considering an attack on civil nuclear facilities.

(N&G)

0058 Beaumont, Roger A. Military Elite Forces : Surrogate War, Terrorism, and the New Battlefield. *Parameters, Journal of the U.S. Army War College*, March 19, 1979. pp. 17-29.

A useful overview of the historical and contemporary role of elite forces, which have recently been used with some success to counter terrorism. The growth of such forces from 170,00 in 1974 to almost a million in 1977, indicates the pertinence of the topic.

(N&G)

0059 Becker, Jillian. Another Final Battle on the Stage of History. *Terrorism : An International Journal*, Volume 5, Numbers 1-2, 1981-82.

Taking its point of departure in remarks made by Ulrike Meinhof during the 1972 trial in West Germany of Horst Mahler, this paper goes on to examine

some of the ideas and assumptions of the members of the terrorist group to which he belonged. Meinhof's as well as Mahler's views of the Jews in Germany and their fate, including their charge of a conspiracy on the part of the malevolent powers, are quoted and make it clear that as terrorists they conformed to a grandiose millenarian tradition. This millenarian tradition has had a long history in Germany, comprising anarchic, egalitarian, and communistic elements. Examples are the followers of John Hus and Thomas Muntzer. The need for group identification is also strong in the millenarians of the present day who believe in and act unquestioningly upon tenets such as those of terrorist groups like the Red Army Faction which, fortunately, has not gained the following of such predecessors as Hilter's Third Reich.

(T)

0060 Becker, Jillian. *Hitler's Children : The Story of the Baader-Meinhof Terrorist Gang*. Philadelphia, Lippincott, 1977.

Although the title is problematic, *Hitler's Children* is the most thorough account of the West German terrorists available. While Becker is less than systematic, the information she provides on terrorist activities is both interesting and useful. On the whole she weaves a story of terrorists-cum-criminals who could claim upper-middle class backgrounds, at least some university education and a basic contempt for authority. It is also interesting to note the degree to which the central members shared disruptive familial backgrounds. In contrast to the notion that terrorists are systematic, efficient and dedicated to their tasks, Becker's terrorists often lack purpose, political objectives or an organizing intellectual framework or ideology. Key instances of ineptitudes are also illuminating. Becker also provides an essential who's who of West German terrorists (7 p.).

(N&G)

0061 Beeson, Trevor. The British and the I.R.A. *Christian Century*, Volume 1003, Number 3, January 28, 1976, pp. 60-62.

The majority of British people favour withdrawal, though there can be little doubt that an Irish civil war would result. So the politicians have to take an unpopular stand, but they have the support of the Churches and of most of the thinking people in Britain.

(PRAJ: PRID)

0062 Begin, Menachem. *The Revolt*. Revised ed. New York, Dell Publishing Co., Inc., 1977.

The complete text of the 1952 edition with addition of a brief preface (2 pages) written in 1977, and a 10 page preface written in 1972. Clearly one of the best auto-biographical accounts of a terrorist campaign available. Perhaps no other book better illustrates the oft-repeated dictum -- "one man's freedom fighter is another man's terrorist." Begin's omissions are frequently as revealing as his text.

(N&G)

0063 Beichman, Arnold. A War without End. *The American Spectator*, 11 April 1978, pp. 20-23.

After reviewing the phenomena of contemporary terrorism, Beichman concludes with the suggestion that the terrorist - the "literal killer of the literal innocent" - be treated as an enemy agent caught behind the lines. He should face capital punishment, and he must know in advance that a "drumhead court-martial" will follow his capture.

(N&G)

0064 Beichman, Arnold. An Angry Fancy : The 'Politics' of Terror. *Lugano Review*, Volume 2, 1975, pp. 18-24f.

Beichman argues that there is a relationship between the diminishment of the revolutionary order of the USSR and the PRC and the obsolense of violent revolution as a form of social change in industrially advanced democratic societies. He concludes the "permanent Revolution" is no longer with us; but the "Permanent Revolutionaries" (Terrorists) still are. He sees the "main tendency" in the world as the slaughter of the innocents, rather than revolution. All of this compounded by the terrorists' frustrations, workers not heeding the call to revolution and the reluctance of left's intellectuals to act. Since there is no way a democracy - which by nature *assumes* an obedient populace can prevent terrorism, more lives will be lost.

(N&G)

0065 Bell, J. Bowyer, Jr. The Escalation of Insurgency : The Provisional Irish Republican Army's Experience, 1969-1971. *The Review of Politics*, Volume 35, July 1973, pp. 398-411.

This article generalizes on the conditions of insurgency, using the provisional IRA as example. Against a background of British political drift and military policy of status-quo order between Protestant majority and Catholic minority, the Provos pursued a strategy of "fomenting a sufficient level of violence" to invoke British responses, i.e., use of gas on civilian population and internment, that would gain support for Provos. Author cites Provos' capacity for pragmatism, patriotism, and ruthlessness as factors in successful insurrection, as opposed to imported techniques that are idealistic, alien, and unknown to the subjected population.

(PRAJ: PRID)

0066 Bell, J. Bowyer. *The Secret Army : The IRA 1916-1970*. New York John Day Company, 1971.

The violence of the Irish Republican Army is justified, and the pro-army bias is not hidden in this thoroughly researched book. The IRA as a revolutionary movement is evaluated in detail. The 404 pages disclose a long history of revolutionary activity; "to dig into the history of the IRA is to uncover not only what to avoid, but how to persist, to endure, to suffer disaster and to maintain the ideals and the organization."

(PRAJ: PRID)

0067 Bell, J. Bowyer. *Terror out of Zion : Irgun Zuaileumi, LEHI, and the Palestine Underground, 1929-1949*. New York, St. Martin's Press, 1977.

A very ample chronicle of terrorism in mandatory Palestine. Extensive attention is directed to the Irgun Zuai Leumi and Lehamey Heruth Israel (LEHI - popularly known as the Stern Gang). Bell's Treatment is clearly the best descriptive work on the subject in English, although a more explicit analytical focus would have enhanced its value. A brief bibliographic section is noteworthy, as are the numerous photographs produced throughout the book.

(N&G)

0068 Bell, J. Bowyer; Chipembere, Henry B. Masauko; M'Gabe, Davis; Hawley, Edward A.; Diamond, Robert A.; Fouquest, David; and

Lofchie, Michael F. Guerrilla Warfare. *Africa today*, Volume 19, Winter 1972, 92 pp. illus.

Entire issue devoted to guerrilla warfare. Partial contents -- The future of guerrilla - revolution in southern Africa, by J. Bowyer Bill. Guerilla warfare in Southern Africa : myth and prognosis, by Henry B. Masauko Chipembere. -- The reality of guerrilla warfare, by Davis M'gabe. -- Guerrilla warfare : then, now and tomorrow, by Edward A. Hawley. -- American military aid to Ethiopia and Eritrean insurgency, by Robert A. Diamond and David Fouquet. -- The British - Rhodesian agreement and United States policy, by Michael F. Lofchie.

Articles examining the problems and prospects of guerrilla warfare in southern Africa. The general consensus is that this part of Africa will be plagued by guerrilla warfare for some time to come.

(PRAJ: PRID)

0069 Bell, J. Bowyer. *A Time of Terror : How Democratic Societies Respond to Revolutionary Violence*. New York, Basic Books, Inc., Publishers, 1978.

The prolific J. Bowyer Bell has prepared an intelligent and highly readable work of journalism (in the flattering sense of the term). While the book is less than the subtitle suggests in terms of treating the response to terrorism, it does provide extended discussions of recent terrorism (from 1968-on), with particularly good chapters on Italy and Ireland. In addition, a very detailed chronicle of the September 1976 hijacking of a TWA flight by Croation terrorists is presented. A bibliography, with comprehensive commentary, deserves the reader's attention as well.

(N&G)

0070 Bell, J. Bowyer. *On Revolt : Strategies of National Liberation*. Cambridge, Harvard University Press, 1976.

Includes case material from mandatory Palestine, Gold Coast, Malaya, Kenya, Cyprus, the contemporary Middle East, Ireland and South Arabia. *On Revolt* is admirably prepared by any standard for a descriptive work, but its lack of an appropriàte theoretical framework will leave many scholars unsatisfied.

(N&G)

0071 Bell, J. Bowyer. *Transnational Terror*. Washington, D.C. American Enterprise Institute for Public Policy Research; and Stanford, Calif., Hoover Institution on War, Revolution and Peace, 1975.

This 90-page monograph offers a concise introduction to the problem of terror-violence; its breadth is far wider than the title "transnational terror" would indicate. It is probably most useful for the concerned layman. Bell categorizes "terror" (perhaps excessively) as follows : Psychotic, criminal, endemic, authorized, vigilante and revolutionary (including organizational, allegiance, functional, provocation, manipulation and symbolic terrorism). He discusses terrorism as it has appeared in Palestine, Ireland, Venezuela, Argentina and among the fedayeen. Bell allows that there has been *ad hoc* "transnational" cooperation between groups, but he does not find assertions of a global or regional conspiracy convincing, thus leaving the reader to wonder why the author chose the title that he did.

(N&G)

0072 Bell, J. Bowyer. Revolutionary Organizations : Special Cases and Imperfect Models. In Carlton David and Schaerf Carlo (Eds.). *In-*

*ternational Terrorism and World Security*. London, Croom Helm, 1975, pp. 78-92.

Espouses a national (vs. cross-national) perspective for understanding terrorism. Analyses of the Provisonal IRA, the EOKA and the Eritrean Liberation Front are offered.

(N&G)

0073 Bell, J. Bowyer. *The Myth of the Guerrilla : Revolutionary Theory and Malpractice*. New Delhi, Alfred A. Knopf.

A new generation of guerrilla fighters appeared in the 1960s. Previous situations considered are the Irish Easter Rebellion of 1916; the Chinese Communists in the 1930s; colonized areas during World War II; the French war in Indochina which culminated at Dien Bien Phu; and theory enunciated by Fanon, Castro and Guevara. With Guevara's new "myth of the guerrilla", fantasies of the "desperate and naive" became frequent and with some replaced "the old orthodoxies of political mobilization, parliamentary infiltration, tradeunion militance and balanced insurrections". Cases studied of this new current are the wars of liberation in southern Africa, the Palestine Fedayeen, and Guevara's effort to create "another Viet Nam" in Bolivia. All of these failed. The idea that "repeated failure paid repeated benefits" has been not only "ineffectual", but also often self-defeating.

(PRAJ: PRID)

0074 Bell, J. Bowyer. Violence and Italian Politics Conflict : *An International Journal for Conflict and Policy Studies*, Volume 1, 1978, pp. 49-69.

Bell sees the violence of the last decade in Italy as a reflection of the inability of the political system to accommodate dissent. To buttress his argument he points not only to the activism of the extreme right and left, but also to the "Neo-Luddites" of Northern Italy who have engaged in violence and destruction not out of ideological impetuses, but from the frustration and discontent produced by the system. His portrait of the intricate web of conspiracy, provocation, violence and counter violence involving the left and the right is nicely done, although he clearly underestimates the potential of several of the groups (esp. Brigate Rosee, in light of the Moro-murder--which occurred after the article was written). He makes much of the payment of $ 800,000 (U.S.) to General Miceli who was later implicated in the abortive coup of 1970, but here he leaves the reader with a matter which could probably stand further scholarly investigation.

(N&G)

0075 Bell, Robert G. The U.S. Response to Terrorism against International Civil Aviation. *Orbis*, Winter 1976, pp. 1326-1343.

Bell traces the history of attacks on civil aviation from its beginnings in the 1920s through to the present. He outlines the moves adopted by the U.S. and notes its failure to get international agreement. "This review has shown that the American effort to stop attacks on civil aircraft was in no way perfect. The government's recognition that mandatory electronic screening was necessary came far too late. The American contention that states should relinquish their right to grant political asylum in cases of aerial hijacking was rejected by the international community. The attempt to obtain an enforcement convention turned into a diplomatic fiasco..."

"The price of future aviation security is constant vigilance; defences cannot be relaxed. At best, though, these defences can succeed only in diverting ter-

rorists to other targets. Without a fundamental resolution of the rivalries, strife and injustices that spawn terrorism, the future promises recurring violence. In the case of international civil aviation, the United States won one battle, but the war with terrorism goes on."

(PRAJ: PRID)

0076 Belz, Mary; Parker, Ellen E.; Sank, Lawrence L.; Shapiro, Joan; and Striber, Linda. Is there a Treatment for Terror? *Psychology Today*, Volume 11, Number 5, October 1977, pp. 54-56, 108-112.

Six therapists report on their work with hostages held by the Hanafis. Terrorism being one of the ugly, inescapable realities of the future, we should not only do everything in our power to stop it, but develop sophisticated and compassionate treatment for the victims.

(PRAJ: PRID)

0077 Ben-Porat, Yeshayahu; Haber, Eitani and Schiff, Zeev. *Entebbe Rescue*. New York, Delacourte Press, 1977.

The authors recreate and reexamine the hijacking and rescue of an Air-France plane from Entebbe Airport in June and early July 1976. They also discuss the history of Arab terrorist activities, the plight of the Palestinians, the changing nature of Israeli Ugandan relations over the past decades, and the backgrounds and personalities of the political and military leaders involved in the confrontation.

(BRD)

0078 Beres, Louis Rene. Terrorism and International Security: The Nuclear Threat. *Chitty's Law Journal*, Volume 26, March 1978, pp. 73-90.

A report commissioned by the U.S. Arms Control and Disarmament Agency in 1977. Beres argues that government efforts aimed at thwarting nuclear terrorism have emphasized the "technological" aspects of the problem and ignored the "behavioral" and "contextual" elements. Beres offers a description of six principal types of terrorist groups, a discussion of the considerations which will influence decision-making within the respective groups and an extended argument for placing the problem within an international perspective. In a rather controversial proposal, Beres posits that the pattern of deterrence and reactive measures against terrorism may be complemented by a reward system. Such positive reinforcement is deemed to be especially apropos when dealing with the political terrorist who evidences a high degree of commitment (with the *fedayeeo* being prototypical).

(N&G)

0079 Beres, Louis Rene. International Terrorism and World Order: The Nuclear Threat. *The Stanford Journal of International Studies*, Volume 12, Spring 1977, pp. 131-146.

Explores the factors underlying the argument that the prospect of nuclear terrorism is both credible and perilous. Beres attributes this acute threat to easy terrorist access to nuclear weapons, the contemporary changes in the terrorists "political code", and the tendency for terrorism to be condoned or at least tolerated within the international system. Beres offers three basic responses to attenuate the threat : technical fixes to render the nuclear materials less accessible, international agreements to control traffic in nuclear goods, and attempts to change the behavior of the terrorists. It is the last proposal which is the most

controversial, for such attempts at behaviour modification may conceivably backfire.

(N&G)

0080 Beres, Louis Rene. *Terrorism and Global Security : The Nuclear Threat*. Boulder, Westview Press, (Special Studies in National and International Terrorism), 1980.

While other recent books, such as *A Time of Terror* by J. Bowyer Bell have sections devoted to the possibility of nuclear terrorism, Beres I is the only one devoted exclusively to the subject. The author examines modern terrorism and shows how its various elements could combine to produce a nuclear threat. He discusses possible forms and consequences of nuclear terrorism and proposes what he believes to be an effective preventive plan based on international cooperation. Beres has constructed "a theory of counter-nuclear terrorism from which viable strategies, should they ever be needed, can be systematically derived." The book is well documented.

(PRAJ: PRID)

0081 Beres, Louis Rene. The Nuclear Threat of Terrorism. *International Journal of Group Tensions*, Volume 6, Numbers 1-2, 1976, pp. 63-66.

The world system is presently confronted with a frightening array of hazards to kindle the apocalyptic imagination. Although it would probably be senseless to rank-order these hazards in terms of their relative urgency for the residents of a beleaguered planet, one argument remains essentially unassailable : the nuclear threat of terrorism is particularly potentious. Without appropriate preventive action from many quarters, this threat is likely to signal the onset of genuinely intolerable global conditions.

(IPSA)

0082 Berger, Peter L. (assoc. editor). Excursus III, Elements of Terrorism. *Worldview*, Volume 19, Number 5, May 1976, pp. 29-30.

Berger defines terrorism and distinguishes it from ordinary crime and acts of violence, e.g., sabotage. It is not necessarily directed against civilians (Che Guevara) but, alarmingly, it is increasingly directed indiscriminately against civilian targets. Societies that are *both* technologically sophisticated and relatively humane in law enforcement (democracies) are most vulnerable. The Soviet Union, e.g., has the first, but represses the second, and seems immune to terrorism. Totalitarian states control everything, including terrorism. Dictatorships are another political phenomenon, not as effective against terrorism, but more so than democracies. Brazil, Chile and Argentina have used counterterror, an effective but dictatorial means of self-defence. Berger thinks that the death penalty in any country is likely to heighten violence.

Terrorism provides personal satisfaction for its devotees, especially those who receive through it a sense of power. Do we face only the alterntive of terrorism of counter terror? Berger hopes not and suggests techniques of self-defence used in hijackings, more effective humane legal systems, use of public opinion against both terrorism and counter terror. Even if terrorism continues, totalitarianism is not the answer, because the state only monopolizes such acts. Perhaps individual acts of terrorism are preferable, but the danger to our value system is that they force the public to opt for any kind of a security, including rejecting democracy - a possibility in our lifetimes.

(PRAJ: PRID)

0083 Beristain, A. Terrorism and Aircraft Hijacking. *International Journal of Criminology and Penology*, London, Volume 2, November 1974, pp. 347-389.

Results of a survey of 875 persons in Madrid, and 131 university students in San Sebastian, Spain, students (who were of Basque origins) were more likely to consider hijacking a political rather that a common crime, when compared to the former sample.

(N&G)

0084 Berkowitz, B.J. et al. *Superviolence : The Civil Threat of Mass Destruction Weapons*. Santa Barbara, Calif, A.D. C.O.N. Corp., 1972.

This study by the Advanced Concept Research Corp., includes chapters on chemical, biological and nuclear weapons.

(N&G)

0085 Bernetel, Paul. Those Three Days Which Shook Brazil (In French). *Jeune Afrique*, Number 455, September 23-29, 1969, pp. 40-43.

Earlier this month, the American ambassador to Brazil, Charles D. Elbrick, was kidnapped by a revolutionary commando, led probably by Carlos Marighela. The conditions of his release were as follows: the Brazilian government (military junta), must publish a declaration violently attacking their regime in the newspapers and have it read on radio and television; fifteen political prisoners must be liberated and sent to Chile, Mexico or Nigeria (they were sent to Mexico).

The kidnapping was important in that it showed how bound to the U.S. the military junta is. Soon after news of the kidnapping hit the media, President Nixon sent word that he wanted his "ambassador alive at any cost". The Brazilian government was forced to comply with the revolutionaries' conditions, although nationalist elements in the Army were against acceptance. Secondly, the kidnapping was important in that it showed the strength of those forces which oppose the regime, in power since April 1964, and the division in the Army (or regime) between pro-American and nationalist factions.

(PRA)

0086 Bernstein, Alvin H. Iran's Low-intensity War Against the United States. *Orbis*, 30, Spring 1986, pp. 149-167.

Actions of the Iranian Revolutionary Guards against American targets in Lebanon and elsewhere; a counter-terrorist strategy for the U.S.

(PAISB)

0087 Berri, Younes. Palestinians : Unified, Divided Resistance (In French). *Jeune Afrique*, Number 706, July 20, 1974, pp. 40-44.

Berri analyses the state of Palestinian resistance movements. Gathered together in the Palestinian Liberation Organization (PLO) are six movements : FATH, SAIKA, the People's Liberation Front of Palastine (FPLP), the People's Democratic Liberation Front of Palestine (FDPLP), the General Command of the People's Libertion Front of Palestine, and the Arab Liberation Front. Berri also discusses the Black September group.

(PRAJ: PRID)

0088 Bienen, Henry and Gilpin, Robert Economic Sanctions as a Response to Terrorism. *Journal of Strategic Studies*, Volume 3, Number 1, May 1980, pp. 89-98.

Economic sanctions can play a limited role in dealing with the problem of international terrorism. Such economic sanctions should preferably be multilateral rather than unilateral. Sanctions should be tailored to the specific areas of activity which pertain to terrorism. In seeking to combat terrorism through the unilateral imposition of economic sanctions on offending states the US has been ineffective and has harmed Amrican economic interests.

(IPSA)

0089 Billig, Otto. The Case History of a German Terrorist. *Terrorism: An International Journal*, Volume 7, Number 1, 1984.

Guerrilla fighters and terrorists who have sprung up in recent years, vary in their commitments and causes. Some may be motivated by their violant desire for national liberation, blind to all other considerations. Others have only vague goals speaking of anti-imperialist and anti-authoritarian aims. They are mainly the German, Italian, and possibly Japanese terrorists who seek insoluble answers to their own conflicts. They become involved in a hopeless struggle that they cannot win; they can only destroy. This article reviews the life history of a German "urban guerrilla." Coming from a regionally prominent family known in the arts, he suffered emotional deprivations. An attempt is made to reach an understanding of the interplay between his personal and the socio-cultural conflicts of his time that may have led to his terrorist acts.

(T)

0090 Bishop, Joseph W. Jr. Can Democracy Defend itself against Terrorism. *Commentary*, May 1978, pp. 55-62.

A useful, if marginally polemical, treatment of the legal and extra-legal adaptations which have been made in Northern Ireland by the Stormont and the British government. Bishop compares the remedies that have been applied in North Ireland to those that might be adopted by the U.S. in a period of intense terrorist activity. He concludes that the use of juryless trials, relaxation of rules of evidence and the burden of proof, and the crime of association would raise grave constitutional issues. Arguing from *stare decisis* he asserts that an important legitimate power would be the use of armed force. He finds that internment is probably constitutional, as might be the juryless trial (in the model from the "Diplock Courts" and in North Ireland). Bishop's argument for preemptive reaction to be applied selectively, in order to prevent rescue operations will no doubt be troubling to civil liberatarians and those who oppose capital punishment on principle. Letter to the Editor and Bishop's reply, appearing in *Commentary*, August 1978, should be read in conjunction with the article.

(N&G)

091 Blair, Bruce G. and Brewar, Garry D. The Terrorist Threat to World Nuclear Programs. *The Journal of Conflict Resolution*, Volume 21, September 1977, pp. 379-403.

Key contention is that the attention that has been focused upon the risk to commercial nuclear facilties has obscured a serious vulnerability to the theft or unauthorized use of nuclear weapons by terrorists. Many will quarrel with their conception of terrorism as a means of conflict resolution that is becoming increasingly attractive to "all elements of society". Similarly, it is difficult to understand how nuclear terrorism is "becoming more practical and legitimate"

(emphasis added). Several of the terror scenarios presented are trivial, while others are at best presented incompletely. The central risk posited, that, military officers assigned to launch facilities might collaborate in the arming and launching of Minuteman missiles grossly underestimates the effectiveness of existing internal security procedures, as well as the complexity and sophistication of launch and targeting procedures.

(N&G)

0092 Blischtschenko, I.P. and Zhdanow, N. The Struggle Against Terrorism and the Principle of Diplomatic Immunity (In German). *Deutsche Aussenpolitik*, Volume 18, Number 5, 1973, p. 1089, p. 16.

The Soviet Union has proposed that crimes, against the above mentioned persons should qualify as serious international crimes, requiring cooperation in carrying the duty of states to prevent and suppress such acts, make provision for them, and proceed against persons, in accordance with their own legislation, who have been guilty of preparing for, attempting and carrying out such crimes, together with accomplices in such acts as serious criminals.

(PRAJ: PRID)

0093 Blum, Yehuda, Z. State Response to Acts of Terrorism. *German Yearbook of International Law.* 19, 1976, pp. 223-237.

Externally stimulated terrorism operating from a sanctuary state against a target state poses serious problems for international law, while indigenous terrorism is normally dealt with under domestic criminal law. From the legal point of view, the target state, in responding to an act of terrorism, is entitled to regard the sanctury state itself as the aggressive attacker, irrespective of whether that state has been unwilling or merely unable to curb the terrorist activities from its territory.

(IPSA)

0094 Bonanate, Luigi. II Teorema del Terrorismo ( The terrorist theorem/Le theoreme du terrorisme). *II Mulino*, 258, Juil aout 78, pp. 574-595.

*II existe differentes formes de terrorisme (contre l'Etat ou exerce par l'Etat) et differentes echelles (terrorisme tactique) ou strategique) qui repondent a une logique propre dans chaque cas. C'est le terrorisme tactique qui a le plus de succes mais c'est toujours sur la violence qu'il repose, et aujourd'hui il reussit a remettre en cause le priniple meme de la qualite du systeme democratique. Mais la violence utilisee par le terrorisme est en meme tamps sa negation et la preuve de l'incepacite de ses partisans as 'imposer autrement.*

(IPSA)

0095 Bonanate, Luigi - terrorismo e governabilita (Terrorism and governa-bility/Terrorisme, et gouvernabilite). *Rivista Italian : Scienza Politca,* Volume 13, Number 1, April 83, pp. 37-64.

The article addresses itself to the problem of the relationship between two contemporary phenomena : the emergence of terrorism and the governability crisis in some political systems. By analyzing the different theories dealing with the causes of terrorism as well as the governability theme the author puts forward the hypothesis that terrorism can be a consequence of specific problems in the functioning of the political system. The concept of blocked system is presented as an useful analytical tool in examining the cause sequence that leads to terrorism. Finally, taking as example the internators system, the paper points

out that the ending of terrorism is not necessarily related to the recovery of the political system. Even after the demise of terrorism the political system can remain "blocked" although men governable.

(IPSA)

0096 Bonanate, Luigi. Some Unanticipated Consequences of Terrorism. *Journal of Peace Research,* Volume 16, Number 3, 1979, pp. 197-211.

The spread of terrorism in democratic societies forces one to examine once more the relationship between society and political violence. From a conceptualization of terrorism based on the cross between two types of characteristics (tactical-strategic : instrumental-finalistic), some observations appear which make common explanations of the causes of terrorism unsatisfactory. For this one might substitute the hypothesis that societies which must cope with terrorism are 'blocked', i.e. incapable of advancing and at the same time immune to disintegration. In this interpretation the appearance of terrorism becomes an indicator that the society in question is only apparently democratic. But, at the same time, this study denounces the inability of terrorism to eliminate the block, to the point of involuntarily acting as a restabilizing element.

(IPSA)

0097 Bonanate, Luigi. Terrorism and International Political Analysis. *Terrorism : An International Journal,*Volume 3, Numbers 1-2, 1979-80.

The international spread of terrorism requires more careful study of its ability to influence the international order. Therefore, it is first of all necessary to distinguish the purposes for which terrorism is set up on the international level, also exactly assessing its actual transnational links. In this way, it will be possible to proceed toward a comparative analysis of terrorism in different regions of the international system. The purpose of such an analysis is to evaluate the influence that terrorism has, from the methodological standpoint, on the studies of the international system, and from the substantial standpoint the actual ability of terrorism to weaken that very system. Clarifying the implications of these aspects, the comparison will be a reflection on the casual relationship that links terrorism and the international system. The former is a consequence of the nature of the latter, caused by the immobility of the international system, and hence by the blocked situation that faces anyone who wants to modify the international order.

(T)

0098 Bouthoul, Gaston. Terrorism. *Etudes Polemologiques,* Volume 3, April 1973, pp. 37-47.

Terrorism has become such an important issue that a special debate on terrorism was held in the United Nations, which resulted only in revealing how confusingly complex the matter is, owing to contradictory positions held by different national delegations. International terrorism has always existed, but recently has become considerably more serious due to technological innovations. Pirates now act quicker with higher stakes. The author outlines different types of terrorism with corresponding effects, including a little resume on the Mafia. These days, it often becomes hard to distinguish between political terrorism and simple crime, as terrorists plead ideological motives as a means of excercising guilt. From the statistical point of view, victims are relatively few compared to murders in the American perspective or car accidents in France. On the other hand,

terrorism occupies an important place, a disproportionate one, in the news and in public opinion. The measurement and comparison of terrorist acts uses, as an objective criterion, the number of murdered victims resulting from the act. But it is difficult to compare or to compile statistics, as some countries, notably the Soviet Union and China, do not make known their criminality statistics.

(PRAJ: PRID)

0099 Bowden, Tom. *Men in the Middle -- The U.K. Police.* London, Institute for the Study of Conflict, 1976.

A treatment of the problems terrorism presents for police in Britain, and the solutions adopted.

(N&G)

0100 Brasher, Christopher and others. The Shambles of Fuerstenfeldbruck. *Observer*, London, September 10, 1972, pp. 9-10.

Step-by-step account of the Olympic tragedy, and speculation on what went wrong in the apparently careful negotiations. Blamed poor communications and poor psychology, as well as unforeseen developments in the course of German strategy.

(PRAJ: PRID)

0101 Brau, Jean-Louis. Guerrilla Weaponry. (In French) Andre Paris Published by Balland, 1974, p. 215. *Reviewed* in Afrique, Contemporaine, No. 74, July-August, 1974, p. 36.

Brau attempts to give a general history of the "guerrillero"; the beginnings, the weaponry, the training. Many examples are taken from Africa; the Sudan, Mozambique, Angola, etc.

(PRAJ: PRID)

0102 Breemer, Jan S. Offshore Energy Terrorism : Perspectives on a Problem. *Terrorism : An International Journal,* Volume 6, Number 3, 1982-83.

This essay examines prevailing perspectives on the prospect of terrorist sabotage against the offshore oil and gas industry in the Gulf of Mexico. It contrasts the dominant "wait-and-see" attitude in the United States with counterterrorist preparations by the North Sea countries, and suggests some of the reasons for this difference in attitudes.

(T)

0103 Buckley, Alan, D. (Ed.). International Terrorism. *Journal of International Affairs,* Volume 32, Spring/Summer 1978.

A collection of articles dealing with terrorism; most of the contributions are conscientiously analytical rather than merely descriptive. Topics range from a typology of terrorism; assassination in Belfast; mass destruction terror; to terrorism, the media and the police.

(N&G)

0104 Burton, Anthony M. *Urban Terrorism: Theory, Practice and Response.* New York, The Free Press, 1975.

Burton's treatment is not as narrow as the title would indicate, nor as probing as the subtitle might hint. He has provided a competent, readable and useful introduction to political terrorism however. The "theorists," from Bakunin to Fanon are surveyed, with nice sections on Debray and Marighella. The whole panoply of terrorist groups is surveyed including the FLN, BOKA, IRA, Irgun,

OAS and the Nazis. Information on the government response to terrorism, particularly the British cases, is of value as well. Several useful appendices (in chart form) are provided including a listing of organizations and personalities in Northern Ireland. The author formerly served in the British Army for sixteen years.

(N&G)

0105 Burton, Anthony. *Revolutionary Violence : The Theories*. New York, Crane, Russak, 1978.

Burton examines terrorism in a Series of short essays, on Lenin, Trotsky, Mao, Hitler, Lawrence, Giap, Guevara and other revolutionary warriors of the present century.

(BRD)

0106 Burton, John. *Deviance Terrorism and War : The Process of Solving Unsolved Social and Political Problems*. Oxford, Martin Robertson and Company Ltd., 1979.

This book focusses on the common features of unsolved social and political problems which exist at all levels in a society and in inter-state relations and suggests processes for solving them.

0107 Buscenko, I.P. and Zdanov, N.V. Sotrudnicestvo gosudarstv v bor'be protiv terroristiceskikh aktov mezdunarodnogo haraktera (The co-operation of States in the Struggle against acts of terrorism of international character/La cooperation des Etats dans la lutte contre les actes de terrorisme de caractere international). *Sovetskoe Gosudarstov i Pravo*, Volume 8, August 1981, pp. 110-119.

The increased number of acts of terrorism which threaten a normal course of international relations posed before the UN the problem of the elaboration of international legal norms in this field. Differences in positions of states in relation to "international terrorism" have led to situation when neither the 28th session of the UN General Assembly nor its subsequent sessions could work out concrete measures for fighting terrorism of international character. The article presents an attempt to work out criteria to refer some acts of terrorism to the sphere regulated by international law, to define optimal forms of states co-operation for the prevention of international acts of terrorism and at ensuring the inevitability of punishment for their commitment. The article unmasks hypocritical campaign launched by the US Administration relating to the USSR involvement in "international terrorism". The authors come to the conclusion that, a conventional mechanism is the most optimal one, since this method ensures not only the unification of the definition of corpus delicti but provides special protection to persons or property which in accordance with international law and their status are entitled to it.

(IPSA)

0108 Bush, George. *Prelude to Retaliation: Building a Governmental Consensus on Terrorism. SAIS* (School Advanced Internat Studies), R7 : 1-9, Winter-Spring 1987.

Policymaking process preceding the Apr. 1986 U.S. bombing of Tripoli,

done in response to terrorist attacks on Americans, allegedly sponsored by Libya.

(PAISB)

0109 Busuttil, James J. The Bonn Declaration on International Terrorism: A Non-binding International Agreement on Aircraft Hijacking. *International and Comparativve Law Quarterly*.

The 1978 Bonn Declaration outlines how the participating states (Canada, Federal Republic of Germany, France, Italy, Japan, the United Kingdom, the United States, et al) intend to deal with states who harbor hijackers. However, the Bonn Declaration itself may not be legally enforced. It is not a standing international agreement because its terms are imprecise, it has not been treated as a binding international agreement, and the language employed is informal. While it is a non-binding agreement, it does stop a participant from claiming the Declaration is without force, it directs the internal and external agendas of the participants, and it opens to joint discussion the treatment of hijackings by participants.

(IPSA)

0110 California, State of. *Nuclear Blackmail or Nuclear Theft Emergency Response Plan*. Sacramento, Office of Emergency Services, 1976.

A very extensive and commendable plan. Available (microfiche copy) without charge from: U.S. Dept. of Justice, Law Enforcement Assistance Administration, National Criminal Justice Reference Service, Washington, D.C. 20530. Refer to NCJ 39358 when ordering.

(N&G)

0111 Callvita, Kitty (Middlebury Coll, VT 05753). "Law and Order" and the Anti-Terrorist Act of 1983. *LM Crime and Social Justice*, Volume 20, 1983, pp. 138-143.

The 1980s have seen a return from a more liberal approach to criminal justice to a stricter law and order approach. Legislation limiting bail and parole, modifying rules of evidence, and generally toughening up against suspected criminals has been enacted. The Extradition Act of 1983, an anti-terrorist bill to be put before the Ninety-Eight Congress, is seen as the international equivalent of domestic law and order legislation. The provisions of the bill allow for political and criminal suspects to be rounded up and detained on request by a foreign nation with which an extradition agreement exists. Here, it is argued that the bill, if passed, would be a serious erosion of individual rights and a preparation for a future period in which terrorism and civil disobedience are common place.

( SAJ)

0112 Carlton, David and Schaerf, Carlo. (Eds.). *International Terrorism and World Society*. London, Croom Helm, 1975.

Every other year the Italian Pugwash movement organizes a conference for postgraduate students and for young teachers in the field of International Relations in the general area of Arms Control and Disarmament. This volume represents the papers given at the 1974 Conference. In the first section of terrorism, Brian Jenkins points out that there is not really a good definition of what he calls International Terrorism. There follows a chapter by Gaston Bouthoul. In the essay by Steven Rosen and Robert Frank on Measures Against International Terrorism there is no analysis, but rather a selected catalogue of terrorist acts and the measures that have been attempted internationally to curb them. The piece on the legal aspects of terrorism by George Sliwowski summarizes the

legal debate prior to the Second World War as well as after. It advocates an international criminal court with compulsory jurisdiction. The penultimate essay in the first part is by J. Bowyer Bell on Revolutionary Organizations, in which he gives histories of the Provisional IRA, EOKA-B and the Eritrean Liberation Front. The final chapter in this section by Daniel Heradsveit looks at the Middle East and especially the Palestinians.

The second part of the book deals with the arms race. In part three, which deals with European and Middle East Security generally, there are essays by Pierre Hassner, Ciro Zoppo (survey of naval developments in the Mediterranean), and David Carlton.

The final section, on peace education and the study of conflict, starts off with a sceptical view of Michael Nicolson on Peace Education.

(PRAJ: PRID)

0113 Carlton, David and Schaerf, Carlo (Eds.). *Contemporary Terror Studies in Sub-State Violence*. New York, St. Martin's Press, 1981.

Besides a number of country case studies, this collection offers essays on a wide range of topics, including nuclear terrorism, the role of the news media, and Chinese and Soviet attitudes towards international terrorism.

(PRAJ: PRID)

0114 Carlton, David and Schaerf, carlo (Eds.). *International Terrorism and World Security*. London, Croom Helm, 1975.

Just about one-third of this book actually treats terrorism (about 100 pages of some 330), with the remaining sections treating the arms race, European and Middle East security, and peace studies and the study of conflict The contributions treating terrorism are relatively general in focus, with some exceptions.

(N&G)

0115 Carmichael, D.J.C. Of Beasts, Gods, and Civilized Men : The Justification of Terrorism and of Counter terrorist Measures. *Terrorism: An International Journal*, Volume 6, Number 1, 1982-83.

This essay argues that the practical difficulties of dealing effectively with terrorism reveal a basic problem in the terms of conventional moral understanding. Specifically, current moral principles permit us to condemn any act of terrorism as categorically unjustifiable only in terms which impose crippling restrictions upon the range of justifiable counterterrorist measures. This problem arises from an abstract individualism which pervades current moral and political thought. If this abstract individualism is rejected, then it is possible to construe acts of terrorism as savage in a special sense, insofar as they reject the prior moral authority of the community to determine its own standards. On this basis, such acts may be condemned as inherently incapable of moral justification and in terms which license vigorous counterterrorist measures.

(T)

0116 Carrere, Rene and Valat-Morio, Pierre. Measurement of Terrorism from 1968 to 1972 (In French). *Etudes Polemologiques 8*, Volume 3, April 1973, pp. 47-58.

As terrorism has continued to grow rapidly, the authors focussed their attention on the problem, analyzing manifestations of collective violence during the 1968-72 period. Of 2, 256 instances, 717, or 31% were considered acts of terrorism. The latter were defined as attempts against persons or goods, political assassinations, the taking of political hostages, air hijackings, Guerrilla tangles or violent demonstrations leading to clashes, were not considered as terrorist

acts. The number of terrorist acts increased considerably year by year. In 1968, terrorist acts formed 18% of the manifestations of violence, whereas in 1969 there were 20%, in 1970, 30%, in 1971, 38%, and in 1972, 49%. The authors note also the increasing sophistication of techniques used and the increasing seriousness of the acts, according to what is threatened (a threat against a car as opposed to threatening a nuclear installation). It is also striking to note that terrorist acts are infrequent in nations where police action is strong or where ideology is vigorous, in war zones or areas of open combat, and in the countries of Western Europe or North America, where opposition to terrorism can make itself heard through legal channels. On the other hand, terrorist acts are intense and frequent in nations with weak ideology or structure (Latin America), in war situations where active combat has stopped (the Middle East), and in conflict situations where the weaker party has insufficient means to use guerrilla tactics or external terrorism (the liberation organizations in Portuguese Africa). The largest acceleration of terrorism is occurring clearly in the Arab world and the Latin American World.

(PRAJ: PRID)

0117 Cassidy, William L. *Political Kidnapping: An Introductory Overview*. Boulder, Sycamore Island Books, 1978

An exercise in vacuousness by a security consultant. This brief (28 printed pages of large type) monograph is purported to be a sanitized "extension" from a "classified study" prepared in the summer of 1977 for a "major international police organization."

(N&G)

0118 Chalfont, Lord. Terrorism and International Security. *Terrorism: An International Journal*, Volume 5, Number 4, 1981-82.

Of the major threats to the security and survival of Western political institutions, international terrorism is surely the greatest. Terrorism rejects morality and the political process promotes totalitarianism and threatens only democratic systems. It has now become an international phenomenon, with links between terrorist groups of all types and nationalities, irrespective of their political, religious, or ideological origins. International terrorism is sponsored by the Soviet Union and its allies, and its activities are frequently encouraged, consciously or unwittingly, by irresponsible behaviour on the part of the press and the other media of information. There is urgent need for international action to deal with what is now a serious international problem.

(T)

0119 Chaliand, Gerard. Munich: Palestinian Terrorism and International Politics. *Liberation*, Volume 17, Number 8, January 1972, pp. 5-7.

Using the "Munich massacre" as a case in point, this article discusses the political strategies and relative sophistication of the Palestinian leadership and the Israeli government. The author claims that the general international support for the Israeli cause must not be understood as a "plot" to humiliate the Palestinians, but must be seen against the background of the bad conscience of Western nations about their passive attitude toward the genocide of Jews in Europe and the fact that Israeli violence is presented as highly technical, methodical and taking place only in response to provocation; on the other hand, "the Palestinian militants are using terrorism simultaneously as a last resort, as a platform and as a means of agitation".

(PRAJ: PRID)

0120 Chaliand, Gerard. Palestinian Terrorism and Internationnal Politics. *Liberation*, January 1973, pp. 5-7

The author perceives the Palestinian resistance as a movement of "hopeless impotence", where the militants are using terrorism simultaneously as an act of desperation, as a platform, and as a means of agitation. He is afraid that they will fail to aid in achieving even a partial solution to the Palestinian national problem. His principal criticisms are: (1) most of the leaderships of the movements have failed to produce any "coherent political strategy"; (2) most of the Palestinian armed forces were utterly destroyed in September 1970; (3) there is a fundamental inability to comprehend the mentality of the West (which is both the enemy and the potential ally?), (4) the movement lacks any "modernizing ideology beyond nationalism."

(PRAJ: PRID)

0121 Challenge of Terrorism. *Statesman*, (Delhi), 16 May, 1985.

The expatriate Sikhs are involved in fomenting violence in India resulting in widespread insecurity all over the country. Also the resignation of Sant Longowal has left the Akalidal in the hands of Extremists.

0122 Chatterjee, S.K. Terrorism and Certain Legal Aspects of Human Rights. *International Relations*, Volume 6, Number 5, May 1980, pp. 749-768.

The purpose(s) of employing terrorism may offer a basis for its classification. Terrorism for liberation movement deserves a special consideration. Despite the conclusion of various international and regional conventions on human rights, state practice suggests that derogations from convention obligations are often justified on the grounds of alleged public policy and public security. An alleged terrorist, whilst in detention, should not be denied basic human rights nor should he be made subject to any punishment. Although no terrorist activity deserves support, the causes of terrorism being manifold, an unorthodox attitude towards terrorist is necessary. Perhaps an alleged terrorist act may best be judged by means of an international mixed inquiry commission rather than a court, although the latter would be necessary for considering attendent legal issues.

(IPSA)

0123 Chopra, V.D. Design behind the Ominous Developments. *Patriot*, 20 May, 1985.

Author sees a great design by foreign countries particularly USA and Pakistan, to destabalise the country. Terrorists are being used but they do not seem to accept this harsh reality.

0124 Chowla, N.L. Terrorism, Violence and Role of Media. *Patriot*, 5 July, 1985.

The article deals with the role of media in reporting Terrorism and Violence.

0125 Civiletti, Benjamin R. Terrorism: The Government's Response Policy. *FBI Law Enforcement Journal*, January 1979, pp. 19-22.

Excerpted from testimony to the Congress, on August 16, 1978. Civiletti is the Deputy Attorney General, and as such has been delegated the responsibility

to oversee government responses to acts of terrorism. He presents a basically optimistic perspective on the capability of the US government to counterterror, while he admits that "upgrading" may be necessary in some areas (e.g., military training and special equipment). Some details of the organization of the government's counter-terrorism structure are provided.

(N&G)

0126 Clark, Richard Charles. *Technological Terrorism*. Devin-Adair, 1980.

The author argues that terrorism using high end technology, has increased the threat to society but unfortunately the government policies have ignored this aspect and is unrecognised.

(BRD)

0127 Clutterbuck, Richard. Management of the Kidnap Risk. *Terrorism: An International Journal*, Volume 5, Numbers 1-2, 1981-82.

Paradoxically, Britain, where kidnapping is rare, has been a pioneer in kidnap insurance, prevention, and negotiation, largely due to the experience of Lloyd's of London in underwriting every kind of risk worldwide. The premium income of Lloyd's for kidnap insurance has grown from $150,000 in 1970 to $ 50 million in 1976. As with fire risks, with kidnap risks Lloyd's found that it saved money both for the underwriters and their clients if they sent specialist consultants to advise on reducing the risk and, in the event of a kidnap, to advise no negotiation. A firm at Lloyd's founded such a consultancy (Control Risks Ltd.) which has now expanded to meet a rising demand, not only from insured client, but also from an increasing number of uninsured clients who engage them on a consultancy fee basis. This article examines the growing attractiveness of kidnapping as a high-yield low-risk crime (whether for political dividends or criminal gain); describes how kidnaps are organized; advises on the various means of protection against it; and discusses the acts of contingency planning and crisis management if a kidnap occurs.

(T)

0128 Clutterbuck, Richard. Terrorism and urban violence. *Proceedings of the Academy of Political Science*, Volume 34, Number 4, 1982, pp. 165-175.

The biggest single motivation of terrorism and violent demonstrations is to gain publicity. Violence is news. Such news reaches more and more people every year, instantly all over the world. There is therefore a natural marriage between the person who uses violence to attract attention and the journalist who wishes to give his readers or viewers what they want. A free investigative press is the only effective guard against corruption and abuse of power, but this freedom must be used responsibly. The journalist has to reconcile his duty to disclose news of public interest with his responsibility as a citizen not to exacerbate violence or put lives at risk. The communications revolution has made the profession of journalism the most influential in the world. To match this power it must enforce higher ethical standards on its members.

(IPSA)

0129 Clutterbuck, Richard. The Cost of Giving in to Terrorists. *Observer*, (London), October 5, 1975, p. 8.

Discusses various methods of countering terrorists, including some, such as repressive legislation, eroding public liberty which can be fatal to a democracy.

Holds that the only effective action comes through efficient police work with active public cooperation.

(PRAJ: PRID)

0130 Clutterbuck, Richard. *Living with Terrorism*. New Rochelle, Arlington House, 1975.

Practical advice for the potential individual victim, with an informed discussion of incidents and perpetrators.

(N&G)

0131 Clutterbuck, Richard. *Kidnap and Ransom*. Boston, Faber and Faber, 1978.

The author examines the aims of terrorist groups, their organization, their techniques and how one should handle the crisis if it occurs.

(PRAJ: PRID)

0132 Cohen, Bernard L. Interview by Richard Brookhiser. Q & A: Understanding a Trillion-Dollar Question. *National Review*, February 2, 1979, pp. 142-155.

Cohen believes the nuclear terror possibility has been considerably overdrawn. In fact, there are experts on terrorism who say it would be a good thing if terrorists became preoccupied with nuclear bombs, since it would distract them from more feasible methods of mass murder.

(N&G)

0133 Cohen, Bernard L. The Potentialities of Terrorism: Plutonium is an over-rated Weapon for Terrorist Use. *Bulletin of the Atomic Scientists*, Volume 32, June 1976, pp. 34-35.

Cohen concludes that it is too late to engage in a dialectic concerning the utility of nuclear power. The time for such a debate was twenty years ago. Furthermore, he finds that the terrorists' concern about their personal safety would lead them to less complicated and less dangerous mass destruction weapons -- poison gas, napalm at a sporting event, the destruction of a dam, or the poisoning of water -- but even these options are out of character with the past activities of terrorists. Finally, he sees yielding to terrorism as a special kind of tyranny which society must avoid for "...to stand fast is a guarantee of eventual victory."

(N&G)

0134 Cohen, David. The Horrors of Hijacks. *New Scientist*, Volume 83, July 12, 1979, pp. 96-97.

Following the hijacking of a Dutch train by South Moluccans in 1975, the psychiatrist who has helped persuade the nijackers to surrender announced that the ex-hostages ran a serious risk of having been mentally disturbed. When the released hostages began criticising the government handling of the affair and expressing sympathy for the South Moluccan case, the government seized upon this warning to discredit them by attributing mental illhealth to them. After a second hijacking in 1977, the government funded a programme of psychiatric assistance for ex-hostages, but the worst ordeal of these people was being treated as psychiatric cases by their friends. These episodes show the contradictions that well-intentioned psychiatric presumptions can lead to.

(PRAJ: PRID)

0135 Cohen, Joel. Tactics Against Terror. *The Spectator*, Number 7608, April 20, 1974, p. 473.

Britain is seriously involved in continuing international war against terrorism. The bombing campaign in Northern Ireland has been extended to London and provincial cities and West European airports resemble military fortresses.

If there were a more positive response from the international community to the grievances of groups demonstrating peacefully, perhaps some potential terrorists could be persuaded to rethink their tactics. Answering force with greater force, showing terrorists that terrorism does not pay off, is a reasonable basis for those who have to deal with terrorism. At the same time the other process of extending a hand to peaceful protesters may spare bloodshed.

(PRAJ: PRID)

0136 Colnando, Ken. Countering Terrorism. *Hindustan Times*, (Delhi), 23 October 1985.

Author recommends that India should create a specialised anti-terrorist force on the lines of SAS of Britain, Delta force of U.S.A., GIGN of France, GSG-9 of West Germany and Spetsnaz of USSR and this force should be trained by SAS of Britian.

0137 Comey, David. The Perfect Trojan Horse. *Bulletin of the Atomic Scientists*, Volume 32, June 1976, pp. 33-34.

Given the risk of nuclear terrorism, Comey sees the growth of civil nuclear power programs as inimicable to civil liberties in the U.S. Comey holds that the terrorist threat is so severe as to "require us to alter our traditional views about citizens' rights and the police powers of the government." Given the problems associated with nuclear power, Comey would prefer to do without the "benefits" of nuclear power rather than suffer the resultant deprivations of liberty.

(N&G)

0138 Conference Proceedings. *International Terrorism*. Proceedings of the Third Annual Conference of Canadian Council of International Law, Ottawa, October 18-19, 1974. Review by Arnold Baichman. *Canadian Journal of Political Science*, Volume 9, Number 3, September 1976, pp.521-523.

The Conference deliberated on "how to stop the metastasis of political terror" and "why it is virtually impossible for the international community...to arrive at some anti-terrorist strategy." Some states (e.g. Libya, Uganda) regard terrorism as legitimate. The technology to reduce the number of certain terrorist acts (e.g. hijacking) exists, and has been applied successfully (mandatory passenger and luggage screening). But terrorist acts against foreign diplomats are more difficult to stop. Debate at the U.N. Ad Hoc Committee has been inconclusive. The Ottawa Conference, too, witnessed a confrontation of views: those, like Paul de Visoher, who differentiates sharply between political and criminal motives, and thinking that political reforms are the answer to the former - and those, like L.C. Green, who stresses protection of the innocent and judging terrorist acts as such regardless of motives. Many ideologies, of both left and right, challenge our bourgeois society - sometimes through terrorism. Some are tiny groups, but can do a lot of damage. Primitive nuclear devices may soon add to their repertoire.

(PRAJ: PRID)

0139 Cooley, John K. *Green March, Black September*. London, Frank Cass and Company Ltd., 1973.

Effective chapters on Arafat, Habash and other Fedayeen leaders. Cooley is the highly respected, former Middle East correspondent for the *Christian Science Monitor*. He writes from a perspective sympathetic to the Palestinians (vis-a-vis the Fedayeen).

(N&G)

0140 Cooper, H.H.A. Terrorism and the Intelligence Function. *Chitty's Law Journal*, Volume 73, March 1976.

Cooper presents a brief and general discussion of the function of intelligence in countering terrorism. He argues that a careful distinction should be drawn between intelligence, counter-intelligence, and preventive intelligence functions in light of the abuses which have been revealed and the resultant concern for eliminating excesses. By clearly distinguishing the one function from the ther, the intelligence agencies (with adequate guidelines) will avoid the "contamination" which programs such as Cointelpro generated, and will be able to continue exercising the intelligence function, which Cooper argues is of the utmost importance in combating terrorism.

(N&G)

0141 Cooper, H.H.A. The International Experience with Terrorism: An Overview. *Disorders and Terrorism*: Washington, pp. 419-442, U.S. Department of Justice, Law Enforcement Assistance Administration *Disorder and Terrorism, Report of the Task Force on Disorder and Terrorism*. Washington, D.C., Government Printing Office, 1976.

A competent overview which stresses the general ineffectiveness of terrorism as a route to political change (through coercion). For a terrorist campaign to succeed in accomplishing its strategic goals (rather than the tactical goals of fear or attention), there must be: "recognizable struggle for self-determination", at least tacit support among the populace, a strong, sustaining ideology, *and* outside sponsorship. Cooper also surveys hard line vs. soft responses, aviation security and legal responses to terrorism.

(N&G)

0142 Cooper, H.H.A. Terrorism and the Media. In Alexander, Yonah, and Finger, Seymeur M. (Eds.). *Terrorism : Interdisciplinary Perspectives*. New York, The John Jay Press, 1977, pp. 141-156.

Addressing the role of the media in the terrorism process, Cooper asserts that the problem is not with straight reporting, but with the propagandizing of terrorism. He argues that the media must content with reporting the inherent drama of an act of terror, rather than providing additional drama. In short, the media must see itself as part of the problem, and this, Cooper suggests, is a step toward solving the problem.

(N&G)

0143 Cooper, H.H.A. Whither Now? Terrorism on the Brink. *Chitty's Law Journal*, Volume-25, Number 6, 1977. In Elliott, John D. and Gibson Leslie K. (Eds.). – Contemporary Terrorism. Gaitherburg,

Maryland International Association of Chief of Police, 1978.

A commentary written in the shadow of the Entebbe success. Cooper suggests that there is a cyclical nature to terrorist activities and at this point the fortunes of terrorist are declining (in what he subsequently identifies as a respite only), whereas state terrorism and repression is on the ascendant--becoming as it were, an alternative form of government. Cooper posits that behind successful (non-state) terrorism we find state support, a questionable conclusion given the more recent adventures of German and Italian terrorists. As a final irony, he postulates that the Entebbe rescue may have taken the world closer to a terrorist Armageddon, with the terrorists seeking to meet state power with mass destructive weapons.

(N&G)

0144 Corsi, Jerome R. Terrorism as a Desperate Game : Fear, Bargaining, and Communication in the Terrorist Event. *Journal of Conflict Resolution*, Volume 25, Number 1, March 1981, pp. 47-85.

This article examines terrorism both theoretically and empirically. A typology is presented to identify different types of terrorist events and characteristics particular to each. Following this, the negotiations involved in hostage situations are examined with emphasis on government/terrorist response options and event outcomes. Throughout the article, assumptions of the theoretical model are empirically tested utilizing the ITERATE data set. Decision routes are mapped as a method for conceptualizing the tactics involved in bargaining communications. Formal game theory is utilized to explore the complexities involved in modelling government/terrorist interaction regarding : (a) developing an extensive game form; (b) specifying utilities; and (c) constructing illustrative games.

(IPSA)

0145 Crelinsten, Ronald D., Laberge-Altmejd, D. and Svablo, D. *Terrorism and Criminal Justice : An International Perspective*. Lexington, Mass, Health Lexington Books, 1978.

A LEAA - sponsored study, provides data from Belgium, Finland, France, U.S., Sweden, Germany and Northern Ireland. The diversity of anti-terror national policies is demonstrated.

(N&G)

0146 Crenshaw, Martha. *Revolutionary Terrorism: The FLN in Algeria, 1954-1962*. Stanford, Calif. Hoover Institution Press, 1978.

The political meaning of terrorism is systematically analyzed in a case study, and useful conclusions are drawn for societies attempting to deal with modern terrorist incidents.

(PRAJ: PRID)

0147 Crenshaw, Martha. The Causes of Terrorism. *Comparative Politics*, Volume 13, Number 4, July 1981, pp. 379-399.

The causes of terrorism directed against the state are imperfectly understood. A useful theoretical approach to the problem of causation focuses on three questions. First, is terrorism more likely in some socio-political contexts than others? Second, what are the reasons for an organization's resort to terrorism? Toward what ends is terrorism a means? Last, what motivates the individual to participate in terrorist activity? Terrorism is usually the product of a disaffected elite, making decisions on behalf of the majority. Survey of sig-

nificant terrorist campaigns of the past century indicates that the answer lies in a complex combination of reactions to the environment, especially to government actions, rational choice of modes of opposition, and psychological commitment to the group and to the cause. Such an answer partially explains why the combat of terrorism is difficult.

(IPSA)

0148 Cross-border Terrorism. *Patriot*, 23 December 1986.

The editorial suggests that recent assurances given by Pakistan that it will not aid and abet terrorism against India, cannot be taken seriously as Pakistan feels duty-bound to foster separatism and disunity in India and its support to anti-India elements is open.

0149 Crozier, Brian, (Ed.). *Annual of Power and Conflict*. London, Institute for the Study of Conflict, 1972-1977.

Annual since 1972. A valuable survey of extremist groups throughout the world, organized by region and by country, this excellent resource is the best book of its kind availabale.

(N&G)

0150 Crozier, Brian. *The Rebels : A Study of Post-War Insurrections*. Boston, Beacon Press, 1960.

While dated in several respects, this book remains a basic source for material on the Algerian FLN, the Cypriot EOKA and the Vietminh. Part IV "Terrorism", discussing terrorism as a "weapon of the weak" deserves a place on any reading list in the field. Crozier sees terrorism as unlikely to succeed unless there is outside support. In the final analysis, he asserts its success or failure will turn not on the intensity of its outrages but on its (in) ability to cause mounting expenditures on the part of the state. "When the question 'Is it worth it?' begins to be asked, the terrorists are winning. When the answer is 'No,' they have won."

(N&G)

0151 Culley, John A. Difusing Human Bombs -- Hostage Negotiations. *FBI Law Enforcement Bulletin*, October 1974, pp. 10-14.

Discussion of New York City's Hostage Negotiating Team which has been noted for its exemplary results when dealing with hostage situations.

(N&G)

0152 Cullinane, Maurice J. Terrorism. A New Era of Criminality. *Terrorism, An International Journal*, Volume 1, 1978, pp. 119-124.

In the context of the 1977 Hanafi terrorists attack in Washington, Cullinane discusses negotiation as it functioned in that incident, and draws conclusions that may be applicable to future incidents. Of particular note are his comments concerning the behaviour of the negotiator who must be chosen carefully; be mature in appearance; never seem to be the final authority; be able to negotiate on all matters except the provision of weapons or additional hostages; only respond to the demands of the terrorists, rather than attempting to be innovative; always receive a *quid Pro quo*; and, always keep the possibility of escape open for the terrorists.

(N&G)

0153 Dang, Satyapal. Fear of Deal with Terrorists. *Times of India*, (Delhi), 22 May 1987.

The imposition of Governor's rule in Punjab has evoked varied reactions.

Article warns the Centre not to make any short term peace which may not be in the nations' interest. Centre should fight terrorism and separatism both on administrative and political levels.

0154 Dang, Satyapal. This Time Deal with Terrorists? *Times of India*, (Delhi), 24 August 1987.

Mr. Darshan Singh Ragi's announcement of his retirement from Panthic Committee and blessings to militants have given a new thrust to Punjab problem. Any attempt by Centre to hold talks with terrorists, will prove counterproductive.

0155 Day, Samuel H., Jr. Some Questions about Entebbe. *Bulletin of Atomic Scientists*, September 1976, p. 7.

Day is critical of the Israeli raid on Entebbe to rescue the hostages captured by the hijackers. The raid has been acclaimed as the proof of the success of a get-tough policy. But is it? Or does it instead just raise the ante? Could bloodshed have been avoided? Yes, by acceding to the demands of the hijackers which Israel refused to do. Did the raid really save lives? Yes, white ones, but the number of blacks killed is not known.

The world will be safe from hijackers only when there is no place for them to go... only when there is an international convention which will deny skyjackers ordinary protection from civil laws wherever they land. If they have no place to land skyjackers will cease to operate. "The Entebbe raid has hampered what little progress the world has been making toward solution of the skyjacking problem through international agreement. Such an agreement would be immensely valuable not only for its own sake, but also as a model for a peaceful, non-violent world in which no nation has a greater stake than Israel Itself."

(PRAJ: PRID)

0156 Debray, Regis. *Revolution in the Revolution*? : *Armed Struggle and Political Struggle in Latin America*. (Trans. by Bobbye Ortiz), New York, Monthly Review Press, 1967.

This brief book has had considerable influence in leftist circles in Latin America and elsewhere. It is strongest on tactics for mobilizing the guerrila potential of the urban and rural masses.

(N&G)

0157 Deeley, Peter. How the Wrath of God came to Ahmed. *Observer*, 5 August, 1973, pp. 1-2.

During the past year, Israeli and Palestinian counter-terror groups have been responsible for a series of killings in Europe, the Middle East and Washington. They have been overshadowed in the news media by hijackings, embassy attacks, etc. Fourteen people have been systematically assassinated, and almost as many injured. Sometimes, very sophisticated modern methods are used.

(PRAJ: PRID)

0158 Delmas, Claude. Terrorism et relations internationales (Terrorism and international relations). *Politique Internationale*, 14 hiver 1981-82, pp. 227-240.

*Au XIX^e siecle, le terrorism etait une forme de revolte auto-destructrice, un defiromantique a la societe. Aujourd'hui il est devenu un moyen pour atteindre un*

*out politique donne comme par example la constitution d'un Etat palestinien. En Allemagne, il existe encore un terrorisme de type nihiliste, egalement en Italie. Les terroristes esperent engendrer la crainte aupres de la population, lui donner un sentiment d'impuissance et de mefiance vis-a-vis des gouvernements en place. Le terrorisme a une dimension internationale en raison de ses repercussions multinationales, des liens entre les groupes et de L'interet evident que l'LRSS Y porte dans les pays occidentaux.*

(IPSA)

0159 Demaris, Orid. *Brothers in Blood: The International Terrorist Network*. New York, Scribner, 1977.

Author has discussed the problem of political terrorism. In five essays he discusses 'carlos' and the web of international terrorist interactions; terrorism in the Middle East; the short careers of Ulrike Meinhof and Andreas Baader in West Germany; the use of terrorism in the long Irish conflict and what would happen if nuclear devices fell into terrorists' hands.

(BRD)

0160 Devine, Philip E.;Rafalko, Robert J. On Terror. *Annals of the American Academy of Political and Social Science*. 463, September 1982, pp. 39-53.

Very little has been written on the subject of terrorism from a philosophical view point. What little exists generally presupposes terrorism to be either senseless brutality of romanticized heroism. We argue that it is neither. Many writers conflate terrorism with either revolutionary or criminal activity. We contend that it is a separate and recent phenomenon, defining terrorism as violence directed, as a matter of political strategy, against innocent persons. We consider three possible arguments that may be offered in defence of terrorism. First, the Economy of Scale argument, which supposes terrorism to be the "cheapest form of warfare". Second, the Consciousness-Raising argument, contending that terrorism is warranted provided that it makes the public aware of institutional injustice. Third, the Collective Guilt argument, which holds that the public is sealed by their silence. We argue that none of these arguments holds up under close scrutiny, and we further consider general objections that can be raised against any terrorist activity. We conclude with a look into the terrorist's mind, noting that he or she interprets the world in starkly polar terms between good and evil. We describe the ideological rift that exists between the liberal democratic tradition - of which our arguments are representative - and the ideologies of terrorism.

(IPSA)

0161 Dobson, Christopher. *Black September: Its Short, Violent History*. New York, Macmillan, 1974.

Popular history with a surfeit of gratuitous ethnocentric and partisan commentary. Dobson's assertion of the Arab's "fatal flow of Violence" is illustrative. He argues that Black September operated under al-Fatah auspices, although the facts would seem to indicate a cooperative relationship. Despite several significant errors, the book contains material of note with respect to Black September. In particular, the identification of Black September principles, as well as an account of the Israeli-Fedayeen "secret war" should be of interest. Dobson is a journalist with the British Sunday Telegraph.

(N&G)

0162 Dobson, Christopher and Robert Payne. *The Carlos Complex: A Study in Terror*. New York, Putnam, 1977.

This work focuses on the interrelatedness of various national terrorist organisations. The authors offer tentative solutions to the terrorism epidemic. 'Carlos complex' is a name given by these authors to denote his connections. These include certain -- communists possibly the KGB, radical extremists' from West Germany and Japan, the Palestinian hijack enthusiasts, Gaddafi and Amin.

(BRD)

0163 Dobson, Christopher and Payne, Ronald. *The Terrorists : Their Weapons, Leaders, and Tactics*. New York, Facts on File, 1979.

An attractive and well-packaged overview of terrorism. In addition to the predictable topics, the book includes a 40 page "who's who" by region and country, in which major groups are given approximately one page of coverage each; a brief (20 page) chronology for the decade through June 1979; fourteen color prints of small arms used by terrorists; and a very handy index. On the whole, a very commendable general work, which holds appeal for the specialist.

(N&G)

0164 Doherty, Frank. The IRA's Deadly Technology. *New Scientist*, Volume 83, 6 September, 1979, p. 708.

Methods used by the Provisional Irish Republican Army for remote detonation of bombs are reviewed. These have become more sophisticated, to circumvent army electronic counter-measure equipment, but remain inexpensive and effective.

(PRAJ: PRID)

0165 Donovan, Robert J. Oppose all Violence Equally (a letter). *Friends Journal*, 15 December, 1982, p. 23.

"Box Nixon's article, 'International Terrorism' (FJ 10/1) seemed to adopt a political viewpoint that violence by isolated individuals or small groups is somehow worse than that of more thoroughly organized armies." If Libya is to be embargoed, there is a stronger case against South Africa, Israel, the United States, and Russia for supporting terrorist infiltrators in various trouble zones.

(PRAJ: PRID)

0166 Dortzback, Karl and Debbie. *Kidnapped*. New York, Harper and Row, 1975.

Memoirs of a missionary who was kidnapped in 1974 by the Eritrean Liberation Front. Some of the names have been changed to protect the guilty.

(N&G)

0167 Dowling, Joseph A. Prolegomera to a Psycho-historical Study of Terrorism. In Livingston, Marious H. (Ed.). with Kressi, Lee B. and Wanek, Marie G. *International Terrorism in the Contemporary World*. Westport, Conn. Green Wood Press, 1978.

Dowling proceeds from a position that the anarchist-terrorist phenomenon is part of an endemic impulse to resolve the existential isolation of man. He touches upon the insights offered by Freud, Erikson and Lifton as vital aspects in any attempt to understand the historical phenomenon of terrorism.

(N&G)

0168 Drastic and Unavoidable. *Tribune*, (Chandigarh), 20 May 1985.

The Terrorist and Disruptive Activities (Prevention) Bill, though more dras-

tic and comprehensive, was unavoidable due to the prevailing circumstances not only in Punjab but in the adjoining States as well.

0169 Edelhertz, Herbert and Walsh, Marilyn. *The White-Collar Challenge to Nuclear Safeguards*. Lexington, Mass, Lexington Books, D.C. Health and Company, 1978.

The authors contend that the extensive attention devoted to the nuclear terrorist threat has overshadowed another serious threat, the diversion of nuclear materials by employees of the industry. This book is a competent remedy to this largely ignored problem.

(N&G)

0170 Editorial. A Long Haul Ahead. *Times of India,* (Delhi), 16 May 1985.

Editorial welcomes Rajiv Gandhi's statement that the Government would be tough in fighting the extremists but flexible in its search for political solution with regard to recent unprecedented eruption of terrorist violence in Delhi and five northern states.

0171 Editorial. Battling Terrorism. *Hindustan Times,* (Delhi), 3 August 1985.

Editorial discusses the issue of banning 'mercenary schools' in USA.

0172 Editorial. Black January. *The New Republic*, 22 January, 1977, p. 10.

France's cowardly release of Abu Doaud, PLO terrorist, disappoints those in Europe who are hoping that Europe will stop selling honour for oil.

(PRAJ: PRID)

0173 Editorial. Coping with "Terrorists". *Progressive,* Volume 42, Number 7, July 1978, p. 11.

Get-tough policies with terrorists will only result in needless bloodshed and teach terrorists that violence really works. "If protection of the public is the objective, acquiescence without condemnment is the best short-term tactics" while the long run strategy should address "those larger, less visible, and more pervasive forms of official terrorism to which such atrocities as Moro's killing are just a small and ugly counterpart."

(PRAJ: PRID)

0174 Editorial. Death Penalty for Terrorists? *Christian Century*, Volume 90, Number 12, 21 March, 1973, pp. 333-334.

The recent tragic incident at Khartoum reminds us that the middle East conflict is our conflict, and that the US is one of the nations responsible for imposing on the Middle East an arrangement which has led to hostility and violence.

(PRA)

0175 Editorial. Fighting Terror. *Times of India,* (Delhi), 22 May 1985.

Editorial welcomes the Terrorist and Disruptive (activities) Bill but cautions the Government to raise the morale, cohesion and effectiveness of the police and intelligence machinery to effectively curb the terrorist activities.

0176 Editorial. Freedom to Exploit. *Christian Century*, Volume 94, Number 11, 30 March, 1977, p. 292.

Disturbed individuals and militant groups attract the attention of the media, by the use of violence and the taking of hostages, exploiting the advantages of a free press, to gain their own goals. Media coverage of incidents of terrorism contributes to their recurrence.

(PRAJ: PRID)

0177 Editorial. From Bad to Worse. *Hindustan Times*, (Delhi), 10 August 1987.

The spurt in terrorist violence in Punjab is a planned move by terrorists to discredit President's rule and to achieve their other goals. The hands of police and paramilitary forces should be strengthened and a dialogue should be started with various sections of the Sikh population.

0178 Editorial. Guilty or Innocent. *Tribune*, (Chandigarh), 24 October 1985.

India's accusation and Pakistan's denial of Sikh terrorists being trained in Pakistan, should be amicably solved between Mr. Rajiv Gandhi and President Zia-ul-Haq, as both are in New York.

0179 Editorial. Harsh and Unnecessary. *Tribune*, (Chandigarh), 30 May 1985.

Editorial cirtises the Gujarat Anti-social Activities (Prevention) ordinance and the move by J & K Government to extent the provisions of the recent anti-terrorist law passed by Parliament to the state.

0180 Editorial. It is not Yet too Late. *Patriot*, 9 July 1987.

Extremists have been successful in their plan of phased balkanisation of India and it is now up to the centre to stem the influence of extremists and suppress them otherwise it will have to face more 'Laldengas'.

0181 Editorial. Meeting the Challenge of Terrorism. *The Hindu*, (Madras), 16 May 1985.

Government efforts in consultation with opposition parties to find political solution of the Punjab problem with moderate Akalis are appreciated. Article also warns about terrorist menace to the unity of India.

0182 Editorial. Menace of Terrorism. *National Herald*, 22 July 1985.

The assurance given by British Government to Indian Government that it would counter the Sikh terrorists is welcomed. Editorial asks UN to take steps to combat terrorism by its member states.

0183 Editorial. Nations and Terrorism. *Hindustan Times*, (Delhi), 11 June 1987.

Editorial discusses the lesson learned throughout world for combatting terrorism. It suggests that a measure of morality will have to be injected in to state behaviour to fight terrorism.

0184 Editorial. On the Visit. *Hindustan Times*, 27 May 1985.

Due to the anniversary of Operation Blue Star, the police and intelligence agencies must take every care to stop the extremists in inciting communal riots and violence against innocent people.

0185 Editorial. Papal Bull. *Progressive*, Volume 47, Number 3, March 1983, pp. 10-11.

Despite the findings of Italian judge Ilario Martella rumours continue that Mehement Ali Agea was aided by the Soviet Union or its satellite, Bulgaria, in his attempt to assassinate Pope John Paul II in 1981. While such complicity is possible, American officials should be reminded of a CIA conspiracy to kill the Congo's Patrice Lumumba and at least eight plots against Fidel Castro.

(PRAJ: PRID)

0186 Editorial. Sadat Dead. *The Monitor Weekly*, Volume 1, Number 3, 9-25 October, 1981, Muslim Monitor Ltd., London, p. 27.

Sadat's assassination is not surprising; he had alienated not only the Arab and Muslim world outside, but also vast sections of Egypt's Population, and loss of allegiance by a section of the armed forces cost him his life. Israel's Prime Minister Begin's attitude on Palestinian rights had hardened, leaving Eygpt's President Sadat high and dry. Israel and USA must bear a large degree of responsibility for what has now happened. No end to the cycle of violent changes can be foreseen, unless we learn from the events of October 7th.

(PRAJ: PRID)

0187 Editorial. Statesman like. *Hindustan Times*, (Delhi), 15 May 1985.

Rajiv Gandhi's speech in Parliament emphasising that Government will deal with extremists with firm hand, was welcomed. Editorial praises P.M. emphasis on flexibility on political aspects of the Punjab problem.

0188 Editorial. Strikes Against Terror. *Tribune*, (Chandigarh), 16 July 1987.

Editorial asks for protection for PSEB workers, as nearly 30 of them have been killed in terrorist violence.

0189 Editorial. Systematic Fault. *Indian Express*, (Delhi), 18 May 1985.

Government assertion of the foreign hand in Punjab is not proved by evidence and neither the Bill to amend Arms Act is going to make much difference.

0190 Editorial. Talk of the Town. *The New Yorker*, 3 June, 1974, pp. 27-28.

A comment on a new kind of crime which is epidemic in the world today. This crime is bent on "influencing a world television audience". Such crimes as the abduction of Patty Hearst, the murder of Israelis at Munich, come in this category. "Publicity crimes pose a special problem for the press". This is discussed.

(PRAJ: PRID)

0191 Editorial. Talk with Terrorists? *Patriot*, 20 April 1987.

Terrorists of all shades like Sikh Extremists, TNV, NSCN and GNLF, are now willing to talk with centre, superseding State Governments, through the strategy that sufficient capacity of killing would force centre to negotiate with them willingly. Editorial warns of such negotiations, till killings are stopped.

0192 Editorial. Terrorism rides again. *Statesman,* (Delhi), 29 November 1985.

Editorial suggests that terrorism in Punjab is on decline due to many circumstances, particularly action taken by USA and Canadian Governments against terrorists there and the violence may continue and should be taken as a sign of frustration on the part of terrorists.

0193 Editorial. Terrorists Abroad. *Statesman*, (Delhi), 19 October 1985.

Editorial discusses and welcomes the 'extradition treaty' between Mrs. Thatcher and Mr. Rajiv Gandhi, but warns that until and unless commensurate steps are taken in USA and Canada, the treaty may remain a half measure.

0194 Editorial. Terrorist Act Rules tabled in Parliament. *Indian Express*, (Delhi), 5 December 1986.

Editorial discusses the modalities of the Terrorist and Disruptive Activities (Prevention) Act, 1985.

0195 Editorial. The Cuban Exile Terrorist Network. *NACLA's Latin America and Empire Report*, Volume 8, Number 10, December 1974, pp. 19-27.

It is ironical that the Cuban exile team which was trained by the CIA in 1960 for the purpose of overthrowing the Castro Government were part of the Watergate machinery and the bombing of the OAS headquarters in Washington. It indicates that these mercenary forces are capable of using their "CIA skills" of burglary, sabotage and assassination to intervene in US domestic politics. The exile group are embroiled in internal warfare now and becoming more isolated in the US and abroad. At the same time, they are becoming more dangerous. The exiles are also linked up with other right-wing forces, particularly the Chilean junta. Revolutionary Cuba, however, is gaining support in the US as well as abroad. This article also contains the transcript of the news conference with former Cuban exile carlos Rivero Collado, who became a double agent in the terrorist groups. This term presents a complete account of the range of activities of the Cuban exiles.

(PRAJ: PRID)

0196 Editorial. The Real Nuclear Terrorists. *Progressive*, Volume 41, Number 4, April 1977, p. 7.

The Nuclear Regulatory Commission has called for stringent security safeguards and a severe restriction of civil liberties to cope with the danger of nuclear terrorism as atomic power plants proliferate. With the threats to safety and freedom, "perhaps these nuclear advocates are the real terrorists."

(PRAJ: PRID)

0197 Editorial. Through Measures to Curb Terrorism. *The Hindu*, (Madras), 22 May 1985.

The terrorist and disruptive activities (Prevention) Bill sho..d be used with extreme care and competence to make to democratic base strong.

0198 Editorial. Time to Get Tough. *Hindustan Times*, (Delhi), 12 May 1985.

After the bomb explosions, editorial asks the government to be strict with extremists and deplores the intelligence agencies of the country. It hopes that opposition parties, instead of partisan politics, would strengthen the hands of government in safeguarding the unity and integrity of the nation.

0199 Editorial. Tracking Down Terrorism. *Tribune*, (Chandigarh), 13 July 1987.

Editorial favours the formation of special cells in seven States and two union Territories, which would help in filling a vital gap in maintaining a constant and heightened watch on the terrorist. It also suggests that a separate minister should be made incharge of these committees.

0200 Editorial. Training Camps Again. *Tribune*, (Chandigarh), 16 July 1985.

India's allegation and Pakistan's denial, about the training camps in Pakistan for Sikh extremists is the focus of the editorial. It suspects the Pakistan's bonafides over the Indian Hijackers trial at Lahore.

0201 Editorial. Use with Care. *Indian Express*, (Delhi), 21 May 1985.

Editorial warns the authorities to implement the Terrorist and Disruptive Activities (Prevention) Bill, with care and caution.

0202 Editorial. War of Nerves. *Times of India*, (Delhi), 12 September 1985.

The issue discussed is whether Frank Camper, warned an official in the Indian consulate in New York about a plot to put bombs abroad two Air-India Aircrafts by Sikh extremists. Editorial concludes that no such warning was conveyed.

0203 Editorial. Wooing the Militants. *Statesman*, (Delhi), 25 May 1987.

Until and unless people moved by Sikh fundamentalism are absorbed into the political mainstream, the solution to Punjab problem is not feasible, though it could give excuses to other fundamentalists to put pressure on government.

0204 Eichelman, B.; Soskis, D.A. and Reid, W.H. (Eds.). *American Psychiatric Association,* Washington, D.C. 1983, Police Work in Relation to Special Types of Offences.

This book contains edited and updated papers presented at a multidisciplinary symposium on the psychiatric aspects of terrorism, held in Baltimore, MD, in September 1979. It represents part of the American Psychiatric Association's attempt to examine the role of psychiatrists and other mental

health professionals involved in terrorist and hostage situations. The first section of the book examines the ethical issues related to the involvement of mental health professionals with law enforcement agencies in terrorist/hostage events. The second section looks at the victims of terrorism and hostage-taking, the victimization and rehabilitative treatment. Section three discusses the training of law enforcement personnel in dealing with terrorist incidents and their cooperation with psychiatry experts in terrorism cases. Section four deals with the research on terrorism (causes of terrorism, hostage situations, victimology, the role of the news media, and terrorist decision-making).

(PRAJ: PRID)

0205 Elahoro, Peter. Africa's Forgotten Wars. *Africa*, (London), Number 7, March 1972, pp.18-20.

Contrary to popular opinion, African guerrilla movements cannot convincingly prove that they are effectively removing white domination in southern Africa even eleven years after they began with the Angolan revolt against Portuguese colonialism. The guerrilla struggles in Angola, Mozambique and Guinea Bissau have all bogged down into stalemates. The credibility of the African guerrillas is questioned because of their tendency to make exaggerated claims of success, and the well-known sympathy of the reporters for the guerrillas. Some of the difficulties playing the guerrillas involve unlimited Portuguese access to weapons through NATO, lip-service only from the big powers in support of the guerrillas, the lack of protective terrain in many areas, declining morale from prolonged war, the fanaticism of the white supremacists, and the reluctance of the African states to actively support the guerrillas. The Liberation Committee of the Organization of African Unity has been in decline since its formation in 1963. The succession of leadership, rivalries, ideological conflicts, ethnic clashes and the desertions within the liberation movements have been embarrassing and can only hearten the white colonial regimes.

(PRAJ: PRID)

0206 Elliott-Bateman, Michael. et al. *The Fourth Dimension of Warfare. Volume 2: Revolt to Revolution Studies in the 19th and 20th Century European Experience.* Totowa, N.J.: Rowman and Battlefield, 1975.

This volume argues that the "modern phase" of guerrilla warfare goes back at least to the French Revolution, though since 1945 it has greatly accelerated. "The doctrines of a Mao or a Giap should not be regarded as a qualititative break-through in militarized revolution, but rather as a more successful attempt to grapple with problems that had already been faced, and sometimes solved, in previous centuries" (p. 144). The collection includes an essay by T.E. Lawrence on the Arab revolt of 1916 and several by other authors on revolution in Ireland. Closing essays by Elliott-Bateman generalize about "conditions" and "battlefronts".

(PRAJ: PRID)

0207 Elliott, John D., and Gibson, Leslie K., (Eds.). *Contemporary Terrorism*. Gaitherburg, Maryland International Association of Chiefs of Police, 1978.

On the whole a useful collection of previously published materials, but not without significant faults. Unfortunately, several areas of concern, in particular nuclear terrorism and terrorist tactics, are incompletely treated or not treated at all. By editorial design, terrorism in its regional manifestations is omitted, thus leaving the reader with only a segment of the picture. Of special note are con-

tributions by David Fromkin, Ian Smart, Andrew Pierre, David Milbank, Brian Jenkins, Jay Mallin, Walter Laqueur, and Edward Mickolus.

(N&G)

0208 Elwin, Goran. Swedish Anti-terrorist Legislation. *Contemporary Crises*, Volume 1, Number 3, July 1977, pp. 289-301.

Through an analysis of Swedish anti-terrorist legislation the author points out fundamental contradiction in Swedish policy. The Government has supported liberation movements in different parts of the world. It has supported them by words and money. But it has also passed a law which works against the interests of these groups. This is the same contradiction that characterizes Swedish policy towards the underdeveloped countries. It urges them to throwoff the yoke of imperialism, but since it is dependent on exports Sweden is also an interested state.

(IPSA)

0209 Epstein, Edward C. The uses of "Terrorism" : A Study in Media Bias. *Stanford Journal of International Studies*, Volume 12, Spring 1977, pp. 67-78.

The use of the value-laden term "terrorism" represents a subtle means of portraying the acts in a highly negative fashion to the papers' readers. The usage of the term "terrorism" is symbolic of an overall type of press bias found in varying degrees in all the newspapers studied. The press in the US may be free with respect to external censorship, but it is clearly not free from internally generated bias. The press plays an essential role in conditioning the public to accept policies without serious discussion of either their implications or their alternatives.

(IPSA)

0210 Evans, Ernest. *Calling a Truce to Terror : The American Response to International Terrorism*. Westport, Greenwood Press, 1979.

The thesis of this book is that the 'no concessions' policy of the American government has not prevented terrorist incidents and must therefore, be reassessed. Evans shows, using the experience of West Germany and Japan, that negotiations will usually save the lives of the hostages and, if conducted properly, can discredit the terrorist organisation... Evans suggests that terrorism be treated as a political act, and terrorist tactics be examined in relation to their goals. This book includes a unique examination of deterrence literature that shows how it is relevant for businesses and other organizations as well as governments.

(BRD)

0211 Fattah, Ezzat A. Some Reflections on the Victimology of Terrorism. *Terrorism : An International Journal*, Volume, 3, Number 1-2, 1979-80.

Literature on terrorists and terrorism is abundant, but very little is written on the victim. Whether the studies are published by psychologists or political scientists, by psychiatrists or sociologists, data on the victim are conspicuous by their absence. There is hardly any mention of how victims of terrorism are chosen, their characteristics, the role they play, if any, in preparing or triggering the terrorist acts, their behavior during the ordeal, and their postvictimization condition. The dearth of empirical data renders the systematic study of the vic-

tims of terrorism particularly difficult. This paper presents a series of reflections on some victimological aspects of terrorism and offers a number of suggestions for future research.

(T)

0212 Fendt, William. Portrait of a Terrorist. *Observer*, (London), 30 October, 1977, p. 2.

Profile of West German (25-year-old) Christian Klar, wanted in connection with Schleyer's murder, and three attempted murders. He is an ex-university student, of gentle manner, self-styled pacifist; he plays the guitar, and paints. His background is middle-class, both parents teachers; he had a special attachment to his mother who has not seen him for a year. At school, his political views were vaguely humanitarian, and he was not easily roused, but any evidence of injustice inflamed him.

(PRAJ: PRID)

0213 Ferracuti, Franco. A Socio-psychiatric Interpretation of Terrorism. *Annals of the American Academy of Political and Social Science*, Number 463, September 1982, pp. 129-140.

Forecasting events, particularly middle and long-range, would improve if we could provide a valid theoretical formulation. This would have to be interdisciplinary and should encompass both the idioverse of the terrorist and the universe of the terrorist events. Psychiatric contributions are few and they lack general validity. Violence and death wishes, which translate into fantasy war, are generally accepted characteristics. Four theories are briefly discussed: (1) frustration - aggression, (2) unbalance of the social system, (3) Olson's rational choice, and (4) Marxist theory.

(PRAJ: PRID)

0214 Fine, Allan M. Attributes of Potential Adversaries to US Nuclear Programs. In US Department of Commerce, National Bureau of Standards. *The Role of Behavioral Science in Physical Security*: Proceedings of the Second Annual Symposium, 23-24 March, Washington, 1977, pp. 27-33.

Data indicates that the requisite combinations of dedication and technical skill have not been coextensive. "For the non-war, subnational, potential US - based adversary, a group possessing all the attributes of the composite high-level profile would be expected to be exceedingly rare." Fine is affiliated with the Sandia Laboratories.

(N&G)

0215 Finger, Seymour Maxwell. Security of International Aviation: The Role of ICAO. *Terrorism : An International Journal*, Volume 6, Number 4, 1982-83.

The International Civil Aviation Organization in the last twenty years has marshalled support of the overwhelming majority of its 150 member states in developing security programs and establishing a legal framework of international cooperation against terrorism in international aviation. The Tokyo Convention of 1963 establishes jurisdiction over offense while an aircraft is in flight and grants a wide spectrum of powers to the aircraft commander to restrain a passenger. The Hague Convention of 1970 obliges states to punish the unlawful seizure of aircraft with severe penalties and to either extradite the offender or try him. The Montreal Convention of 1971 establishes a system of suppression

of acts against aircarft, covering mostly acts on the ground that might endanger an aircraft in flight, and requires states to take practicable measures to prevent such offenses. In the past few years the number of countries adhering to these pacts and instituting improved security measures has increased significantly. Accompanying this trend has been a downward trend in acts of unlawful interference and seizure of aircraft to 147 in the 1978-1980 period compared to 245 in the 1969-1971 period. Nevertheless, only steadfast efforts by all nations can complete the job of eliminating unlawful interference with international civil aviation.

(T)

0216 Fiorillo, Ernesto. Terrorism in Itlay: Analysis of a Problem. *Terrorism : An International Journal*, Volume 2, Number 3-4, 1979.

The author, after a short premise in which the phenomenon under examination is analyzed on the basis of the study of individual motivations, considers, in the context of the present Italian moral crisis, the social and interpersonal factors that violent terrorism generate.

The inquiry then moves on to attempt to identify the aims of terrorism through the observation of the subsequent phases through which it develops.

After a short survey of some sociological and psychological theories of the causes of the phenomenon, the author concludes that the problem of terrorism cannot be solved through the threat of more serious sanctions for the crimes committed but through the reorganization and restructuring of the state, and the elimination of the insecurity and tension that are among the main causes of the phenomenon.

(T)

0217 Flood, Michael. Nuclear Sabotage. *Bulletin of the Atomic Scientists*, Volume 32, October 1976, pp. 29-36.

Rather than addressing illicit bomb construction, which is the want of many commentators, Flood addresses a problem that he argues has been neglected - the possibility that a civil nuclear power facility might be the target of terrorists. Of particular interest are the tables which accompany the article, detailing past incidents involving nuclear facilities.

(N&G)

0218 Foland, M. Frances. Uruguay's Urban Guerrillas. *The New Leader*, 9 October, 1971, pp.8-12.

This article describes the urban guerrillas of Uruguay the Tupamaros. The author writes of the different personalities involved, the ideologies, problems encountered, and political occurrences within the country that make this movement so popular among the people. The author points out the effect they have had on other guerrilla organizations. Other Latin American organizations have shifted from the Cuban model to the Uruguayan model because of their success. The article also deals with the possibility of foreign intervention should urban guerrillas start an armed revolt. The author discusses the reasons why the Tupamaros have become so popular in a country that was once called the "Switzerland of South America". The author maintains that the guerrillas, should they come to power, would become reformists rather than radicals.

(PRAJ: PRID)

0219 Foley, Charles. Do-it-Yourself Mexico Snubs Disaster. *Observer*, 2 September, 1973, p. 4.

People in the earthquake city of Quzaba resent the government's refusal of

international relief, though its own relief is inadequate. The 43-year old government is locally accused of sterility and corruption; left-wing guerrilla groups are rife; right-wing terrorist groups (said to be encouraged by the government) attack them and the peasants; students and peasants are joining in protest, and political assassination result.

(PRAJ: PRID)

0220 Frank, Forrest. Nuclear Terrorism and the Escalation of International Conflict. *Naval War College Review*, Volume 29, Fall 1976, pp. 12-27.

After rehearsing the now familiar vulnerabilities that combine to create the threat of nuclear terrorism, Frank provides some interesting preliminary commentary on the possible effects that an act of nuclear terrorism might have for international relations. Proceeding from a position that views nuclear terror as an act possessed of (inherent?) ambiguity, he sees considerable risk that the act could precipitate interstate conflict. The risks range from crises resultant of retributory acts to a catalytic war.

(N&G)

0221 Frank, Forrest R. Suppressing Nuclear Terrorism : A Modest Proposal. In US Congress, Senate, Committee on Government Operations. *Export Reorganization Act of 1976, Hearings before the Committee on S. 1439*, 94th Cong., Ist Sess., June 1975, pp. 1413-1451.

Proposed treaty language for an international convention to suppress the theft or unlawful use of the nuclear materials or weapons. The proposal is modeled after the Convention for the Suppression of Unlawful seizure of Aircraft.

(N&G)

0222 Frank, Gerald. *The Deed*. New York, Simon and Schuster, 1963.

An account of Lord Moyne's assassination by a reporter who covered the trial of the assassins.

(N&G)

0223 Friedlander, Robert A. The Origins of International Terrorism : A Micro Legal - Historical Perspective. *Israel Yearbook on Human Rights*, Volume 6, 1976, pp. 49-61.

Friedlander argues that despite contemporary intellectual sentiments to the contrary we can be reasonably clear as to the historical origins and composition of international terrorism. To support his assertion, Friedlander offers an overview of terrorism in history, culminating with the outbreak of terrorist activity and state repression in Mandatory Palestine.

(N&G)

0224 Friedlander, Robert A. *Terrorism : Documents of International and Local Control*. Volume 2. Dobbs Ferry, New York, Oceana Publications, 1979.

An outstanding and encyclopedic work that is an absolute necessity for any serious reference collection on terrorism, includes 150 pages of commentary, 93 documents, a bibliography and an index. Documents range from the League of Nations Council debate on terrorism and the assassination of King Alexander (1934); to the UN General Assembly, Report of the *ad hoc* Committee on the

Drafting of an International Convention against the Taking of Hostages (1978).

(N&G)

0225 Friedlander, Robert A. "Terrorism: What Behind One Passive Acceptance of Transnational Mugging". *Barrister*, Volume 2, Summer 1975, pp. 10-13 ff.

Friedlander sees terrorism as "primarily a manifestation of rebellion and revolution against law-oriented society." He describes the lack of involvement of the American Bar Association and regional and local law associations in the matter of terrorism. Similarly, he criticizes the community of nations for their inaction and the imposition of an "international double standard" when dealing with the question; this inertia flying in the face of basic human rights concepts which have become a component of "public international law" since World War II. Friedlander concludes by suggesting statutes which would make submitting to a kidnapper's ransom demands a crime, for to "acquiesce in evil is to condone it."

(N&G)

0226 Friedlander, Robert A. The Ultimate Nightmare : What if Terrorists go Nuclear? *Denver Journal of International Law and Policy*, Volume 12, Number 1, Fall 1982, pp.1-11.

The author discusses "the possible global consequences" of how international nuclear proliferation and the phenomenon of an international arms race have created opportunities for terrorists to utilize nuclear weaponry. Focusing upon several nuclear terrorists attacks which have taken place over recent years, the author notes that "the basic question relating to the nuclear threat is no longer if, but when an episode of mass destruction will occur." He observes that "Terrorists emulate states" and then concludes that the international legal system has not provided remedies which deal with the threat of nuclear terrorism. This is so because a sizeable number of nation-states have voiced their support for terrorist activities, thus splitting the ranks of any international legal order. However, international safeguards may potentially include sanctions against those nations who sponsor terrorist groups as well as direct counterforce response to individual, nuclear terrorist attacks. In closing, he notes that because the world community has failed to develop strong and effective means of controlling terrorists and their mastery of nuclear weapons, nations are "on a collision course with scientific catastrophe".

(IPSA)

0227 Friedlander, Robert A. Sowing the Wind : Rebellion and Terror - Violence in Theory and Practice. *Denver Journal of International Law and Policy*, Spring 1976, pp. 83-94.

Terror-violence presents a severe threat to the legal order and to democratic society itself. Professor Friedlander analyses the background and causes of terrorism, and relates it to rebellion and revolution. The author discusses ways to control terrorism while at the same time preserving democratic freedoms. He concludes that international action must be taken to curb the spread of terror-violence before it destroys the very fabric of international, and national, society.

(PRAJ: PRID)

0228 Friedlander, Robert A. Terrorism and Political Violence. Do the Ends Justify the Means? *Chitty's Law Journal*, Volume 24, September 1976, pp. 240-245.

Friedlander defines terrorism as "the slaughter of the innocent," and he exhorts the civilized community to label it for what it is, a criminal activity. "To say that randomized terror-violence utilized as a political legal strategy for ostensible revolutionary ends can be condoned and even encouraged, simply because there is no peaceful or legitimate remedy for redress, is to replace the rule of law with the ancient credo of might makes right."

(N&G)

0229 Fromkin, David. The Strategy of Terrorism. *Foreign Affairs*, Volume 53, July 1975, pp. 683-698.

Traces terrorism from the Reign of Terror to the 1970s. Incisive comments on modern terrorism are provided, although the anarchist/nihilist variety is ignored. Key conclusion is that the terrorist succeeds or fails depending upon the response of the victim government, which must recognize that the act of terror is merely a means by which the terrorist seeks to force a response.

(N&G)

0230 Fulton, Arthur B. *Countermeasures to Combat Terrorism at Major Events*. Washington, US Dept. of State, 1976.

Includes treatment of the Black September attack at the Munich Olympics, as well as the security preparations for the 1976 Olympics.

(N&G)

0231 Gandhi, Rajmohan. Acceptable Terrorism? *Indian Express*, (Delhi), 10 September 1985.

The notion that one nation's terrorist is another's freedom fighter, is aptly exemplified in the case of Israel and South-Africa, though it is doubtful whether the people in whose name terrorism is practised or espoused will gain anything out of it. Author denounces terrorism against Pretoria.

0232 Gandhi, Rajmohan. Putting Terrorists to Use, *Indian Express*, (Delhi), 28 January 1987.

Author suggests how we should overcome, what he calls the anti-terrorist in ourselves.

0233 Gaucher, Roland. *The Terrorists : From Tsarist Russia to the OAS*. London, Secker and Warburg, 1968. Translated by Paula Spurlin.

Apparently withdrawn by the publisher due to a successful libel suit, this book traces terrorism to 19th century anarchism in Russia, through German, Rumanian, Irish and Jewish cases. Its treatment of the Algerian war is by far the most extensive section in the book.

(N&G)

0234 Gellner, John. *Bayonets in the Streets : Urban Guerrilla at Home and Abroad*. Collier-Macmillan Canada, Ltd., Don Mills, Ontarion, (Hardcover) 1972.

In this book on present-day terrorism, John Gellner not only answers the questions why and how, but also what should we do about it? It is only too true that life in our times is a breeding ground of armed revolution, but it is also

true, as Mr. Gellner fiercely believes, that it is still the kind of life which the great majority want to improve, not to uproot. Defending it against the minority who attack it, is thus equally important as understanding why those assailants act as they do.

The book is concerned with both these issues. The Front de Liberation du Quabec (FLOC) and the crisis it provoked in October 1970, provide its central theme, but the author's view is world-wide. He deals with the urban guerrilla warfare, which is the current fashion. He also shows how ill-prepared Canada and other democracies have been, and still are, for 'the onslaught'. A permanent organization is needed to combat terrorism, and this includes proper intelligence, planning, equipment and a regular counter-insurgency force.

The author maintains that building such a counter-insurgency organization need not result in the weakening of democratic institutions or the curtailment of individual liberties. Quite the contrary. There would be no call for emergency laws or for "bayonets in the streets" - if the lessons learned in these past years were taken to heart and translated into practice.

(PRAJ: PRID)

0235 Genscher, Hans-Dietrich. Hostage, The Securing of Peace, World Economic Cooperation. (In German). *Vereinte Nationen*, Volume 24, Number 5, 1976, p. 129. 8 columns.

The principles of the policy of the Federal Government consist of the unity of Europe, the Atlantic Alliance, the policy of detente and international disarmament. To guarantee peace makes in particular increased demands in the Middle East (Lebanon) and Southern Africa. The efforts of the community of States to bring the application of force under control must, however, extend also to the new, non-national forms of violence, including in particular, hostage-taking. The Federal (German) Government believes it to be necessary that the United Nations should draft a convention that will regard kidnapping as international violence and will ensure that those who do it are extradited or are brought to trial in the country where they were captured. The world-wide securing of human rights demands the creation of an independent, objective, decision-making international court. The aim of creating an international court of justice for human rights should not, in the light of European experience, be seen in too pessimistic a light.

(PRAJ: PRID)

0236 Ghosh, Saliendranath. Ideological Setting for Terrorists. *Hindustan Times*, (Delhi), 28 June 1985.

The terrorist inflictions in Punjab masterminded and operated from a number of foreign countries are very different from the earlier ones by Naxalites. Author reviews the ideological moorings of the Akalidal in the light of the teachings of the Sikh Gurus and analyses the emotional logic that runs through the phenomenon of terrorism.

0237 Gilboa, Eytan. The Use of Simulation in Combating Terrorism. *Terrorism : An International Journal*, Volume 5, Number 3, 1981-82.

Combating the continuing and growing threats of domestic and international terrorism requires new and bold efforts on the part of the industrial democracies. This article suggests that the simulation technique becomes one central element in these efforts. The article briefly presents the technique and

shows how it has been used so far, and how it can be used in four different areas of combating terrorism: training, research, planning and education.

(T)

0238 Gill, P.P.S. Only 10 p.c. of Terrorists Khalistanis. *Tribune*, 12 March 1987.

A study of the arrested Sikh youths and terrorists, reveals that only 10 per cent are committed to "Khalistan". About 50 percent take to the gun out of a spirit of adventure and 40 percent are driven simply by sheer poverty.

0239 Ginossar, Shalev. Outlawing Terrorism. *Israel Law Review*, Volume 13, Number 2, April 1978, pp. 150-159.

Although the size of terrorist atttacks is still far from reaching that of genocide as it was carried out during World War II, terrorism should be considered a sort of "bit-by-bit genocide" and dealt with as such. In order to eradicate terrorism, it is necessary to eliminate all the agents of terrorism, both physically and morally. Trial should be short and speedy. The mere fact of belonging to a terrorist movement should call for the same penalty as that incurred by its leader. Any one actively involved in terrorist activity should be treated with equal severity regardless of the degree of involvement. Offenders should be given a mandatory sentence of death, or of life imprisonment in countries where this penalty has not been abolished.

(IPSA)

0240 Glaser, Herman. The Debate on Terrorism. A Dossier (In German). *Aus Politik and Zeitgeschichte, Deilage zu "Das Parlement"*, Number 25, 1978, pp. 3-47.

This "dossier" provides information on the journalistic discussion on terrorism, national and international terrorism; the generation of the father less; violence against women and violence by women; Rightist and Leftist "voyeurs", feminism and Marxism; Hitler's children decline in political belief; the unwanted generation; the prodigal son and the stay-at-home son; Sponti ideology the "secret joy" of Mescaleros; isolation and self-isolation of higher education; Narcissus- a new form of socialization; the technical school under practical testing; critical sympathy; how far can one go too far? internal censorship; the resolution of extremists; the splendor and the misery of the intellectuals; new sensuality; intelligence and politics, linguistic doubt; danger from the Right, the dispute about educational emancipation; the evil power of words; "sympathizers" express themselves; what is the "Left" today? The need for continual discussion.

(PRAJ: PRID)

0241 Godfrey, David. Terrorism and Banking. *Terrorism : An International Journal*, Volume 5, Number 4, 1981-82.

This paper is primarily concerned with what actions banks, mainly Canadian ones, are taking and ought to take in order to guard themselves against various manifestations of terrorism. Canadian banks generally do not perceive any immediate threats from terrorist per se, but measures are now being adopted that have helped to reduce such crimes as extortion, hostage-taking and kidnapping. The author recommends various countermeasures, including the creation of an executive committee in all larger banks and corporations in addition to crisis management teams which should be aware of potential threats and, in cooperation with law enforcement agencies, are skilled in bringing such terrorist events to a successful conclusion for the victims.

(T)

0242 Goren, Roberta. *Soviet Union and Terrorism*. Winchester, George Allen and Unwin, 1984.

Soviet Union's support of international terrorism outside the Soviet block has been part of Soviet Government policy since 1917 and is consistent with its ideology, on the other hand any act perpetrated against the Soviet Union is defined as criminal. PLO is the paramilitary surrogate of USSR. USSR will depend more on this method (terrorism) of warfare in future.

0243 Govea, Rodger M. Terrorism as a Political Science Offering. *Teaching Political Science*, Volume 8, Number 1, October 1980, pp. 3-19.

This article is a discussion of teaching courses in terrorism. The discussion includes a set of educational objectives for such a course, a review of some prominent literature in the field, and the results of a survey demonstrating the educational effects of instruction on the subject. The article concludes that terrorism is an important vehicle for teaching a variety of topics relevant to the study of political science.

(IPSA)

0244 Goyal, D.R. Paradox of Democracy, Terrorism, Private Enterprises. *National Herald,* 10 July 1985.

In India, not only terrorist groups but also some other organisations like RSS, Shivsena, Dalkhalsa, Hindu Raksha Samiti, called Private Enterprises by the author are endangering the democratic institutions and traditions. To combat such ideas and methods, the only democratic way is to create mass consciousness accompanied by government intervention not to permit activities which negate democratically accepted norms and values.

0245 Green, Leslie C. *Nature and Control of International Terrorism*. Alberta, Canada, University of Alberta, 1974.

Examines cases of hijackings, kidnappings and bombings. Proposes UN initiatives, creation of international criminal courts, and the possiblity of an international anti-terrorism convention as prospective solutions to the terrorism problem.

(N&G)

0246 Green, L.C. Terrorism and its Responses. *Terrorism : An International Journal*, Volume 8, Number 1, 1985, pp.33-77.

The purpose of this paper is to provide a critical analysis of a number of recent works devoted to different problems relating to terrorism paying particular attention to suggested responses, including those that might be made by victims of terrorist activity. This has been done against the background of works dealing with problems of self-determination and insurgency, for many movements claiming to be seeking self-determination or to be engaged in insurgency resort to terrorist acts, while terrorist movements invariably assert that they are true insurgents or are seeking self-determination, and that the end justifies the means. In addition, this paper explores the role of the media in estimating the extent to which public reporting aids terrorism and hinders anti-terrorist activity. The amount of writing now being produced in this field is immense, and one can only find one's way through the morass with the assistance of specialized or general bibliographies. Reference is made to some of these biblio-

graphies, and attention is drawn to their advantages and drawbacks.

(PSA)

0247 Greenwood, Ted. Discouraging Proliferation in the Next Decade and Beyond: Non-State Entities. *In Nuclear Proliferation: Motivations, Capabilities and Strategies for Control*, 1980's Project of the Council on Foreign Relations, by Ted Greenwood, Harold A. Feiveson and Theodore B. Taylor; New York McGraw-Hill Book Company, 1977, pp. 99-107.

While Greenwood does not foreclose the possibility of terrorists aspiring to nuclear terrorism, he does find that the most capable groups are likely to be dissuaded by the tacit threats of retaliation, loss of prestige and reprisal. Furthermore, he finds that terrorist-inflicted casualties have been relatively limited and indeed, have been very far from the levels of wanton human destruction that many would associate with nuclear terrorism. His assertion that all states share an interest in maintaining the taboo against non-state possession of nuclear weapons may be convincing, but could stand further development in terms of policy implications and opportunities for diplomatic action.

(N&G)

0248 Gregor, A. James and Chang, Maria Hsia. Terrorism : The View from Taiwan. *Terrorism: An International Journal*, Volume 5, Number 3, 1981-82.

Pointing out that the circumstances as regards terrorism in Taiwan are far different from those prevailing in, say, Israel or Italy, the authors describe the conditions that have faced the ROC since 1949, the beleaguered fortress mentality, the emergency legislation, and the anti-terrorist measures, including restrictions on political and civil rights, taken in what may be called a period of protracted crisis. In the author's view, the goal of a fundamentally democratic political system will depend to a great extent on outside forces and influences.

(T)

0249 Gregory, Frank. *Protest and Violence : The Police Response - A Comparative Analysis of Democratic Methods*. London, Institute for the Study of Conflict, 1976.

A sketchy account, including case material from France, West Germany, Italy, Japan, UK and the US.

(N&G)

0250 Greisman, H.C. Social Meanings of Terrorism: Reification, Violence and Social Control. *Contemporary Crises*, (Amsterdam), Number 1, July 1977, pp. 303-318.

An argument to either dispense with the term "terrorism" or apply it equally to state actor and non-state actor alike.

(N&G)

0251 Grivas-Dighenes, General George. *Guerrilla Warfare and EOKA's Struggle - A Politicomilitary Study*. trans., by A.A. Pallis., London, Longmans, 1964.

An important treatment by the leader of the National Organization of Cypriot Fighters (EOKA).

(N&G)

0252 Gross, Robert A. *The Minutemen and their World*. New York, Hill and Wang, 1976.

The best tools of social history are applied to an early guerrilla war, resulting in an incisive portrayal of what makes some men revolt and others stay at home.

(PRAJ: PRID)

0253 Groussard, Serge. *The Blood of Israel : The Massacre of the Israeli Athletes, the Olympics,* 1972. trans. by Harold J. Salemson., New York, Morrow, 1975.

Regarding negotiations between the terrorists and German authorities.

0254 Grundy, Kenneth W. *Guerrilla Struggle in Africa : An Analysis and Preview*. A World Order Book, New York, Grossman, 1971.

The author is aware of his impossible task: to predict the outcome of the political and military struggle in Africa. As most future-oriented studies usually do, this book will probably prove of more use for the understanding of the future shape, of the continent. However, scenarios like those used by Kenneth Grundy, have been applied as tools for imaginative thinking at other times and other places as well.

That this method is not too convincing here may be due to the variety of forces in operation - and our shallow understanding of these forces in general. As an analysis it is not too penetrating, but useful as an introduction.

(PRAJ: PRID)

0255 Gupta, R.S. Anatomy of a Terrorist. *Indian Express,* (Delhi), 17 May 1987.

The author highlights the new Urban middle class posture being adopted by terrorists and setting up of business, commercial fronts for terrorist activities. Presenting short biographies of well known Punjab terrorists he concludes that with one exception none of them show any real ideological commitment.

0256 Gunter, Michael. Contemporary Armenian Terrorism. *Terrorism : An International Journal*, Volume 8, Number 3, 1985-86.

In the past decade Armenian terrorists have assassinated 30 Turkish diplomats or members of their immediate families, as well as an approximately equal number of non-Turk. In addition, well over 300 other people around the world have been wounded by their attacks. The purpose of this article is to move beyond the analysis in my earlier studies of the subject by analyzing the present state of the Armenian terrorist movement with regard to (1) its theoretically stated positions and goals, (2) its actual operations and current dissensions, and (3) the personal characteristics of its perpetrators.

(T)

0257 Gutteridge, William (Ed.). *The New Terrorism*. London, Mansell Publishing Limited, 1986.

In this volume an attempt has been made to bring together a number of significant studies of terrorist activity published by the Institute for the Study of Conflict.

In the first part of the book an analysis of the problems terrorism poses for democratic governments alongwith their international dimensions, has been taken up.

In part second a series of case studies (histories) relating to major countries in western Europe particularly France, Spain, Italy and West Germany have been presented.

0258 Hacker, Frederick J. *Crusaders, Criminals, Crazies : Terror and Terrorism in our Time*. New York, Bantam Books, 1978.

A wordy and somewhat systematic account of terrorism by an informed psychiatrist, who distinguishes between state terrorism and terror by non-state entities while condemning both. Hacker's message is that the response to terrorism must encompass both flexibility and restraint. He condemns both surrender and "no-negotiation" responses although his criticism of the latter is far more pronounced than of the former. His professional involvement with the Hearst incident and the September 1973 Fedayeen action in Austria makes his accounts of both cases interesting reading.

(N&G)

0259 Hall, Richard. Mozambeque Regime Battles Guerrillas. *Observer*, (London), June 20, 1982, p. 15.

Guerrilla attacks now supported by South Africa and led by wealthy Portuguese who had been associated with Salazar, are increasing to such a degree that President Machel has felt impelled to cancel a four-day official visit to Britain. The forces, known as the Movimiento Resistancia Nacional (MRN), operate in all ten provinces. Author reports on the best known of the leaders, and suggests that President Banda of Malawi may be implicated.

(PRAJ: PRID)

0260 Halliday, Fred. The Shifting Sands Beneath the House of Saud. *Progressive*, Volume 44, Number 3, March 1980, pp. 39-40.

On November 20, several hundred armed men seized the Grand Mosque of Mecca. On December 5, riots in the eastern provinces of Seihat and Qatif led to five deaths. Both incidents indicate instability in Saudi Arabia. While not under the intense religious control experienced in Iran, Saudi Arabian oil development has created new social conflicts similar to Iran's. "The educated commoners resent the dictatorship of the Saudi family, the radical Moslems resent the close alliance with the United States." America's closest ally in the Middle East is weak and vulnerable.

(PRAJ: PRID)

0261 Helperin, Ernst. *Terrorism in Latin America*. Calif., Beverly Hills, Sage Publications, 1976.

Analyzing the strategy, tactics, social origins, and ideology of terrorism, this paper declares that it is "a vigorous reaction against economic stagnation and social putrefaction" by the most energetic members of the young educated class a bid for power and simultaneously a bid for employment.

(PRAJ: PRID)

0262 Halperin, Ernst. *Terrorism in Latin America*. The Washington Papers, April 1976, 12 pp.

This article analyzes terrorism through its tactics, ideology, members and activities. Terrorist acts are not meant to win worldwide support, but to show the helplessness of the Government and to bring about its downfall. Discussed are tactics used - kidnapping, requisitioning, seizure of domicile, and armed propaganda - and the motives for each. Various liberation movements such as the MLN Tupamaros of Uruguay and the montaneros of Argentina are

described and analyzed. The members of these movements are usually young university students, graduates and professional people. Their dissatisfaction is not so much with what their parents wanted, but that they (the parents) failed to follow through with ideas. In many countries in Latin America there is a high literacy rate and good social legislation. The problem is that the economies are stagnant. So, aggression is directed toward what is perceived to be the cause of economic despair - namely, North America and the local regimes that support North American imperialism.

The book refers to this idea as paranoid, psychotic and labels it "The Vampire Complex", comparing the blood sucking bat to imperialism. The author feels that this scapegoating is based more on a failure to evaluate Latin American shortcomings than a realistic evaluation of foreign investors.

In conclusion, change must come and will come. But it must be of internal attitudes and social systems. Although other nations are partly responsible for Latin American problems, the real trouble lies within.

(PRAJ: PRID)

0263 Hamid, Rashid. What is the PLO? *Journal of Palestinian Studies*, Volume 4, 1975, pp.90-109.

Basic summary of the organizational development of the PLO. A useful chronological piece, including a chart on p. 102 showing the organizational structure, but no names.

(N&G)

0264 Hamilton, Lawerence C; Hamilton James D. Dynamics of Terrorism. *International Studies Quarterly*, Volume 27, Number 1, March 83, pp. 39-54.

These are important controversies over the dynamics of terrorism which have not yet been formally addressed in quantitative social research. We suggest a class of stochastic models for social contagion which may help to shed light on these controversies. Empirical estimates of model parameters were obtained from data on international terrorism in 16 countries over 1968-78. We find some evidence suggesting that the tendency of acts of terrorism to incite further violence is more easily reversed in less democratic, poorer, and less well educated societies. This suggests that reversal of the terrorism "epidemic" is more likely under conditions facilitating represson rather than reform, and that more open societies face particular difficulties in responding to terrorism effectively.

(IPSA)

0265 Hannay, William M. International Terrorism and the Political Offense Exception to Extradition. *Columbia Journal of Transnational Law*, Volume 18, Number 3, 1980, pp. 381-412.

Three recent extradition cases involving terrorists - Peter Mcmullen and Ziyad Abu Eain in the US and Francesco Piperno in France - illustrate the difficulties associated with traditional terrorism and problems with the "political offense" exception to extradition treaties. Consideration of these cases suggests two conclusions : first, that the Castioni test used in Anglo-American jurisprudence to determine whether or not to grant extradition of criminals alleging a political motivation for their acts is seriously outmoded in our violent and rapidly changing world; and, second, that a courtroom is an inappropriate forum in which to attempt an evaluation of the complex internal political struggles within foreign countries that the political offense exception calls for. As the international community grapples with the implications of "the right of

self-determination" and liberation movements, it must be recognized that political passion, however deeply held, cannot be a justification for criminal violence against innocent persons. To be considered a true "political offense", there must be a fair proportionality and reasonable relationship between the political goal espoused and the means used to try to achieve it.

(IPSA)

0266 Hassel, Conrad V. Terror : The Crime of the Privileged - An Examination and Prognosis. *Terrorism : An International Journal*, Volume 1, 1977, pp. 1-16.

Apparently inspired by the notion of "future shock" Hassel traces the appeal of terrorism for the young (17-20 years old), middle class, college-educated individual to the rootlessness and doubt engendered by modern society. He finds the psychological foundations of terrorism in sadism, masochism and necrophilia (erotic attraction to dead bodies). As for the noted participation of women, Hassel asserts such participation an aberrant extension of the feminist movement and the strivings it represents. For the few who become terrorists, the frustrations of seeking peaceful change are said to explain the manifestation of aggression (terrorism). In the end, he concludes that the ecstasy of the revolutions becomes the goal, obscuring we suppose any ostensible goal.

(N&G)

0267 Havens, Murray C. *Assassination, Violence and National Policy*. A paper presented at the 1976 Conference of the Section on Military Studies of the International Studies Association.

Assassination (and other violence) as an instrument of national policy against other governments is examined and Havens concludes that such tactics are rarely appropriate (if ever).

(N&G)

0268 Hawkes, Nigel, et al. Carlos: Cold Killer who wants to be Loved. *Observer*, (London), December 28, 1975. pp. 1-2.

Illich Ramirez Sanchez, better known as Carlos Martinez, and the man believed to have led the recent raid on OPEC's headquarters in Vienna, seems to be living quietly in Algeria. Discusses whether he is a ruthless and subtle opponent, or a playboy who likes killing. Sketches briefly his life, from his birth into a communist family in Venezuela. Question as to whether he is actually dead, and the OPEC raid leader used his name.

(PRAJ: PRID)

0269 Hayes, Denis. Nuclear Terrorism. *Gamaliel*, Volume 3, Number 4, Winter, 1977, pp. 5-6.

Nuclear terrorist weapons can be fabricated with technologies in the public domain. Critical masses are low enough to make such weapons convenient to use, and materials management at nuclear storage sites imprecise enough to ease supply for such use.

(PRAJ: PRID)

0270 Henissart, Paul. *Wolves in the City*. New York, Simon and Schuster, 1970.

An extensive history of the OAS.

(N&G)

0271 Heradstveit, Daniel. A Profile of the Palestine Guerrillas. *Cooperation and Conflict*, Number 1, 1972, pp. 13-36.

The objectives and strategy of the Palestinian guerrilla movement as well as the immediate problems faced by it are analyzed. It is concluded that future development will depend on the internal evolution of the guerrilla movement, which is confronted with serious internal power struggles. Developments will also be determined by the future pattern of politics among the Arab States. The Arab world, including the Palestinians themselves, is divided over whether or not to support the Palestine guerrilla movement, and about the form and extent of any such support.

(PRAJ: PRID)

0272 Herman, Edward S. *The Real Terror Network : Terrorism in Fact and Propaganda*. Boston, South End Pr., 1982.

The author presents an analysis of the US media's imbalanced coverage of terror and its impact upon public perception of the problem. The author says that the human rights violations of the US and its third-world client states are worse than those of communist nations and second that terrorism by revolutionary movements is an insignificant problem.

(BRD)

0273 Heskin, Ken. *Northern Ireland : A Psychological Analysis*. Columbia Univ. Press, 1980.

Heskin has attempted to bring a psychological framework to bear upon the current problems of Ulster. His main theme is the impact of violence upon the general mass of population: but he also discusses the psychological make up of terrorists, the qualities of successful political leadership in Ulster and the problem of growing up there.

(BRD)

0274 Hixson, Bob. International Terrorism : The Tiger Burning Bright. *Friends Journal*, October 1982, pp. 12-14.

Terrorists are people fanatically committed to a cause, but politically weak, whose basic strategy is the use of violence to provoke reaction and upset the existing order. They rarely aim at reform, but seek to bring about revolution through worsening conditions. Essentially a form of war, terrorism has become so common as to be almost accepted in geopolitics, with 3,013 incidents in the decade 1968-78. The Quaker response to this rise of terrorism is to continue trying to alleviate poverty, injustice and intolerance (which foster terrorism); to work for civil liberties (under-cutting terrorist tactics); to support non-military international actions against terrorism (such as that which has almost eliminated hijacking of airplanes); and to maintain their witness against violence, pointing out the lack of success terrorists have had in achieving their goals, and the contrasting record of Gandhian methods.

(PRAJ: PRID)

0275 Hobsbawn, Eric. An Appraisal of Terrorism. *Canadian Dimension*, Volume 9, Number 1, pp. 11-14.

Recent U.S. history has shown that political asassinations are not effective means of changing government policy; individual or small-group terrorism amounts to private enterprise revolution which is tempting to a frustrated activist. The cloak-and-dagger life with all its risks and its sensation of secret superiority is not the same as making a revolution. The terrorists of this age are romantic revolutionaries. How many of them would honestly prefer the more

effective but boring action to the less effective but more spectacular terrorism?

(PRAJ: PRID)

0276 Holton, Gerald. Reflections on Modern Terrorism. *Bulletin of Atomic Scientists*, November 1976, pp. 8-9.

Holton identifies different kinds of terrorism. Type I is an act that imposes terror by *individuals* or small groups on other individuals or groups, e.g. skyjacking. Type II involves governments co-opting and arming terrorist groups for transnational purposes, such as the training, arming and financing by Libya of a network of international terrorists, or the use by the US of the atom bomb. There may be a hybrid coming, a Type III, that "exploits the potential of new technology to produce catastrophes on a scale that destroys the natural setting of human life". Three developments can be expected: (1) "The attempt by one or more states to disseminate both the technology and also the cultural ground of successful terror." (2) A nation chosen for Type III terrorism will not have capacity for deterrence. (3) The new terrorist may experience technical failures which will cause devastating damage. The catastrophic side effects will tell us that Type III has arrived, failures and all.

(PRAJ: PRID)

0277 Holz, Hans Heinz. Has Terrorism a Theoretical Foundation? *Blatter fur deutsche und internationale politik*. Koln (Cologne) Volume 23, November 3, 1978, pp. 317-329.

Terrorism is lack of theory par excellence. It has a fictitious ideological frame and springs from events that betray its connection with the society to which it belongs, although it pretends to be the absolute negation of society.

(PRAJ: PRID)

0278 Honderich, Ted. *Three Essays on Political Violence*. Oxford, Basil Blackwell, 1976.

These three essays discuss the morality of political violence, particularly, political Violence of Left.

0279 Hopple, Gerald W. Transnational Terrorism : Prospectus for a Causal Modelling Approach. *Terrorism : An International Journal*, Volume 6, Number 1, 1982-83.

There has been an avalanche of published and unpublished analyses of the phenomenon of terrorism. There have been few explicit attempts, however, to determine empirically the more systematic precursors or causes and measurable effects of terrorist phenomena. The voluminous literature on terrorism can be subdivided into general works, definitional/conceptual discussions, case studies of particular regions, countries, and/or movements, counterterrorism and crisis management, and terrorist event data. Following a review of the research literature, models of transnational terrorism are delineated. An analytical strategy is also specified; the strategy entails the application of "soft modeling" techniques. A very basic causal model of transnational terrorism is sketched out. The ultimate goal of a causal modeling research program would be to mesh the substance of terrorism research with the social science methodology of causal modeling - simultaneously drawing on the strengths of both while recognizing the weaknesses of each.

(T)

0280 Horchem, Hans J. West Germany's Red Army Anarchists. *Conflict Studies*, Volume 46, June 1974.

Horchem concludes that the Rote Armee Franktion (Baader Meinhof Gang) was engaged in anarchistic conflict, despite its activist's claims to the contrary. In contrast to international terrorism, the domestic terrorism of the RAF is unlikely to succeed-although it will not die out either. This overview is noteworthy for its reference to terrorist's documents in German, many of which are not readily available in English.

(N&G)

0281 Horchem, Hans Josef. European Terrorism : A German Perspective. *Terrorism : An International Journal*, Volume 6, Number 1, 1982-83.

Concentrating on terrorism in West Germany, Italy, and the Basque provinces of Spain, the author presents a detailed picture of the motivations, the strategies, and the "achievements" of a number of the best known groups which for alleged political purposes take the law into their own hands. The Red Armee Faction, perhaps the best known West German terrorist group, and the 2nd of June Movement as well as such organizations as the Revolutionary Cells and the Guerilla Diffusa are described and their aims and activities are scrutinized. German right-wing terrorism is also shown to wield great power, its contacts with terrorists in Lebanon and Algeria rivaling those of leftist organizations. Italian terrorism is also fully covered in this paper, with activities of the Red Brigades, the best-known of the leftist organizations, and its international connections, as well as other groups and the individuals involved being dealt with in some detail. The events in Spain, past and present, due especially to Basque terrorism, are considered, and the Soviet influence, represented by terrorist organizations in Europe, the Middle East, Africa and Cuba is discussed as is also the outlook for the future.

(T)

0282 Horowitz, Irving L. Transnational Terrorism, Civil Liberties and Social Science. In Alexander Yonah and Finger, Seymour M. (Eds). *Terrorism : Interdisciplinary Perspectives*, New York, The John Jay Press, 1977. pp. 283-297.

Horowitz describes the dangers of terrorism as an undemocratic process that violates the Civil rights of the innocents and by passes the due process of law. Correspondingly he identifies the danger that counter terrorism (sometimes anticipatory) may "decimate the social and political fabric." He argues the need to address the consequences of terrorism - its social impact - as well as to engage in the study of its micro effects (e.g., the aggregate casualties wrought by terrorists). Horowitz exhorts social scientists to avoid being bought, to avoid tailoring research and its assumptions, to the sponsoring agencies or groups. Finally, he is concerned that social change not be stifled at the cost of democracy. "To prevent social change in the name of democracy is already to have lost the battle."

(N&G)

0283 Horowitz, Irving L. Unicorns and Terrorists. Delivered at the *Conference on International Terrorism*, U.S. Department of State, 25-26 March, 1976.

Stresses the need to understand the political system and understand ter-

rorism as a national - as opposed to international - phenomenon.

(N&G)

0284 Horowitz, Irving L. Political Terrorism and State Power. *Journal of Political and Military Sociology*, Volume 1, Spring 1973, pp. 147-157.

Horowitz urges that careful distinctions be drawn between "terrorist" groups to avoid the inappropriate labelling of national liberation movements. While it is not clear, using his criteria that a national group, operating internationally, can ever be classified "terrorist", his argument is nonetheless an important rejoinder to assertions of "transnational and international terrorist networks." A provocative, though less than faultless profile of a terrorist is also offered.

(N&G)

0285 Horne, Alistair. The Guerrillas of Teaponte. *Encounter,* (Great Britain), Volume 37, Number 6, 1977, pp. 76-83.

In April 1970 a group of 70 Left-wing students at La Paz University, Bolivia, in emulation of the Che Guevara, instituted an ill-prepared guerrilla operation in the wild forest area of the Alto Beni, beginning at Teoponte. The diaries of two of the student leaders, extracts from which are quoted with a detailed commentary, graphically describe the operation, "the terrible problems of survival in the wilderness, and .... moral stresses and strains within the guerrilla itself." The diaries "demand attention because of the special relevance of their contemporary setting - a turbulent Bolivia when anything could happen."

(PRAJ: PRID)

0286 Hostage Release Operations. *International Law Enforcement*, Volume 1, Number 4, 1984, pp. 5-7, 9, 11-12, 14-16, 18, 20.

In this article, an in-depth-look is taken at hostage release operations and at the techniques and equipment utilized by specialist anti-terrorist units.

(PSA)

0287 Hottinger, Arnold. The Increase of Power of the Arab Guerrilla Movement and the Clash with the Jordanian Government (In German). *Europa-Archiv*, Volume 25, Number 20, 1970, p. 737, 10 pp.

The activity of Palestinian guerrillas, which is split into more or less radical groups such as Fatah, FPIP, FPDLP, is bound to lead to contradictions and tensions in the Arab- Israeli conflict, as the happenings in Jordan during the summer of 1970 have shown: (1) on one hand, the Fedayeen have established themseleves, as the legitimate representatives and the embodiment of the Palestinian population. At last "the essence of the Arab fight with Israel became the adoption of the Palestinian cause by the Arabs". (2) On the other hand, the sequence of events showed that the "Arab states were not willing to have their sovereignty challenged by the Palestinians."

(PRAJ: PRID)

0288 Hoveyda, F. The Problem of International Terrorism at the United Nations. *Terrorism : An International Journal*, Volume 1,1977, pp. 71-83.

Hoveyda, formerly permanent representative of Iran to the United Nations, reviews UN proceedings on the subject of terrorism from 1972. The author argues that a "step by step" approach may have yielded a better result than the

attempt to attain comprehensive solutions.

(T)

0289 Hubbard, David G. *Winning Back the Sky : A Tactical Analysis of Terrorism*. New York, Say-brook Publications, 1986.

This book examines terrorism, terrorists and the US Response. The author suggests that the terrorist act to get their 'message to the world' though they are docile, unsuccessful and self-centered. The author criticises the US attitudes and actions towards terrorism, making their acts into massive threats through mass media. Author suggests specific ways of controlling terrorist situations.

(BRD)

0290 Hudson, Michael C. The Palestinian Factor in the Lebanese Civil War. *Middle East Journal*, Volume 32, Summer 1978, pp. 261-278.

Discusses the fragmentation of the Fedayeen into three main tendencies: pro-Syrian, middle of the road and rejectionist.

(N&G)

0291 Hudson, R.A. Cartro's America Department : Systemizing Insurgencies in Latin America. *Terrorism : An International Journal*, Volume 9, Number 2, 1987.

Since the success of the Cuban-Soviet "political military" revolutionary model in Nicargua in 1979, Cuba, in tandem with the sandinists, has worked to introduce and systemize such a model throughout much of latin America. This is done by Cuban support of insurgent group in a given country being made a condition of their forming, together with the local Moscow-line commuist party, a marxist-Leninist alliance under Cuban direction. This paper traces the development of Cuba's America Department and documents the extent of its activities in support of extremist groups in Latin America and Puerto Rico, including its use of Nicaragua as a regional subversive centre.

(T)

0292 Hutchinson, Martha Crenshaw. Defining Future Threats : Terrorists and Nuclear Proliferation. In Alexander Yonah and Finger Seymour M. (Eds). *Terrorism : Interdisciplinary Perspectives,* New York, John Jay Press, 1977.

Hutchinson's analysis of contemporary terrorism leads her to the conclusion that the harm done by terrorists will continue to increase and thus the possibility of nuclear terrorism is a real one. The essence of terrorism is said to be the willingness to accept risks in order to achieve political goals, such a willingness prevails in this analysis. In addition, Hutchinson does not find that the prospect of mass casualties will deter at least some terrorists from employing nuclear weapons. Her concluding comments on the actions that governments may adopt to prevent nuclear terrorism, or failing that, to cope with nuclear terrorism, are likely to be interesting to even those who may object to her earlier conclusions.

(N&G)

0293 Hutchinson, Martha Crenshaw. *Revolutionary Terrorism : The FLN in Algeria, 1954-1962*. Calif; Stanford, Hoover Institution Press, 1978.

A study of the use of terrorism by the FLN. Hutchinson identifies several functions for terrorism including compliance, endorsement, disorientation, isolation and organizational.

Concludes that the FLN "victory" in Algeria was less a case of the terrorists "winning" than it was of a government "losing". She sees the confluence of a number of fortuitous factors producing the victory, and she asserts that terrorism as the "unique means of resistance" can only succeed in "rare circumstances." The book should be read with a competent history of the conflict (e.g., Alistair Horne's *A Savage War of Peace*).

(N&G)

0294 Hutchinson, Martha Crenshaw. Terrorism and the Diffusion of Nuclear Power. *International Studies Association*, Toronto, February 25-29, 1976.

Although nuclear material may be safeguarded if a state is able to incur the cost, from the terrorist's viewpoint, the potential benefits of nuclear terrorism may exceed the high risks involved. In such a scenario, what governmental responses, e.g., military intervention, are possible?

(PRAJ: PRID)

0295 Hutchinson, Martha Crenshaw. The Concept of Revolutionary Terrorism. *Journal Conflict Resol.*, Volume 16, Number 3, September 1972, pp. 383-396.

This paper deals with the definition and explanation of the concept of revolutionary terrorism, considered a part of insurgent strategy in international War. It contends that such terrorism is a rational method of action employing acts of extra ordinary violence against selected physical victims deliberately creating a psychological effect and thereby influencing political behaviour and attitudes. This definition is tested against the activity of the FLN during the Algerian War and used as a basis to explain the theoretical and empirical significance of terrorism. The paper compares the relative costs and benefits of a terrorist strategy from the revolutionary point of view.

(IPSA)

0296 Hutchinson, Martha Crenshaw. Transnational Terrorism and World Politics. *Jerusalem Journal of International Relations*, Volume 1, Winter 1975, pp. 109-129.

Hutchinson finds that terrorist operations have produced: (1) superficial compliance among third party states and multinational organizations; (2) recognition, whether in the form of praise or denunciation; (3) counterviolence (with Israel as key example); (4) imitation by other minority, political or criminal groups. She is not optimistic about the prospect for international cooperation against terrorists, but instead points to the possibility (now realized) that states will choose the Israeli solution of direct retaliation. Finally, she does not accept the assertion of a formal global terrorist network.

(N&G)

0297 Hyams, Edward. *Terrorists and Terrorism*. New York, St. Martin's Press, Inc., 1974.

Proceeding from a relativistic conception of law and morality, Hyams - who betrays an ecletic, but largely anarchistic personal ideology-provides a rather sympathetic account of terrorism to buttress his argument that terrorism has indeed been an effective instrument of political change. His argument is flawed by an over-emphasis on the terroristic aspects of political struggle (e.g., the role of the Stern Gang in mandatory Palestine) and a number of explicable errors (e.g., he credits the bombing of the King David Hotel to the Stern Gang instead

of the Irgun). Nonetheless, much of the book is highly readable and useful. In particular, his treatment of Ievno Azev, the infamous Russian double agent, who shared his services between the Okhrano (Secret police) and the social Revolutionary Party, is well worth consulting.

(N&G)

0298 Imaik, Ryukichi. Nuclear Safeguards. *Adelphi Papers*, Number 86, London, International Institute for Strategic Studies, March 1972.

An excellent primer on safeguards, and thus in turn an important reference for those concerned with the technical feasibility of nuclear terrorism.

(N&G)

0299 Institute for the Study of Conflict. Nuclear Power, Protest and Violence. *Conflict Studies*, Volume 102, December 1978.

A useful survey of anti-nuclear movements in the US, West Germany, France, UK and Japan. A Chronology of incidents is included.

(N&G)

0300 Institute for the Study of Conflict. The Surrogate Forces of the Soviet Union. *Conflict Studies Security Report* Number 92, February 1978.

See esp. pp. 5-7, "Surrogate terrorists and guerrillas " and the "Role of Libya."

(N&G)

0301 Institute for the Study of Conflict. Croat Separatism : Nationalism, Dissidence and Terrorism. *Conflict Studies*, Volume 103, January 1979.

An up-to-date overview Croatian resistance to the concept and the reality of Yugoslavia. Begins with the founding of the Ustase, surveys the wartime Croat State, post-war subversion, links to Moscow and the activities of the 1970s. Projects enhanced separtist militancy (hence : terrorism) in the post-Tito era.

(N&G)

0302 International Institute for Strategic Studies. *Civil Violence and the International System*, Parts I and II. London, Idem. 1971.

Published in the Adelphi Papers series (number 82 and 83), Part I is subtitled, "The Scope of Civil Violence," and Part II is subtitled, "Violence and International Security."

(N&G)

0303 Israel. Accessories to Terror : The Responsibility of Arab Government for the Organizations of Terrorist Activities. *Middle East Information Series*. Jerusalem : Ministry for Foreign Affairs, Division of Information, Israel Information Centre, July 1973.

1968-1973 chronology of Arab terrorist activities, with information on Arab governmental aid to terrorist groups.

(N&G)

0304 Iwakawa, Takashi. The Making of a Terrorist. *Atlas*, January 1976, pp. 33-34. From *Bungei Shungu*, Tokyo, December 1974.

Iwakawa tells the story of Tsuyoshi and Junzo Okudaira, members of the Japanese Red Army. Both were good students. Tsuyoshi was brilliant. They both attended a good university. Both became involved in leftist students' groups.

0321 Jenkins, B.M. The Potential for Nuclear Terrorism. *Rand Report*, P-5876, May 1977, 11 pp.

The possibility that criminals or political extremists might sabotage nuclear facilities, fabricate a nuclear explosive device, or disperse radioactive material has been the subject of numerous studies. What conclusions can we draw? (1) It can be done. (2) There are political extremists and criminal groups today that possess or could acquire the necessary resources. (3) The historical record provides no evidence that such groups have attempted to acquire nuclear material for illicit use; there have been low-level incidents involving nuclear facilities or material. (4) There is no inexorable progression from the currently identified spectrum of potential nuclear terrorists to actual nuclear terrorists, or from the nuclear incidents that have occurred to actions of greater consequence. (5) Whether any of the current potential nuclear terrorists will actually go nuclear remains an unanswerable question. (6) There may appear new kinds of adversaries more likely to take nuclear action. (7) The level and nature of the threat may change. (Presented at Conference on Nuclear Arms Proliferation and Nuclear Terrorism. Arms Control Association, Washington, D.C., 8 May 1977.)

(PRAJ: PRID)

0322 Jenkins, B. An Urban Strategy for Guerrillas and Governments. *Rand Abstract*, P-04670/1, August 1972, p. 13.

The author synthesizes a five stage strategy by which urban guerrillas could take over a city, and suggests government countermeasures. The guerrilla struggle appears to follow a sequence of (1) dramatizing their cause by terrorist bombings and assassinations, (2) expanding and reinforcing their organization, (3) launching an offensive to control the streets and isolate the police, (4) provoking repression to win mass support, and (5) coordinating mass support with guerrilla warfare to wage full-scale urban warfare. The proposed government strategy capitalizes on the government's advantages in legitimacy and superior resources. It includes preventing exploitation of dissatisfaction by providing jobs, giving dissidents a voice, and coopting guerrilla demands that have wide popular support -- all with the goal of out-persuading and out-mobilizing, not merely out-fighting, the guerrillas. Most important, the government must maintain the rule of law and use only minimal force.

(PRAJ: PRID)

0323 Jenkins, B. and Johnson, J. International Terrorism : A Chronology, 1968-1974. *Rand Report*, R-1597-DOS/ARPA, March 1975, p. 58.

A chronology of incidents of international terrorism that took place between 1968 and 1974. Most of the material is based on press reports, although other sources were used. Only incidents that had clear international repercussions were included - incidents in which terrorists went abroad to strike their targets, selected victims or targets that had connections with a foreign state (e.g., diplomats, executives or the offices of foreign corporations), or created international incidents by attacking airline passengers, personnel and equipment. Incidents in which groups such as the Irish Republican Army or the Tupamaros of Uruguay directed activities against their own government or citizens in their own territory were excluded, but the international activities of such groups - an IRA bombing in London, for example, or the kidnapping of a foreign diplomat in Uruguay - were included. The thousands of reported acts of terrorism in Indo-China and the numerous cross-border raids by Arab guerrillas and Israeli com-

mandos were excluded, except for the major episodes.

(PRAJ: PRID)

0324 Jenkins, B. Terrorism and the Nuclear Safeguards Issue. *Rand Report,* P5611, March 1976, p. 7.

Terrorism for the most part is not mindless violence. Mass casualties do not serve the terrorists' goals and could alienate the population. Thus the detonation of a nuclear bomb or the deliberate dispersal of toxic nuclear material seem the least likely terrorist threats. However, terrorists might contemplate carrying out low level nuclear incidents and hoaxes. The inconvenience and political repercussions will probably exceed the actual danger to public safety. At a far more gradual rate the possibilities of serious nuclear incidents may increase simply because the number of nuclear facilities will increase, and technical knowledge regarding nuclear devices will spread. Before then, however, more effective safeguards can be developed.

(PRAJ: PRID)

0326 Jenkins, B. Will Terrorists Go Nuclear. *Rand Report,* P-5541, November 1975, p. 10.

Testimony given before the California State Assembly Committee on Energy and Diminishing Materials regarding the possibility that terrorists might steal fissionable material or nuclear weapons, attack nuclear facilities, or create nuclear hoaxes. In the author's view, the primary attraction of nuclear material for terrorists is not causing mass casualties, but the fact that terrorist action associated with the word "nuclear" attracts attention and generates fear. Mass casualties do not serve the terrorists' goals and could alienate their constituents. The same constraints may not apply to nihilistic groups or lunatics; however, those most willing to cause widespread death may be the least able to do so. As the nuclear industry expands during the next few years, there may be a growing number of hoaxes and minor acts of sabotage, simply because the number of nuclear facilities has increased; however, the inconvenience and political repercussions these incidents produce probably will exceed the actual danger to public safety.

(PRAJ: PRID)

0326 Jenkins, Brian M. Statements About Terrorism. *Annals of the American Academy of Political and Social Science, 463,* September 82, pp. 11-23.

Terrorism has proved to be a far more serious problem than we anticipated 10 or 12 years ago. After more than a decade of terrorism to observe and nearly 10 years of research on the topic, we can say few things for certain. One is that terrorism has increased in volume and severity, although despite the increasing bloodshed, terrorists still operate within self-imposed constraints. Although terrorism is a widespread phenomenon, it affects the world unequally. There is no single factor that explains why some societies suffer higher levels of terrorist violence than others. Terrorists operate with a limited technical repertoire that has changed little over time. Diplomats and businessmen are the most frequent target of incidents of international terrorism. Terrorists share a common demographic profile and certain common attitudes, but we do not know enough about them as individuals to identify a common terrorist personality. Authoritarian regimes have characterstically reacted to terrorism with repressive measures, while nations with strong democratic traditions have cautiously limited certain liberties. Generally, the rhetoric against terrorism exceeds the commitment of resources to combat it, and international cooperation is limited.

(IPSA)

0327 Jenkins, Brian M. *Urban Strategy for Guerrillas and Governments*. Santa Monica, Calif., Rand Corporation, 1972.

A strategy for forestalling and perhaps avoiding urban terrorism. Applicable to developing countries.

(N&G)

0328 Jenkins, Brian M. *Five States of Urban Guerrilla Warfare: The Challenge of the 1970s*. Santa Monica, CA, Rand Corporation, 1971.

Five stages: gaining publicity, buttressing organization, isolating police from the populace, producing government repression and coordination between the emerging mass movements and the organizers.

(N&G)

0329 Jenkins, B. The Terrorist Mindset and Terrorist Decision Making: Two Areas of Ignorance. *Rand Report*, P-6340, June 1979, 6pp.

Governments have acquired considerable data about terrorists and behaviourists have offered a number of hypotheses regarding their thinking, but no one can say with confidence that they have penetrated the terrorists' mind. Psychologists can identify a cluster of behavioral traits common to most terrorists, and perhaps identify a personality type predisposed to such activity. But these could be a reflection of their present circumstances rather than a reason for becoming a terrorist. Another area of uncertainty is understanding terrorist decision-making, such as what factors terrorists consider more important than others and how they measure the success of their operations. (Paper submitted to the International Scientific Conference on Terrorism, West Berlin, November 1978.)

(PRAJ: PRID)

0330 Jenkins, B. Terrorism Works - Sometimes. *Rand Report*, P-5217, April 1974, 9pp.

What is terrorism? Who are the terrorists? What direction will terrorism take in the future? What will the consequences be? The author provides some insights into these four questions, based on his definition of terrorism as violence that "recognizes fewer civilians," than other forms of warfare, and of terrorists as a mixed bag of "disparate groups and individuals whom history will judge to be murderers, or patriots, or lunatics." While the terrorists' record in achieving political goals is dismal, their tactics have been successful in terms of headlines captured; TV coverage; diversion of resources due to alarm; costs of protective measures; intimidation of governments, compelling them to abandon their law enforcement function. Some future trends can be discerned: increasing links and cooperation between terrorists in various parts of the world; and, given the creation of new social vulnerabilities and new sophisticated weapons, more spectacular and destructive acts.

(PRAJ: PRID)

0331 Jenkins, Brian; Johnson, Janera and Ronfeldt, David. Numbered Lives: Some Statistical Observations from 77 International Hostage Episodes. *Conflict : An International Journal for Conflict and Policy*, Volume 1, 1978, pp. 71-111.

Among the most interesting conclusions reached by Jenkins et al. are the following: the terrorist stands roughly an 80% chance of survival in a hostage venture; the likelihood of gaining at least some demands is roughly 50%; standard kidnapping tends to occur on the "home turf" of the terrorists; barricade

and hostage situations are more likely to be international; American diplomats and other US representatives (official or non-official) tend to be favorite targets, yet only in 3 incidents have explicit demands been made on the US government; no-concession policies have not deterred, but only reshaped the act, so that propaganda replaces concessions as the objective; and more hostages die during assault by anti-terrorist forces than from the direct action of the terrorists. A very useful chronological list of annotated hostage situations is appended.

(N&G)

0332 Jenkins, Brain M. and Johnson, Janera. *International Terrorism : A Chronology*, Rand Corporation, A. Johnson, 1976.

It is a supplement to an earlier Rand Report by Brain M. Jenkins and Janera Johnson, about the incidents of International terrorism that occurred between January 1968 to April 1974. In this supplement 57 additional incidents that occurred during that period and 109 incidents that occurred during the remaining seven months of 1974 have been incorporated.

This report does not contain accounts of what they call 'Internal terrorist Violence' carried out by governments against their own citizens and by terrorists operating within their own country and against their own nationals. This report also includes an Index of the terrorist groups and organisations.

0333 Jit, Inder. New Anti-Terrorist Strategy. *Tribune*, (Chandigarh), 6 August 1986.

Article deals with the Indian government's proposal of creating a security belt along the entire Indo-Pak border. Author suggests the adoption of the approach used by General Templer in tackling terrorism in Malaysia in the fifties.

0334 Johnson, Chalmers. *Perspectives on Terrorism*. Berkeley, CA, University of California, 1976.

Discussion of the 1976 Department of State Conference on International Terrorism identify the following typology of terrorism : ethnic, nationalistic, ideological and pathological.

(N&G)

0335 Johnson, Chalmers. Terror. *Society*, 15 November/December 1977, pp. 48-52.

Explains the increase in international terrorism a reflection of "new targets" susceptible to terrorist attacks, "new technologies" of weaponary and media capabilities, and "new toleration" of terrorists through direct and indirect support by nations. To counter terrorism, Johnson urges action by elected assemblies in the form of "special powers enacted 'for the duration'" of the war against terrorism.

(N&G)

0336 Judd, Judith. Protest at Funds for Terrorists. *Observer,* (London), August 22, 1982, p. 5.

According to a report of the *Catholic Institute for International Relations*, the *Commonwealth Development Corporation* is considering investing funds, borrowed from the British Government, in a Philippine plantation controlled by the *Lost Command*, a group of ex-soldiers and criminals who, the Institute alleges, are a paramilitary terrorist organization responsible for tortures and murders. The plantation is being developed by a partnership of the Philippines Govern-

ment and the Malaysian company, *Guthrie Overseas Holdings*, which uses the Lost Command as its security force. None of the Lost Command has ever been brought to trial, seemingly because the philippine police fear the danger to their men.

(PRAJ: PRID)

0337 Karber, Phillip, and McMengel, R.W. A Behavioral Analysis of the Adversary Threat to the Commercial Nuclear Industry. In Fine, Allan M. Attributes of Potential Adversaries to US Nuclear Programmes. In US Department of Commerce, National Bureau of Standards. *The Role of Behavioural Science in Physical Security.* Proceedings of the Second Annual Symposium, March 23-24, 1977. Washington, 1977 pp. 27-33.

(1) "Very few groups, particularly those engaged in terrorism, have the organization, training or level of force necessary to carry out an attack against the nuclear industry with major societal consequences." (2) Such groups which do have the resources have not operated in the US. (3) There are a number of non-terrorist groups that do have the resources.

(N&G)

0338 Karlekar, Hirammay. The Anatomy of Terrorism. *Indian Express*, (Delhi), 2 June 1985.

Author analyses the phenomenon of terrorism down the ages in India and Abroad and concludes that with firmness and concessions it can be defeated.

0339 Kasch, Wilhelm F. Attempted Explanations of Terrorism. Results and Theories of Sociological Research (In German). *Stimmen der Zeit*, Volume 103, Number 10, 1978, pp. 674 with 16 references.

There has been criticism of the "personagrams" (Personal profiles) which were provided by a Federal and Provincial-working group, as well as of theories of sociological research on terrorism. The interpretation which is based on the term 'violence' fails especially - a fact which is recognizable in the example of the theory of structural violence of the Norwegian sociologist Johan Galtung. It is a moral Phenomenon that has to be heeded when formulating questions and when setting up research methods and the research has to investigate the reasons which make people decide in favour of terrorism.

(PRAJ: PRID)

0340 Katz, Robert. *Days of Wrath : The Ordeal of Aldo Moro, the Kidnapping, the Execution, the Aftermath*, Garden City New York, Doubleday, 1980.

This book concerns the 1978 abduction of Moro, President of Italy's leading party, the Christian Democrats by the terrorist Red Brigades. Fifty-four days later, Moro was murdered, after the Italian government, with worldwide support, had maintained a 'hard line' position refusing to consider Red Brigade Ultimatums. Katz directs his Wrath against the architects of the 'hard line'.

(BRD)

0341 Kelly, Kelvin. *The Longest War : Northern Ireland and the IRA.* Hill, 1983.

The first part of the book is an overview of the Irish history from the Anglo-Norman invasion to 1962. Author regards British imperialism as the chief obstacle to Irish unity. The Reminder of the text is devoted to a review of events since 1962 in or relating to Northern Ireland.

(BRD)

0342 Kelly, Orr. If Terrorists Go After US Nuclear Bombs. *US News and World Report*, March 12, 1979, pp. 43-45.

An informed discussion of the problem, written with more than tacit cooperation of responsible government officials.

(N&G)

0343 Kiejman, Claude. Tupamaros. (In French) *Jeune Afrique*, Number 493, June 16, 1970, pp. 36-37.

The Tupamaros are the well-loved terrorists of Uruguay. Recently, the government of Uruguay forbade all verbal references to the Tupamaros. Thus, the authorities are of the opinion that the guerrillas will lose their best weapon : propaganda. The Tupamaros, however, are gaining in strength. Furthermore, they are being emulated by most other urban guerrilla movements in Latin America.

(PRAJ: PRID)

0344 Kielmansegg, Peter. Political Science and Problems of Violence : On the Dangers of Loss of A Sense of Reality (In German), *DGFK-Information : Friendens - und Konflikt forschung*, volume - 1/79, June 1979, pp. 20-23.

There are two dangers of looking for causes of terrorism in the FRG : (1) Finding that almost everything that happend in recent years has some link to it, and (2) confusing casual influence with guilt and responsibility. A German magazine has blamed political scientists for the outbreak of terrorism. Yet political scientists know very little about its causes. Most theories are too general, try to explain a broad range phenomena such as "political violence", or "why men rebel." (Ted Gurr). But even if we narrow it down to "political terrorism in democratically governed industrial societies of the Western type", we still find two types of terrorism : national-separatist (the IRA or the Basques) and social-revolutionary. For the latter, the revolt is often against a reality as perceived by the terrorist which may be far removed from objective reality. The explanation of the "causes" of terrorism might then better come from psychology than from political science. Did political or social sciencce contribute to the outbreak of terrorism? (1) The widening of the definition of violence to include dictatorship, exploitation, dependence etc. i.e. "Structural violence" - has meant a justification of traditionally understood anti-regime violence. According to Galtung's definition, all existing societies partake to various degrees in structural violence (because they are not ideally just societies) and therefore revolutionary violence against them seems justified. This is the modern restatement of the classical "right to revolution" against tyranny - but New Left writers, such as Marcuse, explicitly call all Western democracies "totalitarian" (i.e. tyrannical). Such a concept means that the great experiment, to "domesticate" (tame) violence through government, must be given up. The "right to revolution", traditionally an exception under strictly limited unusual circumstances, becomes universalized. All this comes from striving for a perfectly just socity. (2) The

over-ambitious application of the postulates of democracy - sovereignty of the people, self-determination, political equality - must always mean that all existing socieites fall short of the ideal. If they do, must this totally destroy their claim to legitimacy? Democratic ideals are being used - sometimes with malicious intent- to undermine states that are *relatively* democratic, within human possibilities. If no society can be truly democratic, then we must accept anarchy - so goes the argument. (3) "Loss of a sense of reality" shows up in the alienation of young people, who feel no loyalty to their country. This might well stem from political science: (1) ideologial blindness (e.g. Marxist explanations which claim that the FRG is "a fascist state"). (2) Professional blindness (the excessively theoretical explanations put forward by social science) and (3) "prejudice against that which exists" ("opposition science", which is just as perniciously biased as the "establishment science" we used to have, which assumed that "what exists must be right") - all these may contribute to the alienation of students from the state. The alienation (and the terrorism rooted in it) has many causes, of which political science is only one — but a real one.

(PRAJ: PRID)

0345 Kitson, Frank. *Low Intensity Operations: Subversion, Insurgency, Peacekeeping*. London, Faber, 1971.

Partial contents. — pt. 1. Trends and background : Future trends in the use of force. Enemy aims and methods. Civil Military relations. —pt. 2. The army's contribution : They preparatory period. The non-violent phase. Insurgency part 1: tactics, the handling of information. Insurgency part 2; direction, unit and equipment. Peace-keeing --pt. 3. Preparation required: Education and training. Provision of units, specialists and equipments. Conclusions and after thoughts. -- Bibliography. - Index.

Suggests several measures to increase the British Army's capability to deal with insurgency, subversion and domestic peacekeeping operations. Kitson argues that conventional land warfare is becoming obsolete and that the army's future lies in fighting or even inciting subversion. Part 1 analyzes the future trends in the use of the military in domestic situations, while part 2 discusses the contributions and insurgency. Part 3 collects the requirements arising from the previous sections and stresses ways of dealing with insurgents.

(PRAJ: PRID)

0346 Kittrie, Nicholas. Reconciling the Irreconcilable : The Quest for International Agreement over Political Crime and Terrorism. *Year Book of World Affairs*, Volume 32, 1978, pp. 208-236.

There is no single or simple solution offered for the international regulation of the violence posed by political crime and terrorism. It would be premature at this time to call for a new anti-terrorism convention or for the creation of an international body to deal with terrorism.

(IPSA)

0347 Klevans, Edward M. Film Review. *American Journal of Physics*, Volume 44, April 1976, pp. 406-407.

Two "educational" films treating nuclear terrorism are the subject of this review. Of particular note is the "NOVA" presentation.

(N&G)

0348 Knorr, Klaus. Is International Coercion Waning or Rising? *International Security*, Volume 1, Spring 1977, pp. 92-110.

See esp. pp. 100-102, where Knorr speculates on the great leverage that

would obtain for the terrorist bent on international coercion based on threats of large-scale destruction. He muses that to pay blackmail under suh circumstances may be the lesser evil.

(N&G)

0349 Krieger, David. What Happens if...? Terrorists, Revolutionaries, and Nuclear Weapons. *Annals of the American Academy of Political and Social Science*, Number 430, March 1977, pp. 44-57.

Krieger finds that the continuing expansion of peaceful nuclear technology will increase the possibility that tomorrow's terrorist will be armed with nuclear weapons. In addition, he argues the plausibility of a nuclear bomb being provided by a sympathetic government, particularly in a Middle Eastern setting. His description of the problems which nuclear armed terrorists might precipitate would rank such an event with history's greatest crises.

(N&G)

0350 Krieger, David. When Terrorists go Nuclear. *The Center Report*, June 1974, p. 13.

"Trends in terrorist tactics in recent years have shifted from bomb-throwing to hijacking and kidnapping. There may be a further shift which will subject whole cities to terrorist demands. Many of the same people who empathized with Patricia Hearst and her parents may one day find themselves part of a city held ransom to nuclear-armed terrorists." Fissionable material suitable for making nuclear weapons is a by product of the fuel cycle in nuclear power plants. By the end of the century, it is estimated there will be 750 tons produced each year. All of this must be safeguarded from terrorists.

In the US the physical security systems around power plants have been found to be ineffective, and there is "inevitably a small loss of nuclear materials in the nuclear fuel cycle." Also when nuclear materials are transported there is a possibility of diversion of this material, which is worth some $5,000 a pound. The opportunities are there for terrorists to get material.

Security measures to prevent theft will create a sort of garrison society and this security can be broken by smuggling materials from other nations.

The social cost as well as the economic cost of such a garrison society are "so negative that we should halt all development of nuclear power plants and try to achieve a moratorium on the whole nuclear power industry, both nationally and globally."

(PRAJ: PRID)

0351 Kreis, Karl Markus. International Terrorism. An Unsolved Problem of the Community of States. (In German) Extract from : New Tasks Facing Security Policy (German) Published by Karl Kaiser and Karl Markus Kveis, Frankfurt/Main, 1976). *Europa-Archiv*, Volume 31, Number 11, 1976, p. 367, 9pp. with references/notes.

"The rise of present-day international terrorism attributed to "five main elements" : instability in Third World countires; global concentration of communications; the role of the Palestinians; new radical activities in Western countries; international contacts between terrorsits. Terrorism is explained as "a tool of the revolutionary struggle", "a demonstration of anarchical revolt", and as "a feature of a substitute war". To counteract international terrorism, the removal of its social causes must interlock with the development of police

cooperation, also the possibilities of the retreat of terrorists to sheltering countries must be restricted or prevented.

(PRAJ: PRID)

0352 Kupperman, Robert H. Treating the Symptoms of Terrorism : Some Principles of Good Hygiene. *Terrorism : An International Journal*, Volume, 1, 1977, pp. 35-49.

The Chief Scientist of the US Arms Control and Disarmament Agency suggests that as the publicity value of the current levels of terror subsidies, terrorists may escalate their threats to keep the public's attention. Kupperman speculates that "mass destruction extortion" may attract criminal elements to its lucrative possibilities.

(N&G)

0353 Kupperman, Robert H. Terror, the Strategic Tool : Response and Control. *Annals of the American Academy of Political and Social Science*, Number 463, September 1982, pp. 24-38.

The United States appears ill-prepared to deal with an emerging form of interstate rivalry, that is, the use of terror as an unconventional weapon to achieve conventional political ends. The terror event represents a powerful form of leverage simply because of its media value. Using media coverage to amplify their impact, acts of terrorist violence have paralyzed Western governments and undermined their credibility. In a destabilized international environment, the vectored terrorist threat offers additional advantages to radical nations or superpowers in pursuit of foreign policy objectives. Under the guise of criminality, it can become a low-cost, low-risk, high-leverage tool of low-intensity warfare, difficult to combat because uncertainty about the origin of the threat limits the full range of diplomatic and military responses.

(PRAJ: PRID)

0354 Kupperman, Robert H. *Facing Tomorrow's Terrorist Incident Today*. A report prepared for the Law Enforcement Assistance Administration, Washington, D.C., October 1977.

This important report by the Chief Scientist of the Arms Control and Disarmament Agency, reviews and summarizes the results of extensive research funded by the Law Enforcement Assistance Administration. Kupperman takes a wide view of macro-terror, including nuclear, biological and chemical options, as well as other significantly disruptive acts (e.g.,terrorist interdiction of electrical gride). Special consideration is devoted to target hardening, policy choices (including cooption), incident management and damage limitation. An appendix summarized several of the more impressive recent efforts at even modelling and adversary description.

(N&G)

0355 Kupperman, Robert H. Nuclear Terrorism : Armchair Pastime or Genuine Threat? *Jerusalem Journal of International Relations*, Volume 3, Number 4, Summer 1978, pp. 19-26.

Although nuclear terrorism is feasible, it is a nontrivial technical task. The amateur is likely to get killed, and the sophisticated terrorist is likely to feel that the costs of inflicting mass destruction are far too great. Nevertheless, the possibility should not be ignored. When viewed in conjuction with the menace of nuclear weapons proliferation among nations, the idea of a terrorist brandishing an atom bomb is not so bizarre. Nuclear terrorism must be viewed in context

with a wide variety of technically sophisticated, highly destructive acts. Various lines of defense are indispensable. These include an active intelligence collection apparatus, the hardening of critical targets in society to block the admission of amateurish terrorists and increase the costs to more talented ones, the development of a counter terrorism technology whose cost-effectiveness must be assessed in light of the perceived threat, and the creation of thoughtful, broadly gauged crisis management mechanisms intended to deal efficiently with serious incidents.

(IPSA)

0356 Kupperman, Robert H.; Smith, Harvey A. Waiting for Terror. *Washington Review of Strategic and International Studies*, Volume 1, Number 1, January 1978, pp. 50-61.

There are deeply rooted causes for terrorism, especially in groups that are politically driven and habitually subjected to repressive conditions. Greater concern for human rights and the settlement of international disputes by creative application of diplomacy and international law are crucial if the world is to be rid of the source. Dealing with terrorism on a symptomatic bases, rather than examining its underlying etiology requires a focus on national and international means needed to combat terrorism. Governments must cooperate in intelligence collection, physical security and the ability to manage crises efficiently.

(IPSA)

0357 Kupperman, Robert H., and Trent, Darrell M. *Terrorism : Threat, Reality, Response*. Stanford, CA, Hoover Institution Press, Stanford University, 1979.

This book contains about 180 pages of original material with eight selected readings. Kupperman and Trent treat the possibility of "nationally disruptive terrorism" as well as the appropriate government response to such acts. Walter Laqueur has contributed a ten page preface to the book, and a twelve page bibliography is included. Kupperman is the Chief Scientist for the Arms Control and Disarmament Agency.

(N&G)

0358 Kuriyama, Yoshihiro. Terrorism at Tel Aviv Airport and a "New Left" Group in Japan. *Asian Survey*, Volume 13, March 1973, pp. 336-346.

Focuses upon the emergence of the United Red Army, as well as its tactics and ideology.

(N&G)

0359 Labrousse, Alain. *The Tupamaros* (In French). Published by Seuil, Collection "Combats", 1971.

Labrousse presents .n amply-documented history of the Tupamaros, an ultrasecret organisation of urban guerrillas in Uruguay.

(PRAJ: PRID)

0360 Lador-Lederer, J.J. On Certain Trivialties Written on Terrorism. *International Problems*, Volume 12, Numbers 3-4 (24), October 1973, pp. 25-28.

The author argues that the laws providing for the punishment of those who commit acts of terrorism are ineffective, because, in these instances, the individuality of the victim counts far less than the mass media value of the act. The

nature of terrorism — i.e., instilling terror and paralysis in the victim's mind - allows for neither self-defence against the material act nor reprisal against it; thus, the author advocates active intervention in the planning of terrorist acts (i.e., "forceful intervention with a policy rather than a single act"). He maintains that any group of terrorists is capable of threatening world peace and he criticizes the concept that acts of terrorism should only be outlawed on the condition that they are crimes of 'international significance', this argument fails to take into account that crimes which are directed against the security of innocent persons are of 'international significance'.

(PRAJ: PRID)

0361 Laffin, John. *Fedayeen : The Arab - Israeli Dilemma*. New York, The Free Press, 1973.

Pro-Israeli, though the author alleges that he has written a fair account. The theme of the work is that the Fedayeen really do not represent the Palestinian people, but only themselves. Laffin portrays a movement splintered that would best serve the Palestinians by disappearing. "But, this will not happen. Resistance has become an industry; the fedayeen organizations have become entrenched bureaucracies in which the hierarchy are reluctant to eliminate their own authority."

(N&G)

0362 Lagoni, Rainer. The United Nations and International Terrorism (In German). *Universitas*, Volume 33, Number 4, 1978, pp. 369-376.

Initiatives in regional organizations appear at present to be more promising in the enforcement of measures against international terrorism than the United Nations. Yet, even under Current majority conditions, the United Nations are able to make a contribution towards the solution of this problem. A first step in the path towards the establishment of a furher legal principle is an international agreement against the taking of hostages.

(PRAJ: PRID)

0363 Lambrick, H.T., trans. *The Terrorist*. London, Ernest Benn Ltd., 1972.

Deals with the Sind region of present-day Pakistan during the last years of the British colonial period.

0364 Lamadrid, Sergio Araoz de. Guerrilla Environment. *Marine Corps, Gazette*, Volume 58, Number 10, 1974, pp. 25-30.

"The 'indirect strategy' espoused by Mao Tse-tung continues to be employed by subversive forces in Latin America."

(PRAJ: PRID)

0365 Lang, Daniel. A Reporter at Large : The Bank Drama. *The New Yorker*, volume 25, 1974, pp. 56-126.

On the Relationships between captors and captives during the August 1973 incident at the Kreditbank, Stockholm, Sweden.

(N&G)

0366 Larus, Jocl. *Nuclear Weapons Safety and the Common Defence*. Columbus, Ohio., Ohio State University Press, 1967.

An early study concerned less with illicit acquisition by terrorists than with faulty control procedures.

(N&G)

0367 Laqueur, Walter. The Continuing Failure of Terrorism *Harper's*, November 1976, pp. 69-76.

Laqueur's studies show that terrorism has decreased from its peak in 1970. This is not widely known because of the media, which play up every terrorist attack. Terrorism makes news. This is one of the misconceptions about Terrorism; the other is the vagueness with which the term is used. Terrorism was once characteristic of highly repressive regimes; today "terrorism occurs only in democratic societies and in half-hearted authoritarian regimes. There have been countless studies of the causes of terrorism, ranging from lack of vitamins to frustration as causes. The old theory was that terrorism grew out of injustice, inequality, poverty, etc. and the cure was to remove these. But it isn't that easy. Concessions to one group will result in injustice to another. One thing is clear: "the more the injustice and repression, the less terrorism there is." Appeasing terrorism isn't the answer either. "Terrorism, to summarize, is not more than a nuisance at present. One day mankind will be threatened by weapons of superviolence... There is the certainty that society will not be able to satisfy the demands, justified or unjustified, of all its members. There is equally the certainly that some individuals will at some future date have the skill and the determination to dictate their wishes to society. Such action would, of course, be irrational, leading sooner or later to destruction without precedent. It is not certain, unfortunately, whether this perspective will deter individuals or small groups of people, convinced that society or the whole world ought to be punished if their demands are not met."

(PRAJ: PRID)

0368 Laqueur, Walter. The Futility of Terrorism, *Harper's Magazine* March 1976, pp. 99-105.

Terrorism has increased, but how much is it accomplishing? Laqueur gives as an example the terrorist action in Vienna. Few people have any idea what the terrorists wanted, and when it was all over, they were no nearer their objective. There are a number of myths about terrorism; (1) That it is something new. False, it has been with us for centuries. (2) It is left-wing and revolutionary in character. False, terrorists are usually elitist, sometimes they are rightist, sometimes leftist. (3) Terrorism appears when there are legitimate grievances; remove the grievance and terrorism stops. False, there are always grievances; sometimes a minor one will produce terrorists, other more serious may not. The only bit of truth is that the terrorist sees a grievance. (4) Terror is highly effective. False, it catches the headlines, but seldom has a lasting effect. (5) Importance of terrorism will increase as the power of their weapons increases. Partly true, but a terrorist movement is not needed, a mad man can do as much damage. (6) Political terrorists are more intelligent and less cruel than criminals. False, political terror attends to be less humane than ordinary criminals. Often political terrorists are better educated, but not necessarily more intelligent. (7) Terrorists are poor, hungry and desperate human beings. False, modern terrorists hardly fit into this class. Most of them are well financed. Terrorism makes headlines, but it is politically ineffective. "Compared with other dangers facing mankind, it is almost irrelevant."

(PRAJ: PRID)

0369 Laqueur, Walter. *Terrorism*. A Balance Sheet *Harpers Magazine*, March and November 1976.

Laqueur argues that terrorism, which is "no more than a nuisance at present, "has been blown out of proportion by those who equate headlines with

power. He commends a stiffbacked policy against terrorists and argues that to do otherwise would invite constant tyranny and blackmail by small groups. His argument that terrorism occurs in cycles and that the current cyclic momentum is downward will be challenged by many.

(N&G)

0370 Laqueur, Walter. (Ed.). *The Terrorism Reader : A Historical Anthology*. New York, New American Library, 1978.

A nice reader including selections from antiquity (Aristotle, Cicero, etc.), the 19th century (Bakuin, Most, Kropotkin, etc.), to the present (Paul Wilkinson, Feliks Gross, Hans Josef Horchem, etc.). Unfortunately, many of the selections are only excerpts, rather than complete materials, so the specialist will have to look elsewhere for sources which have not been "trained" by the hands of an editor.

(N&G)

0371 Laqueur, Walter. *Terrorism*. Boston, Little, Brown and Company, 1977.

A masterful, yet flawed book which surveys terrorism in broad literary and historical sweeps. Laqueur criticizes the synchronic thrust of much of the contemporary work on terrorism, and offers instead the insight that terrorism has been with us for quite some time. He is particularly enamored of the Russian terrorists of the 19th century, in particular the Narodnaya Volya, which one suspects he sees as representative of what a "moral" terrorist group should look like. Juxtasposed to the continuity of contemporary terrorism, he sees several important discontinuities between the old and new terrorist, prominent among such factors is the lack of restraint and discriminateness which characterized modern terrorism. He posits--briefly--a cyclic notion of terrorism in which the phenomenon ebbs and flows from generation to generation. However, this cyclic "theory" is not convincing at this stage, but instead would demand careful analysis and research. In interpreting a brief subsidence in terror-violence (which coincided with the writing of his book) as the beginning of a downward trend. While the book is buttressed with an impressive collection of footnotes, the footnote system he employs is erratic and confusing at times. A number of quotes are unreferenced or ambiguously referenced. Furthermore, a number of incidents are mentioned in passing, and while they might impress the reader with the breadth of Laqueur's scholarship, they demand too much of even the well-informed reader (who might, for example, desire at least some explanation of the Chittagon raid in 1930, rather, than seeing it mentioned *passim*.

(N&G)

0372 Laqueur, Walter. *Terrorism*. London, Weidenfeld and Nicolson, 1977.

Author has analyzed the so called mythology of terrorism and has highlighted the basic differences between the strategy of rural guerrilla warfare and urban terrorism.

Prof. Laqueur argues that terrorist groups will not use chemical and guerrilla warfare as a matter of principle and also because it would defeat their purposes. Compromise with terrorists in some cases may be useful but consistent conciliation is bound to claim a higher toll in human life in the long run than resisting it.

0373 Lee, Alfred McClung. The Dynamics of Terrorism in Northern Ireland, 1968-1980. *Social Research*, Volume 48, Number 1, Spring 1981, pp. 100-134.

Terrorism in Northern Ireland involves or confronts people as (1) strategic procedure, (2) theatre, (3) direct personal involvement, and/or (4) indirect involvement or confrontation. Some at least try to assess its role in (5) social change. Persons and groups sympathetic to or participant in (a) official, enforcement, "peacekeeping" or (b) subversive, agitational, "guerrilla" terrorism act or react rather differently in each of these five perspectives. The contrast of the groups arises chiefly from the sense of an established and secure claim on legitimacy among official or enforcement terrorists and an ideological legitimacy-on-trial sense among the subversive or agitational and their friends. In discussing the first point, policy bases of terrorist activities are summarized. The second is discussed in terms of specific illustrations. Certain social surveys help to portray the third and fourth. The fifth is an effort to look into social consequences as they are variously observed or predicted.

(IPSA)

0374 Leiser, Burton M. Terrorism, Guerrilla Warfare, and International Morality. *Stanford Journal of International Studies*, Volume 12, Spring 1977, pp. 39-65.

No state should give refuge to terrorists or permit any person under i.. jurisdiction to protect, conceal, or assist them in any manner whatever. Every nation should endeavor to punish all persons guilty of such acts. Granting refuge to terrorists who are engaging in depredations against sister states is an act of war. Terrorists should be entitled to a fair trial before an impartial tribunal, humane treatment during confinement, and no cruel and inhuman punishment. But a significant increase in the number of dead terrorists might discourage some who might otherwise succumb to the romance of the terrorist's life.

(IPSA)

0375 Lens, Sydney. Quiet Violence in Guatemala. *Peace News*, 12 January 1973, p.9.

This article describes and comments on the many killings in Guatemala during the past year. Fear is widespread. It seems likely that the army and the Arana regime are responsible for most of the deaths.

(PRAJ: PRID)

0376 Letman, Solan T. Some Sociological Aspects of Terror Violence in a Colonial Setting. In Basiouni, M. Cherif., (Ed) *International Terrorism and Political Crimes*. Springfield, Illionids, Charles C. Thomas, 1975, pp.33-42.

Letman focuses on the relationship between colonialism and terrorism as a manifestation of the alienation (economic, political, cultural and military), which interact and inevitably lead to eruptions of violence. He presents four behaviour models : "passing", "zombi", "revolutionary violence" (inspired by Fanon) and "isolated terrorism". Fanon's keen influence is clearest in Letman's assertion that colonial alienation breeds *liberating* violence.

(N&G)

0377 Linebery, William P. (Ed.). *The Struggle Against Terrorism*. New York, The H.W. Wilson Company, 1977.

A collection of previously published materials on Terrorism. Includes articles by Fromkin, Hoffacker, et.al.

(N&G)

0378 Liston, Robert A. *Terrorism*. Nashville, Thomas Nelson, Inc., Publishers, 1977.

*Terrorism* is a diatribe against terrorism by states, terrorism by revolutionaries and terrorism by criminals. Liston tells us very little about the phenomenon other than the "fact" that it is almost always unnecessary. The attentive newspaper reader will find very little new information in this book, although a chapter-anecdotal in focus—which treats efforts to combat terrorism may be marginally useful.

(N&G)

0379 Livingston, Marius H. (Ed.). with Kress, Lee B., and Wanek, Marie G. *International Terrorism in the Contemporary World*. Westport, Conn., Greenwood Press, 1978.

Over 40 papers from the International Symposium on Terrorism held at Glassboro State College (N.J.) in 1976. Contributors include Robert A. Fearey, J. Bowyer Bell, Edward Mickolus, Edgar O'Ballance, Brooks McClure, H.H.A. Cooper, Robert Friedlander, Jay Mallin, R. William Mengel, Ernest Evans, etc. Unfortunately, several of the contributions, at least a third, appeared in print subsequent to the conference and in more comprehensive form than they appear in the present volume. An 18 pp. summary of the symposium, prepared by Marie Wanek is provided, as is a 30-page bibliography, which was prepared by Lee Kress.

(N&G)

0380 Livingstone, Neil C. States in Opposition : The War Against Terrorism, *Conflict*, Volume 3, Numbers 2-3, 1981, pp. 83-141.

Although there is no special solution to the problem of terrorism, an effort must be made to eradicate the causes of terrorism, especially when it is rooted in desperation, injustice and deprivation. One of the most effective methods of dealing with terrorism today, especially hostage situations, is a swift and harsh counterattack. However, because a commando response does not strike at the real heart of the problem, it cannot be regarded as a long-term solution.

(IPSA)

0381 Livingstone, Neil C. Fighting Terrorism : The Private Sector. *Conflict*, Volume 3, Numbers 2-3, 1981, pp. 177-219.

Government action alone is not enough to contain the spreading disequilibrium caused by terrorist violence. The private sector, both individuals and corporations, must look to themselves as the ultimate guarantors of their own security. The first step in developing an effective security program or system is a comprehensive analysis of the threat. However, there is a tendency for many in the private sector concerned about their security to create a defense before they analyze the threat.

(IPSA)

0382 Livingstone, Neil C. and Terrell E. Arnold (Eds.). *Fighting Back : Winning the War Against Terrorism*. Lexington, Lexington Books, 1986.

This book deals with the 'policy issues' with regard to terrorism within the US, i.e., how US should respond to international terrorism and especially state sponsored terrorism in view of repeated attack on US soldiers, diplomats and facilities abroad.

Some policy makers in the administration are of the view that US must be prepared to use force against terrorists and accept the necessary risks involved. Others argue that the problem does not warrant a resort to such drastic methods.

The articles by authors examine the rise of State sponsored terrorism and solutions to this problem.

0383 Livingstone, Neil C. Low Level Violence and Future Targets. *Conflict.* Volume 2, Number 4, 1980, pp. 351-382.

The rapid progress of technology has provided terrorists and other techno aggressors with a seemingly limitless horizon of diverse and vulnerable new targets. Whole societies and their complex economies, food production and distribution systems, communications networks and energy production, storage and transport systems present the contemporary terrorist with unparalleled opportunities for disruption. The most vulnerable societies, moreover, are those that are the most open, where the highest degree of personal mobility and the most extensive personal freedoms exist along with government safeguards against arbitrary action by state. As a result of the routinization and trivialization of violence in contemporary societies, terrorists will have to constantly strive to achieve new heights of horror in order to capture public attention, and this will likely result in a historic departure from past and even present levels of violence as they strike out at targets of unprecedented, real or symbolic importance.

(IPSA)

0384 Lodge, Juliet (Ed.). *Terrorism : A Challenge to the State*. New York St. Martins Press, 1981.

This is a collection of original essays on contemporary terrorism and government response in Western Europe. The work includes case studies of terrorism in West Germany, Italy, France, the Netherlands and Northern Ireland. It also contains analyses of the problems at the European level : a study of the European community's attempts to provide for the extradition or punishment of terrorists and an overview of the legal problems of a coordinated European response.

(BRD)

0385 Lopez, George A. Teaching about Terrorism : Notes on Methods and Materials. *Terrorism : An International Journal*, Volume 3, Number 1-2, 1979-80.

That terrorism presents scholars and policy makers alike with new challenges is well documented. But the fact that transnational terrorism and societal responses to it have also placed new demands on those who teach international affairs in the undergraduate classroom is less widely discussed. This article identifies a basic set of educational objectives for teaching about terrorism as well as materials and methods for achieving those objectives with a reasonable degree of success. Through a discussion of the uses of library research exercises, films,

role playing and simulation, and values clarification approaches, the article provides a scheme for educating a nucleus of future citizens who will better understand the policy and value choices confronting them in a world beset by terrorism.

(T)

0386 Low, Konrad. Does the Rule of Law Favor Terrorism? (In German), *Aus Politik und Zeitgeschichte, Beilage zu " Das Parlament"*, Number 20, 1978, pp. 3-21.

The constitutional state should not allow itself to be restricted in enacting laws governing behaviour. The limits to anti-terrorism measures which it is permissible to set from the standpoints of the rule of law are still very far from being reached. Effective prosecution and crime prevention are permissible under the rule of law. The best way to counteract terrorism is, however, to remove the causes of terrorism. Since all terrorists call themselves Marxists, anyone taking seriously the strategy of the Marxists against our society must expect ruthless attempts to change the existing order.

(PRAJ: PRID)

0387 Lynch, Edward A. International Terrorism : The Search for a Policy. *Terrorism : An International Journal*, Volume 9, Number 1, 1987.

The United States has come to a point in its history which demands it form a coherent and comprehensive policy to address the odious threat of terrorism. The lack of such a coherent policy is one of the conditions that makes the United States a frequent target of terrorist attack. Developing such a policy is admittedly difficult given the nature of terrorism and difficulties it poses for the United States. State-sponsored terrorism has emerged as an effective and almost cost-free type of warfare for Iran, Libya, the Soviet Union, Cuba and Nicaragua. Narco-Terrorism is a particularly heinous form of attack on the United States. In spite of all the difficulties, recognizing the links between terrorist sponsoring states and understanding their objectives is the first step towards developing a policy. There are specific defensive and offensive strategies the Western democracies can employ to fight back.

(T)

0388 Mackey, Janet (Ed.). *Terrorism and Political Self-Determination : A Tragic Marriage we could help Decouple.* Chicago, World without War Publications, 1980.

Introduces the relationship between terrorism and the pursuit of self-determination, offers standards for evaluating and testing claims, and suggests how they might apply in specific situations.

(RW)

0389 Macstiofain, Sean (pseud). *Revolutionary in Ireland*. Farnborough, UK, Gordon Cremonesi, 1975.

Apparently the autobiography of the Chief of staff of the Provisional IRA, John Edward Drayton Stephenson. Stephenson was largely responsible for the split between the Provos and the officials. As expected, he argues the case for violence as a political tool.

(N&G)

0390 Mairowita, David Zane. Scissors in the Mind. *Harper's*, May 1978, pp. 28-31.

The reaction to terrorism in West Germany has been in itself terrifying. "There is a mounting fear of engaging in extraparliamentary political activity; hesitation about signing even liberal petitions for groups like Amnesty International; anxiety about associating with the 'wrong' people; isolated instances in which wives up for promotion have been asked to dissociate themselves from their husbands' political convictions (and vice versa); and what political theorist Wolf-Dieter Narr refers to as a 'general uncertainty as to what may or may not be articulated, written, learned or even taught.'" The target seems to be liberal opinion rather than extremist action. The effect has been on the middle-of-the-road rather than anyone remotely linked to terrorism. As a protest, the Third Bertrand Russell International Tribunal on the Situation of Human Rights in the Federal Republic of Germany and West Berlin has been convened and has questioned whether citizens are being denied the right to exercise their professions on account of their political views, whether censorship is being exercised through provisions of criminal and civil law and through extra legal measures, and whether human and constitutional rights are being eroded or eliminated. It is apparent that actual acts of unconstitutionality do not have to be proved, but attitudes can be prosecuted. An author's presumed intention can be prosecuted.

Anyone who deals in printed matter — even the truck-drivers who deliver it - can be prosecuted. Self-censorship of 'scissors in the head' has become the pattern. The extremity of the reaction against terrorism causes as much concern as the terrorism.

(PRAJ: PRID)

0391 Malik, K.N. This is the Politics of Terrorism. *Times of India*, (Delhi), 8 September 1985.

Author discusses the role of Sikh Extremists in UK and the extent of terror they have been able to instil in the minds of moderates. Also the part played by Indian High Commission in resolving the rift between Sikhs and Hindus, is discussed.

0392 Mallin, Jay (Comp.). *Terror and Urban Guerrillas : A Study of Tactics and Documents*. Coral Gables, Fla., University of Miami Press, 1971.

Contents - Introduction, by Jay Mallin. -- Partisan warfare, by N. Lenin. - A Viet Cong directive on "repression." - The Palestine terrorists : statements by Yasser Arafat and William Khoury. - Terror in the United States : "an introduction to elementary tactics : and "some questions on tactics" by George Prosser. - Minimanual of the Urban guerrilla, by Carlos Marighella. - One hundred fifty questions to a guerrilla, by Alberto Bayo Giround. Notes. -- Sources... Bibliography. - Index.

"This volume is aimed at setting forth the theory and techniques of terror, as described by its leading proponents and practitioners." Lenin's 1906 article urges "partisan actions" or "armed struggle" (which Mallin calls "an euphemism for terrorism") as one-but not the only-means of advancing the proletarian revolution. The captured 1965 Viet Cong directive spells out in detail policies, conditions, and methods for the repression of "counter revolutionary elements." In short statements, Arafat and Khourty justify the use of "armed struggle" and "special tactics" to achieve the liberation of Palestine. The excerpts from articles by George Prosser (a pseudonym) suggest terrorist tactics that might prove use-

ful in the United States. The Brazilian revolutionary carlos Marighella outlines the role and functions of the Urban guerrilla terrorist. Bayo's popular 1955 treatise, used in training Cuban guerrillas, details guerrilla organization weapons-making and tactics in a question and answer format.

(PRAJ: PRID)

0393 Mallin, Jay. Terrorism as a Military Weapon. *Air University Review*, Volume 22, January/February 1977, pp. 54-64.

Mallin's controversial thesis is that military tactics subsume terrorism. Thus he sees the Black September attack at the 1972 Olympics as "fundamentally a military move." Mallin asserts that "when soliders fail, terrorists take over," and yet many terrorists are soldiers. Terrorism is a military tactic when : it substitutes for regular warfare, when it is used in conjuction with other military activities and when it is used as a chosen weapon by a population segment against another segment or foreign power. Terror as a military weapon can have the following functions : psychological warfare, material destruction, and economic damage. Problematically, Mallin seems to blur the distinction between counter-terror actions by a state and state-terrorism. He concludes by criticizing the military's lack of appreciation of the importance of terrorism.

(N&G)

0394 Manor, F.S. Liberal Terror. *The American Spectator,* October, 1978, pp. 19-21.

In a rejoinder to Merritt, Manor passionately argues in favor of the restrictions that the Federal Republic has put into force to forestall terrorism. Stripping away the polemic, Manor's argument is that communism ("of whatever hue") actively seeks the establishment of a replacement regime which would "supplant free democracy and abolish human rights," an argument which is *ipso facto* justification for the measures instituted in West Germany. Unfortunately, Manor does not address the possibility of an over reaction in a rightward direction, obviously a matter that deserves equal time (viz. at what point do the preventive measures themselves become excessive?).

(N&G)

0395 Margolin, Joseph. *Psychological Perspectives in Terrorism.* In Alexander, Yonah and Finger, Seymour M. (Eds.). *Terrorism Interdisciplinary Perspectives,* New York, The John Jay Press, 1977, pp. 270-282.

A pithy survey of the possibly fruitful directions that behavioural research into terrorism may travel. Margolin is critical of much of the behaviorally-oriented works to date because of their parochialism ( "the unproven assumption that the terrorist is sick"). Included are brief discussions of the frustration-aggression theory, the goal gradient, Ziegarnik effect, uncertainty principle, cognitive style, the study of stimulus deprivation and projected research needs. On a whole a very well-argued piece with significant "hints" for additional research.

(N&G)

0396 Martin, L. John. The Media's Role in International Terrorism. *Terrorism : An International Journal*, Volume 8, Number 2, 1985-86.

Terrorism, like propaganda, is a form of persuasive communication. Like propaganda, it is a pejorative term. Some have referred to it as propaganda of the deed. It is hard to define because its definition depends on whether one agrees with the message. If one does, neither propaganda nor terrorism is the term that is normally used to describe such activity.

After considering various definitions and examples of what is and is not terrorism, this paper looks at the symbiotic relationship that exists between terrorism and mass media. Each exploits the other and terrorism has no meaning without media coverage in this age of mass communication. Terrorists use mass media for both tactical and strategic purposes.

While the mass media do, generally, cover terrorism at a rate of at least nine incidents per day worldwide, according to a pilot study undertaken for this paper, the press uses the term "terrorist" sparingly, preferring such neutral terms as guerrilla, rebel, and paramilitary, or using no value-laden adjectives at all. (Each country in the study, except Egypt, did, however, have its pet terrorists). This raises the question of the effectiveness of terrorism. The Press gives terrorists publicity but often omits the propaganda message that terrorists would like to see accompanying reports of their exploits, thus reducing terrorism to mere crime or sabotage.

Terrorism has much in common with propaganda. Both are forms or vehicles of communication. Both are persuasive in intent, rather than, say, informative. Both are expressed in verbal as well as non-verbal terms. And both are pejorative in connotation. One does not refer to friends as terrorists or propagandists. These are terms reserved for one's enemies. The mass media we found in this preliminary study may quote someone verbatim using "terror" or "terrorism" in reference to an act performed by a group toward which the medium is either neutral or opposed, but the press will never use these terms in a headline unless it not only disapproves of the act but has no sympathy for its perpetrators.

(T)

0397 Martino, Antonio. "Making Democracy Unsafe for Italy." *The American Sepectator*, June/July 1978, pp. 15-16.

This University of Naples economics professor and official in the Italian Liberal Party, argues that a symbiotic relationship (at least) exists between the *Brigate Rosse* and the Italian Communist Party, in that the actions of the terrorists enable the PCI to assert its identification with the political establishment and the concomitant necessity that it be included in any national government.

(N&G)

0398 Mather, Ian. Red Brigades Strike at the Heart of Italy, *Observer*, (London), 19 March, 1978, p. 17.

The Moro kidnapping focusses attention on the nature and increase of terrorism in Italy - there are estimated to be several hundred groups (most of them middle - class students) first formed in 1969, and all of them coldly brutal. Includes brief profiles of Renato Curcio and Roberto Ognibene. The Brigades are condemned by the Communist party, although extreme Leftists, and they in turn are violently critical of the Communist compromises with the Christian Democrats. Much is speculated about the Brigades, but little is known.

(PRAJ: PRID)

0399 Mather, Ian. The Shining Path ot Death. *Observer,* (London), 24 October, 1982, p. 12.

Describes *Shining Path*, the Peruvian guerrilla organization which is carrying out raids throughout the country, as a Maoist group, which speaks especially for Peruvian Indians who live in the central Andean provinces, and are in a state of utter depression. Their leader is Comrade Gonzalo (See Abimael Guzman), formerly a philosophy lecturer at the University of Ayacucho. These guerrillas are concentrating on a people's war in the countryside, later to be extended to the

cities. The guerrillas are now so powerful that President Belaunde, head of the first civilian, democratically-elected government in 12 years, has suspended constitutional rights, and holds about 300 political prisoners without trial.

(PRAJ: PRID)

0400 Mather, Ian and others. Secret Tricks Beat the Hijackers. *Observer,* (London), 23 October, 1977, p. 6.

Describes the elaborate preparations that made possible the capture of the hijacked Lufthansa airliner in Mogadishu airport - international preparations, the shadowing of the hijacked plane, training of commandos for the job. Many countries were involved and there appears to be a growing reluctance of Arab capitals to play host to hijackers - Lebanon, Oman, Iraq, Kuwait, South Yemen, Egypt all refused them. This is partly because the PLO has given up hijacking as an instrument of propaganda.

(PRAJ: PRID)

0401 Mather, Ian and others. Arab War Games in the West End. *Observer,* (London), January 1978, p. 11.

There have been three incidents in London in nine months, involving violent deaths of Arabs, the last being Eve Said Hammani, the PLO's representative in London - a moderate who recognized the need of a dialogue with Israel. Speculates on probable perpetrators of the murders - in particular on two extremist Palestinians, Abu Nidal and Wadi Haddad.

(PRAJ: PRID)

0402 Matsushita, T. *Youthful Extremism in Japan.* Tokyo, United Nations, Asia and Far East Institute for the Prevention of Crime and Treatment of Offenders, 1977.

A brief (8 pp.) report dealing with the trends in extremist activities by Japanese students, the causes of such extremism, and criminal sanctions appropriate to the problem.

(N&G)

0403 McClure, Brooks. Hostage Survival. *Conflict : An International Journal for Conflict and Policy Studies*, Volume 1, 1978, pp. 21-48.

This treatment of hostage situations in the context of terrorism is a fascinating summary of many of the lessons learned from past incidents. The specialist is unlikely to find any new information, but McClure's competent synthesis should be of particular value to those whose professions might render them potential targets for terrorists, as well as those with academic interests in the dynamics of hostage survival.

(N&G)

0404 McClure, Brooks. *The Dynamics of Terrorism.* Gaithersburg, Md., International Association of Chiefs of Police, 1976.

This monography is intended for a professional police audience. The scope of the effort is wide-ranging, including brief discussions of the variants of terrorism, its origins, causes and recruitment patterns. Useful sections treat reactions to terrorism and countermeasures.

(N&G)

0405 McGuire, Maria. I Accuse Sean Mac Stiofan, *Observer,* (London), 3 September, 1972, pp. 9-10; 10 September, 1972, p. 25; and 17 September, 1972, p. 7.

Member of the Provisional IRA charges Mac Stiofan, its Chief of Staff, with abusing and using the members for his own interests; charges that he is a

bigoted murderer, willing to permit sectarian killings as a means of keeping in power. Describes her work with the IRA.

(PRAJ: PRID)

,406 McKnight, Gerald. *The Terrorist mind : Why they Hijack, Kidnap, Bomb and Kill.* Indianapolis, The Bobbs-Merrill Company, Inc., 1974.

A disappointing book which delivers far less than the title suggests. Rather than a systematic treatment of the terrorist mind, the reader instead encounters a series of interviews, anecdotal in focus, which vary in their value. The most useful materials concern the Fedayeen, IRA and Latin American terrorists.

(N&G)

0407 McPhee, John. *The Curve of Binding Energy.* New York, Farrar, Straus and Giroux, 1974.

Originally published as a series in *The New Yorker*, this is a popularized treatment of Theodore Taylor, and the possibility of the illicit fabrication of nuclear weapons.

(N&G)

0408 McWhinney, Edward. *The Illegal Diversion of Aircraft and International Law.* Leyden, Sitjhoff, 1975.

McWhinney complains that hijacking is usually treated as a single problem, although the motives for the act can be quite diverse. More than half the book is devoted to various "problem-solving techniques", mainly international treaties, both multilateral and bilateral. The Tokyo (1963), Hague (1970) and Montreal (1971) Conventions introduced the principle "aut dedere, aut punire", but left prosecution to the competent authorities without guaranteeing punishment. Since there is no sanction against a treaty, state's non-compliance, bilateral treaties are probably better than multilateral, since the latter are more frequently ignored. Also of value are actions by such bodies as IATA (International Air Transport Association) or the International Federation of Air Line Pilots, when they threaten a total cut-off of all flights to and from a delinquent state which harbors hijackers. Individual states have also taken such actions as amending their penal codes or instituting security searches at airports. The greatest problem in international legal action against hijackers is political sympathy of the "refuge" state with the hijacker. McWhinney favors considering each case on its special merits, since "political defence" may sometimes be justified, and "freedom of the air" is not part of international "juscogens". The "special legal community of the air" should develop its own control measures and cooperate in their enforcement.

(PRAJ: PRID)

0409 Melucci, Alberto. New Movements, Terrorism, and the Political System : Reflections on the Italian Case. *Socialist Review*, Volume 11, Number 2, March-April 1981, pp. 97-136.

Terrorism is both the most radical result and the radical antithesis of new "class" movements. The terrorist groups have all the characteristics of fundamentalist sects : the sectarian organization and the symbolic framework which structures even the personality of the members. In Italy, terrorism has increasingly lost its Marxist origins after 1977. Terrorism in mature societies is not only a response to crisis, but the desperate indicator of points of social conflict.

(IPSA)

0410 Mengel, R.W. Terrorism and New Technologies of Destruction : An Overview of the Potential Risk. In *US Department of Justice, Law Enforcement Assistance Administration. Disorder and Terrorism* Report of the task force on Disorder and Terrorism, Washington, D.C. Government Printing Office, 1976, pp. 443-473.

Proceeding within a costs-benefits scheme. Mengal finds that terrorists-particularly the US - are not likely to assume the high risk associated with "new technology terrorism" (i.e., in particular, nuclear, chemical and biological terrorism). Alluding to-but not presenting - a data base of more than 4500 acts of terrorism, Mengel finds that terrorists are decidedly non-suicidal, that terrorists generally opt for "controllable weapons", and that their activities are reducible to patterns (a significant factor for further research). Rejecting the "lone-individual" scenarios, it is asserted that high technology terror is more appropriately a (skilled) team effort. This analysis does support the conclusion that high technology terror could be attractive to those wishing to escalate their efforts when faced with likely failure at lower levels of violence. A matrix of violent behavior is presented which distinguishes between terrorism and seven other violent behaviors (e.g., criminal, psychopathic, etc.); however, since terrorism is never clearly defined, its utility (i.e., the matrix) is rather questionable. This article concludes with extended commentary and prescription on the law enforcement and incident-management aspects of the problem."

(N&G)

0411 Merrit, Richard L. From Munich to Mogadishu. *The American Spectator*, June/July 1978, pp. 17-19.

Addressing the possibility of an authoritarian reaction by the West German government to the terrorist exploits of the Red Army Faction, inter alia, Merritt finds the danger lies not in what has occurred to date, but what might develop in the future. Summarizing the legal and administrative steps that have been taken to dampen the terrorist threat, he argues that pressure from the right may result in measures which will place "state security above personal freedoms," and thus play into the hands of the terrorists. The most significant problem is said to arise from the superheated political environment, resultant of terrorism, which precludes rational debate and consequently could lead to a breakdown in political consensus.

(N&G)

0412 Mickolus, Edward F. Statistical Approaches to the Study of Terrorism. In Alexander, Yonah and Finger, Seymour M. (Eds.). *Terrorism : Interdisciplinary Perspectives.* New York, The John Jay Press, 1977, pp. 209-269.

A useful compilation from the ITERATE (International Terrorism : Attributes of Terrorist Events) project. Data includes : incidents by type, 1968-1975; casualties, 1969-1975; location of incidents; nationality of victims and targets; groups by type of incident and region; as well as supporting bibliographic cites. In addition the ITERATE coding sheet (107 items) is reproduced.

(N&G)

0413 Midlarsky, Manus I.; Crenshaw, Martha and Yoshida, Fumihiko. Why Violence Spreads. The Contagion of International Terrorism.

*International Studies Quarterly*, Volume 24, Number 2, June 1980, p. 262-298.

The study examines the spread of international terrorism from 1968 to 1974. Using Poisson and negative binomial probability models, a diffusion of international terrorism was found in the first segment of the time period (1968-1971) and contagion as a direct modelling process in the second (1973-1974). Accordingly, the theory of hierarchies in which the diplomatic status of a country predicts its degree of imitability was found to operate among Latin American countries during the second portion of the overall period, but not during the first. An inverse hierarchy is suggested as an explanation for the contagion of violence from Latin America and other third world countries to Western Europe. Autocorrelation functions were used to assess which forms of terrorism were most contagious in which regions.

(IPSA)

0414 Milbank, David L. *Research Study : International and Transnational Terrorism : Diagnosis and Prognosis*. Washington, D.C., Office of Political Research, Central Intelligence Agency, PR 76 10030, April 1976.

A solid study notable for its prognosis that "transnational terrorism" (carried out by autonomous non-state actors) is more likely to pose an increasing problem for the future than "international terrorism" (carried out by terrorists controlled by a sovereign state). Among Milbank's predictations is the -- as yet unrealized -- assertion that transnational terrorism will be more sharply felt in the US in the years ahead.

(N&G)

0415 Miller, Abraham H. *Terrorism and Hostage Negotiations*. Boulder, Westview Press, 1980.

Miller's study focuses on a single aspect of terrorism: the techniques used in hostage and barricade situations ...where hostages are taken, a barricade situation ensues, and demands are made on the authorities for the hostages' release. He examines the effectiveness of techniques such as government policy of 'no negotiations' with terrorists and makes predictions as to the future efficacy of these policies in hostage and barricade situations. He points out that there is a limit to how far a government can take any policy and that even the Israelis with their stated policy of 'no negotiations with terrorists,' attempted negotiations at Maalot in May 1974.

(BRD)

0416 Miller, Abraham H. On Terrorism. *Public Administration Review*, July/August 1977, pp. 429-435.

Comprehensive review essay treating works by Yonah Alexander, J. Bowyer Bell and Christopher Dobson. Miller criticizes the literature in general for its failure to address the public policy aspects of the terrorism problem.

(N&G)

0417 Miller, Bowman H. Terrorism and Language: A Text-Based Analysis of the German Case. *Terrorism : An International Journal*, Volume 9, Number 4, 1987.

Contemporary terrorism combines selective violence with reliance on language to articulate motivations, beliefs and objectives. Focussing on language, this interdisciplinary approach applies insights from content and propaganda

analysis, psycholinguistics, structural linguistics and political and sociobiographical analysis to major event-related statements issued between 1972 and 1986 by the West German terrorist group Red Army Faction (RAF).

Semantic, lexial and syntactic means used to produce altered meanings and achieve persuasion are isolated in the texts. RAF awareness of the need for an manipulability of language is contrasted with their rejection of language as a political tool. The terrorists' verbal objective is to usurp the West German government's claim to legitimacy, morality, monopoly on the use of force, and popular support.

The analysis concludes that the RAF's language component fails because of the unacceptability of terrorist claims and their feeble effort to articulate aims and politics to a wider audience. By combining linguistic assessment of texts with indepth knowledge of the history and nature of terrorism in West Germany, the study illustrates the need to analyze terrorist statements as one aspect of understanding and coping with terrorism.

(T)

0418 Miron, N.S. *Hostage*. Kalamazoo, Michigan, Behaviordlia, Inc., 1978.

Discusses the nature of the hostage-taker and the characteristics of an effective negotiator. Includes case material from US hostage situations.

(N&G)

0419 Moddie, A.D. The Posts of Terrorism : System Against Counter System. *Statesman*, (Delhi), 6 April 1987.

Author gives a brief history of terrorism world-wide and differenciates between terrorism and guerrilla warfare.

Terrorism can be controlled through political processes and not by appeasement or corrupt politics. The failure so far in Punjab is primarily the failure of politics and only secondarily that of the police. People should be involved through informal bodies of public opinion to fight this menace. Unfortunately this has not been done either by the centre or the state government.

0420 Mommsen, Wolgang J. and Hirschfeld, Gerhard. (Eds.). *Social Protest, Violence and Terror in Nineteenth and Twentieth - Century Europe*. London, The MacMillan Press Ltd., 1982.

The essays in this volume are the papers presented in a conference on social protest, violence and terror: strategies of violence resorted to by social and political fringe groups in the nineteenth and twentieth centuries, organized by the German Historical Institute from 15 to 17 November 1979, at the Werner-Reimers-Stijtung in Bad Homburg.

The papers attempt to assess many political groups and movements which in the course of the last one and-a-half century in Europe have resorted to means of violence and individual terror to press certain political and economic demands and in some cases to pave the way for radical change and revolutionary up heaval upon reluctant governments - no matter whether authoritarian, constitutional or democratic. Articles describe the typical patterns or terrorist strategies of violence as well as the social conditions within which these groups operated-focussing on the rise of terrorist groups within specific historical developments. Finally an attempt has been made to produce a typology of various forms of terrorism or non-legal violence in modern European history along with the present day terrorist activities namely (1) Social Protest Movements, (2) National emancipation movements, (3) Terrorist movements or

groups of anarchist persuasion, (4) Anarcho-syndicalist groups, (5) Movements of integral nationalism, (6) Fascist movements, (7) Neo-fascist groupings and lastly (8) Neo-marxist or pseudo-marxist movements.

0421 Momboisse, Raymond M. *Blueprint of Revolution : The Rebel, The Party, The Technique of Revolt.* Springfield, Illinois, Charles C. Thomas, 1970.

Includes useful treatments of terror, assassination and urban guerrilla warfare.

(N&G)

0422 Monroe, Charles P. Addressing Terrorism in the United States. *Annals of the American Academy of Political and Social Science*, Number 463, September 1982, pp. 141-148.

Terrorism presents a serious threat to democratic governments that must protect themselves without trampling individual rights. Federal Bureau of Investigation successes have shown that the US government can effectively deal with this threat while protecting the constitutional rights of citizens.

(PRAJ: PRID)

0423 Moodie, Michael. Political Terrorism : A Unique Kind of Tyranny. *Osterreichische Zeitschrift fur Aussenpolitik,* Volume 18, Number 1, 1978, pp. 27-38.

Developing countermeasures to illicit traffic in arms raises the general question of the international response to political terrorism. The fact that some states actively support terrorist activities makes the international regulation of the problem difficult. To date, governments have responded to terrorist violence by substituting a sort of technical concern about the resolution of *adhoc* situations for a comprehensive solution to the problem. It must be remembered that terrorism is a political problem which must be countered by political policies.

(IPSA)

0424 Moorehead, C. Terrorism In the Air. *New Society,* Volume 72/1174, 1985, pp. 471-472.

The author provides a brief overview of the terrorism problem today, looks at the increase of terrorism of all varieties, especially of hostage-taking and at what psychiatrists have learned of hostage behaviour.

(IPSA)

0425 Morris, Michael. *Armed Conflict in Southern Africa : A Survey of Regional Terrorism from their Beginnings to the Present, with a Comprehensive Examination of the Portuguese Position.* Cape Town, South Africa, Jeremy Spence, 1974.

Includes useful case material, maps and bibliographies for groups active since 1950 in Rhodesia, Mozambique, Angola, Portuguese, Guinea, Zambia, Tanzania, Malawi, South-West Africa, South Africa and Botswana.

(N&G)

0426 Moss, David. The Kidnapping and Murder of Aldo Moro. *Archives Europeennes de Sociologie*, Volume 21, Number 2, 1981, pp. 265-295.

In order to understand the kidnapping and murder of the Italian political

leader Aldo Moro by Red Brigade terrorists, it is necessary to take into account the context of contemporary Italian politics. From this viewpoint, the events appear as a tactic appropriate to the pursuit of political identity; they create a frame for the sequence of symbolic actions designed to transform the group's identity. The transformation was achieved through the intellectual co-operation of the Red Brigades' antagonists, by publicly reading and interpreting the texts circulated by Moro's captors. They did not achieve political recognition, but achieved a characteristic paradox: Moro's passage into a redescribed political world, his becoming an independent agent challenging the old boundaries. In the history of political leaders' deaths, Moro finds an original place.

(IPSA)

0427 Moss, Robert. International Terrorism and Western Societies. *International Journal*, Volume 28, Number 3, Summer, 1973, pp. 418-430.

Proceeding from the finding that the modern city is singularly vulnerable to terrorists who are increasingly becoming an international phenomenon, finds that the danger for western societies is not that they will be overturned, but rather that they will be provoked into repression measures which will corrode democratic institutions. Moss sees the solution in more effective cooperation among target states, complemented by a heightened concern with the problem.

(N&G)

0428 Moss, Robert. *The War for the Cities*. New York, Coward, MacCann and Geoghaghan, 1972.

Although somewhat overtaken by events, this book, by a renowned British authority, remains a masterful, descriptive survey of urban terrorism. Moss's overarching theme is that "terrorism is a faulty weapon that often misfires." Notable sections of the book treat terrorism as exercised in Cyprus, Northern Ireland, Brazil, Venezuela, Guatemala, Uruguay and Tsarist Russia. Discussions of terrorists' ideologies also merit attention. Symptomatic of the analytical problems that plague the literature, Moss's distinction between the "urban guerrilla" and the "terrorist" is less than rigorous and is at times even contradictory to the case examples he provides.

(N&G)

0429 Moss, Robert. "Urban Guerrilla War". *Adelphi Papers*, Number 79, (1971). London, International Institute for Strategic Studies, 1971.

A terse monograph which neatly summarizes many of the analytical points made by Moss in his *The War for the Cities*. Marighella's Minimanual *of the Urban Guerrilla* is appended.

(N&G)

0430 Moskin, J. Robert (Ed.). World Beat.The PLO's Latin Beat. *World Press Review*, August 1982, p.7.

Neue Zurcher Zeitung, Zurich, charges that the Palestine Liberation Organization (PLO) supports revolutionary movements all over the world aimed against the US. "Aside from Cuba and Nicaragua, the PLO has bureaus in only 3 Latin American countries : Mexico, Peru and Ecuador." Their greatest success has been in Nicaragua. In July 1979 they sent a plane-load of weapons from Beirut. Israel had sold weapons to the former Nicaraguan dictator Somoza, so the PLO were happy to send arms to the governments overthrowing him. In 1980 Arafat visited Nicaragua and the PLO later loaned Nicaragua $10 million. Later Salvadoran guerrillas received aid from the PLO. In January Arafat said that the PLO

had pilots in Nicaragua and soldiers in El Salvador.

(PRAJ: PRID)

0431 Moskin, J. Robert. (Ed.). World Beat - Terrorist Capital. *World Press Review*, November 1982, p. 8.

Paris is called "the undisputed terrorist capital of Western Europe", by the RAND DAILY MAIL, Johannesburg. First it was Corsican and Breton nationalists, and then terrorists, from all over Europe began to use it as a base for operations. ACTION DIRECTE, which began as an anarchist group, joined with French Arabs, and were converted to the Palestinian cause. When Mitterand declared a political amnesty, the Action Directe was free to plot new campaigns. It is almost the only growth industry left.

(PRAJ: PRID)

0432 Moughrabi, Fouad. The Refusal Front : A Study of High Risk Politics in the Palestine Resistance Movement. *International Studies Association*, Toronto, 25-29 February, 1976.

The Palestine Resistance Movement contains at least two distinct patterns of political behaviour, one pragmatic and flexible,the other committed to armed struggle and a no compromise position. This paper discusses the latter, "high risk politics," as a function of personality and situational variables.

(PRAJ: PRID)

0433 Mulgaokar, S. Defiling the Statute Book. *Indian Express,* (Delhi), 29 May 1985.

Author describes the Terrorist and Disruptive Activities (Prevention) Act as the one among the blackest pieces of legislation to defile independent India's statute book - the dark days of the emergency always excluded. The powers provided to police under this particular law will result in converting at least half of the people arrested, into hardcore terrorists with or without a cause. Only a political solution of the Punjab problem can resolve this crisis.

0434 Mullen, Robert K. Mass Destruction and Terrorism. *Journal of International Affairs*, Volume 32, Spring/Summer 1978, pp. 63-90.

Probably one of the best analyses published to date on the macro-terrorist problem (i.e. nuclear, biological and chemical). Mullen offers an informed discussion of chemical and biological agents with mass destructive capabilities, and then proceeds to identify the production and delivery considerations which will affront the terrorists. His presentation supports his conclusion that mass destruction threats from terrorists are "vanishingly remote."

(N&G)

0435 Murray, Mark. Japan's "Red Army" at War with World. *Observer,* (London), June 4, 1972, p. 4.

The author interviewed young radical Japanese, who explained the formation of Japan's most militant ultra-leftist organization, Sekigun-ha (Red Army), three of whose members, recruited by the Palestinian PFLP, were responsible for the massacre at Israel's Lod airport. The young Japanese interviewed said the Japanese society is so rigid and dominated by the past that it is impossible for them to change it, and they are forced to go international to have some effect on the corrupt world. Cooperation with the PFLP is one way. The Sekigun-ha consists of a cross section of young upper-class Japanese, many of them scholars, doctors, engineers and nurses. The members are severely disciplined to

the point of assassination among themselves, and they are politically uninvolved, calling themselves Maoist, Tronskyist or anarchist. A number are on trial for murder.

(PRAJ: PRID)

0436 Murray, Russell. Killings of Local Security Forces in Northern Ireland 1969-1981. *Terrorism: An International Journal*, Volume 7, Number 1, 1984.

Governments faced with insurgency often prefer to deploy local security units rather than regular troops; they in turn may become the primary targets of guerrillas or terrorists. This paper examines the circumstances in which police officers and Ulster Defence Regiment personnel have been killed by the Provisional IRA and similar groups since 1969. Significant differences are found between the victims from the two forces; police officers are most likely to be killed on duty and in urban areas; nearly all UDR members are killed off-duty in rural areas. These are related to the different threats that the police and UDR present to the IRA's operations and objectives. In carrying on with their ordinary duties the police undermine the IRA's attempts to render the country ungovernable. The UDR personnel who live in rural areas represent an invaluable source of intelligence for the government.

(T)

0437 Naar, Joseph L. Rise in Anti-Capitalist Terrorism. *American Journal of Economics and Sociology*, January 1980, p. 82.

Risks International Inc., a consulting firm which monitors international terrorism, has compiled data from the U.S. State Department, the CIA, and the Rand Corporation which shows a rise in terrorist incidents from 572 in 1975, to 728 in 1976, to 1,256 in 1977 and 1,511 in 1978. Nearly 3/4 of the incidents took place in 14 countries. The top 5 are the U.S., Argentina, Italy, Colombia and Peurto Rico. Business and its employees are the prime targets. Business executives accounted for 55% and diplomats 28%, military and police 8% and news personnel 4%. The incidents reported include assassinations, kidnapping, bombings and personal assaults.

More and more multinationals are taking steps to protect their employees by providing guards and advice, purchasing kidnap insurance, improving physical security. Ransom demands have also risen. Before 1972 no group demanded as much as $ 1 million. In 1978 there were 12 demands of a million or more. The report finds that the norm now is $5 to $ 10 million.

(PRAJ: PRID)

0438 Nader, Ralph and Abbotts, John. *The Menace of Atomic Energy*. New York, W.W. Norton and Co., Inc., 1977.

Chapter XII, "The Plutonium Fuel Cycle," discusses the danger of the illicit diversion of plutonium by terrorists and others.

(N&G)

0439 Nath, Shaileshwar. *Terrorism in India*. New Delhi, National Publishing House, 1980.

This work is the study of the Revolutionary Movement in Bihar from 1902 to 1935, particularly in post-1912 period, when Bihar was separated from Bengal in 1912. This movement was well connected with mainstream revolutionary movement and was broadbased.

0440 Neale, William D. Terror - Oldest Weapon in the Arsenal. *Army*, August 1973, pp. 10-17.

A workman-like treatment marred by several important errors, in particular the role of terrorism in mandatory Palestine and the support engendered by the Irgun. Neale identifies three variants: vigilante terror, reign of terror (state terrorism) and siege of terror (revolutionary terrorism). He ignores the anarchist nihilist variant. The treatment suffers from the tendency to call every "terrible" act terrorism, thus we find the Dresden attack and Hiroshima offered as examples because they were terrifying, rather than constituting a program of terrorism (cf. Stalin's terrorism, Hitler's genocide and the French Reign of Terror).

(N&G)

0441 Nedava, Yosef. Some Aspects of Individual Terrorism : A Case Study of the Schwartzbard Affair. *Terrorism : An International Journal*, Volume, 3, Number 1-2, 1979-80.

The literature dealing with individual terrorism through the ages is voluminous. Assassinations have occurred since the dawn of civilization, and tyrannicide has been the subject of philosophical discussion and analysis since the formative stages of human society. At first, the act of killing a tyrant was not frowned upon, and it carried no suggestion of moral obloquy. On the contrary, it was considered a legitimate means of meting out justice where no other remedy was available to the afflicted; it thus reflected commendable, and not only justifiable, vengeance. With the growth of "some semblance of an organized, democratic society, assassinations came to be regarded as at hreat to recognized authority. Such a resort to extra legal means seemed likely to lead to anarchy, thus endangering the very basis of existence of society. Assassinations soon came under the heading of criminal acts and were dealt with accordingly.

Nowadays both democratic and authoritarian regimes alike look askance at acts of individual terrorism. To be sure, Soviet rule, more particularly during the "black years" of Stalinism, has applied both mass and individual terror to ensure obedience, but such terrorism was used as a means to an end. Marxism does not condemn terrorism from an ideological point of view; it simply does not believe in its practicability in bringing about a substantial change in society.

(T)

42 Netanyahu, Benjamin (Ed.). *Terrorism : How the West can win.* Farrar, Straus and Giroux, 1986.

In this connection the contributors examine the moral, political, legal, historical, military and journalistic aspects of terrorism. The premise of this book is that clarification will lend support to intelligent and decisive action, led by the US and supported by other democracies.

(BRD)

0443 Netanyahu, Benjamin (Ed.). *International Terrorism : Challenge and Response*. Proceedings of the Jerusalem Conference on International Terrorism. Israel, The Jonathan Institute 1981.

This volume contains papers read at the Jerusalem conference on International Terrorism, conducted by the Jonathan Institute on July 2-5, 1979.
The papers discuss the origin, nature and future of terrorism and the measures for combating and defeating the international terrorist movements, while protecting the fundamental civil liberties of the citizens.

0444 Niezing, J. (Ed.). *Urban Guerrilla Studies on the Theory Strategy and Practice of Political Violence in Modern Societies*. Rotterdam, Rotterdam University Press, 1974.

Proceedings of the First International Working Conference on Violence and Non-Violent Action in Industrialized Societies, Brussels, March 13-15, 1974, Part I, with an introduction by J. Niezing, Professor of Sociology and Polemology at the Free University of Brussels and Director of the Polemological Centre of the Free University of Brussels.

The study of political violence and of the urban guerrilla in particular, can be tackled from several angles. In this book, much attention is paid to the relation between socio-political change and political violence in general, and to the strategy and tactics of the urban guerrilla in particular. This volume consists of studies on a theoretical and strategic nature as well as descriptions of specific guerrilla movements. Together, these studies demonstrate the broad range of reflections on political violence that can be found within contemporary peace research. Contributors: John Niezing, Hakon Wiberg, Andrew Mack, Otthein Ramstedt, Edi Clijsters,Rob Kreg, Charles Reid, Ger Teitler, Godfried Van Bentahem, Van den Berg, H.C.F. Mansilla, Johan E. Huetling.

(PRAJ: PRID)

0445 Nisan, Mordechai. PLO Messianism : Diagnosis of a Modern Gnostic Sect. *Terrorism: An International Journal*, Volume 7, Number 3,1984.

Placed against the backdrop of the recent war in Lebabnon, this original analysis of the PLO rests upon the conviction that this movement is not merely a military-political body, but is a kind of "religious" sect in meaning, intent, and form. This philosophical interpretation of the PLO draws upon a gnostic model in order to uncover the psychological universe of the PLO. In so doing, the author employs the interdisciplinary method of linking religion and politics (which is a view of political culture in the Arab-Muslim world) to penetrate to the ultimate inner reality of the PLO. In this search, it is difficult to avoid concluding that the PLO represents a highly disorderly force in the Mid-eastern and global settings.

(T)

0446 Norman, Lloyd. Our Nuclear Weapons Sites : Next Target of Terrorists? *Army*, June 1977, pp. 28-31.

One of the Oft-discussed routes to weapons states is the theft of an intact device. In this informative and informed article, Norman draws extensively from an interview with the Defense Department official charged with the security of nuclear weapons sites. Security procedures are outlined, as are the safety devices which preclude unauthorized use of nuclear weapons. It is conceded that a highly-skilled perpetrator might be able to disassemble and reconstruct even a weapon equipped with security devices, thus pointing up the key importance of site security.

(N&G)

0447 Norton, Augustus R. *Moscow and the Palestinians*. Miami, Center for Advancd International Studies, University of Miami, 1974.

Traces the evolving relationship through the summer of 1974, with special emphasis upon the soviet perspective.

(N&G)

0448 Norton, Augustus R. *The Palestinian State Under PLO Leadership.* A paper presented at the April 1976 annual meeting of the Mid-West Political Science Association, Chicago, Illinois.

An examination of the "aura of responsibility thesis" which holds that a revolutionary movement, once established in a state, will turn inward to the tasks of development and administration, and away from terrorism and violence.

(N&G)

0449 Norton, Augustus R., with the assistance of Martin H. Greenberg. *Understanding the Nuclear Terrorism Problem.* Gaithersburg, Md., International Association of Chiefs of Police, Inc., 1979.

A thorough examination of the nuclear terrorism problem. Although this publication is intended for senior police officials, much of it will be of wider interest. Includes a primer on the pertinent technologies, an analysis of the contending assessments of the problem, as well as an overview of the physical security and technical vulnerabilities that characterize nuclear facilities. Prospective nuclear terrorists are discussed with detailed assessments of the PLO and the FALN. The study concludes with a commentary on the implications of the nuclear terror threat -- both the wider implications for constitutional protections.

(N&G)

0450 Norton, Augustus R. Terror by Fission : An Analysis and Critique. *Chitty's Law Journal*, 1979.

A critical monograph which addresses most of the literature on the nuclear terrorism question. Norton is critical of the perspective which holds that the technical feasibility of nuclear terrorism (which is itself a controversial question) demonstrates the likelihood of such an act. Instead he proposes that the motives, morals, rationality, and objectives of the terrorists must be taken into account, and that when this is done the likelihood of nuclear terrorism is at least far less than a certainty. A model of terrorists' decision-making is offered. The most important conclusion is that the terrorist groups most competent relative to an act of nuclear terror, and precisely those who would have the least to gain through such an act; the converse is also said to be true.

(N&G)

0451 Norton, Augustus R. Nuclear Terrorism and the Middle East. *Military Review,* Volume 56, April 1976, pp. 3-11.

The Middle East is an often-mentioned setting for nuclear terrorism, with the Fedayeen (Palestinian terrorists) cited as the likely perpetrators. In this selection Norton investigates the Middle Eastern case, with particular emphasis on the aquisition of nuclear weapons, the motivation for doing so, and considerations of threat effectuation. He finds a lack of motivation among the most technically capable Fedayeen, and a number of here-to-force unrecognized problems for the terrorist bent on carrying out an act of nuclear terrorism.

(N&G)

0452 Norton, Augustus R. and Greenberg, Martin H. (Eds.). *Studies in Nuclear Terrorism*. Boston, G.K. Hall and Co., 1979.

An extensive anthology on the subject with an original introduction by Norton. Robert Friedlander provides a thoughful and incisive foreward. Indexed, with a glossary and technical primer.

(N&G)

0453 Nuclear Energy, Policy Study Group. *Nuclear Power : Issues and Choices*. Cambridge, Mass, Ballinger Publishing Company, 1977.

See esp. pp. 301-315. While the participants in this Ford Foundation Study are concerned about inadequacies in the physical security of nuclear reactors in the US and abroad, they find that the difficulties involved with designing, planning, and constructing a nuclear weapon from reactor grade materials are considerably greater than many experts have claimed.

(N&G)

0454 O'Ballance, Edgar. *Arab Guerrilla Power, 1967-1972*. Hamden, Conn., Archon Books, 1973.

A competent journalistic treatise by an author who has written extensively about conflict in the Middle East, *inter alia*.

(N&G)

0455 O'Ballance, Edgar. *Terror in Ireland: The Heritage of Hate*. Pamaron Way, Novato, Presidio Press, 1981.

O'Ballance presents a recitation of events in Northern Ireland since the 1960s, with several introductory chapters on Irish history and the IRA.

(BRD)

0456 O'Ballance, Edgar. IRA Leadership Problems. *Terrorism: An International Journal*, Volume 5, Number 1-2, 1981-82.

The present leadership of the IRA has been in power for about five years, and appears to be a tight, collective one, with determination to fight a long terrorist campaign until the British government is forced to abandon Northern Ireland. Behind that firm facade are doubts and uncertainties, such as whether the IRA will in fact, be able to sustain a long campaign in the face of improved antiterrorist measures. The article traces the development of the leadership, its differences, the reasons for the split between the "Officials" and the "Provisionals," and the appearance of the Irish National Liberation Army splinter.

(T)

0457 O'Brien, Cornor Cruise. The Long Shadow of the Terrorist. *Observer*, (London), 5 February, 1978, p. 10.

Reports a debate on "Terrorism in the Democratic Society", in which the civil servants, industrialists and police blame the educators who taught a Leftist ideology; the academics felt that the student terrorists were disappointed idealists in despair of realizing their egalitarian ideals by other means. The author, in his own experience, found that many of the extremists were seeking release of aggression, intimidation of opponents, and love of power.

(PRAJ: PRID)

0458 O'Brien, Cornor Cruise. Ireland Will Not Have Peace. *Harper's*, December 1976, pp. 33-42.

O'Brien rejects outright the concept that the IRA are "freedom-fighters". The immediate withdrawal of the British forces would not bring peace. Eire has specifically rejected the IRA and many Northern Ireland Catholics are equally strong in their rejection. These have suffered enormously as a result of the IRA, at the hands of the Protestants, at the hands of the British and from the IRA directly. O'Brien traces the history of the IRA and points out the differences between the original struggle for freedom and the present one. The only similarity is the concept that all connection with England should be dropped. It is not now

the economic conditions or anything else except terrorism which invokes a response from the IRA. "So when will Ireland be free and at peace?" The IRA say "When British stops interfering in Ireland." But if they withdrew, the IRA would look upon the Ulster Protestants as stooges for Britain. The judges of whether Ireland is free would be the IRA, not the people of Ireland. There could be no political agreement between the two communities in Northern Ireland and Dublin, if the IRA were to continue to exist. Should the British withdraw, sectarian violence would increase, from both the Protestants and the Catholics. The IRA talks of peace by agreement if the British leave, but it would be peace at a terrible price. Nor does O'Brien see the IRA as fading away. Those in America and elsewhere who provide help to the IRA are prolonging Ireland's agony. The peace offensive by Irish women may take support away from the IRA, but it is a slow process. The immediate future holds little hope for peace.

(PRAJ: PRID)

0459 O'Brien, Conor Cruise. Liberty and Terrorism. *International Security*, Volume 2, Number 2, Fall, 1977, pp. 56-67.

O'Brien's distinction between the millenarian and the secessionist/irredentist terrorist is probably worthy of adoption (of the loose use of the anarchist/nihilist label).

(N&G)

0460 O'Brien, Conor Cruise. Liberty and Terror. Illusions of Violence, Delusions of Liberation. *Encounter*, Volume 49, Number 4, October 1977, pp. 34-41.

The democratic version of liberty is imperfect but known. The terrorist versions combine the perfections of fantasy with the reality of arbitrary power over whatever can be covered by the barrel of that gun. However, long it takes, the democratic struggle against the underground terrorist empires, whatever slogans they may use, is a struggle for real liberty for real people. The people understand that other better than some of those who seek to advise and instruct them.

(IPSA)

0461 Ochberg, Frank. (Ed.). *Victims of Terrorism*. Boulder, Colorado, Westview Press, 1979.

This book centers on hostage situations, with particular attention to the victim's physiological and psychological reactions, as well as on the phenomenon of victim/terrorist alliance--the so-called Stockholm Syndrome. An annotated bibliography is included.

(N&G)

0462 Ochberg, Frank M. and Soskis, David A. (Eds.). *Victims of Terrorism*. Boulder, Westview Press, 1982.

As the title itself suggests this volume is about the victims of Political terrorism. An attempt has been made to integrate the expertise on stress, coping, and captivity in order to understand the victimization by political terrorists or to relate this expertise to the work of those chargd with combating terrorism. Attempt has been made to relate and explain the relationship between the concepts of stress, coping, and the effects of captivity, that is how people react to major stress on a short term basis.

0463 O'Neill, Major Bard E.; Alberts, D.J.; and Rossetti, Stephen (Eds.). *Political Violence and Insurgency*. Arvada, Colorado, Phoenix Press, 1974.

Case studies dealing with insurgents in Ireland, Thailand, Uruguay, Guatemala, Iraq, and the Portuguese African colonies. The emphasis is upon what has happened, rather than why.

(N&G)

0464 O'Neill, Major Bard E. Israel and the Fedayeen : Persistence of Transformation. *Strategic Review*, Volume 4, Spring 1976, pp. 89-101.

The article is a faint cry for Israeli-Palestinian talks aimed at the emergence of a ministate, based on guarantees, provisions for Israeli sanctions, a moderate PLO government, no purge of non-Fedayeen, and joint economic ties, as well as the continued existence of Jordan.

(N&G)

0465 O'Neill, Major Bard E. Towards a Typology of Political Terrorism: The Palestinian Resistance Movement. *Journal of International Affairs*, Volume 32, Number 1, Spring - Summer 78, pp. 17-42.

A number of variables account for Palestinian terrorism. With respect to long term causes, relative deprivation (both political and economic) and ideology are most important. Crucial short-term factors include the June war, the struggle for power and influence within the Palestinian movement, the gradually increasing success of the Israeli counter-insurgency program between 1968 and 1970, and the deficiencies in Palestinian capabilities. Palestinian weaknesses stem from an incoherent and poorly conceived strategy, organizational failures (disunity and the absence of a parallel hierarchy in Israel and the occupied areas), marginal active popular support in the occupied territories, and limited military assets. The general proposition that terrorism is a "weapon of the weak" is underlined in this case.

(IPSA)

0466 Ontiveros, Suzaune Robitaille. (Ed.). *Global Terrorism - A Historical Bibliography*. Santa Barbara, ABC-CLIO, 1986.

This volume presents abstracts from some 600 journal articles. These are presented in a regional arrangement, followed by author and subject indexes and a chronology of terrorist related events from 1975-1985.

(BRD)

0467 Organized by Ankara University, 1984. *International Terrorism and the Drug Connection*.

The work is the result of a 'Symposium on International Terrorism' organized by Ankara University. The main objective of this Symposium was to shed light on all aspects of international terrorism, with special emphasis on Armenian terrorism, which is of immediate concern to Turkey.

The different papers in this collection have attempted to examine the anatomy of international terrorism and its involvement with the illegal narcotic traffic, particularly the linkages between ASALA (Armenian Secret Army for the Liberation of Armenia) a terrorist group and other underground groups with narcotic traffic and other terrorist groups.

0468 Orlow, Dietrich. Political Violence in Pre-Coup Turkey. *Terrorism : An International Journal*, Volume 6, Number 1, 1982-83.

The long-standing and pervasive patterns of political violence in Turkey, which were only abated by the military coup of September 1980, are examined in terms of their historical and socio-political antecedents. The paper concludes that political violence in Turkey is the result on the one hand of the specific forms of Kemalist modernization to which the country was subjected from 1920 to 1945. Kemalism led to modern political and legal institutions, but left much of Turkey's cultural and economic life subject to traditional values. In addition, Kemalism bequeathed a legacy of political parties that saw the national good identified solely with each political organization's success, which in turn subjectively legitimized violence against political opponents as acceptable in the struggle for the national welfare. After 1945 the legacy of Kemalism was joined by severe developmental problems in the area of economics and social welfare, a resurgence of hypernationalism over the Cyprus issue, and an anti-modernist backlash through a revival of Islamic traditions. The results were conflicts in a society already strained by the symptoms of second stage modernization that could not be compromised within the parameters of the Turkish political system.

(T)

0469 O'Shaughnessy, Hugh. Guerrillas Backing Angry Indians' Revolt. *Observer*, (London), 28 November, 1971, p. 9.

The sudden emergence of a full-fledged movement of nationalism and self-assertion, among several Indian tribes in Colombia, took everyone by surprise. It appears that they have been holding secret meetings for years. Their first political movement, the Comite Regional Indigena del Cauca (CRIC) is agitating for the return of lands they felt were stolen from them by the Whites early this century. They are occupying these lands, and violence is expected between the 70,000 Indians and the troops. The Army is studying the correlation between the several guerrilla movements and the Indians' increasing political awareness.

(PRAJ: PRID)

0470 O'Sullivan, Noel. (Ed.). *Terrorism, Ideology and Revolution : The Origins of Modern Political Violence*. Sussex, Harvester Press, 1986.

In this volume IRA along with Nazism has been studied to see how a opposition group, by practising terrorism, establishes a state or acquires power and after the acquisition of office, how such group or regime destroys all legal forms whatsoever.

0471 Paine, Lauran. *Terrorists*. London, Robert Hale and Co., 1975.

Material is included on Palestinian and Canadian terrorists, the Tupamaros, Black Panthers and the IRA.

(N&G)

0472 Pankov, Yu. (Ed.). *Political Terrorism - An Indictment of Imperialism*. Moscow, Progressive Publishers, 1983.

In 1980 USA started a propaganda campaign against USSR alleging that it was involved in international terrorism.

In 1960s and 1970s imperialist reaction has turned to the most extreme form of violence, terrorism. The spread of violence in the capitalist world testifies to a new crisis of bourgeois establishment. Terrorism sponsored by imperialist regimes has many faces, but its classic essence and its anti-popular, anti democratic orientation remains the same. The use of mercenaries, another form

of terrorism sponsored by imperialist states has a similar political content. Hired terrorism is a permanent feature of capitalist society. Imperialist powers use terrorism to interfere directly in the domestic affairs of their former colonies.

0473 Panter-Downes, Millie. Letter from London. *The New Yorker*, 24 March, 1973, pp. 131-133.

A note on London's reaction to IRA's setting off of bombs in the city, in early March. A description of the continuous series of strikes which is plaguing the city and the country, with reference to the measures, Prime Minister Health is bringing forth to copy with the situation.

(PRAJ: PRID)

0474 Parry, Albert. *Terrorism : From Robespierre to Arafat*. New York, Vanguard Press, 1976.

A polemic against terrorism, particularly in its "leftwing" variants and Marxism. Parry holds the Soviet Union to blame for much of the world's contemporary terrorism. While the breadth of his treatment is far-reaching and promising, his lack of detachment limits the scholarly value of the book. Furthermore, there is a very discernible tendency to call all political violence terrorism, which must raise certain questions about the author's understanding of terrorism.

(N&G)

0475 Paust, Jordan J. Response to Terrorism : A Prologue to Decisions Concerning Private Measures of Sanction. *Stanford Journal of International Studies*, Volume 12, Spring 1977, pp. 79-130.

Individuals, groups, and private institutions can and do participate in response to terrorism creatively or destructively in terms of serving minimum public order and human dignity. Forms of private response can be as varied as private patterns of social interaction. Choice as to permissibility must consider both context and relevant legal policies at stake in given cases. The power of public protest and the sanction of public opinion should not be ignored by those who seek effective responses to terrorism.

(IPSA)

0476 Paust, Jordàn J. A definitional Focus. In Alexander, Yonah and Finger, Seymour M. (Eds.). *Terrorism : Interdisciplinary Perspectives,* New York, The John Jay Press, 1977, pp. 18-29.

An excursus on the problem of defining terrorism. Paust argues for a working definition that would be preferable to confusion resultant of attempts at absolute precision (e.g. in the UN).

(N&G)

0477 Pepper, Curtis B. The Possessed. *New York Times - Magazine,* 18 February, 1979, 29-32 ff.

A journalistic account of the rise of the Brigate Rosse, including biographical data on its founder Renato Curcio.

(N&G)

0478 Pepper, Curtis B. *Kidnapped : 17 Days of Terror*. New York, Harmony, 1978.

A narrative account of the 1978 kidnapping of Paolo Lazzaroni, 40 year old son of a wealthy Milanese manufacturer. The kidnapping, apparently carried out by the Mafia, was yet another example of the rash of kidnappings—for-profit

which have been so much a feature of contemporary Italy.

(N&G)

0479 Pepper, Crutis B. Kidnapped. *New York Times Magazine,* 20 November, 1977, 42-ff.

A factual account of an Italian Kidnapping based on the fascinating chronicle of victim.

(N&G)

0480 Perlmutter, Phillip. Israeli, Irish and Arab Terrorism. *Christian Century,* Volume 1002, Number 18, 14 May, 1975, pp.486-487.

People who claim similarities between Ireland and Israel only confuse the issues. Ireland, unlike Israel, is *not* in danger of total extinction.

(PRAJ: PRID)

0481 Perrott, Roy. The Quest of the Student Guerrillas. *Observer,* (London), 17 January, 1971, p. 9, 10.

The author, just back from South America, reports the story of how 75 young followers of the Che Guevara - many from the elite governing classes tried to start a revolution, and were hunted down in the jungles by the Bolivian army.

(PSA)

0482 Peterson, R.W. *International Terrorism Threat Analysis.* Springfield, VA, National Technical Information Service, 1977.

Using the CIA's International Terrorism: Attributes of Terrorist Events (ITERATE) file, an attempt is made to identify future threats. The results were quite inconclusive.

(N&G)

0483 Pfaff, William. Reflections Terrorism. *The New Yorker,* 18 September, 1978, 135 ff.

Discusses the anarchic terrorists of Italy and Germany and concludes that they more nearly manifest fascism than any leftist ideology. Pfaff argues that the terrorists' significance lies in what they "reveal to us about the deep preoccupations and anxieties of the national societies in which they act," factors which are resultant of long standing intellectual trends which are only now experienced *de novo.*

(N&G)

0484 Pierre, Andrew J. The Politics of International Terrorism. *Orbis,* Volume 19, Winter 1976, pp. 1251-1269. (Abbreviated version in *Survival,* May/April 1976, pp. 60-67).

Pierre presents an overview of terrorism in which he identifies six motivations for the terrorist: gaining political goals, seeking attention and publicity, eroding or undermining support for the state, compensating for lack of political access, liberating colleagues, and gaining financial rewards. He surveys the recent history of hijacking, kidnapping and UN attempts to seek solution of the problem. He proposes that counter-efforts combine "prevention" with deterrence. Prevention including acting on legitimate grievances and rewarding groups which abstain from terrorism. As to deterrence, he promotes; agreements to the effect that terrorists will be punished for their acts; international sanctions against those who harbor terrorists; the sharing of intelligence; a reveiw of "no ransom policies"; and, the seeking of a consensus that certain acts are beyond the pale of legal and moral acceptability. Pierre was a Senior

Research Fellow with the Council on Foreign Relations when he wrote this article.

(N&G)

0485 Pilon, Juliana Geran. The Bulgarian Connection: Drugs, Weapons and Terrorism. *Terrorism: An International Journal*, Volume 9, Number 4, 1987.

The Bulgarian government is involved in subversion of Western governments, almost certainly orchestrated in Moscow, involving drugs, weapons and terrorism. Despite US efforts to work with Bulgaria to curb the illicit traffic of drugs and weapons, cooperation has been virtually nil. This has prompted some members of the congress to probe Bulgaria's motives. and on February 26, 1985, senator Alphonse D'Amato introduced a bill, S. 515, the Bulgarian International Review Act, directing the President to conduct a comprehensive review of US policy towards Bulgaria. This article analyses that legislation, the dimension of the drugs and terrorism Connection in Bulgaria, and offers further recommendations in dealing with the issue.

(T)

0486 Pincus, Walter. Scenario for a Nuclear Scare. *San Francisco Chronicle*, 1 October, 1978.

A report of a US Department of Energy exercise that presumed terrorists had hidden a home-made atomic bomb in an urban area, and demanded $ 325 million to forestall detonation. Search teams reportedly found the "device" in less than 4 hours in 900 sq. mile area.

(N&G)

0487 Pisano, Vittorfranco S. A Survey of Terrorism of the Left in Italy : 1970-78. *Terrorism: An International Journal*, Volume 2, Numbers 3-4, 1979.

The terrorists who have ravaged Italy over the past several years are not totally faceless. The names and backgrounds of many are well known, as are their habitual modes of operations and the ideologies by which they are moved. After a brief catalog of the terrorists' actions, the article outlines the physiognomy of Italy's major terrorist groups. A substantial part of this consists of a list of each groups' victims, since any assessment of the terrorist groups' effects must begin with an awareness of which sectors of Italian society have been struck. The backgrounds of the terrorists, the political language they speak, and the list of their victims point unambiguously to the conclusion that terrorism in Italy is overwhelmingly a phenomenon of the left and that it conceives of itself as a means of bringing about a Communist regime. The terrorists regard themselves as the competitors and reformers of the Italian Communist Party. But at the same time they have made good their claim as the mortal enemies of the Communist Party. The question regarding the Italian terrorists' international connections cannot be answered definitely. Such evidence as exists however, suggests that today's self-declared communist terrorists may be acting in ways similar to their predecessors of the 1940s and early 1950s, who found safe haven in the Communist regimes of Eastern Europe.

(T)

0488 Platero, D. To be Prepared not to be Prepared. *Assets Protection*, Volume 1, 1976, pp. 16-20.

Advice for coping with the kidnapping of loved ones.

(N&G)

0489 Pockrass, Robert M. Terroristic Murder in Northern Ireland: Who is Killed and Why? *Terrorism: An International Journal*, Volume 9, Number 4, 1987.

Terrorism can be characterized as planned acts of violence, directed at civilians and carried out for the purpose of obtaining a political goal. This paper shows the changing pattern of terrorist murders in Northern Ireland for the period 1969 through 1984. He purposes a model of motivation which will help to explain terroristic murders. In addition, terroristic violence has changed its focus with members of the security forces becoming the prime target in the late 1970s and 1980s.

(T)

0490 Porzecanski, Arturo C. *Uruguay's Tupamaros : The Urban Guerrila*. New York, Praeger, 1973.

This is the first scholarly study of Uruguay's famed Tupamaros. Based on primary materials and on-the-scene research, the book covers the period 1962-1972, examining virtually all aspects of the Tupamaro movement : ideology; strategy; the motives behind the guerrillas' emergence; their objectives and tactics; their composition and internal organization and their challenge to, interaction with, and destruction by Uruguay's government. The author emphasizes the significance of the guerrillas' shift from the rural to the urban areas of Uruguay and the lessons to be derived from the Tupamaro experience.

(PRAJ: PRID)

0491 Post, Jerrold M. Notes on a Psychodynamic Theory of Terrorist Behaviour. *Terrorism : An International Journal*, Volume 7, Number 3, 1984.

Because of the diversity of terrorist groups and causes, there is no one terrorist "mindset." Within this diversity it is useful to distinguish two major categories: the "anarchic-ideologies," such as the Red Army Faction, committed to destroying the world of their fathers; and the "nationalist-secessionists," such as ETA of the Basques, who carry on the mission of their fathers.

There is a tendency for marginal, isolated, and inadequate individuals from troubled family backgrounds to be attracted to the path of terrorism, so that for many, belonging to the terrorist group is the first time they truly belonged, and the group comes to represent family. This creates powerful pressures to conform within the group, for to disagree is to be seen as disloyal, and to risk losing the group. Organized against society, the group is seen as all good, and the outside society as all bad, this being the rationale for committing violent anti-society acts.

(T)

0492 Poston, Lawrence. Letter to Editor. *Progressive*, Volume 42, Number 10, October 1978, p. 63.

Questions the assertion that the assassination of Aldo Moro was a response to the terrorist policies of the Italian state, and the implicit justification of the assassination.

(PRAJ: PRID)

0493 Powell, W. *The Anarchist Cookbook*. New York, Lyle Stuart, 1971.

A how-to manual for the aspiring terrorist: From garrote to bomb.

(N&G)

0494 Price, D.L. Institute for the Study of Conflict. *Ulster : Consensus and Coercion*. London, *Idem*, 1973.

Most noteworthy for its examination of the effects of government security activities on the tactics of the terrorist in Northern Ireland.

(N&G)

0495 Price, H. Edward Jr. The Strategy and Tactics of Revolutionary Terrorism. *Comparative Studies in Society and History*, Volume 19, January 1977, pp. 52-66.

A competent review of the literature in which-following Chalmers Johnson--Price suggests that terrorism may be the revolutionary paradigm of the 1970s

(N&G)

0496 Puri, Rakshat. Meeting Terrorist. *Hindustan Times*, 2 July 1985.

The acts of terrorism in its many forms, by extremists is a long term policy to achieve intended results. To counter it, a long term action plan has to be built taking in view, social, political and cultural causes of the acts of terrorism.

0497 Ra'anan Uri.; Pfaltzgraff (Jr) Robert L.; Shultz, Richard H.; Halperin, Ernst.; and Lukes, Igor. *Hydra of Carnage-International Linkages of Terrorism*. Lexington Lexington Books, 1986.

This volume contains a collection of documents consisting of interviews with persons formerly involved in terrorism and papers captured in the invasions of Grenada and Lebanon and the contributions to a conference held at Tufts University in 1985.

The second half of this lengthy book includes documents demonstrating the links between soviet foreign policy and unconventional warfare. 'Surrogates' in the Caribbean, especially Grenada and the Middle East receive the most attention.

(BRD)

0498 Radlick, Amy Sands. Transnational Factors affecting Quebec Separatist Terrorism. *International Studies Association*, Toronto, 25-29 February, 1976.

Although the underlying reasons for the mid 1960s violence in Quebec were unique to Quebec--centuries of deprivation being quickly overturned by the processes of industrialization, urbanization, and secularization--some precipitating force may have come from the international flows of concepts, information, and tactics, as well as from other transnational groups. This analysis will describe many of these external, foreign factors which may have influenced the Quebec separatists/terrorists of the 1960s. Some specific trends concerning the role of transnational flows of ideas, concepts, and information in an unstable situation should emerge and help to mold some general hypotheses dealing with this type of phenomenon.

(PRAJ: PRID)

0499 Rapoport, David C. *Assassination and Terrorism*. Toronto, Canadian Broadcasting Co., 1971.

First presented by the CBC, this book is an expanded version of the series. Includes historical survey of assassination and its perpetrators, and a treatment of modern terrorism and its antecedents. Nachayev's *Revolutionary Catechism* is

reproduced and a bibliography on assassination (and terrorism) is provided.

(N&G)

0500 Rapoport, David C., and Alexander, Y. (Eds.). *The Morality of Terrorism : Religious and Secular Justifications*. New York, Pergamon Press, 1982.

*The Morality of Terrorism* weaves an original and profound portrait of modern terrorism by gathering the common threads of terrorist activities through history. The authors examine the moral climate that produces terrorism, the doctrines used to justify it, the moral predicaments terrorists create and, most interestingly, the paradox by which terrorists gain moral sympathy through morally repugnant acts. *Contents*: Terror and the Messiah: an ancient experience and some modern parallels, D.C. Rapoport; Models of rebellion, V. Kavolis; the unravelling of the myth of progress, M. Amon; International terrorism and the just war, J. Dugard; Liberation theology; its methodological foundation for violence, J.R. Pottenger; the French revolution: Jacobin terror, M. Carter; Fascism's philosophy of violence and the concept of terror, A.J., Gregor; Nazi terrorism: the complete trap and the final solution, S, Aronson; Document on terror; The moral issue: some aspects of individual terror, Z. Ivianski; Terrorism: the immorality of a belief, A. Louch; Guilt transfer, M. Tugwell; The laws of war and terrorism, P. Wilkinson; Do terrorists have rights R. Gerstein; Eliminating the terrorist opportunity, G. Quester; Selected bibliography; Index; About the contributors.

(PRAJ: PRID)

0501 Rasmussen, Norman C. Electric power -- the Nuclear Option. *National Forum : The Phiappa Phi Journal*, Volume 58, Fall 1978, pp. 13-17.

Good terse, non-technical summary of the influential reactor safety study--the Rasmussen Report--by the primary author.

(N&G)

0502 Rees, Merlyn. Terror in Ireland-and Britain's Response. *Terrorism: An International Journal*, Volume 5, Numbers 1-2, 1981-82.

Reacting to the last of four distinct terrorist campaigns in Northern Ireland, the British Parliament in 1973 passed the Northern Ireland (Emergency Provisions) Act, which was amended in 1974. The act marks the first time in United Kingdom statute law that terrorism is defined as the use of violence for political ends. British efforts are aimed at the development of the police to the point where the military is no longer required. Terroristic acts in Great Britain, usually connected with Northern Irish affairs, have led to the introduction of the Prevention of Terrorism (Temporary Provisions) Act, the powers of which are also described in this paper. The author also discusses the problem of the safeguarding of civil liberties as well as the European Convention on the Suppression of Terrorism, drawn up by the Council of Europe.

(T)

0503 Report on the Brinks Incident: New York State Policy Study Group on Terrorism. *Terrorism: An International Journal*, Volume 9, Number 2, 1987.

At the initial session of the New York State Policy Study Group on Terrorism, a decision was made to examine the Brinks armored car robbery/murder case that occurred in Nyack, New York on October 20, 1981. The Brinks case

was selected for study because it provides a rare chance to examine the responses of the various elements of the criminal justice system to a real case. As a result, this provides an opportunity for studying issues such as law enforcement response, inter-agency coordination, resource availability and management, security and prosecution.

(T)

0504 Richards, Colman. Boost for Mac Stiofan. *Observer*, (London), 10 September, 1972, p. 7.

Maria McGuire's story attacking Sean Mac Stiofan, Provisional IRA Chief of Staff, has had the effect of intensifying support for him, and silencing opposition to him. Both O'Bradaigh and O'Connell deny conversations with Miss McGuire as reported by her.

(PRAJ: PRID)

0505 Ronchey, Alberto. Guns and Gray Matter: Terrorism in Italy. *Foreign Affairs*, Volume 57, Number 4, Spring 1979, pp. 921-940.

In Italy the guerrilla warfare of ideological confrontation advances on two fronts. The closely knit underground of the Red Brigades carries out sensational, military style actions and smaller armed factions are systematically engaged in spreading violence in the form of full-scale guerrilla warfare. The mainstream of far-left terrorism, a resistance movement against democracy tends to strike at well-chosen symbolic individuals while at the same time exploiting the media. Guerrilla terrorism in Italy has succumbed to an urge to commit purely ideological murder, to the violent repression of any reasoning alternative and to obsessive form of class struggle.

(IPRA)

0506 Rosenbaum, H. Jon and Sederberg, Peter C. (Eds.). *Vigilante Politics*. Philadelphia, University of Pennsylvania Press, 1976.

On the use of illegal violence in support of established social and political order. Theory as well as examples from the US, Asia, Africa and Europe.

(PRAJ: PRID)

0507 Rothstein, Raphael. Undercover Terror : The other Mid-East War. *World Magazine*, Volume 2, Number 3, 1973, pp. 18-22.

This article gives considerable background information on the terror activities of the Palestinian Liberation groups fighting Israel and a little on the Israeli attempts to counter it. Several of the Palestinian groups are named as well as several of their leaders. The chief of the Mosad, the Israeli counterpart of the American CIA and the director of its section handling Israel's counter-terror are mentioned. Specific information is given on a number of the terror activities carried out by Palestinian Black September and Fatah groups within the general European area. It appears that until recently the Palestinians had concentrated their efforts along the borders of Israel in Jordan, Syria and Lebanon and Israeli counteractivity was likewise largely limited to these areas. Having failed to infiltrate Israel, however, the Palestinian activity has now spread throughout western Europe, where many Arab nationals in the various embassies help to supply money, weapons, etc. Political factors, such as fear of offending Arab states, is also said to result in leniency for terrorists in many cases. Israeli's counter-terror chief is quoted as believing that the current terrorism will not cease until there is a final settlement of the Palestine problem.

(PRAJ: PRID)

0508 Royal United Services Institute(RUSI) for Defense Studies. *Ten Years of Terrorism : Collected Views*. New York, Crane, Russak, and Co., Inc., 1979.

Despite some sloppy editing, this book has managed to emerge as a notably lucid discussion of terrorism. The book is the result of a lecture series conducted throughout 1977 at the RUSI. While the contributions tend to address British concerns, there remains much of interest to the non-British reader. As might be expected, Northern Ireland is the major focus of *Ten Years of Terrorism*; however, the reader will also find that the space devoted to the media and terrorism is particularly revealing, both in the nature of the Northern Ireland problem, and in the pathology of terrorism in general. Contributors include: Martin Bell, Max Beloff, Lord Caradon, Richard Clutterbuck, and Sir Richard Thompson.

(N&G)

0509 Roucek, Joseph S. Terrorism in its Sociological Aspects. *Sociologia Internationalis*, Volume 18, Numbers 1-2, 1980, pp. 97-110.

Strong measures to counteract terrorism may escalate violence, abridge civil rights and prove a case of the cure being worse than the disease. Possibly political terrorism is inevitable so long as violence is an acceptable means of dealing with distribution of power. If governments overact and become oppressive, the terrorists will have won, for their theory is that repression will eventually lead to revolution. Prosecution of terrorists may provoke new terrorist incidents.

(IPSA)

0510 Rubin, Alfred P. Terrorism and Piracy : A Legal View. *Terrorism : An International Journal*, Volume 3, Numbers 1-2, 1979-80.

Terrorist attacks on persons or property on the high seas or in the newly designated "exclusive economic zones" bear analogy closer to the traditional international law of "piracy" than most observers suspect. In traditional practice"private ends" in the usual sense was not an essential element of the offense; the label and its legal results were attached to unrecognized belligerents too. The latest codifications of the international law relating to piracy, principally those deriving from the 1958 Geneva Convention on the High Seas, are patently defective. A new formulation is proposed, with a commentary that, among other things, points out how international criminal law and universal jurisdiction can be coordinated with the generally accepted international law of armed conflict to clarify what is currently a chaotic legal situation.

(T)

0511 Russell, Charles A. and Miller, Bowman H. Profile of a Terrorist. *Military Review*, August 1977, pp. 21-34.

One of the better attempts to profile terrorists, includes data on age, sex, marital status, rural versus urban origins, socio-economic background, education, and the method-locale of recruitment.

(N&G)

0512 Russel, Charles A.; Banker, Leon J. Jr.; Miller, Bowman.- *Out-Inventing the Terrorist*. Washington : US Air Force, Office of Special Investigations, 1977. In US Congress Senate Committee on

Government Affairs. An Act to combat International Terrorism, Report of the Committe on S.2236. 95th Cong., 2nd Sess., 1978.

A lucid overview which treats terrorist groups, capabilities, motivation and targets, as well as mass disruption terrorism (e.g. operations against transportation or communication networks) and mass destruction terrorism. The authors successfully combine the tools of historical research with speculative analysis. They see the likelihood of terrorism "increasingly becoming an end in itself." "This would result from a nihilist attitude which already appears...quite prevalent..." They point to the possibility of terrorists attempting disruption operations or even small-scale destruction operations using high-technology or bacteriological resources.

(N&G)

0513 Rustamji, K.F. Need for New Approach. *Hindustan Times*, 20 July 1987.

The solution to terrorism according to the author is political which unfortunately has not been tried in Punjab.

Author also criticises the failure of the judiciary and the intelligence agencies. Regarding policing there are genuine problems which have not been taken into consideration. Author suggests that the Law Commission be converted into a statutory Criminal Justice Commission.

0514 Sabetta, Anne R. Transnational Terror: Causes and Implications for Response. *Stanford Journal of International Studies,* Volume 12, Spring 1977, pp. 147-156.

Until it is decided whether terrorist acts are directed against a state or all mankind, that is, until the political or criminal nature of terrorism is agreed upon, an international convention to prevent the phenomenon seems a fruitless endeavour. What might be more expedient are conventions of a more limited scope, such as a convention prohibiting the export of violence to states outside a struggle between another state and a political sub unit. The establishment of such a convention might then provide a more specific and perhaps more justifiable basis for the extradite-or-prosecute principle.

(IPSA)

0515 Saddy, Fehmy. International Terrorism, Human Rights, and World Order. *Terrorism : An International Journal*, Volume 5, Number 4, 1981-82.

This article attempts to summarize the efforts that have been made during the 1970s in the search for an appropriate definition of international terrorism, its causes, and the measures to combat it. It evaluates these efforts in the context of the simultaneous interests in human rights. It advances some propostitions as to how international terrorism could be seen from the perspectives of both social-psychological theories of violence and Western legal practices. In conclusion, the relationship between the individual and the state is evaluated in the context of the present world order and its operative political and legal principles. Although this approach may not solve the problem of international terrorism by advancing any neat scheme of control which can be readily applied by anxious governmental law enforcement agencies, nor succeed in articulating a strategy for the respect of human rights by governments and individuals, it will hopefully generate some ideas about how justice can be rediscovered while searching for viable solutions for both international terrorism and human rights.

(T)

0516 Sahay, Mohan. Special Pak Cell Trains Terrorists. *Statesman*, (Delhi), 7 December 1986.

Government of Pakistan has created a separate cell to deal with sikh terrorists, who take refuge in Pakistan. Author gives the case of one Nishan Singh, who was in Pakistan along with other sikhs.

0517 Saksena, N.S. Terrorism : Fire-fighting Won't Do. *Times of India*, (Delhi), 12 August 1986.

Author blames, Chief Ministers, Secretaries of State and Union, for interfering in the police work and thus demoralising the police force to fight terrorism. Author cautions that time left is very little and till machinery of internal security is not perfected, the situation will worsen.

0518 Saksena, N.S. Terrorism, : Facing the Real Issue. *Times of India*, (Delhi), 16 July, 1985.

Author believes that mere passing of anti-terrorist laws or anti-goonda laws like in Gujarat is not going to solve these (terrorism and violence) problems untill and unless police efficiency is increased by stopping its misuse for political ends, and police apparatus is expanded and modernized.

0519 Saksena, N.S. *Terrorism : History and Facets in the World and India*. New Delhi, Abhinav Publications, 1985.

As the title itself suggests, author has traced the history and analysed different facets of terrorism i.e., both, terror against the state and by the state, in the world and India. Author has laid emphasis on State terrorism in this work. Though the totalitarian states have greater chances of employing terror, the democratic state uses terror mainly against its own minorities.

The Government of India has failed to curb terrorism, mainly because law and order machinery has been made a tool of political manoeuvring. Though author is pessimistic about containment of violence unleashed by terrorists in India he still believes that a political leadership with a strong political will, an efficient administrative machinery can build a strong public opinion against terroristic activities. This might reduce terroristic activities substantially.

0520 Sanctions against Libya. *W. Comp Pres Docs.*, Number 22, 20 January, 1986, pp. 41-45.

President Reagan interviewed by European journalists, Jan. 10, 1986; on economic sanctions imposed in an effort to deter terrorist activities.

(PAISB)

0521 Sandler, Todd.; Tschirhart, John T. and Cauley, Jon. A Theoretical Analysis of Transnational Terrorism. *American Political Science Review*, Volume 77, Number 1, March 1983, pp. 36-54.

The article presents some "rational-actor" models that depict the negotiation process between terrorists and government policymakers for those incidents where hostages or property are seized and demands are issued. The models account for the objectives and constraints faced by both the terrorists and the policymakers. Uncertainty is introduced through probability constraints (i.e., chance constraints) requiring a specific likelihood of some event occuring. Implications are subsequently extracted from the comparative static analysis as

the models' parameters are changed. The last part of the article presents a club theory analysis concerning the sharing of international commando forces.

(IPSA)

0522 Schamis, Gerado. *War and Terrorism in International Affairs*. New Brunswick, Transaction, 1980.

Schamis argues that terrorism is a new form of war against democratic societies and that once recognized as such, it significantly alters our view of international relations.

(R&W)

0523 Schenker, Hillel. The Anti-Peace Amendment. *New Outlook*, Number 30, March 87, pp. 7-9.

Amendment to the Ordinance for the Prevention of terrorism, stipulating that contact by an Israeli citizen with a member of a terrorist organization is a criminal offense, passed Aug. 6, 1986; issue of civil rights.

(PAISB)

0524 Schelling, Thomas C. Thinking About Nuclear Terrorism. *International Security*, Volume 6, Number 4, Spring, 1982, pp. 61-77.

Sometime in the 1980's an organization that is not a national government may acquire a few nuclear weapons. The origin, at least of the fissionable material, will have been national weapon, power, or research programs. The acquires will probably be intelligent, professionally competent, and well organized and will have had motive and opportunity to plan a strategic campaign. "Terrorist" strategies, as for most small nations that might acquire such weapons, will be about the only strategies available. Successful threats will not necessarily end with loss or surrender of unused weapons; whereas most terrorist acts are inherently short-lived and unstable, a nuclear terrorist organization may have a "steady state" existence. It may behave like a nuclear mini-state. The most likely uses will be deterrent threats against military actions. Possession of such weapons by unstable governments may lead to weapons in the hands of dissident military forces, leaders in exile, or unknown parties after turmoil like what has occurred in Iran or Lebanon. Government leaders might be wise to pause before acquiring such potentially divisive weapons. Generally speaking, the problems posed by non-nation organizations with nuclear weapons will be very much like the problems posed by small nuclear arsenals owned by governments.

(IPSA)

0525 Schelling, Thomas C. Who will have the Bomb? *International Security*, Volume 1, Summer 1976, pp. 77-91.

Schelling's lucid article squarely addresses the nuclear terrorism question as an aspect of nuclear proliferation, rather than of political terrorism. He finds that state actors are far more likely proliferators than terrorists. In fact, he sees the task of weapons construction as beyond the capability of today's terrorists. He posits that the Jewish terrorists of mandatory Palestine may be prototypical for the type of organization which would be capable of the task. His comments upon the deterrent uses to which terrorists might employ nuclear weapons are both provocative and original.

(N&G)

0526 Scherer, John L. The Plot to Kill the Pope. *Terrorism : An International Journal*, Volume 7, Number 4, 1984.

This essay analyzes East European operations in the conspiracy to kill Pope John Paul II on May 13, 1981. It describes the seemingly irrational, unexplained behavior of Mehmet Ali Agca and Bulgarians in Rome who allegedly carried out the conspiracy. It finally resolves with a surprise twist, the inconsistencies in East European planning and operations.

(T)

0527 Schiller, David Th. Germany's other Terrorists. *Terrorism : An International Journal,* Volume 9, Number 1, 1987.

When analyzing terrorism in Germany, attention normally focuses on the Rote Armee Fraktion, better known as Baader-Meinhof gang. Already in the early years of the RAF there existed different groups, such as the Movement, 2nd June, which often rivaled and strongly criticized the elitist event-gardism of Andreas Baader, Ulrike Mehinhof, and Gudrun Ensslin. Today only a small fragment of the some 350 terrorist acts and 500 acts of Sabotage (1985 statistics) can be attributed to the RAF. Germany's other terrorists, the Revolutionary Cells and autonomous/anti-imperialist groups have long ago outdone the RAF and become a much graver threat to the internal security of the Federal Republic. Though similarities in rhetoric and operational approach exist between the RAF and these groups, the existing underlying differences are strong and untill recently have prevented cooperation. The hunger strike campaign of the winter 1984/1985 appears to present a change in policies on behalf of the cells.

(T)

0528 Schlesinger, Philip. Terrorism, the Media, and the Liberal - Democratic State : A Critique of the Orthodoxy. *Social Research*, Volume 48, Number 1, Spring, 1981, pp. 74-99.

This paper pursues three themes. First, it argues that current official and semi-official conceptions of "terrorism" in liberal-democracies stress the supposed irrational character of all political violence, at the same time reaffirming the complete legitimacy of liberal-democratic practice. This dominant view is criticised, in particular its blindness to the existence of state repression in democracies. Next, the paper analyses the orthodox assumptions of counter-insurgency writers concerning the ostensible negative symbolic effects of reporting terrorism, and finds them quite unsubstantiated. The assertion that the media are manipulated by terrorists is countered by arguing that they are more often loyal servants of the state. This point is elaborated in the final section, which gives a critical analysis of British media coverage of Northern Ireland and of state media policy. The article concludes by calling for systematic comparative research into the relationships between the state, media and political violence as a practical contribution to the maintenance of civil liberties.

(IPSA)

0529 Schleifer, A. Palestine: The Commandos Unite. (In French), *Jeune Afrique*, Number 433, 21-27 April, 1969, p. 40.

The four Palestinian organizations made a step forward recently forming a unified command for armed action. The Palestinian movement has been hampered in the past by the rivalry of the four factions.

(PRAJ: PRID)

0530 Schmid, Alex P. and Graff, Janny de. *Violence as Communication : Insurgent Terrorism and the Western News Media*. New York, Sage Publications, Book Review by Cruise O'Brien in Observer, (London), 8 August, 1982, p. 9.

Authors believe that the media "plays an important part in the diffusion of terrorism." They support their view with an impressive collection of data and quotations, but they admit that they cannot prove their proposition. An approach which they view with sympathy is for the media to give more attention to frustrated violence-prone people and to frustrating violence-producing situations, before the violence actually breaks out.

(PRAJ: PRID)

0531 Schmitt, David E. Bicommunal Conflict and Accommodation in Northern Ireland. *Terrorism : An International Journal*, Volume 9, Number 3, 1987.

Northern Ireland represents one of the clearest and most intractable instances of Bicommunal conflict in the contemporary world. This paper analyzes the conflict from the stand point of efforts to end violence through specific strategies to achieve accommodation. Law enforcement and anti-discrimination reforms as well as attempts to achieve representative political institution are discussed. The New Ireland Forum Report and the Anglo-Irish agreement of November 1985 are considered in the context of their potential contribution to accommodation and political stability.

(T)

0532 Schreiber, Jan. *The Ultimate Weapon : Terrorists and World Order*. New York, William Morrow and Company, Inc., 1978.

Schreiber's sympathetic treatment of the terrorist fails to seriously challenge prevailing intellectual assessments because the book is simply too sophomoric. Imprecision, confusion, and error confound this attempt to prove that denied legitimate access to power, all men and women are potential terrorists.

(N&G)

0533 Schreiber, Junrgen. Anti-Terrorist Laws? A Survey of Adopted and Projected Limitations of Constitutional Rights in the Name of "International Security". (In German). *Blatter fur deutsche und internationale Politik*, Kole (Cologne). Volume 23, Number 4, 1978, pp. 398-413. 119 references.

In this contribution, the attempt is made to show in detail the limitations of constitutional rights with respect to such fundamental rights as the right to free speech, the privacy of residence, to the principally unrestricted forming of associations, to free choice of counsel etc. In particular, the attempt is made to trace the connection between previous arguments for liberalization of these rights and the beginnings of the demagogic argumentation of people like Strauss and Dregger.

(PRAJ: PRID)

0534 Schutz, Hans-Joachim.; Meyer, Alex.; Faller, Edmund W. and Wille, Jorn. Hijacking (In German) Book Review of : (1) Meyer, Alex, "International Air Transport Agreement:, Vol. VI, "Concept of Air Piracy, Factual Circumstances, countermeasures" (In

German), Cologne, Berlin, Bonn, Munich, 1972. (2) Faller, Edmund W.; "Violent Take-overs of Aircraft from the Viewpoint of International Law (in German), Berlin, Munich, 1972. (3) Wille, Jorn, "Prosecution of Criminal Acts on Boards of Ships and Aircracft" (in German), Berline, New York, 1974. *Jahrbuch fur internationales Recht*, Volume 17, 1974, p. 456, 2 pp.

Seizures of aircraft and other acts of terror against international civil aviation have become a very serious problem, whose solution is predominantly a political task. However, it also concerns international jurisprudence, and thus the science of international law, which also must play an important role. In Anglo-Saxon scholarly circles, awareness of this has been widespread for a long time. Recently, however, German-language international law scholars have also begun to make an important contribution to the discussion about protection of civil aviation from terrorism.

(PRAJ: PRID)

0535 Scotti, Anthony J. *Executive Safety and International Terrorism : A Guide for Travellers*. Englewood cliffs, N.J. Prentice-Hall, 1986.

Precautions and safety tips that can help diminish the likelihood of involvement in a terrorist incident.

(PAISB)

0536 Security Forces in Northern Ireland. *Tables Reinsurance*, (Gt Brit), Number 17, June 1985, pp. 51-3.

Analyzes figures on the number of deaths from terrorist activity in Northern Ireland; implications for underwriting life insurance for British soldiers.

(PAISB)

0537 Selth, Andrew. Diplomats as Terrorist Targets: An Historical Overview. *Australian For. Affairs Rec.*, Number 56, July 1985, pp. 597-603.

Attacks on diplomats and diplomatic facilities worldwide, 1968-82.

(PAISB)

0538 Selzer, Michael. *Terrorist Chic : An Exploration of Violence in Seventies*. Stemons Freeways, Hawthom Books, 1979.

Selzer explores the ethos celebrating brutality, sadomasochism and mindless destruction ... in fashion, photography, sex, media coverage, and popular fiction. His definition of terrorist chic is 'the outer limit society is able to allow itself in expressing the fantasies which terrorists make explicit through their behaviour.

(BRD)

0539 Seminar on the Protection of Victims of Violence in the 1980s: Summary Report. *Terrorism : An International Journal*, Volume 9, Number 2, 1987, pp. 215-24.

Seminar held at the Henri Dunant Institute, Geneva, April 10-12, 1985. Includes protection of victims of terrorism and armed conflicts.

(PAISB)

0540 Shamwell, Horace F. (Jr.). Implementing the Convention on the Prevention and Punishment of Crimes against Internationally Protected Persons, Including Diplomatic Agents. *Terrorism : An*

*International Journal*, Volume 6, Number 4, 1982-83.

The Convention on the Prevention and Punishment of Crimes Against Internationally Protected Persons was negotiated by the Sixth Committee of the UN General Assembly on the basis of a draft by the International Law Commission. The Convention represents a major move against terrorism aimed at diplomats and others who have special status under international law. The United States Government was successful in obtaining fairly rapid approval of the text and also in obtaining the necessary US legislative action to put it into effect. The United States has been hampered, however, by the fact that the two federal agencies, the FBI and the US Marshal's service normally do not engage in the type of activity required to protect persons covered by the Convention. Local US authorities are overburdened with their normal duties and there is extremely limited federal authority to extend financial assistance to the states. More far-reaching measures to counter the growing terrorist threat are needed.

(T)

0541 Shanor, Donald R. Europe Beat - Terrorism in France. *World Press Review*, October 1982, p. 12.

In July and August, there were more than 100 acts of political violence in France. FRANDFURTER ALLEGEMEINE Frankfurt, charges that France has become a haven for terrorists. It puts the blame on civil-liberties' reforms introduced by Mitterand. He has abolished the State Security Court, which provided an overview of the activities of terrorists. There is no general staff gathering together all the threads in the fight against terrorism. Only recently did the Ministry establish an electronic data bank on terrorists. Until then, each separate police force was working on its own. The paper also comments that left-wing police unions want to disband special units that have had success in capturing terrorists.

(PRAJ: PRID)

0542 Shapley, Deborah. Plutonium : Reactor Proliferation Threatens a Nuclear Black Market. *Science*, 9 April, 1971, pp. 143-146.

Notes several incidents of attempted or possible thefts of nuclear materials.

(N&G)

0543 Sharabi, Misham. Liberation or Settlement : The Dialectics of Palestinian Struggle. *Journal of Palestine Studies*, Volume 2, Winter 1973, pp. 33-48.

"The Palestinian experience has tended to develop largely independently of systematic theory, which, as expressed in institutions and behaviour, lagged behind. Theory and rhetoric were indistinguishable, and practice mostly took one form of spontaneous, disorganized activity".

(N&G)

0544 Shaw, Jennifer.; Guefitz, E. F.; and Younger, A.K. *Ten Years of Terrorism - Collected News*. New York, Crane, Russak and Company, INC., 1979.

Terrorism with all its ramifications has been discussed. Terrorism is basically a problem for democracies so it is important for these democracies to protect its citizens without sacrificing the consent of majority.

0545 Shaw, P.D. Extortion Threats : Analytic Techniques and Resources. *Assets Protection*, Volume 1, Summer 1975, pp. 5-16.

A description, the phenomena of Extortion complemented by a discussion of preventive and identification procedures.

(N&G)

0546 Sheehan, Edward R.F. Why Sadat and Faisal Chose Arafat. *New York Times Magazine*, 8 December, 1974, 31 ff.

The article proposes that Sadat engineered the split in the Palestinian resistance movement by having Arafat espouse the acceptance of a limited state.

(N&G)

0547 Shultz, George. Low-intensity warfare : The Challenge of Ambiguity. *Dept. State Bul*, Number 86, March 1986, pp. 15-18.

Address before the Low-Intensity Warfare Conference at the National Defense University, Jan. 15, 1986.

Effect of worldwide terrorism and insurgency on US policies.

((PAISB)

0548 Shultz, George. Protecting US Personnel and Property Overseas. *Dept State Bul.*, Number 85, September 1985, pp. 38-40.

Statement before the Foreign Affairs Committee, U.S. House of Representatives, July 24, 1985.

On the recommendations of the Advisory Panel on Overseas Security, Bobby Inman, Chairman; particularly counter-terrorism efforts.

(PAISB)

0549 Shultz, Richard. Conceptualizing Political Terrorism : A Typology. *Journal of International Affairs*, Volume 32, Spring/Summer 1978, pp. 7-15.

Shultz offers a useful, if not definitive typology of political terrorism that categorizes terrorism into three basic types--and then proposes that these types be examined by variation according to cause, environment, goals, strategy, means, organization and the nature of participants. The value of the proposal is that it offers some hope that the study of terrorism can move somewhat beyond the descriptive and journalistic treatments which are currently in vogue.

(N&G)

0550 Shultz, Richard. The limits of Terrorism in Insurgency Warfare the Case of the Viet Cong. *Policy*, Volume 11, Number 1, Fall 1978, pp. 67-91.

The National Liberation Front of Vietnam closely adhered to the theoretical propositions of the revolutionary warfare theorists and relegated policial terrorism to a purely ancillary status. Such tactics were used mainly to supplement the positive aspects of their program and were generally not as extreme as those used against the representative of the regime. When coercion was used, it tended to follow a continuum of graduated harshness. The Front resorted to extreme method not indiscriminately but rather in a very discriminate, selective, and limited fashion.

(IPSA)

0551 Shultz, R.H., Jr. and Sloan, S. *Responding to the Terrorist Threat : Security and Crisis Management*. New York,Pergamon Press, 1981.

The contemporary use of political terrorism has been marked by a proliferation of targets and techniques chosen by terrorists. In response to this challenge to law enforcement authorities, experts describe and review a wide range of operational programs and policies designed to deter or limit the effectiveness of terrorist groups personnel protection procedures, negotiation strategies, security programs, training of special units, protection of vital installations, organization of law enforcement, and development of predictive models are explained. *Contents* : International terrorism : the nature of the threat; The state of the operational art; A critical review of anti-terrorist programme; restrictions encountered in responding to terrorist sieges: an analysis; responding to the victims of terrorism : psychological and policy implications; Executive protection : the view from the private security sector; Simulating terrorism : an analysis of findings related to tactical, behavioural, and administrative responses of participating police and military forces; Subnational threats to civil nulclear facilities and safeguards institutions; Responding to terrorism : basic and applied research ; The diffusion of transnational terrorism, Terrorism : an objective act, a subjective reality, Index.

(PRAJ: PRID)

0552 Silj, Alessnadro, (tr. by Salvator Attanasio). *Never Again Without a Rifle : The Origions of Italian Terrorism*. New York, Karz Pubs, 1979.

Silj's book is a series of biographical descriptions of arrested and dead members of the Red Brigades and the Armed Proletarian Nuclei - (two of the) Italian terrorist groups of the 1970s... (The book contains) information on the social backgrounds, political experiences, and motivations of individual terrorists, including Renato and Margherita Curcio. It also (attempts to) point out significant differences in the composition and goals of these two organisations.

(BRD)

0553 Silverstein, Martin. Surviving Terrorism. *Washington Quarterly*, Volume 5, Number 4, Autumn 1982, pp. 175-180.

The increasingly random target strategy of terrorist movements presents a significant challenge to potential victims, but also one that can be minimized by adequate target preparation and the use of trans-barricade remote medical care. A logical approach to medical care and survival among victims must be based on our present knowledge of the physical and emotional pathophysiology of captivity, regional epidemiological patterns of disease, dietary patterns, parasitic and other microbiological patterns. Lessons can be learned from similar but not identical captivity situations in prisons, World War II concentration camps and the prisoner of war camps of Korea and Vietnam. Target populations can be identified and should be trained and medically "hardened" by individual training for captivity and the prevention of disease. Emergency medical equipment, including telemetry, should be part of preparatory stockpiles for potential target sites. A small corps of physicians trained in remote populations should be available for deployment overseas to terrorist incident sites.

(IPSA)

0554 Simpson, Howard R. Organizing for Counter-terrorism. *Strategic Review*, Volume 10, Number 1, Winter 1982, pp. 28-33.

Despite a dramatic upsurge in international terrorist actions targeted

against Americans and US interests, the US Government has made slow headway in putting together the elementary machinery for meeting this mushrooming threat. The needed ingredients of an effective counterterrorist strategy are a full-time and streamlined decision-making body, a permanent and integrated strike force, the methodical training of all concerned in sophisticated counterterrorist (with emphasis on the psychological dimensions), and the aggressive US pursuit of hard and explicit arrangements of international cooperation against the danger. The time for mustering these ingredients is growing short in the face of a low-cost, low-risk form of shadowy combat that is rapidly substituting for open warfare as "the continuation" of politics by other means".

(IPSA)

0555 Simpson, Howard R. The Guerrilla and his World. *US Naval Institute. Proceedings*, Volume 95, Number 8, August 1969, pp. 42-54.

This article covers guerrilla warfare in all its aspects from the man doing the fighting, to his purposes, to his methods employed. The guerrilla is seen to possess the qualities of commitment, determination, courage, basic intelligence and physical stamina. Above all, the guerrilla is a person with a mind and it is his political officer who brings out the potential in the man. This officer has proved indispensible to success and an in-depth discussion is given to the purpose and methods employed by this important man. Many examples are given from all over the globe to illustrate points being made Viet Cong., partisan organizations in World War II operations in Algeria and methods of Che Guevara are some examples cited. The primary target of the guerrilla, facing superior forces, is his enemy's most vulnerable point, the brain.

(PRAJ: PRID)

0556 Singer, Eric H. Terrorism, Extradition, and FSIA Relief: The Latelier Case. *Vanderbilt J. Transnational Law*, Number 19, Winter 1986, pp. 57-82.

Use of the US Foreign Sovereign Immunities Act to obtain relief for victims of state-sponsored terrorism; application in the case of the 1976 assassination of former Chilean Foreign Minister Orlando Letelier and his American aide.

(PAISB)

0557 Singh, Baljit and Ko-Wang, Mei. *Theory and Practice of Modern Guerrilla Warfare*. New York, Asia Pub. House, 1971.

Analyzes the revolutionary, political and socio-psychological causes of modern guerrilla warfare, its strategy and tactics and the concept of counter guerrilla warfare. The authors assert that the factor most responsible for the significant role of guerrilla warfare in political change today is the nature of international politics in the atomic age. Since nuclear war, they believe, is a thing of the past, "unconventional methods of political change" are increasingly employed.

(PRAJ: PRID)

0558 Singh, Daljit. Lt. Col. (Retd.). Time for Cool Thinking. *The Hindu*, (Madras), 19 December 1986.

Author's warning about the terrorists play to divide and create hatred among Hindus and Sikhs and that nothing should be done by any agency-government or political party etc, especially author cites the case of Mr. Bal Thakeray, to widen this gulf. According to author there are three ingredients of Punjab problem - Pride, Pakistan and Propaganda.

0559 Slater, Leonard. *The Plege*. New York, Simon and Schuster, 1970.

Useful and worthwhile for the author's chronicle of the arming of the Haganah.

0560 Sloan, Stephen. *Simulating Terrorism*. Hegerstown, Norman Univ. Okla pr., 1981.

Describes ten simulations conducted with police and military forces in the United States and overseas.

(PAISB)

0561 Sloan, Stephen. International Terrorism : Academic Quest, Operational Art and Policy Implications. *Journal of International Affairs*, Volume 32, Number 1, Spring-Summer, 1978, pp. 1-5.

Confronted with the growing recognition of the threat of international terrorism, a number of crucial groups are now employing their particular skills and perspectives to meet this invidious threat to the civil order. Members of the academic community are now in the process of defining the characteristics of international terrorism in order to collect and evaluate data and refine their techniques of comparative analysis. This refinement of techniques has been carried over to the operational realm where law enforcement agencies have developed new tactics and stategies including the use of Special Weapons and Tactics and Hostage Negotiate techniques to respond to potential incidents. Finally, while there is a lack of coherent international policies to meet the dangers of modern terrorism, regional responses and more effective coordination among local domestic jurisdictions are being formulated. All of these groups are increasingly aware of the fact that the rhetoric of concern must be replaced by concrete measures in the holding action that until now has characterized " the war on terrorism"

(IPSA)

0562 Sloan, Stephen and Kearney, Richard. Non-territorial Terrorism : An Empirical Approach to Policy Formation. *Conflict*, Volume 1, Numbers 1-2, 1978, pp. 131-144.

A more precise definition of the phenomenon of international terrorism is needed so that functionally specific concepts may be employed as base points for more rigid analysis. International terrorism can be more precisely defined as Non-Territorial Terrorism - a form of terror not confined to a clearly delineated geographical area. It is important that terrorists no longer continue to escape any form of punishment for their actions. Consistent, long-term sentences should be invoked following the conviction of individual terrorists.

(IPSA)

0563 Smith, Colin. *Carlos : Portrait of a Terrorist*. New York, Holt, Rinehart and Winston, 1976.

Drawing on interviews and eyewitness accounts, as well as secondary sources, Smith provides a commendable biography of Illich Ramirez Sanchez " Carlos" and the PFLP, (the organization with which Carlos has been most closely identified). The best book available on the subject.

(N&G)

0564 Smith, Colin. They Call it Civil War in Ulster Now. *Observer*, (London), 21 May, 1972, p. 2.

What is different in Belfast now is that most civilians are no longer being killed accidentally during a confrontation between the IRA and security forces, but they are being killed deliberately because they are Protestant or Catholic. Details cases. It would seem that the Provisional IRA are trying to touch off a fullscale Civil War. Author discusses several theories as the reason for this - e.g. to counter Ireland's entry into the Common Market, or to force a United Ireland.

(PRAJ: PRID)

0565 Smith, Colin. and McCann, Joe. The Making of a Myth. *Observer*, (London), 30 April, 1972, p. 9.

Describes the building up of martyr, out of a fairly ordinary career of a young IRA guerrilla, shot by the British Army.

(PRAJ: PRID)

0566 Smith, Desmond. Scenario Reality - A New Brand of Terrorism. *The Nation*, Volume 218, 30 March, 1974, pp. 392-394.

The mass media are increasingly influenced by various types of terrorists and terrorist groups which have recently been making special efforts to perform acts which will be fully and sympathetically reported in the mass media, e.g., Patty Hearst's Kidnapping.

(PRAJ: PRID)

0567 Symth, Robin. Schmidt Plays for Time in Civil War. *Observer*, (London), 11 September, 1977, p. 4.

In the wake of the Schleyer kidnapping, estimates of the number of terrorists in West Germany run to 1,200 with some 6,000 active sympathizers. They are frank that they are opening the road to fascism, in the belief that this will provoke a left-wing revolution. The terrorists are largely from middle and upper class families and they are becoming increasingly brutal and more efficient and sophisticated.

(PRAJ: PRID)

0568 Smyth, Robin. Enemy of Israel and Arafat. *Observer*, (London), 15 August, 1982, p. 7.

Reports what is known of the Palestinian terrorist Sabri el-Ganna, who uses the name Abou Nidal. His chief targets are known to be: (1) Jews and (2) all supporters of Yasser Arafat. He has been suspected of the massacre in the Paris cafe of Jo Goldenberg and linked with the shooting of Israel's Ambassador in London (which provided the pretext for Israel's invasion of Lebanon). He was a lieutenant of Arafat until 1974,when he led a breakaway faction accusing Arafat of capitulation and treason. Before the end of 1974, Arafat had condemned Abou Nidal to death for embezzlement, sedition and murder. Since then, Nidal has supported, and was protected by Iraq. until that country made deals with moderate Arab powers and the PLO; then Syria took Iraq's place and there were various attacks by Abou Nidal's men, in Antwerp and in Vienna. He has joined Carlos at the top of France's list of foreign terrorists.

(PRAJ: PRID)

0569 Snitch, Thomas H. Terrorism and Political Assassinations : A Transnational Assessment, 1968-80. *Annals of the American Academy of Political and Social Science*, Number 463, September 1982, pp. 54-68.

The internatioal system is experiencing a growing amount of terroristic violence. During the past five years there has been a marked increase in the yearly number of politically inspired assassinations of prominent public figures. This study presents the results of a seven-years, cross-national survey of political assassinations. An analysis of 721 events reported in 123 nations for the period concludes that there are definite trends and patterns of political assassinations that may provide important lessons for public policymakers. Certain nations, targets and terrorist actors account for a large portion of all assassination activity. Statistical analysis suggests that the academic community may have to rethink its ideas about assassination behavior in general and its relationship to the issue of development in particular. No evidence could be generated by the study to link terrorist-inspired assassinations to the developing world nor was any international network of assassins discovered. The findings point to growing levels of separatist-inspired violence and a distinct shift in target selection towards the international business community and the diplomatic corps. Terrorists appear to be increasingly successful because they are targeting relatively unprotected public individuals.

(IPSA)

0570 Sobel, Lester A. (Ed.). *Palestinian Impasse : Arab Guerrillas and International Terror*. New York, Facts on File, Inc., 1977.

A very handy reference work.

(N&G)

0571 Sobel, Lester A. (Ed.). *Political Terrorism,* Volume I. New York, Facts on File, 1975.

This work is a record of the wave of violence (terrorism) towards the latter half of the 1960s and continued on in to the 1970s. The material comes largely from the reports printed by FACTS ON FILE in its weekly coverage of world events.

0572 Sobel, Lester A. (Ed.). *Political Terrorism,* Volume II 1974-78. New York, Facts on File, 1978.

In this Volume like Volume I, the material is based largely on the records compiled by FACTS ON FILE in its weekly coverage of current world history up to the early part of 1978.

0573 Sofaer, Abraham D. The Political Offense Exception and Terrorism. *Dept. State Bul*, Number 85, December 1985, pp. 58-62.

Statement before the Foreign Realtions Committee, U.S. Senate, Aug. 1 1985.

(PAISB)

0574 Sofaer, Abraham D. The War Powers Resolution and Antiterrorist Operations. *Dept. State. Bul.*, Number 86, August 1986, pp. 68-71.

Statement before the Subcommittee on Arms Control, International

Security and Science, Foreign Affairs Committee, U.S. House of Representatives, Apr. 29, 1986.

(PAISB)

0575 Sofaer, Abraham D. The U.S. - U.K. Supplementary Extradition Treaty. *Terrorism : An International Journal*, Volume 8, Number 4, 1986, pp. 327-43.

Statement before the Committee on Foreign Relations. U.S. Senate, 1 August, 1985.
Relating to international terrorism.

(PAISB)

0576 Sofaer, Abraham D. Terrorism and the Law. *For. Affairs*, Number 64, Summer 1986, pp. 901-22.

Reasons for the failure of international law and cooperation to control recent international terrorism based on lecture.

(PAISB)

0577 Soviet Union. The Soviet Attitude to the Palestine Problem. *Journal of Palestine Studies*, Volume 2, Autumn 1972, pp. 187-212.

An important document (believed to be legitimate), comprising a critique of the political program of the Syrian Communist Party by Soviet officials (asserted to be Mikhail Suslov and Boris Ponomarev). Included in the extensive commentary are arguments against "adventurism" and "extremism" (basically to be understood as counter-productive violence vis-a-vis "revolutionary violence)"

(N&G)

0578 Sparks, Allister. Blacks Angry at Pretoria Bomb. *Observer*, (London), 22 May, 1983, p.1.

Black leaders in South Africa, such as Dr. Ntatho Motlana, Chairman of Soweto's Committee of Ten and Bishop Desmond Tutu, feel that the car bomb attack in Pretoria, which killed 17 and injured up to 200, was an atrocity. Some think that it could not have been the work of the ANC, whose policy is to attack only military targets - that possibly it was done by someone trying to discredit the ANC. They fear, too, that it will move the government to more retaliatory raids on outside ANC bases and to intensified security surveillance.

(PRAJ: PRID)

0579 Spillane, Jay M. Terrorists and Special Status : The British Experience in Northern Ireland. *Hastings Internat and Comparative Law R*, Volume 9, Spring 1986, pp. 481-515.

Argues that Britain's use of special powers creates special status prisoners entitled to human rights protections.

(PAISB)

0580 Stephens, Hugh W. Not Merely the Achille Lauro : The Threat of Maritime Terrorism and Piracy. *Terrorism : An International Journal*, Volume 9, Number 3, 1987, pp. 285-296.

Fighting piracy at the international, the national and the company level.

(PAISB)

0581 Sterling, Claire. The Terrorist Network. *Atlantic*, November 1978, pp. 37-47.

A rather simplistic journalistic account of European terrorism, particularly as practiced by the Red Army Faction and the Red Brigades. Sterling's conclusion that today's urban guerrillas are not unbeatable, raises far more questions than it answers. However, those segments of the article that address state-actor support for terrorists are of some value (esp. with reference to the Cuban and the Warsaw Treaty Organization countries' relationships with terrorists).

(N&G)

0582 Sterling, Claire. *The Terror Network : The Secret War of International Terrorism*. Holt, Rinehart & Winston, 1981.

The author traces back the international network of terror back to the Inter-Continental Conference in Havana in 1966, followed by the KGB takeover of the Cuban Security Forces two years later and the gradual KGB infiltration of the PLO through the Rejection front.

The author's major theme is that there is a network of terrorism at whose centre one finds a Palestinian connection and a Russian patron, and that the prime beneficiary of the terrorism is the Soviet Union.

(BRD)

0583 Stern, Susan. *With the Weathermen*. Garden City, New York, Doubleday and Co., 1975.

An insider's account by a minor leader. The especially illuminating aspect of Ms. Stern's book is that she never tells the reader why she joined the Weathermen and one suspects there is not a very profound explantation or motive. More than anything else her involvement with violent left seems to have been a trip and indeed she states (p. 3) : "It was rare that I wasn't stoned...."

(N&G)

0584 Stevenson, William. *90 Minutes at Entebbe*. New York, Bantaun, 1976.

Author details the planning and successful execution of "operation thunderbold", to rescue the 103 passengers on an Air France Airliner that had been hijacked on June 27 by Arab terrorists while enroute from Athens to Paris. Stevenson gathered much of his material from taped interviews and written reports.

(BRD)

0585 Stohl, Michael. and Geroge A. Lopez, (Eds.). *Government Violence and Repression : an Agenda for Research*. Westport, Greenwood Pr., 1986.

Contributions to the study of state-sponsored terrorism and government use of violence; various countries.

(PAISB)

0586 Stohl, Michael. (Ed.). *The Politics of Terror : A Reader in Theory and Practice*. New York, Marcel Dekker, 1977.

Includes selections by T.R. Gurr (terrorism in the 1960s), P.N. Grabosky (urban terrorism), H.R. Tary (revolutionary terrorism), E. Mickolus (transnational terrorism), R.R. Corrado (European ethnic and student terrorism), M.R. Welfling (sub-Sahara Africa), J.W. Sloan (Latin America), V.F. Bishop (fedayeen), R.C. Hula (Bengal) and F.D. Homer (U.S).

(N&G)

0587 Stohl, Michael. (Ed.). *The Politics of Terrorism*. New York, Dekker, 1979.

The Essays in this volume discuss the theoretical and historical development of political terrorism. After an introduction by the editor the four essays in part one, emphasize concepts and theories. The seven essays in part two focus on case studies of particular geopolitical regions.

(BRD)

0588 Stork, Joe. Mad dogs and Presidents. il MERIP (Middle East Research & Info. Project) *Middle East Rept.*, Number 16, May/June 1986, pp. 6-10.

Background and motivation for the U.S. bombing raid on Libya, Apr. 15, 1986.

(PAISB)

0589 Street, M. Prevention of Terrorism (Temporary Provisions) Act of 1974. *Criminal Law Review*, London, April 1975, pp. 192-199.

A critical assessment of British legislation to control terrorist activities related to Northern Ireland.

(N&G)

0590 Strentz, Thomas. Law Enforcement Policy and Ego Defenses of the Hostage. *FBI Law Enforcement Bulletin*, November 48, April 1979, pp. 2-12.

A lucid treatment of the Stockholm Syndrome in a Freudian context. Strentz argues that the syndrome reflects the regression of the victim to a child-like stage of complete dependence. Various examples of the phenomenon are offered, as are several conditions for its coming into play, the two most important being : The chronological length of interaction between victim and captor, and the nature of interactions i.e., whether they have been positive, negative or neutral.

(N&G)

0591 Suarez, Hector Victor. *The Revolutionary Armed Forces : With Che's Weapons*. In James Kohl and John Litt, Urban Guerrilla Warfare in Latin America. Cambridge, Mass., The MIT Press, 1974.

A brief account of Argentinian (FAR) thinking on the question of urban guerrilla warfare.

(N&G)

0592 Sundberg, Jacob. Operation Leo : Description and Analysis of a European Terrorist Operation. *Terrorism : An International Journal*, Volume 5, Number 3, 1981-82.

Operation Leo, an aborted terrorist action that was to take place in Stockholm in the summer of 1977, had as its goal the kidnapping of former Minister of the Interior Anna-Greta Leijon, who was then to be traded for the release of a number of terrorists in captivity in West Germany. The plan misfired and the perpetrators were brought to book. The present article takes as its point of departure a discussion about the Baader-Meinh of group and Wolfgang Huber's Socialist Patients' Collective in Heidelberg. The background of Norbert Kroecher, the instigator of Operation Leo, his stay in Stockholm, including such

members as Aramando Carillo, Alan Hunter and Manfred Adomeit, together with their plan of action, are brought out partly through quoted testimony at the trial. Much light is thrown on the inner workings of such a conspiratorial group, and questions are raised as to why such foreign refugees with cirminal records were not picked up immediately but remained undetected for a long time, why quite a few middle-class Swedish intellectuals, especially young women, were attracted to terrorist doctrines and to what extent the fault lay with the destruction of the social infrastructure and the lack of family control in a society characterized by a general leftist atmosphere. All these and other factors, it seems, combined to make Sweden into a "giant Socialist Patients' collective," in which German and other terrorists were operating with impunity.

(T)

0593 Sweeney, Jane Chace. State-sponsored Terrorism : Libya's Abuse of Diplomatic Privileges and Immunities. *Dickinson J Internat Law*, Number 5, Fall 1986, pp. 133-65.

The Vienna Convention on Diplomatic Relations viability in the current political arena.

(PAISB)

0594 Syrian Support for International Terrorism : 1983-86. *Dept State Bul*, Number 87, Fall 1987, pp. 73-76.

Prepared by the office of the Ambassador at Large for Counter-Terrorism ; includes a chronology of selected terrorist incidents.

(PAISB)

0595 Tanham, George K. ; Jenkins, Brian.; Wainstein, Eleanor S.; and Sullivan, Gerald. United States Preparation for Future Low-Level Conflict. *Conflict : An International Journal for Conflict and Policy Studies*, Number 1, 1978, pp. 1-19.

Report of a meeting held in Washington, at the Rand Corporation, in October 1976. The subject was the ability of the U.S. to respond to the low-level conflicts which are considered likely to define parameters for the remainder of the century. In nearly every realm, the participants (Government officials and think-tank professionals) found the U.S. capability to be inadequate. Recommendations includes a centralized organization to cope with low-level conflict; enhanced contingency planning, and gaming by top level officials, increased emphasis within the services; further coordination with allies; and a partial redirection of intelligence efforts.

(N&G)

0596 Tayor, Charles. Behind the Kidnapping. Alienation too Profound for the System to Contain. *Canadian Dimension*, Volume 7, Numbers 5-6, pp. 26-29.

A significant segment of the youth of Quebec feels alienated enough from the political system and society to applaud and even participate in acts of terror. There is no confidence in reforming the political and social system through elected representatives. The result of this move towards violence, on the part of some youths is the destruction of the non-violent work others are involved in. The violence of one segment is breeding a back-lash of law and order - thus violence is met with violence.

(PRAJ: PRID)

0597 Taylor, Clyde D. Links between International Narcotics Trafficking and Terrorism. *Dept. State Bul*, Number 85, August 85, pp. 69-74.

Testimony before a joint session of the Committees on Foreign Relations and the Judiciary, U.S. Senate, May 14, 1985; includes country reports.

(PAISB)

0598 Taylor, Robert. (Ed.). Latin America Beat - Guerrilla Conflicts. *World Press Review*, October 1982. p. 16.

Caretas, Lima, Peru, demands swift government action to stop guerrilla violence. It notes the increasing number of attacks by the mountain-based guerrilla group, Sender Luminoso. President Fernando Terry Belaunde declared a state of emergency of August 20. EL COMERCIO, Lima, urges the government forces to eradicate the terrorists bands. EL NACIONAL, Caracas, Venezuela, suggests that President Belaunde's previous overthrow by a 1968 military coup gives him reason not to give the military a free hand. EL TIEMPO, Bogoto, Colombia, comments that President Belisario Betancur has offered to expand negotiations with the leftist gurrillas, and this change in attitude gives some optimism. The guerrillas must understand that now is the time for compromise and peace.

(PRAJ: PRID)

0599 Taylor, Robert W. and Vanden, Harry E. Defining Terrorism in El Salvador : 'La Matanza'. *Annals of the American Academy of Political and Social Science*, Number 463, September 1982, pp. 106-118.

The term "terrorism" has been defined in a number of ways by a variety of scholars. For the most part, each definition has yielded a limited understanding of the actual phenomenon. This is especially true when analyzing the current wave of international situations in contemporary global affairs, such as those occurring in central America. This article explores the various actors and motives operating in EL Salvador in an attempt to clarify the meaning of terrorism.

(PRAJ: PRID)

0600 Taylor, Theodore. In Statement Before Snata Committee on Government Affairs. 266, March 22, 1978.

"... it is highly credible that a small group of people could design and build Fission explosives, using information and non-nuclear materials that are accessible to the public worldwide. Under some circumstances, it is quite conceivable that this could be done by one person, working alone. Such explosives could be transported by automobile. Their probable explosive yields would depend considerably on the knowledge and skills of the group. Relatively crude explosives that would be likely to yield the equivalent of up to about 1000 tons of high explosive would be much easier to build than explosives that could be reliably expected to yield the equivalent of more than 10 kilotons of high explosive. Explosives with yields in the latter range would be much easier to build with highly enriched uranium or uranium — 233 than with plutonium. All three materials including plutonium of all isotopic compositions, could be used for making relatively crude explosives with yields in the vicinity of one kiloton."

(N&G)

0601 Teixeira, Bernardo. *The Fabric of Terror*. New York, The Derin-Adair Company, 1965.

Written by a Portuguese, this book Chronicles a particularly gruesome spate of anti-colonial terrorism which occurred in Angola during March 1961

Whatever the impetus for this book, it was definitely not intended for the faint of heart. Eight pages of gory photographs have been included.

(N&G)

0602 Terchek, Ronald. Conflict and Cleavage in Northern Ireland. *Annals*, Number 433, September 1977, pp. 47-59.

Useful as background material, rather than as a vehicle for studying terrorism in Northern Ireland. Terchek traces the conflict to the conflicts between the Protestant and Catholic communities, as well as the strains produced by any attempt to include the Catholic minority in the government.

(N&G)

0603 Terrorism : Special report. il *Am Legion M*, Number 120, July 1986, pp. 15-21.

Impact of international terrorism on U.S. Foreign policy, International law, and NATO: includes an interview with Vice President George Bush: 5 articles.

(PAISB)

0604 Terrorism. il *Dept State Bul*, Number 86, August 1986, pp. 1-16.

Statements by Ambassadors Robert B. Oakley and Parker W. Borg; Chronology of major American-related terrorist incidents, 1985, statement on the taking of U.S. citizens hostage.

(PAISB)

0605 Terrorism. *World Press* R, Number 32, September 1985, pp. 35-40.

Six articles translated and excerpted from the world press, June 29-July 11, 1985.

(PAISB)

0606 Thakur, Janardan. When will the Terrorists Strike Again? *Hindustan Times*, (Delhi), 12 July 1987.

The government pronouncements after every terrorist incident, that it will not tolerate this maddness, has become useless, empty words. People have lost the confidence. Author asks a very important question, i.e., with whom (group) centre should talk?

0607 Tharp, Paul A. Jr. The Laws of War as a Potential Legal Regime for the Control of Terrorist Activities. *Journal of International Affairs*, Volume 32, Number 1, Spring-Summer 1978, pp. 91-100.

This article offers both a theoretical overview and a legalistic review of the current state of international law in regard to the regulation of those acts of terrorism which transcend national boundaries. The article examines the debate between those who believe that terrorism should be treated as a political matter versus those who wish to see it treated as an international crime. The traditional laws of extradition and the recent conventions on terrorism from the United Nations Organization of American States and the Council of Europe are discussed. The author then suggests that the laws of war might also provide a model for rules of law which could strike a compromise between the political and legalistic approaches to the problem.

(IPSA)

0608 The IRA Death Machine. *Observer*, (London), 10 October, 1971, pp. 25-26; 17 October, 1971, p. 11.

Profile of the IRA - its history, divison into "Provisionals" and "Officials", its hierarchy, brief biographies of its leaders, its present oneness with the Catholics

in Ulster (owing largely to the active political campaign of the Provisions, who adopted the class struggle against Ulster's Protestants) and its ties with Communism.

(PRAJ: PRID)

0609 Thompson, W Scott. Political Violence and the Corelation of Forces. *Orbis*, Winter 1976, pp. 1270-1288.

Thompson thoroughly analyzes the phenomenon of political violence and notes that "one nation's terrorism is another's national liberation". While it is not common in the Second World or communist states, it is growing increasingly common in the First and Third Worlds. It feeds on itself. Once there were tremendous protests when India seized Goa; now there is little international protest when Indonesia invades Timor. And other countries follow the pattern. The successes in Mozambique and Portugal gave fresh impetus to others. Thompson sees several factors contributing to the rise of terrorism : one is a decline in the leadership of the United States; another is the residue of colonialism; and a third the rise in European prosperity. "Violence in the non-communist world is a symptom of the distress of a civilization and could well be the critical medium of its decline." As violence increases, freedom declines. The author examines the shift fromdemocracy to dictatorship in the Philippines, for example. The West and its supportes are the enemy and the USSR and its proteges the breeding groud for terrorists.

"A sober view of how bleak the position is, shared by free men throughout the world, is a necessary first step before anything can be done about political violence within the structure that permits it, the independent nation state."

(PRAJ: PRID)

0610 Thornton, Thomas P. Terrorism as a Weapon of Political Agitation. In *Internal War : Problems and Approaches*, Harry Eckstein, (Ed.). New York, The Free Press, 1974, pp. 71-99.

The seminal article on the subject: Thornton defines terrorism as "...a symbolic act designed to influence poltical behavior by extranormal means, entailing the use of threat of violence."

(N&G)

0611 Tierney, John J. Terror at Home : The American Revolution and Irregular Warfare. *Stanford Journal of International studies*, Number 12, Spring 1977, pp. 1-19.

As a form of warfare; terrorism will remain an integral part of the strategy of those who wish to overthrow the political status quo. As such, terrorism will continue to be "legitimate" for those whose aspirations it serves, and immoral and repugnant for those against whom it is directed. Even in the American Revolution, terrorism was judged in a similarly subjective manner. Although the Americans mastered this form of conflict in their own revolution, they have since forgotten it. [First of a series of a article on "International terrorism"]

(IPSA)

0612 Toker, Metin.Terrorism and Political Violence : Its Causes and Development. *Vierteljahreserichte. Probleme der Entwicklungslander*, Number 86, December 1981. pp. 329-336.

Terrorism in Turkey after 1975 was encouraged by weak governments which reduced the state mechanism to a point where it was unable to perform its duties and incapable of making the state authority felt. This led to anarchy in

every sector of society. Although terrorism still carried political labels in this anarchical environment, it nevertheless started making an effort in the direction of relatively non-political objectives. The main feature in this period of terrorism was the emergence of right-wing terror.

(IPSA)

0613 Tromp, Hyeke. (Polemological Institute, Groningen, Netherlands) *Terrorism and Political Violence; Some Notes on Definitions, Explanations, and Causes*. International Peace Research Association, Konigstein, FRG, 22 August, 1979.

Over 25 million people were killed in wars in 1945-76 - inter-state wars in which armies of 82 states were involved. However, "political violence" also includes civil and guerrilla warfare, whose incidence has gone up during this period, while "classical" inter-state war has gone down. Guerrilla fighters (beginning e.g. with the French Resistance in World War II) have no rights under international laws of war and are usually executed when caught, rather than taken prisoner. Revolutionaries are treated as common criminals; their use of violence is considered "illegitimate"; only governments have the monopoly of "legitimate violence." "Terrorism is another variation on this theme; terrorists are analyzed pscyhologically by social scientists, while their political motives are ignored. Since most come from universities and from upper-class families, do we close the universities and eradicate the upper classes as a preventive? In defining terrorism, we need to deal with the actors, the targets, the nature of terrorist acts, the scale (e.g. number killed) and the legitimacy. In defining the actors, we should not exclude national governments; they too sometimes plot assassinations of other nations' leaders. The targets of armies in classical warfare are, officially, opposing armies - but the distinction between armies and civilians is usually not observed. Terrorist acts are usually aimed at a prominent person (politician or businessman), or a limited group (a plane-load of passengers), while armed forces may wipe out a whole village or city. Are nuclear weapons "legitimate" while a hostage-taking is not? We are all hostages in Mutual Assured Destruction. H.N. There is a distinction between guerrilla warfare (directed against an army) and terrorist acts (directed against civilian targets) - in both cases by irregular forces. Guerrillas apply force to "change the minds" of their targets directly; terrorists attack outsiders or bystanders in order to exert indirect pressure on governments (thus the targets of the act and of the intended pressure are not the same). Both forms of "unconventional" warfare tend to be protracted struggles. Terrorist acts are "criminal" in the sense of breaking existing laws, but we should distinguish between "private" and "public" goals in criminal violent acts. Political terrorists are generally regarded with even more horror than private-gain criminals, because they are seen as "heretics" who have declared war on society. Organized crime (the Mafia) is seen as a normal fringe of the social order; but Political terrorists are not only beyond the law, but beyond the social order. Regarding the scale of violence, political terrorism is low-level violence - from 0 to 400 victims per incident. Moral justification of any violence is difficult - revolutions are usually accepted as legitimate only in retrospect, *if* they are successful (e.g. George Washington). In discussing the "causes of terrorism", we should not try to "explain it away" by "scientific" analyses of sociological background and psychological personality characteristics of the terrorists; such use of science is profoundly supportive of the *status quo* (of mental hospitals for Soviet dissenters H.N.). One valid explanation is that there has been a shift in the spectrum of political violence. There are 11 factors; (1) Arms- extending now to rockets, (2) Mobility - increasing tremendously, (3)

Communication and publicity is instantly widespread, though often distorted, (4) Money seems plentiful - e.g. for the and from Irish Americans, (5) Social alienation of many groups. (6) Failure of the political system to represent all public interests adequately, (7) New supranational reference groups, (8) Organizational complexity of modern states - which makes them more vulnerable, (9) Absence of alternatives for the terrorist. (10) Compulsion to express deeply held emotions, (11) The process like character, the political use of violence, i.e. identification with the primary group terrorist cell and adoption of its norms to the exclusion of all others; and throwing all problems to the simple one of "winning the war". "Sect like behaviour", including the execution of deserters and heretics, is part of this mentality. Terrorism is simply war "continued by other means."

(PRAJ: PRID)

0614 Trotsky, Leon. *Terrorism and Communism*. Ann Arbor, University of Michigan, 1961.

Trotsky defends terror in the Russian Revolution on the grounds that it was necessary to the defense of socialism. He argues that the party can permit no opposition and that terrorism is a necessary means for the highest moral end of humanity: the socialist state. Trotsky himself became a victim of the police state which he helped to create.

(RW)

0615 Truby, J David. *How Terrorists Kill : The Complete Terrorist Arsonal*. Boulder, Paladin Press, 1978.

A treatment of the implements, rather than the mechanics of terrorism. This book is noteworthy for its 50 pages of illustrations and photographs, most depicting weapons used by, or suitable for use by terrorists.

(N&G)

0616 Truby, J David., and Minnery, John. *Improvised Modified Firearms*, Volume I and Volume II, Boulder, Paladin Press, 1975.

These two volumes chronicle improvised weapons from the anti-tank weapons to the zip gun. Given the ready availability of professionally manufactured weapons, only the disinherited terrorist might consider turning to homemade weapons of the type described. Nontheless, the volumes are instructive as to the extent that persons have gone in the past to fabricate weapons. Extensive illustrations.

(N&G)

0617 Truskier, A. Politics of Violence: The Urban Guerrilla in Brazil : Interview with four Revolutionists. *Ramparts Magazine*, Number 9, October, 1970, pp. 30-34.

Interesting interview with four leading Brazilian guerrilla leaders: Angelo Pezzutti, Carlos Eduardo Fleury, Ladislaw Dobor and Fernando Nagle Gabeira.

(N&G)

0618 Turk, Austin T. Social Dynamics of Terrorism. *Annals of the American Academy of Political and Social Science*, Number 463, September 1982, pp. 119-128.

Effective strategies for avoiding the projected "legitimation crisis" presuppose the clarification and resolution of issues regarding the definition, causation, and justification of political violence. It is proposed that terrorism be defined as an ideology or strategy justifying terror-defined as lethal or non-lethal violence intended to deter political opposition by maximizing fear, specifically by random

targeting. On causation, it is argued that terrorism is to be explained as the product not of discrete causes but rather of systemic processes generated in functional and interactive relationships of inequality. Examples of relational dynamics encouraging groups to adopt terrorism are considered. Such dynamics encouraging groups to adopt terrorism are considered. Such dynamics are found to vary among as well as within authority structures. Terrorism is more likely to appear in totalitarian structures, but acts of terror are more frequent in democratic structures which is largely attribuable to the dissemination of terrorist ideologies, the displacement of political conflicts to freer settings and the propensity of totalitarian governments to sponsor terror elsewhere. Terrorism and terror are associated with the breakdown of traditional authority structures and with efforts to create modern ones. Regarding issues of justification, it is concluded that terrorism and terror are unjustifiable on empirical grounds.

(IPSA)

## U.S. CONGRESS AND U.N. HEARINGS AND REPORTS

0619 U.S. Congress. Senate. Committee on Governmental Affairs. *An Act to Combat International Terrorism, Report of the Committee on S. 2236*, 95th Cong., 2nd Sess., 1978.

In addition to the hearing summaries, several important studies are appended, including : B.M. Jenkins, International Terrorism : Trend and Potentialities:" R.H. Kupperman, "Facing Tommorrow's Terrorist Incidents Today"; F.M. Ochberg, "The victim of Terrorism-Psychiatric Considerations;" and L.A. Russell, L.J. Banker, and B. Miller, "Out-Inventing the Terrorist."

(N&G)

0620 United States. *Defense civil preparedness agency. Domestic terrorism.* May'79 120p+v.p. bibl index (Stock no. 008-040-0082-6) Supt docs.

Prepared by the Emergency preparedness project, Center for Policy Research, National governors' association.

(PAISB)

0621 U.S. Department of Justice, Law Enforcement Assistance Administration. *Disorders and Terrorism : Report of the Task Force on Disorders and Terrorism.* Washington, D.C. Government Printing Office, 1976.

While mainly intended for the law enforcement community, this bulky report (661 pp.) deserves wider attention. Subjects include terrorism in general, specific constabulary, executive, and judicial concerns, nuclear terror, and terrorism in its particular regional manifestations (viz. Germany, Argentina, and Canada). Special features : extensive bibliography and chronology.

(N&G)

0622 U.S. Office of Technology Assessment. *The Non-State Adversary. Nuclear Proliferation and Safeguards.* New York, Praeger Publishers, 1977, Chapter V, pp. 115-136.

Prepared by the Congressional Office of Technology Assessment, this reference proceeds from a useful review of terrorist activities, to a consideration of several of the non-state adversaries that may attempt to acquire nuclear weapons those being: the terrorist, the criminal and the mentally defective. The

second part of the section succinctly addresses the impact that nuclear safeguards may have upon civil liberties in the U.S., presenting synopses of the three modes of confronting the question.

(N&G)

0623 United Nations. *Report of the Ad Hoc Committee on Intenational Terrorism.* New York, 1973.

Covers the debate over defining terrorism, the causes of terrorism and measures for prevention.

(N&G)

0624 United Nations. Gen. Assembly. Ad hoc com. on internat. *Terrorism Report.* '79 iii + 34p. (Official recs. : 34th sess. Sup. no. 37 (A/34/37) - New York, NY 10017.

Summary, report and recommendations of meetings held Mar. 19—Apr. 6, 1979.

(PAISB)

0625 United Nations General Assembly. *Report of the Ad Hoc Committee on International Terrorism,* General Assembly, United Nations. Official Records Twenty-eigth Session, Supplement No. 28(A/9028). 34 pp., U.S. $2.00.

The United Nations in various bodies has been struggling with different aspects of "international terrorism" for many years. The emphasis of this particular report is on Interantional Terrorism, but this already raises great difficulties. since many of the causes of the phenomena to be explained are internal, even though their manifestation may be international. The Committee acknowledges this in its stress on the evils of colonial, racist and alien regimes. However, there are other factors not associated with this type of regime which gives rise to international terrorism. Nevertheless, the Committee did recognize that it would have to go for the cause in order to find a successful cure, rather than just indulge in straight repression. The trouble is that the analysis of the causes is essentially selective, and while this does not distract from its validity, it is not the whole truth. Fortunately some representatives did raise the question of state terrorism. and not only in the context of colonial, racist and alien regimes. The Committee set up three sub-committees-one to deal with the definition of "international terrorism", one to deal with its underlying causes, and the third to deal with its prevention. On the whole, the Western Powers were more concerned with prevention and the Third World Powers were more concerned with an analysis of causes (selective).

This Committee Report reviews a wide range of disparate views. There is no consensus on this subject. It also reveals a variety of measures have been taken within the U.N. body of organizations and exist already. Equally it reveals that there has been a thorough discussion of the issues. The question is whether there are any absolute rules which no 'terrorists' can break, as in the case in the law of war. If so, can they be spelled out? If there are no absolute rules, are there any selective causes in the pursuit of which 'terrorism' can be justified, as for example, what can be justified by the theory of just war in the minds of some? These issues are likely to be debated for a long time. The end result, however, will probably not be a general code, but rather some specific or regional agreements on particular matters, such as the recent agreement on hostages. This particular one is universal, but one can well envisage that within different frameworks, such as Latin America or Europe, regional agreement will

be worked out which could not be agreed at the universal level.

(PRAJ: PRID)

626 United States Department of State-Patterns of Global Terrorism : 1984. *Terrorism : An International Journal*, Volume 9, Number 4, 1987.

The pace of international terrorist activity around the world continued unabated during 1984. We recorded nearly 600 international terrorist attacks involving personal injury of property damage, representing an increase over each of the previous four years. Deaths in 1984 exceeded 300. These numbers, when viewed in the context of the past 15 years, suggest that the overall threat may again be increasing.

U.S. citizens and interests remained a prime target of foreign terrorists around the world, followed by those of France and Israel. More than 20 per cent of international terrorist incidents in 1984 involved U.S. targets.

The major trend apparent in 1985 was the growing dominance of the Middle East as the crucible of terrorism. In 1984, nearly half of all international terrorism. In1984, nearly half of all international terrorist attack either occurred in the Middle East or were committed elsewhere by Middle Easterners.

Many of the attacks of the Middle Eastern origin in 1984 were the work of groups or agents who freqently work at the behest of one of the three radical states: Iran, Syria, or Libya. Indeed, sponsorship or support of terrorism by these three countries became the most salient characteristic of international terrorism in 1984-one that has been largely responsible for the increased violence of attacks and the proliferation of Middle Eastern terrorist operations in Western Europe. Resurgent Palestinian terrorism also drove up the level of attacks of Middle Eastern origin.

Western Europe experienced an outbreak of what became known as Euroterrorism — a campaign of seemingly coordinated attacks against NATO and defence-related targets primarily in West Germany, France, and Belgium.

Latin America, as in past years, indigenous terrorist violence associated with the communist backed insurgencies in Elsalvador and Colombia far exceeded the number of international terrorist attacks.

In Asia the most spectacular terrorist incident - the assassination of Indian Prime Minister Indira Gandhi by Sikh members of her security force- was in fact an instance of indigenous, rather than international, terrorism.

Prospects for a slowdown in international terrorist activity are dim. We expect terrorism of indigenous origin in Western Europe to continue at the current level and most Latin American violence to continue to vary according to the success of local governments in dealing with insurgent problem. Moreover, terrorism emanating from the Middle East is unlikely to slacken its pace: Iran, syria and Libya have thus far enjoyed relative success in pursuing their individual foreign policy objectives through the use of terrorism.

(T)

0627 United States. Home Com. on For. Affairs. *Subcom on Internat. Operations.* The diplomatic security Program : hearings and markup, 13 November, 1985-March 6, 1986, on H.R. 4151. '1986 iii+340p tables charts (99th Cong.) (SD Cat. no. Y4.F 76/1 : D 62/33) pa-Supt Docs.

Protecting U.S. diplomatic facilities and their staffs from terrorists actions.

(PAISB)

0628 United States. House. Com. on For. Affairs. *Antiterrorism measures : The Adequacy of Foreign Airport Security : Staff Report,* 8 August, 1986. '86 xi+15p.(99th Cong., 2nd sess.) (Com. print) (SD cat. no. Y 4. F 76/1 : An 8/2) - Supt Docs.

Findings and recommendations of the committee's Task Force on International Terrorism and Diplomatic Security Investigating compliance with the Foreign Airport Security Act: airports in Frankfurt, Rome, London and Athens.

(PAISB)

0629 United States. House Com. on For. Affairs. *Subcom on Inter-Am. Affairs, Review of the presidential certification of Nicaragua's connection to terrorism : hearing,* 30 September, 1980. '80 iii+50p. (96th Cong., 2nd Sess.) pa-Washington, DC 20515.

Whether there is such a connection and whether it should affect United States aid to Nicaragua.

(PAISB)

0630 United States. *House Beirut tragedy : A New Crowd in town and Beirut casualties : care and identification;* report, together with supplemental views of the delegation to Beirut of the Committee on Armed Services and Committee on Veterans' Affaris. '83 ii+14 p. plan (98th Cong. 1st Sess.) (Com. Print no. 12) (SD cat. no Y 4. Ar 5/2 : B 339) - Washington, D.C. 20515.

Views of officials and academics in West Germany and Italy.

(PAISB)

0631 United States. House, Com. on the Judiciary. *Subcom. on Civil and Constitutional Rights. Report on domestic and international terrorism.* '81 v+36p. (97tg cong., 1st sess.) (Com. Print No. 6)-Washington. DC 20515.

Views of officials and academics in West Germany and Italy.

(PAISB)

0632 United States. House. Com. on the Judiciary. *Subcom. on Crime. Antiterrorism Act of 1986:* hearing, 4 March, 1986, on H.R. 4294. '87 iii + 190p (99th Cong., 2nd sess.) (Serial no. 100) (SD cat. no. Y 4. J 89/1:99/100) pa-Supt Docs.

Issue of criminal jurisdiction over terrorist acts that occur outside the borders of the U.S. and updating of the extradition laws.

(PAISB)

0633 United States. House. Com. on For. Affairs. *Iran's seizure of the United States embassy:* hearings, 17 February – 11 March, 1981. '81 iii + 285p. (97th Cong., 1st Sess.) pa-Supt Docs.

A review of the Iran hostage situation; implications for future United States foreign policy, including the deterrence of terrorism.

(PAISB)

0634 United States. House. Com. on For. Affairs. Subcom. on Europe and the Middle East. *The media, diplomacy, and terrorism in the Middle East :* hearing, July 30, 1985. '85 iii + 152p (99th Cong., 1st sess.) (SD cat. no. Y 4.F 76/1-M 46/5) (LC 86-20082) pa-Supt Docs.

Impact of media coverage during acts against the U.S.

(PAISB)

0635 United States. House. Com. on the Judiciary. Subcom. on Civil and Constitutional Rights. *Terrorism :* oversight hearings, August 26–May 15, 1986. '87 iii + 327p. tables charts maps (99th Cong., 1st and 2nd sess.) (Serial no. 91) (SD cat. no. Y 4 J 89/1 : 99/91) pa-Supt Docs.

Terrorism against Americans; includes data on incidents in the U.S., 1981-85.

(PAISB)

0636 United States. House. Com., on For. Affairs. *The Central American Counterterrorism Act of 1985:* hearings, October 24 and November 19, 1985. '86 vi + 321 p. tables charts (99th Cong., 1st sess.) pa-Washington, DC 20515.

U.S. programs to provide military training and equipment and civilian law enforcement assistance.

(PAISB)

0637 United States. Senate. Com. on governmental affairs. *Ombibus anti-terrorism act 1979:* hearings, March 30 and May 7, 1979, on S. 333, to effect certain reorganization of the federal government to strengthen federal programs and policies for combating international and domestic terrorism. '79 iv+448 p il tables (96th Cong., 1st sess): pa-Supt docs.

Emphasis on the addition of chemical taggants to explosives to aid in their detection and identification.

(PAISB)

0638 United States. Senate. Com. the Judiciary. Subcom. On Security and Terrorism. *Soviet, East German and Cuban involvement in fomenting terrorism in southern Africa :* report. '82 v+28p. (97th Cong., 2nd sess.) (Com. print) - Washington, DC 20510.

Emphasis on the role of the Soviet Union in the African National Congress and the South West Africa People's Organization.

(PAISB)

0639 United States, Senate. Com. on the Judiciary. Subcom. On Security and Terrorism. *The Anti-terrorism and Foreign Mercenary Act : Hearing,* September 23, 1982, on S. 2255. '83 iv+79p (97th Cong., 2d sess). (Serial No. J-97-140) pa-Washington, DC 20510.

Bill to amend Title 18, United States Code, to establish criminal penalties to control the mercenary activities of American citizens on behalf of foreign

powers and terrorist groups that are hostile to the United States.

(PAISB)

0640 United States. Senate. Com. on the Judiciary. Subcom. on Security and Terrorism. *Terrorism : the role of Moscow and its subcontractors : hearing,* June 26, 1981. '82 iii+55p. (97the Cong., 1st sess.) (Serial No. 97-44) pa-Washington, DC 20510.

Testimony of Robert Moss, a writer and syndicated columinst with the London daily telegraph.

(PAISB)

0641 United States, Senate. Com. on labor and Human resources. Subcom. on *Alcoholism and Drug Abuse and terrorism.* '84 iii+120p maps (98th Cong., 2d sess.) (S. hearing 98-1046 (SD cat. No. Y 4. L 11/4 : S. Hrg. 98-1046) pa-Washington, DC 20510.

Alleged international drug trafficking by terrorist groups in various parts of the world.

(PAISB)

0642 United States. Senate. Com. on For. Relations. *International terrorism : hearing,* June 10, 1981, on S. 873, a bill to strengthen federal programs and policies for combating international and domestic terrorism; the Convention on the Physical Protection of Nuclear Material (Exec. H, 96-2); the International Convention Against the Taking of Hostages (Exec. N, 96-2). '81 iii+94p. il tables charts (97th Cong., 1st Sess.) pa-Washington, DC 20510.

(PAISB)

0643 United States. Senate. Com. on For Relations. Subcom. on Near Eastern and South Asian Affairs. *Regulation changes on exports : hearning,* March 18, 1982, on the change in Department of Commerce regulations on exports to Iraq, South Africa, Syria, and South Yemen. '82 iii+44p table (97th Cong., 2d sess.) - Washington, DC 20510.

Concerning export of materials or equipment capable of being used for terrorist, military or policing purposes, to countries felt to be supportive of international terrorist activities; issue of whether the commerce department consulted with the Congress before changing export control regulations.

(PAISB)

0644 H 401-24.
*FAA review of security at foreign international airports.*
September - 18, 1986, 99-2.
iii+102 p. GPO $ 3.00.
CIS/MF/4. Item 1016-A; 1016-B.
.YU G74/7:F31/70.
LC 87-601228.

Hearing before the subcom. on Government Activities and Transportation

to review the adequacy of the FAA program for assessing foreign international airport security to prevent airline hijacking and other terrorist activities against U.S. airlines.

Appendix (p. 79-102) includes a submitted statement and : House Foreign Affairs committee, 'Anti-Terrorism measures : The adequacy of foreign Airport Security. '8 August, 1986 (p. 80-102).

(CIS)

0645 H-6

181-36. 6:Apr. 1, 1987 p. 621-671.

Witness: Feldman, Roger B. Compt. State Dept. Budget

Explanation: State Dept FY 88 request for :

(a) Emergency requirements of the diplomatic and consular service, including loans to destitute U.S. citizens over-seas, evacuation of citizens and Government employees from crisis areas and rewards for information about terrorist acts (submitted justifications, p. 622-627).

(b) American Institute in Taiwan activities for maintenance of U.S. commercial and cultural relations with Taiwan (submitted justifications, p. 644-650)

(c) Foregin service Retirement and disability Fund (Submitted justifications p. 660-661)

(CIS)

0646 H-521-40

Anti-terrorism Act of 1986.

March 4, 1986. 99-2. iii+190p. GPO $5.50 CIS/MF/4.

Item 1020-A; 1020-B. J89/1:99/100.

MC 87-8615. LC 87-601018.

Committee serial No. 100. Hearing before the subcom. on Crime to consider the Anti-terrorism Act of 1986. (draft tert, p. 145-171), to establish Federal Criminal Jurisdiction over and revised extradition procedures relating to act of international terrorism. Title II is cited as the extradition Act of 1986.

Also consider H.R. 4288 (text, p. S-7) and similar S.1929 (text p. 13-16 and both the terrorist prosecution Act to Authorize Federal Prosecution of and criminal penalties for terrorist attacks against U.S. citizens abroad. Supplementary material (p. 3-12-181-190) includes a submitted statement, correspondence and :

(CIS)

0647 H 521-25

Terrorism.

August 26, 1985, February 28, May 14-15, 1986. 99-1; 99-2, iii + 327 p. GPO $ 9.50 CIS/MF/6 Item 1020-A; 1020-B. .Y 4. J 89/1:99/91. MC 87-674. LC-600875.

Committee Serial No. 91. Hearing before the subcom. on civil and constitutional rights to examine the characteristics of international and domestic terrorism and U.S. anti-terrorism programmes and politics. Also reviews state and local law enforcement agency roles in preventing domestic terrorism.

(CIS)

0648 H-181- 30.2 April 28, 1977 P. 111-266.

Witness : SAMPSON, Arthur F., Commr, Public Building Service; accompanied by Sanders, Wilbur H; Rep. Commr;

Mankin, Hart T., GSA Dir of Budget; and Johnson W.L. Jr., GSA Asst. Administrator for Admin.

Statement : Budget explanation for the public Building Service FY 72 request, emphasizing raising of cleaning standards, improvement of Federal Protective Service, needs of newly organized U.S. Postal Service and use of the lease construction concept as opposed to direct federal building construction (p. 111-115, 194-266).

Discussion : Potential rent savings and cost benefits from lease construction projects, guidelines and policies used on new building architectural design; problems in transferring funding Mechanisms from Post office Dept off to new U.S. Postal Service; GSA experience and policies for protecting Public buildings in event of bomb threats. (p. 116-158)

Factors governing site selection of and provision of parking facilities for, new government building, GSA role in minority hiring contract compliance regarding Federal building construction (p. 159-193).

(CIS)

0649 H. 381-5

Safety of U.S. Diplomats.

April 27, 1970. 91-2 + Item 1017. iii + 10p.

Yu. F 76/1 : D62/27.

9217 (71). 75-611444.

Hearing before the subcom on Inter-American Affairs on problems raised by terrorist attacks upon U.S. diplomatic personnel abroad. Hearings later adjorned to executive session.

(CIS)

0650 H 641-9. Security in Federal Buildings.

March 10, 11, 1971. 92-1 +. Item 1024.

iv + 150 P. Yu. p 96/11 : 92-2. 9229 (71).

Committee Serial No. 92-2. Hearings before the subcom on Public Buildings and Grounds on Security measures necessary to protect life and property in the capital building and all other Federal buildings. Includes submitted statements and correspondence (P. 138-150).

(CIS)

0651 H 381-45.

Northern Ireland.

February 28 - March 1, 1972. 92-2 +. Item 1017.

vi + 639 p. Index. Yu. F76/1 : Ir 2/3.

13477 (72)72-602621.

Hearing before the subcom on Europe to consider origins and possible settlement of the civil conflict in Northern Ireland, includes discussion on various legislative proposals supporting on official U.S. position, including H. Res. 653, similar to S. Res 180 and H Con. Res 523, to urge an end to British internment of political prisoners, withdrawal of British forces from Ulster, end to direct rule from London and the convening of a conference of all parties to pave the way for unification of Ireland, includes submitted statement by Members of Congress (p. 313-344), and a subject Index (p. 633-639). Appendix (p. 345-631) contains submitted statements, correspondence, resolution and press reports and article, including :

(a) Appeal of conscience Foundation "Tension Northern Ireland "Fact finding report" (p. 347-359).
(b) Commentary by a group of Northern Ireland citizens on Northern Ireland government white paper, a record of constructive change "August 20, 1971". (p.401-423)
(c) Kramer, Jane "Letter from Ireland" From New Yorker, February 19, 1972 (p. 484-501).
(d) Government of Northern Ireland White paper "A Record of constructive change" presented to Parliament by command of the Governer of Northern Ireland, Aug. 1971, text (p. 528-537).
(e) Power, Paul F. "Conflict and pluralism the case of Northern Ireland" Paper, 1971 annual meeting of Intl. Studies Assn, San Juan, Puerto Rico (p. 543-558).
(f) Northern Ireland "Troubles in perspective," Statement prepared by Ulster citizens living in Great Britain (p. 559-567).
(g) Ulster Unionist Party "Ulster-the Facts" September 1969 (p. 592-618).

(CIS)

0652 H 482-2

Political Kidnappings, 1968-73.
Aug. 1, 1973. 93-1. S/N 5270-01924.
iii + 54 + VP. Index.
Y. In 8/15: P 75/96, 8-73.

29920 (73) 73-602521.

Staff study on political kidnappings, 1968-73, of U.S. and foreign diplomats and businessmen in various parts of world. Reviews motivations of kidnappers and preventive security measures by U.S. and international organisations, presents case studies of major political kidnappings and describes terrorist groups alleged to participate in kidnappings. Appendices (p. 34-54) contain chronological list of major political kidnappings and papers, "Trotskyism and Terrorism." Includes index (p. I.V.).

(CIS)

0653 H 481-3

Theory and Practice of Communism,
Part-3.
(Expocuba).
October 17, 18, 1973. 93-1.
V + 2191-2372 + ix P. il. Index.
S/N 5270-02225.
CIS/MF/4. Item 1026.
Yu. In 8/15:C73/973/Pt. 3.

73-603236. 09085(74).

Continuation of hearings on communist activities and policies. This volume focuses on Cuban Communist influence in the U.S. and Latin America and includes information on EXPOCUBA, a pro-Castro regime exposition held July 26-29, 1973, in NYC to show films, publication and other exhibits on life in present day cuba.

Appendices (p. 2229-2372) include:

(a) Material on EXPOCUBA, including committee Staff Study (p. 2238-2257) of American sponsors (p. 2229-2257).

(b) Correspondence and photos depicting revolutionary activity in Cuba (p. 2260-2271). Material submitted by H. Romersation.
(c) Ramirez, Carlos (et al), "The only Road Workers, Power and socialism", Argentinian Trotskyite rationale for need for terrorism in Argentina, from International Information Bulletin, Published by Socialist Workers Party (SWP), NYC, October 1972 (p. 2277-2314).
(d) Resolutions of the fifth congress of the Revolutionary workers party, on establishing Argentine guerrilla warfare units, from International Internal Discussion Bulletin, SWP, April 1973 (p.2315-2360).
(e) "The Barzman Letter", and related correspondence and analytic article allegedly showing connection between minority group in SWP and International Trotskyites, from SWP Discussion Bulletin, July 1973 (p. 2361-2369).

(CIS)

0654 H 481-08.

Terrorism, Part 1.

February 27, 28, March 21, 22, 26, 1974, 93-2.

vi+2951-3083+vi P. Index.

S/N 52 70-02477.

CIS/MF/4 .Item 1026.

Yu. In 8/15: T27/Pt. 1.

Hearing to acquire knowledge on world-wide terrorist activities including relationship of terrorism to U.S. internal security, and to assess adequacy of existing Federal legislation. This volume focuses on possible consistencies of character structure in persons committing terrorist crimes and examines potential methods of preventing and controlling terrorism. Hearing on Feb. 28 held in executive session. Includes index of individuals, organisations and Publications (p. i-vi).

(CIS)

0655 H. 482-4

Terrorism.

August 1, 1974. 93. 2.

iv+246+xxxiii P. il. Index.

S/N 5270-02496.

CIS/MF/5 Yu. In 8/15: T 27/2.

Staff study on U.S. and foreign terrorist groups recently involved in violent activities while claiming political objectives. Contains following chapters :

I Latin America Terrorist Organisation (p. 9-27).
II Palestinian and other Middle East Terrorist Organisation (p. 29-47).
III African Terrorist Organisation (p. 49-64).
IV European Terrorist Organisations (p. 65-70).
V Far Eastern Terrorist Organisations (p. 71-75).
VI U.S. Communist Positions on the use of Terror and Guerrilla Tactics (p. 76-96).
VII Terrorist Acts in the U.S. Includes review of alleged activities of Weatherman,. black extremist groups including Black liberation Army, and Symbionese Liberation Army (SLA) (p. 97-164).

Appendices (p. 165-246) includes.

(a) FAA statistics on aircraft hijackings (p. 165-167).
(b) Newspaper articles relating to SLA activities (p.169-19).

(c) FBI articles on terrorism. From FBI Law Enforcement Bulletins and other journals, 1970-73 (p. 199-232).
(d) Footnotes to text (p. 233-246).

(CIS)

0656 H. 482-1.
The Symbionese Liberation Army.
February 18, 1974, 93-2. v+13+iii P. Index.
+CIS/MF/3 Yu. In 8/15: Sy 6.

74-600973.

Staff Study presenting available information on the Symbionese Liberation Army (SLA). Contains : a review of SLA activities, including details of the Oakland School Superintendent murder and the Patricia Hearst Kidnapping; profiles of Known SLA members and associates; description of materials found in searches of SLA headquarters and members' residences, and analyses of SLA correspondence and tactics. Includes an Index to individuals, organisations and publications (p. ii-iii).

(CIS)

0657 H 641-15.1 : March 21, 1974. P. 3-12.
Witness: Knight, H. Stuart, Dir. US Secret Service.

Statement and Discussion : Potential benefits to foreign diplomatic missions of increasing Executive Protective Service Force, particularly in light of International terrorism increase.

(CIS)

0658 H 181-48. 11: March 6, 1974. P. 451-574.
Witness : Kelley, Clearence M. Dir., FBI accompanied by Callahan, Nicholar., Assoc Dir. Budget Explanation : FBI request for Fy 75 (Submitted justification, p. 452-480) for the following activities :

(a) Criminal investigations of kidnapping, extortion, aircraft crimes, bank robbery and other federal offenses.
(b) Domestic intelligence relating to espionage, counter-espionage, sabotage, treason, sedition and subversion.
(c) Coordination and dissemination of security data.
(d) Specialized security programs concerning sensitive government application and employee investigations.
(e) Uniform crime reporting and compilations of statistics on extent and fluctuations of crime, arrests, convictions and related crime data.
(f) National crime information to centre to computerize national index of documented law enforcement information relating to identifiable property, wanted persons, and criminal histories.
(g) Identification function and scientific crime detection.
(h) Training activities and operations of FBI Academy, Quantico, Va.

Discussion : Explanation of FBI employee promotion system; extent of FBI fingerprint identification activities (graphs, p. 504-509); summary of internal studies of FBI operations; Work of national crime information centre and review (groups, p. 526-534) of nation-wide crime trends (p. 428-536).

Review of FBI activities relating to extremist and revolutionary groups (summar p. 537-541); accomplishments of FBI organized crime activities (Summar, P. 548-550); overview of civil rights cases handed by FBI Fy 73 inves-

tigative accomplishments by category and surveillance procedures (p. 537-574).
(CIS)

0659 H 381-8
International Terrorism.
June 11, 18, 19, 24, 1974.
93-2. vii + 219 P. + CIS/MF/5.
.Item 1017.
Yu. F 76/1 : T 27.
02044 (75) 74-603160.

Hearing before the subcom on near East and South Asia on the nature and forms of international terrorism, analyzes cycles of violence in the Middle East, problems posed for the U.S., and psychology and evolution of terrorism. Appendix (p. 161-219) includes witness biographies and articles, including:

(a) CRS, "International Terrorism". (p. 170-175).

(b) Hutchinson, Martha C., "The concept of Revolutionary Terrorism" from conflict Resolution, Vol. 16 (p. 176-188).

(c) Wolf, John B., "Mideast Profile: The cycle of Terror and counter Terror", from Intl Perspectives No. V-Dec. 1973. (p. 189-195).

(CIS)

0660 H 481-1 Terrorism, Part 2.
May 8, 14, 16, 22, 29, 30,
June 13, 1974. 93-".
vi=3085-3322+viii p. 11 . Index.
$2.30 CIS/MF/5.
.Item 1026.
Y4. In8/15:T27/pt.2.
13404 (75) 74-602406.

Continuation of hearings to acquire knowledge on worldwide terrorist activities, including the relationship of terrorism to U.S. internal security and to assess the adequacy of existing Federal legislation.

Appendices (p. 3233-3321) include :

(a) Burns International Investigation Bureau, Executive Protection Handbook, 1974 (p. 3233-3259).

(b) Prosser, George, "Terror in the U.S. : An Introduction to Elementary Tactics and Some Questions on Tactics" from Terror and Urban Guerrillas, (p. 3264-3280).

(c) Mallin, Jay, "The Military vs. Urban Guerrillas" from Marine Corps Gazette (p. 3281-3288).

(d) Luks, Allan, "Revolution in the Blood" (p. 3289-3298).

(e) State Dept. States signatory or parties to the Tokyo, Hague and Montreal Conventions, list (p. 3301-3308).

(f) State Dept, Anti-terrorism proposals in the UN, resume and voting list (p. 3310-3318).

(g) Joint Soviet-Syrian statement, from Moscow. News, Apr. 27, 1974 (p. 3319-3321).

Includes the individual, organisation and publication index (p. i-viii).

(CIS)

0661 H 481-2 Terrorism, Part 3.
June 26, 27 July 10, 11, 23.
August 13, 1974. 93-2.
vi+3915-4130+vip. il. Index.
$2.15 CIS/MF/5.
*Item 1026.
Y4. In 8/15:T27/pt.3.
13405 (75) 74-602406.

Continuation of hearings on terrorism and national security. Includes testimony on ethics of media coverage, personal experience with terrorists, detailed histories of terrorist groups and advisability of multidiscipline study action advisory groups for combating terrorism. Appendix (p. 4029-4130) contains exhibits submitted by witnesses, including :

(a) Pamphlets and literature from the Symbionese Liberation Army (SLA) (p.4029-4059) and the Black Muslims (p. 4060-4089).
(b) Unpublished articles by Claude L. Fly on kidnapping and capital punishment (p. 4091-4110).
(c) State Dept views on terrorists kidnappings, including suggested personal security measures (p. 4111-4130).

Also includes an Index (p. i-iv) of individuals, organisations, and publications.

(CIS)

0662 H 481-3
Terrorism, Part 4.
July 30, August 1, 15, 20, 1974.
93-2. vi+4131-4477+xi p.
Index. $3.15.
S/N 5270-02654. CIS/MF/6.
.Item 1026.
Y4. In8/15:T27/pt.4.
03664 (75) 74-602406.

Continuation of hearings on terrorism and national security. Includes testimony by law enforcement agencies and social science researchers. Appendix (p. 4221-4477) contains correspondence, papers on urban guerrilla's groups and submitted responses to questions from the subcom including:

(a) Rosenbaum, David M., "Interviews with Members of Urban Undergrounds" interviews with Irish and Zionist underground figures (p. 4252-4321).
(b) Justice Dept information regarding U.S. citizens' support of terrorism in Northern Ireland (p.4345-4422).
(c) Jenkins, Brian M. (Rand Corp.), "An Urban Strategy for Guerrillas and Governments," Aug. 1972 (p. 4448-4460).
(d) Jenkins, B.M., "Soldiers versus Gunmen: The Challenge of Urban Guerrilla Warfare," Mar. 1974 (p. 4461-4469).
(e) Jenkins, B.M., "Should Corporations be Prevented From Paying Ransom?" Sept. 1974 (p. 4470-4477).

Also includes an Index (p. i-xi) of individuals, organisations and publications.

(CIS)

0663 H 461-18.2 October, 28, 1975. p. 79-98.

Witness : Taylor, Theodore B., bd chm, Intt. Research and Technology Corp.

Statement and Discussion : Analysis of dangers from possible terrorist use of nuclear weapons.

(CIS)

0664 H461-21-1: September 30, 1975. p. 2-62.

Witness : Abu Lughod, Ibrahim, Prof.

Northwestern Univ.

SAID, Edward W., Prof. Columbia, Univ., fellow, Center for Advanced Study in Behavioral Sciences, Stanford, Calif. Statements and Discussion : Review of PLO formation and efforts to establish a Palestinian State; Explanation of PLO policies, internal differences and attitude towards terrorism; alleged U.S. hostility toward's Palestinians evidenced by support for Israel, non-recognition of the PLO and charged inhibition of public discussion on the Palestinian situation.

(CIS)

0665 H521-5

Internationally Protected Persons.

Bills; Unsworn Declarations Bills.

June 30, 1976. 94-2.

iii+110p. + CIS/MF/4.

.Item 1020. Y4. J89/1:94-45.

MC977-2532. LC 76-603517.

Committee serial no. 45. Hearing before the subcom. on criminal Justice to consider H.R. 12942 and identical H.R. 13709 (texts p. 36-58), the act for the Prevention and Punishment of crimes. Against Internationally Protected Persons, to implement : the convention to Prevent and Punish the Acts of Terrorism taking the forms of crimes against persons and related extortion that are of International significance; and the convention on the Prevention and Punishment of crimes against Internationally Protected Persons, including Diplomatic Agents. Bill was reported out Sept. 18, 1976, as H.R. 15552 (text committee rcpt. p. 59 85).

Includes brief testimony on H.R. 11106 and Identical H.R. 11217 (texts, p. 86-91), to authorize the use of unsworn declarations under penalty of perjury as evidence in Federal proceedings. Bill was reported out September 20, 1976. as H.R. 15531 (text, committee rpt. p. 92-110). Includes correspondence (p. 4-7).

(CIS)

0666 H523-39

Implementing International Conventions.

Against Terrorism.

September 18, 1976. 94-2. 16p.

+CIS/MF/3 .Item 1008-A.

H. Rpt. 94-1614.

Recommends passage of H.R. 15552, to implement : the convention to prevent and punish the Acts of Terrorism taking the form of crimes against persons and related extortion that are of international significance and the conven-

tion on the prevention and punishment of crimes against internationally protected persons, including diplomatic agents.

Includes dissenting views (p. 15-16) H.R. 15552 is related to H.R. 12942 and H.R. 13709.

(CIS)

0667 H461-80.3 August 3, 1978 p. 97-156.
Witnesses : Ledeen, Michael A., exeeditor,
Washington Review of Strategic and Intl. Studies.

Sr research staff member, Centre for strategic and Intl Studies, Georgetown Univ. Berger, Suzananne, political science prof. MIT. Statements: Review of the Social Economic and Political conditions contributing to domestic instability in France and Italy; examination of French and Italian communist parties; including extent of ties with soviet union and reasons for recent losses in electorate support; differing views on need for U.S. reassertion of opposition to communist presence in Western Europe. (p. 97-140) Discussion: Advocacy of coherent U.S. foreign policy, with recommendations; assessment of possibility for totalitarian rule following communist party selection by voters; conflicting opinion on French and Italian communist parties linkages with terrorist groups. (p. 141-156).

(ICS)

0668 H643-19
Act to combat International Terrorism.
October 15, 1978. 95-2, 20 p.
+CIS/MF/3 .Item 1008-A.
1+Rpt. 95-1801, pt. 1.

Recommends passage, with an amendment in the nature of substitute of H.R. 13387, the Act to combat International terrorism, to strengthen federal programs and domestic terrorism. Includes provisions for: Presidential reports to congress on and sanctions against nations supporting terrorism; DOT assessment of foreign airport security measures and mandatory identification and detection taggants in certain explosives. Also amends the Federal Aviation Act to strengthen aircraft sabotage and piracy sanctions.

H.R. 13387 is related to S. 2236.

(CIS)

0669 H522-10
Federal capabilities in crisis management and terrorism.
December 1978. 95-2. iii+232 p.
+CIS/MF/5 .Item 1020.
.Y4. J89/1:c 86/11.
LC 79-602918.

Committee Print no. 27. subcom on civil and constitutional rights staff Report examining federal policies and capabilities for preventing and responding to terrorism. Appendices (p. 19-232) include text (p. 35-51) of Executive order 12036, US. Intelligence Activities Jan 24, 1978 and news media views on Press coverage of terrorist incidents within the U.S. (p. 63-232).

(CIS)

0670 H521-13

Federal capabilities in crisis management and Terrorism.
August 16, September 15, October 4, 1978, 95-2.
iii+116 p. +CIS/MF/4..Item 1020.
.Y4. J89/1:95/77. MC 79-930. LC 79-601159.

Committee Serial no. 77. oversight hearings before the subcom on civil and constitutional rights to examine federal policies and capabilities for preventing and responding to acts of terrorism.

(CIS)

0671 H961-20

Investigation of the Assassination of Martin Luther King Jr. Vol. 6.
No. 17, 20, 21, 1978, 95-2.
iii+608 p. $500.
S/N 052-070-04876-0.
CIS/MF/9 .Item 1009.
.Y4 AS7:K 58/V-6.
MC 79-14371. LC 79 601289.

Continuation of hear'ng before the select committee on assassination to examine evidence relating to the Apr. 4, 1968 assassination in Memphis Tenn. of Martin Luther King Jr. This volume focuses on allegation regarding FBI complicity in the kind of assassination, including charges that :

(a) FBI 1967-68 counter intelligence activities against King and the Southern Christian Leadership Conference (SCLC) served to create a climate conducive to assassination.

(b) FBI made payments to or used informants in the Invader a Memphis group of young black activists, to provoke violence in Mar.-28 in which King participated to support striking sanitation workers in order to manoeuvre kings' return to Memphis several days later. Committee Staff members participate in examination of witnesses. Where relevant, former affiliations are cited representing witnesses 1968 employment. Includes transcript of committee staff interview with former FBI agent Theron D. Rushing No. 16, 1978 (p. 376-404) and marralions by committee chief counsel G. Robert Blackey (p. 407-413) for abstract of most significant narration.

(CIS)

0672 H 961-20. 1: No. 17, 21, 1978, p 58-96;
607-608.

Witness: Blakey, G. Robert, Committee Chief Counsel and staff Dir. Narration: Failure of committee investigation to develop evidence of direct FBI involvement in King' assassination; possibility of indirect FBI contribution resulting from 1962. Initiation of a campaign to discredit King; Chronology of anti King activities and assessment of personal motivations of FBI Director J Edgar Hoover; goals and mechanics of intensified 1967-68 counter-intelligence programs targeting king and black nationalist group. (p. 58-90). Inability to uncover evidence of FBI link to convicted assassin James Earl Ray suggesting existence of conspiracy. (p. 607-608).

(CIS)

0673 H 641-1.

International Terrorism.

July 18-20, 25, 1978. 95-2.

vi+392 p. il+CIS/MF/6.

.Item 1024.

.Y4. p 96/11:95-61.

MC 79-5/36. LC 78-603737.

Committee Serial no. 95-61. Hearings before the subcom. on Aviation on H.R. 13261 (text, p. 1-22), the act to combat International terrorism to strengthen Federal programs and policies for combating international and domestic terrorism includes provisions to :

(a) Require periodic report by the president on acts of international terrorism, nations supporting terrorism and U.S. and international actions which assisted in positive termination of incidents.

(b) Authorize the president to terminate assistance under the foreign Assistance Act of 1961 and the Arms Export Control Act, approve no export licenses, and extend no duty free treatment to nations supporting terrorism.

(c) Amend the Federal Aviation Act of 1958 to require DOT to assess and publicize findings on security of foreign airports and suspend commercial air service to airports not having appropriate security standard. Also would provide additional sanctions for hijacking threats, and hoaxes.

(d) Require Treasure Dept. to establish standards for identification and detection taggants, substances add to an explosive material during manufacture which permit identification of manufacturer following detonation, or detection of explosives prior to detonation.

Full committee chairman Harold T. Johnson (D-Calif) presents a statement on July 18. Full Committee member Don H. Clansen (R-Calif) presents a statement and questions witness on July 18, includes "Evaluation of the needs and Benefits of Explosives Tagging program," Juhius Rath (Mgmt. Science Assocs) final rpt MSA 317-1, prepare for But of Alcohol, Tobacco and Firearms, Mar. 1978, with tables and graphs (p. 207-392).

(CIS)

0674 H641-10

Aircraft Piracy International Terrorism.

February 28, March 1, 1979, 96-1.

iv+437 p. il. + CIS/MF/7.

.Item 1024. .Y4 p96/11:96-2.

MC79-15912. LC 79-602451.

Committee Serial no. 96-2. Hearings before the subcom. on Aviation to consider H.R. 1834 and similar H.R. 2441 (texts p. 3-54), both the Act to combat International Terrorism to amend the Federal Aviation Act of 1958 to strengthen Federal Programs for confronting international domestic terrorism, particularly aircraft hajackings.

Focuses on bills' provisions to require addition of substances to certain explosives for purpose of identifying manufacturers and users of detonated explosives (identification taggants) or for purpose of locating bombs prior to detonation (detection taggants).

Supplementary material (p. 311-437).

Includes submitted statements, correspondence and "compatibility of iden-

tification taggants with explosives," Aerospace corp., prepared for Bureau of Alcohol, Tobacco and Firearms (BATE) Aug. 1978, with tables. (p.348-389).

(CIS)

0675 H643-12. Act to combat International Terrorism.
September 11, 1979. 96-1. 26 p.
+CIS/MF/3. Item 1008-A.
H. Rpt. 96-424, pt. 1.
MC 79-23492.

Recommends passage, with an amendment in the nature of a substitute, of H.R. 2441, the Act to combat International Terrorism, to Amend the Federal programs for confronting international and domestic terrorism particularly aircraft hijackings by :

(a) Requiring biannual reports by the President on international terrorist acts, nations supporting terrorism, and U.S. and international action contributing to ending terrorist incidents.

(b) Authorizing the President to terminate assistance under the foreign Assistance Act, to prohibit defense sales and credit extension under the arms export control act and to deny licenses for defense and technical materials export under the arms export control Act and the Export Administration Act sanctions would be applied against countries supporting terrorism.

(c) Requiring DOT to assess foreign airports' security and to suspend commercial air service to airports not meeting security standards Bill also would provide additional Federal penalties for hijacking, threats, and hoaxes.

(CIS)

0676 H381-36. 1:April 2, 1979. p. 2-40.

Witness : McLaughlin, Sister Janice, Washington office on Africa, former press sec, catholic commission for justice and Peace in Rhodesia. Smart, Malcolm, head Africa section research dept, Amnesty Intl. Statement and Discussion : Overview of current situation in Zimbabwe-Rhodesia. Focusing on causes of conflict, terrorist tactics of the government' counter-insurgency campaign, plight of the refugees, and complicity of the U.S. opposition to lifting sanctions, description of human rights violations resulting from government legislation and policy with emphasis on detention without trial, political trials, torture and executions.

(CIS)

0677 H522-19
Claim Settlement under Nato-Status of Forces.
Agreements; Criminal justice; and other.
Legal Issues. (Germany, Italy, and England).
December 1978. 95-2.
vii+346p. + CIS/MF/6.
.Item 1020.
.Y4. J89/1:C52/7. LC 79-604205.

Committee Print No. 31. Report of a study mission headed by George E. Danielson (D-Calif) to West Germany, Italy and Great Britain, conducted Dec. 7-17, 1978; to gather information on legal and diplomatic issues including;

(a) Criminal jurisdiction and claims settlement under NATO-Status of Forces Agreement (p. 13-27).

(b) Immunity of States and their diplomatic personnel in civil actions (p. 29-39).
(c) Patents and copyrights (p. 47-57).
(d) Dispute processing by English masters and American magistrates (p. 59-66).
(e) Attorney's fees and legal aid in England (p. 67-78)

Appendices (p. 79-346) contain texts of international conventions, West German, Italian and English laws and U.S. bills, articles and reports, including :

(a) Great Britain, State Immunity Act 1978, text, July 20, 1978 (p. 84-92).
(b) Council of Europe, European Convention on State Immunity, English texts of convention and additional protocol, signed in Basle, Switzerland, May 16, 1972 (p. 92-104).
(c) Great Britain, Diplomatic Privileges Act 1964, text, July 31, 1964 (p. 105-111).
(d) Council of Europe, European Convention on the Suppression of Terrorism, English text, signed in Strasbourg, France, Jan. 27, 1977, with explanatory rpt. (p. 112-125).
(e) Pisano, Vittorfranco S. (LC Law Library), "Study of the Restructured Italian Intelligence and Security Services" May 26, 1978 (p. 129-208).
(f) U.S., patent and copyright legislation, texts of 95th Congress H.R. 2101, H.R. 6063, the Performance Rights Amendment of 1977 and H.R. 8261, the Visual Artists' Moral Rights Amendment of 1977, Jan.-July 1977 (p. 224-251).
(g) West Germany, employee invention law, text, July 25, 1957 as amended through June 27, 1970, with regulations governing compensation to be paid for employees' inventions made in private employment, July 20, 1959, excerpts, Industrial Property, Sept. 1972 (p. 252-275).
(h) International Convention for the Protection of Performers, Producers of Phonograms and Broadcasting Organizations (Rome Convention), English text, UNESCO copyright Bull, 1961 (p. 277-284).
(i) U.S., Magistrate Act of 1978, 95th Congress S. 1613, to improve access to Fed Courts by increasing magistrates jurisdiction, text as reported to House, July 17, 1978 (p. 296-313).
(j) Camden Community Law Center, Great Britain, annual report 1977/78 and five-year review (p. 317-338).
(k) "Law Society : History, Organization and Work of Solicitors in England and Wales" Apr. 1978 (p. 339-349).

(CIS)

0678 H181-20. 5: Feb. 21, 1980. p. 599-669.
Witness: Slayton, William L., Dep Asst Sec,
Foreign Bldgs, State Dept.

Budget Explanation: State Dept FY81 request (submitted justifications, 600-653) for acquisition, operation, and maintenance of buildings abroad under direct appropriations and under special foreign currency program.

Insertions: Foreign Service post requiring improvement in counter-terrorist physical security to control public access, summary (p. 660-664).

(CIS)

0679 H481-1
Terrorism, Part 2.
May 8, 14, 16, 22, 29, 30.
June 13, 1974, 93-2.
vi+3085-3322+viii p. il. Index.
$2.30 CIS/MF/5.

.Item 1026.

.Y4. In 8/15:T27/pt. 2.

13404 (75) 74-602406

Continuation of hearings to acquire knowledge on worldwide terrorist activities including the relationship of terrorism to U.S. internal security and to assess the adequacy of existing Federal legislation. Appendices (p. 3233-3321) includes:

(a) Burns International Investigation Bureau, Executive Protection Handbook, 1974 (p. 3222-3259).

(b) Prosser, George, "Terror in the U.S.: An Introduction to Elementary Tactics and some Questions on Tactic's" from Terror and Urban Guerrillas, (p. 3264-3280).

(c) Mallin, Jay, "Military vs. Urban Guerrillas" from Marine Corps Gazette (p. 3281-3288).

(d) Luks, Allan, "Revolution in the Blood" (p. 3289-3298).

(e) State Dept, States signatory or parties to the Tokyo, Hague and Montreal conventions, list (p. 3301-3308).

(f) State Dept, Anti-Terrorism proposals in the U.N. resume and voting list (p. 3310-3318).

(g) Joint Soviet-Syrian statement, from Moscow News, Apr. 27, 1974 (p. 3319-3321).

Includes individual, organisation and publication index (p. i-viii).

(CIS)

0680 H481-3

Terrorism Part 4.

July 30, August 1, 15, 20, 1974.

93-2. vi+4131-4477+xi p.

Index. $3.15.

S/N 5270-02654. CIS/MF/6.

.Item 1026.

.Y4. In 8/15. T27/pt. 4.

03664 (75). 74-602406

Continuation of hearings on terrorism and national security. Includes testimony law enforcement agencies and social science researchers.

Appendix (p. 4221-4477) contains correspondence, papers on urban guerrilla groups, and submitted responses to questions from the subcom including:

(a) Rosenbaum, David M., "Interviews with members of urban underground" Interviews with Irish and Zionist underground figures (p. 4252-4321).

(b) Justice Dept information regarding O.S. citizen's support of terrorism in Northern Ireland (p. 4345-4422).

(c) Jenkins, Brian M. (Rand Corp.), "An Urban Strategy for Guerrillas and Governments," Aug. 1972 (p. 4448-4460).

(d) Jenkins, B.M., "Soldiers versus Gunmen, The Challenge of Urban Guerrilla Warfare," Mar. 1974 (. 4461-4469).

(e) Jenkins, B.M., "Should corporations be Prevented from Paying Ransom?" Sept. 1974 (p. 4470-4477).

Also includes an Index (p. i-xi) of individuals, organisations and publications.

(CIS)

0681 H481-2

Terrorism, Part 3.
June 26, 27, July 10, 11, 23,
August 13, 1974. 93-2.
vi+3915-4130+vi p. il. Index.
$2.15 CIS/MF/5.
.Item 1026.
.Y4. In8/15 : T27/pt. 3

13405 (75) 74-602406

Continuation of hearings on terrorism and national security includes testimony on ethics of media coverage, personal experience with terrorists, detailed histories of terrorist groups and advisability of multidiscipline study/action advisory groups for combating terrorism.

Appendix.(p. 4029-4130) contains exhibits submitted by witnesses, including:

(a) Pamphlets and Literature from the symbionese Liberation Army(SLA) (p. 4029-4059) and the Black Muslims (p. 4060-4089).

(b) Unpublished articles by Claude L. Fly on kidnapping and capital punishment (p. 4091-4110).

(c) State Dept views on terrorist kidnappings, including suggested personal security measures (p. 4111-4130).

Also includes an Index (p. i-vi) of individuals, organisations and publications.

(CIS)

0682 H433-3

Intelligence Authorization Act for FY 81.
May 7, 1980. 96-2. 11p.
+CIS/MF/3. Item 1008-C.
H.Rpt. 96-926-pt. 1. MC 80-17228.

Recommends passage of H.R. 7152, to authorize Fy 81 appropriation for CIA, DOD and other agencies' foreign intelligence programmes, the Intelligence community staff, CIA Retirement and Disability system and FBI counter-terrorism programme.

(CIS)

0683 H621-11

H.R. 1956 and H.R. 2019. Benefits to federal employees who are victims of terrorism. June 12, 24, 1985 99-1 v+195 p + CIS/MF/4. Item 1022-B, 1022-C.
Y4. p84/10; 99-12. LC 86-600996.

Committee Serial no. 99-12. Joint hearings before subcom on civil service, the subcom on compensation and employee benefits and the house foreign affairs committee, subcom on International operations to consider H.R. 1956, to amend the Hostage Relief Act of 1980 and related H.R. 2014, both to provide educational and medical benefits and other compensation to Federal employees and their families who are held captive, disabled, or killed as a result of terrorism or other hostile action encountered in foreign countries due to their relationship to the U.S.

H.R. 2019 also applies to hostile actions occuring within the U.S., but does

not cover members of the armed services. Suplementary material (p. 50-54, 154-195) includes correspondence and President's commission on Hostage compensation, final report and recommendations, September 21, 1981 (p. 157-195).

(CIS)

0684 H380-1

Economic sanctions against Libya. Communications from the President. January 21, 1986. 99. 2. 1+2 p. +CIS/MF/3. Item 996-A, 1-996-B.

H. Doc. 99-148.

Transmittal of Jan. 8, 1986 executive order, under the International Emergency Economic Power Act and the National Emergencies Act, to block Libyan Government and Central Bank Properties and other assets in U.S. Possession.

Action is intended to aid dissolution of U.S. Libya economic ties and to preclude possible unlawful Libyan Acts against U.S. interest.

(CIS)

0685 H380-2

National Emergency with Respect to Libya communication from the President.

January 21, 1986, 99-2 k+4p+CIS/MF/13.

Item 996-A; 996-B.

H DOC 99-153.

Y I I/7:99-153

Transmittal of Jan. 7, 1986 executive order, under the International Emergency Economic Powers Act, the International Security and Development Corporation Act of 1985 and the National Emergencies Act, to prohibit;

(a) Exports to and imports from Libya.
(b) Lilbyan air carrier and ship entry to the U.S.
(c) U.S. contractor support of Libyan projects.
(d) U.S. citizen loans to Libya.
(e) U.S. citizen travel to Libya.

Action is in response to Libyan Government policies and activities supporting international terrorism.

(CIS)

0686 H381-3

American Missing in South-East Asia.

June 27, 1985 99-1.

iii+109p. + CIS/MF/4.

Item 1017-A; 1017-B.

Y4. F76/1: 508/39.

LC 85 603366.

Hearing before the subcom on Asian and Pacific Affairs to examine continued U.S. efforts to account for prisoners of war (POWS) and personnel missing in actions (MIAS) in Southeast Asia. Full committee Members Benjamin A. Civilman (R-NY) and Robert J. Lagomarsino (R-Calif) present statements (p. 6-7, 11) and participate in questioning witnesses. Full Committee Members, John Mclain (R-Ariz) and Christopher H. Smith (R.NJ) and Reps. Bill Hindon (R-NC) and Robert C. Smith (R.NH) participate in questioning witnesses. Tes-

timony from former POW Robert Garwood was received in executive session and is not included in featuring transcript.

(CIS)

0687 H381-8

Islamic Fundamentalism and Islam.

June 24, July 15, September 30, 1985, 99-1.

iv+443 p. + CIS/MF/7.

Item 1017-A; 1017-B.

Y4. F76/1. IS4.

LC 86-600981

Hearing before the subcom on Europe and the Middle East to examine the growth of Islamic fundamentalist and radical organizations and to assess implication for U.S. interest and policies in the Middle East.

Also reviews the status and implications of the Iran-Iraq war.

Full Committee Member Stephen J. Solaqi Z (D-NY) presents a statement (p. 149-150) and participates in questioning witnesses on July 15.

Appendices (p. 281-443) includes submitted statements, articles, correspondence witnesses, biographies, and;

(a) subcom staff, "Major Attack of Islamic Jihad and other Radical Islamic Groups" (p. 281-286).

(b) Esposito, John L. (Coll of the Holy Guess) "Islamic Revivalism" with bibl. (p. 298-313)

(c) Nader, George, "Interview with Sheikh Muhammed Hussen Fadl Allah" Middle East Insight, Vol-4, no. 2, 1985 (p. 326-335).

(d) Norton, Augustus R. (US Military Academy), "Harakat Amal" book chapter from the Emergence of a New Lebanan; Fantasy or reality 1984 (p. 336-378).

(e) Norton, Augustus R. (US Military Academy), "Political and Religious Extremism in the Middle East" (p. 376-390).

(f) Akhani, Shahrough (Uni. of SC), "Power Structure of the Islamic Republic of Iran" (p. 391-403).

(CIS)

0688 H383-7

Omnibus Diplomatic Security and Anti-terrorism Act of 1986.

March 12, 1986. 99-2.

iv+106p. +CIS/MF/4.

Item 1008-C; 1008-D.

H. Rept. 99-494.

Y1.1/8; 99-494.

Recommends passage, with an amendment in the nature of substitute, of H.R. 415, the omnibus Diplomatic Security and Anti-Terrorism Act of 1986, in the following titles:

Titles I through IV, the Diplomatic Security Act, to Authorize FY 96-FY90 appropriations for a restructure, State Dept Comprehensive security enhancement program for diplomatic missions and personnel abroad and foreign missions in the U.S.

Title, V, to amend the State Department Basic Authorities Act of 1956 to authorize state dept FY86-FY87 appropriations for rewards for information regarding international terrorism and major drug trafficking offenses, and to

amend Export Administration Act of 1979 to restrict U.S. exports to terrorist countries.

Title VI, to amend the Atomic Energy Act of 1954 to direct the President to take action to combat international nuclear terrorism, including suspension of nuclear cooperation with nations which have not rectified the convention on the Physical Security of nuclear Material.

Title VII, to direct the President to pursue multilateral cooperation and negotiations regarding measures to combat international terrorism.

Title VIII, the victims of Terrorism Compensations Act to authorize Federal agencies to pay medical and educational benefits and other compensation to civilian and military Federal employees and their families who are held captive, disabled, or killed as a result of hostile actions encountered in the U.S. or foreign countries due to their relationship to the U.S.

Title IX, the International maritime and port Security Act to amend the ports and Waterways Safety Act of 1972 to authorize coast Guard appropriations to improve the security of port, harbor, and coastal facilities. Includes provisions relating to passenger ship-security.

Title X, the Fascell Fellowship Act to establish a Fellowship program to provide scholars, Student and teachers in Russian and East European languages and area studies with temporary positions at diplomatic post in the Soviet Union and Eastern European Countries.

(CIS)

0689 H383-3

Supporting the Contradora-Process.
February 26, 1986, 99-2.
iii+55 p. + CIS/MF/3.
Item 1008-C; 1008-D.
H. Rpt. 99-474.
Y1.11/8. 99-474.

Recommends passage of H. Con. Res. 282, to reaffirm congressional support for Latin American Contradora Group country initiatives for negotiating a Peaceful settlement of Central American Conflicts, focusing on Nicaragua and El Salvador.

(CIS)

0690 H381-25.

Central American Counter-terrorism Act of 1985.
October 24, November 1985, 99-1.
iv+321 p. +CIS/MF/6.
Item 1017-A; 1017-B.
Y4. F76/1: C 83/985.

Hearing to consider H.R. 3463 (p. 221-223), (text, p. 221-223), the Central American counter-terrorism Act of 1985, the Administration bill, to amend the Foreign Assistance Act of 1961 to authorize FY 86 appropriation for military and civilian counter-terrorism assistance and law enforcement agency improvement for El Salvador, Honduras, Panama, Guatemala and Costa Rica. Includes a submitted statement (p. 319-321).

0691 H181-24-2:

March 4, 1986 p. 123-319.

Witness: Webster, William H., Dir., FBI, Budget Explanation: FBI request for FY 87 (submitted Justifications p. 124-258) for :

(a) Criminal and Security investigations concentrated on organized and white collar cirme, drug crime, civil rights violations, terrorism and foreign counter-intelligence.

(b) Investigative support, including FBI agent training, forensic laboratory services formation and retrieval services and maintenance of legal attaches in foreign countries.

(c) State and local assistance, and criminal justice, and statistical services through the national crime information on center and uniform crime Reporting Program.

(CIS)

0692 H381-19

Victims of Terrorism Compensation.

Act. October 8, 29, 1985. 99-1.

iii + 106 p. + CIS/MF/4.

Item 1017-A; 1017-B.

Y4.F76/1:V66.

LC 86-601198.

Contains transcript (p. 1-57) of subcom. on International Operations Oct. 8 markup session on H.R. 2851 (text, p. 13-28; dept rept, p. 45-47), the victims of Terrorism Compensation Act, to authorize Federal agencies to pay medical and educational benefits and other compensation to civilian and military Federal Employees and their families including foreign national and contract employees, who are held captive, disabled, or killed as a result of hostile action encountered in the U.S. or foreign countries due to their relationship to the U.S. Bill also provides cash payments to Government employees held captive in Iran between Nov. 1979 and Jan. 1981. Amended bill (text, p. 30-41) was favorably reported to the full committee.

Also contains transcript (p. 59-106) of Oct. 29 full Committee markup session to consider the subcom report on H.R. 2851, presented by Rep. Olympia J. Snowe (R.Maine) Amended bill (text, p. 80-93, draft subcom rpt. p. 95-106) was favorably reported to the House.

(CIS)

0693 H381-26

Human Rights in Peru.

November 13, 1985. 99-1.

iii + 103 p. + CIS/MF/4.

Item 1017-A; 1017-B.

Y4. F76/1:H88/39.

Hearing before the subcom on Human Rights and International Organizations and the subcom on Western Hemisphere Affairs to examine the prospects for democratic reforms in Peru, including the ability of recently elected President Alan Garcia to deal with guerrilla movement terrorist activities and human rights' abuses by military and national police forces.

(CIS)

0694 H380-10

Use of U.S. Armed Forces in Libya.
Communication from the President
April 16, 1986. 99-2.
i+1p. +CIS/MF/3.
Item 996-A; 996-B.
H. DOC. 99-201.
Y 1.1/7: 99-201.

Transmittal of report, in accordance with the war powers resolution notifying congress of U.S. air and naval force April 14, 1986 bombing strikes against selected targets in Tripoli and Benghazi, Libya in response to Libyan-sponsored terrorist attacks against U.S. citizens and installations and to deter further acts of Libyan supported terrorism.

(CIS)

0695 H381-39.1

January 28, 1986. p. 2-48.

Witness: Murphy, Richard, W., Asst. Sec., Bur of Near Eastern and South Asian Aff. State Dept. Statement and Discussion: Overview of Middle East political and economic developments; perspectives on efforts to resolve Middle East conflicts, considerations involved in proposed U.S. arms' sales to Jordan and other nations; review of efforts to reduce terrorist attacks in the Middle East.

(CIS)

0696 H381-21

Aftermath of the Achille Lauro Incident.
October 30, November 6,7, 1985.
99-1, iii+74 p. +CIS/MF/3.
Item 1017-A, 1017-B.
Y4. F76/1. AC 4.

Hearing before the subcom on International Operation to review U.S. Counter-terrorism activities in light of the Oct. 7, 1985 hijacking of the Guise ship Achille Lauro and the murder of passenger Leers Killing Hopper.

Includes transcript (p. 62-63) of Nov. 6, subcom markup session on H. Con. Res. 213 (Text, p. 55-56), to express the sense of congress that the U.S. should negotiate a multinational agreement with Western allies establishing a strategy for responding to a sharing intelligence on international terrorist incidents and that the U.S. should terminate foreign aid to nations that fail to prosecute terrorists. Amended bill was favorably reported.

Also includes transcript (p. 65-74) of Nov. 7 full committee markup session to receive report presented by subcom Chairman Dan Mica (D Fla) on H. Con. Res. 228 (text, p. 66-70) to condemn acts of terrorism and urge improvement of international collaboration against terrorism. Bill was favorably reported.

(CIS)

0697 H381-18

Legislation to Combat International Terrorism :
98th Congress.

November 9, 1983, June 7, 13, 19, September 26, 1984.
98-1; 98-2.
IV+461 p. il. CIS/MF/7.
Item 1017-A; 1017-B.
Y4, F76/1: L52/8.
MC 85-16260. LC 85-601445.

Hearings before the *Subcom on International Security and Scientific Affairs* to consider the following bills and resolutions to address international terrorism problems.

H. Res. 233 (text, p. 187-188), to urge the President to enter into negotiations with the Soviet Union to provide for mutual cooperation in dealing with the threat of accidental nuclear war caused by the acts of terrorism. H.R. 5612 (draft text, sectional analysis, p. 214-219 text, p. 220-326), the Acts for rewards for information concerning Terrorist acts, and administrative bill, to authorize Justice Dept and State Dept payment of rewards for information leading to prevention of terrorist activities against U.S. persons or property, or for information leading to arrest or conviction of terrorists. Includes provisions for informant eligibility for resident alien status and protection under the Federal Witness Security Programs.

(CIS)

0698 H521-50

Terrorism Legislation.
September 26, 1984. 98-2. iii+42p. 1-CIS/MF/3.
Item 1020-A; 1020-B.
Y4. J 89/1:98/155.
MC 85-18710. LC 85-601697.

Committee Serial No. 155: Hearing before the *Subcom on Crime* to consider the following Administration bills to Strengthen Federal programs for Combating International and Domestic terrorism:

H.R. 5612 (text, p. 3-9), the Act for Rewards for Information Concerning Terrorists' Acts, to authorize Justice and State Dept rewards for information regarding terrorist activity.

H.R. 5689 (text, p. 10-14), the Act for the Prevention and Punishment of the Crime of Hostage—Taking, to establish Federal Jurisdiction and Penalties in certain hostage taking cases. Bill would implement the International Convention Against the taking of Hostages.

H.R. 5690 (text, p. 15-24), the Aircraft Sabotage Act, to amend the Federal Aviation Act of 1959 to implement the Montreal Convention Strengthening aircraft piracy and sabotage sanctions.

(CIS)

0699 H521-25

Prohibition against the Training or Support of Terrorist Organisations Act of 1984.
August 2, 1984. 98-2.
iii+75. +CIS/MF/3
Item 1020-A; 1020-B.
Y4. J89/1: 98/82.

MC 85-11782. LC 85-601153.

Committee Serial No. 82, Hearing before the *Subcom on Civil and Constitutional Rights* to consider H.R. 5613 (text, p. 61-69), the Prohibition Against the Training or Support of Terrorist Organizations Act of 1984, the Administration bill, to impose criminal penalties on U.S.

Citizens or business providing military or intelligence assistance to international terrorist groups and governments which support terrorism. Supplementary material (p. 30-60, 70-75) include submitted statements, correspondence, and:

(a) Maechling, Charles, Jr., "Containing Terrorism" Foreign service, J. July/Aug. 1984 (p. 55-60)

(b) Act to combat International Terrorism, draft bill to amend the state Department Basic Authorities Act of 1986, related to H.R. S613, text (p. 70-75)

(c) Draft bill to amend the State Department Basic Authorities Act of 1956, related to H.R. S5613, text (p. 75).

(CIS)

0700 H.R. 5613 (draft text, sectional analysis, p. 206-214. text p. 227-235).

The Prohibition Against the Training or Support of Terrorist Organizations Act of 1984, an Administration Bill, to impose criminal penalties on U.S. Citizens or businesses providing military or intelligence assistance to international groups or foreign governments that support terrorism.

July 7 and 19 hearings were held jointly with the Subcom on International Operations. June 13 and Sep. 26 hearings were held before the full committee. Includes transcript (p. 182-186) of Sep. 26 full committee markup session on H.R. 6311 (text, p. 239-246), the 1984 Act to Combat International Terrorism, a clear bill, to amend the State Dept. Basic Authorities Act of 1956 to authorise State Dept payment of rewards for information regarding terrorist activity to urge the President to seek more effective international cooperation in combating terrorism, and to authorise additional appropriations for enhancement of security at U.S. missions abroad. Bill was favourably reported.

Appendices (p. 187-461) include submitted statements, witness written responses to Sub-Com. questions, and; H. Con. Res. 339, to convey the sense of Congress that the President seek an international convention for the suppression of terrorism, text (p. 236-238) Appendices also include Apr. 26. 1984 Presidential message (p. 189-219) transmitting draft texts of the Act for Rewards for information concerning Terrorist Acts, the Prohibition Against the training or support of Terrorist Organizations Act of 1984, and additional proposals as follows:

(a) The Act for the Prevention and Punishment of the Crime of Hostage-Taking, to implement the International Convention Against the Taking of Hostage by establishing Federal Jurisdiction and Penalties in certain hostage-taking cases, text and sectional analysis (p. 193-197).

(b) The Aircraft Sabotage Act, to amend the Federal Aviation Act of 1958 to implement the 1971 Montreal Convention for the Suppression of Unlawful Acts Against the Safety of Civil Aviation by expanding Federal Jurisdiction over terrorist acts involving hijacking and aricraft or aircraft facility sabotage, text and sectional analysis. (p. 197-206).

(CIS)

0701 J892-3

Basket I;

Implementation of the final act of the conference on security and cooperation in Europe : Findings Eleven Years, after Helsinki: Nov. 1986 99-2, IV+419p. GOP $12.00 CIS/ MF/7. Item 1089-C; 1089-D. Y4. Se 2:Eu7.

Commission on Security and Cooperation in Europe report assessing signatory nations, compliance with conference on security and cooperation in Europe (CSCE) 1975. Helsinki Final Act principles regarding human rights and East-West political and security relations.

Review background of CSCE process and review activities (p. 3-27) evaluated status of security in Europe (p. 28-43) and assesses human rights conditions and developments in East European nations and the Soviet Union (p. 44-231) Appendices (p. 237-419) include, "Chronology of major terrorist events, Nov. 1982-Sept. 1986" (p. 237-247).

(CIS)

0702 J952-53

*Nuclear Proliferation and Safeguards. Vol. 11.*

Appendix: Part 1.

June 1977. 95-1.

607 p. Var Paging. i1. Oversized. CIS/MF/9.

Publication No. OTA-E 50. Appendices to June 1977 Office of Technology Assessment (OTA) report analysing the risk of nuclear weapons proliferation, and technical institutional, and political options for control (for report summary, see 1977 CIS/Annual J 952-16). This volume contains the following separately paged background papers; including OTA revision as required:

(a) Stanford Research Institute, nuclear weapons, acquisition incentives and disincentives for industrialized and developing nations (48 p.)

(b) Levi, Barbara G., "Peaceful Nuclear Explosions" with program and research chronologies (36 p.)

(c) Jenkins, Brian M. and Krofcheck, Joseph L. (Rand Corp.), "Potentional Nuclear non-state Adversary" incentives for terrorist organized crime and non-govt agents to acquire nuclear capabilities, with review and commentary by Douglas Denike (128 p.)

(d) Westin, Alan F., "Civil Liberties Implications of U.S. Domestic Safeguards" with bibl. (54 p.)

(e) Stanford Research Institute, "Interantional Nuclear Industry" including assessment of U.S. nuclear exports with tables (86 p.)

(f) Science Applications Inc., "Technical description of Fuel Cycle Facilities and Evaluation of Diversion Potential" with illus. tables (237 p.)

Notes: Report copies are available from National Technical Information Service, PB. 275, 844, $28.00 Hard Copy.

(CIS)

0703 PL94-467

*Act for the Prevention And Punishment of Crimes Against Internationally Protected Persons.*

October 8, 1976. 94-2. 5p.

CIS/MF/3. Item 575.

LC 90 STAT : 1977.

"To amend title 18, United States Code, to implement the convention to Prevent and Punish the Acts of Terrorism Taking the form of Crimes Against

Persons and Related Extortion that are of International Significance and the convention on the prevention and Punishment of crimes Against Internationally Protected Persons, Including Diplomatic Agents, and for other Purposes". Legislative history: (H.R. 15552 and related bills):

1976 CIS/Annual :

Hanse Report : S523-47 (No. 94. 1614) Senate Report : S523-47 (No. 94-1273) accompanying S. 3646 Congressional Record Vol. 122 (1976): Sept. 21, Considered and passed Hanse. Sept. 24, considered and passed Senate; Weekly compilation of Presidential Documents vol. 12, No. 42 (1976): Oct. 10, Presidential Statement CIS, Index to publications of the United States congress.

(CIS)

0704 Vol. 18, No. 5, During May 1987

Terrorism characteristics and US anti-terrorism policies and programs.

Committee Serial No. 91. Hearings before the Subcom on civil and constitutional rights to examine the characteristics of international and domestic terrorism and U.S. anti-terrorism programs and policies. Also reviews state and local law enforcement agency roles in preventing domestic terrorism.

(CIS)

0705 Vol. 18, No. 5.

Terrorism Legislation.

May 7, 1986. 99-2. iii+72p. GPO $2.25.

CIS/MF/3.

Hearing to consider provisions of H.R. 4151, the Omnibus Diplomatic Security and Anti-Terrorism Act of 1986, and related bills to expand U.S. measures to combat international terrorism.

(CIS)

0706 S 385-6.

*Supplementary Extradition Treaty with the Federal Republic of Germany.* Message from the President. Republic of Germany. Message from the President. June 25, 1987. 100-1.

vii + 3p. S Doc Ram CIS/MF/3. Item 996-A;

999-B. Treaty Doc. 100-6. Y1.1/4:100-6.

Recommends senate advice and consent to ratification of an amended supplementary extradition treaty between U.S. and West Germany, Signed Oct. 21, 1986, excluding certain terrorist crimes from the scope of the political offence exceptions to extradition.

(CIS)

0707 S381-11 *Terrorism Legislation.*

May 7, 1986. 99-2. iii+72p. GPO. $ 2.25.

CIS/MF/3. Item 1039-A; 1039-B.

S Hrg. 99-952. MC 877-6720. LC 87-600689.

Hearing to consider provisions H.R. 4151, the Omnibus Diplomatic Security and Anti-terrorism Act of 1986 and related bills to expand U.S. measures to combat international terrorism.

(CIS)

0708 S-383-6

*International Security and Development Cooperation Act of 1987.*
May 22, 1987. 100-1. VI + 183 PS Doc Rm CIS/MF/14.
Item 1008-C; 1008-D.S. RPt. 100-60. Yi. 1/5; 100-60.

Recommends passages of S-1274, the international Security and Development Cooperation Act of 1987, to amend the Foreign Assistance Act of 1961 and the Arms Export Control Act to authorize FY88 appropriations for international security and economic development assistance program including military aid, foreign military sales (FMS), economic support fund international organisation and programme, anti-terrorism, peace-keeping operation, AID, American Schools and Hospitals Abroad, Asian Development Fund Bank includes provision to:

(a) Review FMS assistance terms including authorization of a new category of FMS grants.
(b) Increase military aid to the Philippines.
(c) Revise military assistance term for Turkey and Greece.
(d) Prohibit further transfer or arms to Iran,
(e) Authorize FY88 appropriations for Africa's famine recovery and development program Title, V. Part A is entitled the Africa Famine Recovery and Development Act.
(f) Set forth the sense of congress regarding alternative to administration policy in central America.
(g) Amend the Peace Corps Act to authorize FY88 appropriations for Peace Corps programs.
(h) Require Treasury Dept promotion of multilateral development bank procedures to increase lending for environmentally beneficial project in borrowing countries.

Authorize FY88 appropriations for international population planning and health activities, educational and human resources development programs, and international narcotics control programs. Includes additional views (p. 135-183); S. 1274 is related to 14 other bills.

(CIS)

0709 S641-11

Security on the capital ground relating to the Bombing of the U.S. Capital.
March 2, 1971. 92-1. + Item 1045. iii+21 p.
Y4. p 96/10:92-H7.
9290 (71) 74-611441

Committee Serial No. 92-H 7. Hearing before the subcom. on public buildings and grounds to review circumstances surrounding the bomb explosion at the U.S. Capital on Mar. 1, 1971, and to consider the adequacy of existing laws relating to protection of public buildings.

(CIS)

0710 S521-38

Testimony of Thomas Edward Mosher, Part 2.
March 10,11, 15, 1971; 92-1.
+Item 1042.
ii+81-159+ixp. Index. Y4. J89/2:M85.

12/pt. 2.
10805(71). (79-612276

Continuation of hearings before the subcom on Internal Security to question Thomas Edward Masher on: Origins and history of the organisation of solidarity of the peoples of Africa, Asia, and Latin America (Tricontinental) and its alleged role in development of "urban guerrilla warfare" tactics by U.S. radical groups, and alleged relationship to the Black Panther Party. Che Guevarcis' role in Tricontinental; Personal affirmation of existence of an organized underground in the U.S. (p. 81-100). Alleged relationships between Cuban government, the National Liberation Front in Vietnam, North Korea, and U.S. guerrilla movement; witness experiences with civil right groups in the south, alleged SDS radicalizing efforts within federally sponsored community action agencies. (p. 100-132).

Witness experience, following his Cuban visit, connected with an explosives and weapons cache in the Santa Cruz Mountains, and various terrorist activities in the San Francisco Bay Area (p. 132-159).

(CIS)

0711 S385-5

Convention to prevent and punish the acts of terrorism taking the form of crimes against persons and related extortion that are of international significance, Message from the President,
May 11, 1971. 92-1. +13p.
Exec. Doc. D. 92-1.
Y1. 92/1 : D.
10724 (71).

Recommends senate advice and consent to the convention, which is aimed at kidnapping and other acts of terrorism against diplomats and officials of Foreign governments.

(CIS)

0712 S522-3

Human Cost of Communism in Vietnam.
1972. 92-2. iii+123+xp.

Compendium prepared for the Subcom on Internal Security of excerpts from newspapers, magazines and books, highlighting the nature and extent of communist terrorism in both north and south Vietnam and estimating probable terrorism should the Communists win in SE Asia. Includes author, subject index. (p. 1-x).

(CIS)

0713 S263-55

Crimes Committed Aboard Aircraft.
September 19, 1972, 92-2+. Item 1008-A, 10p.
S Rpt. 92-1183.
17186 (73).

Recommends passage with amendments of S. 2567 the Aircraft Pirarcy Amendments of 1972, to facilitate prosecutions for certain crimes and offence committed aboard aircraft. S. 2567 is related to S. 2280 as amended.

(CIS)

0714 S384-20

Convention on International Liability for Damage caused by space objects.
October 4, 1972, 92-2. + 14p.
Exec. Rpt. 92-38.
Y1-92/2: rp. 38.
17127 (73).

Recommends that the senate give its advice and consent to ratification of the convention, signed at Washington, London and Moscow, March 29, 1972, to provide for compensation payment in the event of damage to a member state by a space object of another member state. Appendix contains statements and correspondence with State Dept. concerning simultaneous ratification instruments' deposits by Soviet Union and the U.S. (p. 5-14)

(CIS)

0715 S384-16

Aircraft Sabotage Convention.
October 2, 1972, 92-2. + 27 p.
Exec. Rpt. 92-34.
Y1. 92/2 : rp. 34.

Recommends that the Senate give its advice and consent to ratification of the convention for the Suppression of Unlawful Acts Against the Safety of Civil Aviation, which supplement the Hijacking convention by requiring the extradition or prosecution of persons who commit acts of sabotage or destroy aircraft or who endanger the safe flight of an aircraft by damaging it or air navigation facilities. Appendix (p. 5-27) contains a reprint of the hearing held on Sept. 22, 1972, on the convention.

(CIS)

0716 S348-4

Convention to Prevent and Punish the acts of Terrorism.
June 5, 1972. 92-2+5p.
Exec. Rpt. 92-23.
Y1. 92/2:rp. 23.
10836 (72).

Recommends that the Senate give its advice and consent to ratification of the convention to prevent and punish the acts of terrorism taking the form of crimes against persons and related extortions that are of international significance. Convention is aimed at kidnapping and other acts of terrorism against diplomats and officials of foreign governments by excluding such crimes, for purpose of extradition and asylum, from being treated as political offenses.

(CIS)

0717 S381-11. 15

April 4, 1973 p. 431-448.
Witness : Harrop, William C., Press, Amer Foreign Service Assn: accompanied by Harris, F. Allen, Counselor and pd member.

Statement and Discussion. Assessment of Foreign Affairs Specialist (FAS) program: current concerns and requirements of foreign service members includ-

ing proposed legislation (text, p. 443-445) to compensate survivors of terrorist victims.

(CIS)

0718 S181-28. 27: July 24, 1973. P. 2433-2474.

Witness: Hoffacker, Lewis, Coord. Committee for Combating Terrorism, accompanied by Murray, Richard W. Dep. Asst. Sec for Budget and finance, State Dept. Gentile, G. Marvin, Dep. Asst. Sec for. Security; and Peters, Edward, office of communications.

Statement and Discussion: Budget explanation for state Dept FY74 amendment request for the committee for combating terrorism to increase protection for government overseas and domestic personnel and property; proposed protective measures, including additional security guards, building security protected vehicles, and improved communications network.

(CIS)

0719 S521-14.

Human Cost of Communism in Vietnam Part II;
The Myth of no Bloodbath.
January 5, 1973. 93-1 $0.30; $0.50 ppd.
Item 1042. ii+55 p. Index.
Y4. J89/2: C73/64/pt. 2.
23062(73) (73-601011)

Hearing before the subcom on Internal Security to receive testimony from Danial H Teodoru, Eastern Regional Secretary for the nation students coordinating committee for freedom in Vietnam and South East Asia disputing earlier claims from other sources that no bloodbath occurred during implementation of radical land reform programmes in North Vietnam between 1953 and 1956.

Appendix contains additional articles and correspondence (p. 31-49).

(CIS)

0720 S521-72

Terroristic Activity.
Part 4: International Terrorism.
May 14, 1975. 94-1. iii+177-260+x p.
Index. CIS/MF/3. Item 1042.
Y4. J89/2: T27/4/pt. 4.
13606(75) 75-600818

Continuation of hearings before the subcom on Internal Security on the nature and extent of terroristic activity. This volume examines the threat to public safety and other repercussions of politically motivated acts of international terrorism and violent subversion. Also considers U.S. and other governmental responses to escalating terrorist incidents. Appendix (p. 253-260) contains CRS paper entitled "International Terrorism" by Vita Bite, Iuuse Brief No. 1 B 74042 including record of congressional activities to help stem international terrorism includes subject index (p. i-x).

(CIS)

0721 S521-27

Terrorist Activity, Part I.
September 23, 1974. 93-2.
ii+96p. ip. Index.
CIS/MF/3 Item 1042.
Y4 J89/2: T27/4/pt.1.
08489 (75) 75-600818

Hearing before the Subcom on International Security on the nature and extent of terrorist operations in California. Includes index (p. 91-96) of individuals, organization and publication.

(CIS)

0722 S521-29

Terrorist Activity, Part - 3.
July 5. 1974. 93-2.
ii+155-176+iii p Index.
S/N 052-070-02724.
CIS/MF/3 Item 1042.
Y4. J89/2: T27/4/pt. 3.
05291 (75) 75-600818.

Hearing before the Subcom on International Security to receive testimony concerning the composition, variety, tactics, goals and influence of selected domestic and foreign terrorist groups and organizations.

(CIS)

0723 S521-17

State Department Bombing by Weatherman Underground.
January 31, 1975. 94-1.
ii+29p. il+CIS/MF/3. Item.
1042. Y4. J89/2:B63.
03794 (75) 75-600934

Hearing before Subcom on Internal Security to determine responsibility for Jan. 29 1975, bomb explosion in main State Dept building. J-G. Sourwine (Subcom Chief Counsel) directs witness interrogation.

(CIS)

0724 S402-18

Peaceful Nuclear Exports and Weapons Proliferation,
A Compendium.
April 1975. 94-1.
xii+1355 p. $11. 70.
CIS/MF/16 Item 1037.
Y4. G74/6:N88/2.
75-601849.

Compilation, prepared with CRS assistance, of selected reports, technical and confernece papers, newspaper and journal articles, Congressional Record

excerpts and other materials on the potential dangers associated with international acquisition of peaceful nuclear technology. Focuses on the issue of nuclear materials safeguards and the specter of unlimited nuclear weapons proliferation.

Contents:

Overview (p. 1-10).

(a) Donnelly, Warren H. (CRS) "Special Nuclear Materials: Safeguards" May 9, 1974, updated Jan. 31, 1975 (p.1-10). Perspectives on the Problem (p. 11-126). Includes:

(b) Kinderman, E.M. (Stanford Research Inst.) "Plutonium: Home Made Bombs?" Paper presented at Atomic Industrial Forum Conference on Nuclear Public Information, Mar. 6, 1972 (p. 20-28).

(c) Willrich, Mason and Taylor, Theodore B., "Nuclear Theft: Risks and Safeguards," 1974, Chapter 2 and 6 excerpts (p. 45-83).

(d) Phillips, James G., "Energy Report/Safeguards, Recycling Broadened Nuclear Power Debate," from National Journal Reports, Mar. 22, 1975 (115-125).

Historical Background (p. 127-286). Includes:

(a) State Dept, "A Report on the International Control of Atomic Energy," prepared for former State Dept committee on Atomic Energy, Mar. 16, 1946 (p. 127-198).

(b) Baruch, Bernard M., "The Baruch Plan," statement before UN Atomic Energy Commission, June 14, 1946 (p. 203-213).

(c) State Dept, "Report of the Advisory Committee on U.S. Policy Toward the International Atomic Energy Agency" ("Symthe Report"), May 19, 1962 (p. 221-246).

(d) Quester, George H., "Can Proliferation now be Stopped?" from Foreign Affairs, Oct. 1974 (p. 266-286).

Treaties, Federal Laws and Regulation (p. 287-422). Includes:

(a) Statute of the International Atomic Energy Agency (IAEA), as amended to June 1, 1973, Text (p. 292-311).

(b) P.L. 93-438, P.L. 93-485, P.L. 93-500, and Exec. Order 10841, texts and text excerpts regarding international cooperation in nuclear exports and uses (p. 312-325).

(c) Code of Federal Regulations, Title 10-Energy: Chapter 1, AEC rules and regulations, excerpts (p. 326-367).

(d) Spodak, William M. (Westinghouse Corp.), "Legal Framework for the Transfer of Nuclear Material, Equipment and Faciliteis Overseas" Feb. 10, 1975 9p. 384-405).

(e) McWhinney, Robert T., Jr. (AEC), "Safeguards: Regulatory Requirement," remarks before Atomic Industrial Forum's Pub Aff Workshop on Plutonium, Sateguards and the Breeder, Oct. 9,1974 (p. 4060418).

Congressional Views and Initiatives (p. 423-551). Includes:

(a) Donnelly, Warren H. (CRS), "Congress and Nuclear Safeguards, prepared for Atomic Industrial Forum's Workshop on Plutonium, Safeguards, and the Breeder, Oct. 23, 1974, revised Apr. 9, 1975 (p. 423-454).

(b) Rosenbaum, David M., "The Threat of Nuclear Theft and Sabotage" rpt. of AEC Special Safeguards Study, Apr. 30, 1974 (p. 467-482).

Executive Branch activities (p. 552-722). Includes:

(a) Ad Hoc Advisory Panel on Safeguarding Special Nuclear Material, "Report to the Atomic Energy Commission" ("Lumb Report"), excerpt, Mar. 10, 1967 (p. 563-572).

(b) AEC, mixed oxide fuel draft environmental statement, excerpt on plutonium recycling safeguards, Aug. 1974 (p. 575-579).

(c) Ray, Dixy Lee (Chm, AEC), remarks before international conferences on nuclear technology export and transportation safeguards (p. 580-601).
(d) AEC, "Proposed Final Environmental Statement: Liquid Metal Fast Breeder Reactor Program," excerpt form WASH-1535 rtp, Dec. 1974 (p. 602-620).
(e) Presidential message, "14th Annual Report of the U.S. Arms Control and Disarmament Agency," excerpt, H. Doc. 94-64, transmitted Mar. 3, 1975 (p. 633-645).
(f) Nuclear Regulatory Commission export and import licensing regulations, article and press releases, Mar.—Apr. 1975 (p. 649-653).
(g) ERDA, "International Nuclear Export Acitivites," rpt, Apr. 1975 (p. 654-686).
(h) Commerce Dept, "Proposed Findings Supporting Determination Related to International Nuclear Power Export Activities," excerpt, Apr. 1975 (p. 687-713).

International Organizations and Activities (p. 723-1053) Includes:
(a) Marks, Anne W., "NPT : Paradoxes and Problems," excerpt from Arms Control Assn recommendations for nuclear non-proliferation treaties, 1975 (p. 723-731).
(b) IAEA, "Safeguards", Booklet text with bibliography (p. 732-756).
(c) IAEA, "The Structure and Content of Agreement beteween the Agency and States Required in Connection with the Treaty on Non-Proliferation of Nuclear Weapons," June 1974 (p. 757-788).
(d) IAEA, "Recommendations for the Physical Protection of Nuclear Material" ("Grey Book"), June 1972 (p. 789-808).
(e) Donnelly, Warren H. (CRS), "Commercial Nuclear Power in Europe: The Interaction of American Diplomacy with a New Technology," excerpt from committee print (p. 837-883).
(f) Szasz, Paul C., "International Atomic Energy Agency Safeguards" chapter 4 from International Safeguards and Nuclear Industry, Mason Willrich, editor, 1973 (p. 884-952).
(g) Proposed U.S. sale of nuclear reactors and fuel supplies to the Middle East, statements by Administration and public witnesses in July 1974 hearings before Senate Committee on Banking, Housing and Urban Affairs (p. 953-998).
(h) Stanley Foundation, "Fifteenth Strategy for Peace," rpt presented to Oct. 17-20, 1974 conference (p. 999-1009).
(i) Stockholm International Peace Research Institute, "Preventing Nuclear-Weapon Proliferation: An Approach to the Non-Proliferation Treaty Review Conference" Jan. 1975 (p. 1017-1053).

Safeguards (p. 1054-1302). Includes:
(a) Willrich, Mason: and Taylor, Theodore B., "Nuclear Theft: Risks and Safeguards" 1974. chapter 7, 8 and 10 excerpts (p. 1058-1105).
(b) Conlon, Frank B.; and Pettigrew, George L. (Bur of Radiological Health, HEW), "Summary of Federal Regulations for Packing and Transportation of Radioactive Materials" Feb. 1971 (p. 1110-1153).
(c) Brobst, William A. (Chief, Div of Waste Mgmt and Transportation, AEC), "Where, Oh, Where Did My Atoms Go?" presented at Inst of Nuclear Materials'. Management's 13th Annual meeting, June 2, 1972 (p. 1154-1169).
(d) GAO, "Improvements Needed in the Program for the Protection of Special Nuclear Material," rpt, Nov. 7, 1973, with photos (p. 1170-1207).
(e) GAO, "Protecting Special Nuclear Material in Transit: Improvements Made and Existing Problems", rpt, Apr. 12, 1974 (p. 1208-1225).
(f) Special Panel to Study Transportation of Nuclear Materials, "Transportation of Radioactive Material by Passenger, "Transportation of

Radioactive Material by Passenger Aircraft" rpt, Sept. 17, 1974 (p. 1226-1245).

(g) Speth, J. Gustave (et al.) (Natural Resources Def Council), "The Plutonium Decision: A Report on the Risks of Plutonium Recycle" Sept. 1974 (p. 1246-1263).

(h) Cohen, Bernard L. (Inst for Energy Analysis), "The Hazards in Plutonium Dispersal" Mar. 1975 (p. 1278-1302).

Appendices (p. 1303-1335) contain:

(a) Rather, Barbara L. (CRS), "Safeguarding Nuclear Materials: A Selected Bibliography" Apr. 7, 1975 (p. 1303-1316).

(b) AEC, "Safeguards Glossary," WASH-1162 rpt, Dec. 1, 1970 (p. 1317-1341).

(c) S. 1439, the Export Reorganization Act of 1975, to revamp nuclear technology export licensing procedures, text (p. 1342-1355).

(CIS)

0725 S521-500

Terrorist And His Victim.
July 21, 1977, 95-1.
ii+33p. +CIS/MF/3.
Item 1042.
Y4. J89/2: T27/6.
LC 77-604177.

Hearings before the Subcom on Criminal Laws and Procedures to receive briefing on the causes and effects of the possible counter-measures to terrorism.

(CIS)

0726 S521-72

Terroristic Acitivity: Terrorism in the Miami Area.
Part 8.
May 6, 1976. 94-2.
ii+607-662+vi p. Index.
$ 0.75 CIS/MF/3.
.Item 1042.
Y4. J89/2: T27/4/pt. 8.
MC 76-9788. LC 75-600818.

Continuation of hearings before the Subcom on Internal security on the nature extent of worldwide terrorist activity. This volume examines Miami area terrorist bombings and other subversive activities by anti-Castro Cuban exile groups and Cuban communist agents. Appendix (p. 645-662) includes articles and statements on Terrorists' operations and bombing incidents. Includes subject index (p. i-vi).

(CIS)

0727 S523-47

Implementing International Conventions Against Terrorism September 26, 1976. 94-2. 16 p.
+CIS/MF/3 . Item 1008-A.
S. Rpt. 94-1273.
MC 77-1315.

Recommends passage, with an amendment in the nature of substitute, of S. 3646, to implement the convention to Prevent and Punish the Acts of Terrorism

taking the form of cimes against persons and related extortion that are of International Significance and the convention on the Prevention and punishment of Crimes against Internationally Protected Persons, including Diplomatic Agents.

(CIS)

0728 S383-29

Terrorist Attack at Istanbul Airport.
September 16, 1976. 94-2. 5p.
+CIS/MF/3 . Item 1008-A.
S. Rpt. 94-1235.

Recommends passage of S. Res. 524, to urge the President, in light of the Aug. 1976 terrorist attack on the Istanbul Airport and other recent hijacking attempts, to encourage foreign governments to suspend air service to any nation involved in terrorism to undertake international discussions to strengthen aviation safety standards and airport security measures and to consider appropriate domestic actions to deter further support of international terrorism.

(CIS)

0729 S522-14

Panama Canal and the Problem of Security.
October 1976. 94-2. V+42p.
+CIS/MF/3 . Item 1042.
Y4. J89/2: p. 19.
LC 76-603324.

Contains report by staff assistant Harold E. Hughes (former Sen, D-Iowa) and staff member Alfonso L. Tarobochia of the Subcom on Internal Security reviewing their investigatory trip to Panama. Summarizes discussions held with canal-Zone Officials and Panamian government leaders on problems of protecting the security of the Panama canal against possible terrorist activities. Also reviews progress made in improving job opportunities for Panamanians in the Canal Zone.

(CIS)

0730 S521-9

Terroristic Activity: Terrorist Bombings and Law Enforcement Intelligence. Part 7.
October 23, 1975, 94-1.
iii+497-605+ix p. il, Index.
$ 1.90 CIS/MF/4. Item 1042.
Y4. J89/2:T27/4/pt. 7.
MC 07286(76). LC 75-600818.

Continuation of hearings before the Subcom on Internal Security on the nature and extent of worldwide terrorist activity. This volume examines escalating trends in terrorist bombing incidents and the adequacy of law enforcement technical and intelligence tools developed to counteract bomb-related crimes. Includes subject index (p. 1-ix).

(CIS)

0731 S521-73

Terroristic Acitivity-Interlocks between Communism and Terrorism–Part 9.

May 7, 1976. 94-2.

ii+663-749+xp. il foldout.

Index . $ 1.65 CIS/MF/3.

.Item 1042.

Y4. J89/2:T27/4/pt. 9.

MC 76-9788. LC 75-600818.

Continuation of hearings before the subcom on Internal Security on the nature and extent of worldwide terrorist activity. This volume examines interlocks between communism and domestic terrorist groups.

Appendix (p. 685-749) includes exhibit articles, political literature, and:

(a) Luce, Phillip A., terrorist, revolutionary communist and democratic socialist organisations' origins and present divisions, organisational chart, May 1976 (Facing p-688).

(b) Luce, Phillip A., "Contemporary terrorism within the U.S. : Relationships between External Communist Ideology and Internal Communist Terrorism" monograph, May 1976 (p. 705-718).

(c) "Guerrilla Acts of Sabotage and Terrorism in the U.S., 1965-1970," annotated list, Scanlan's, January 1971 (p. 720-747) Includes subject index (p. 1-x)

(CIS)

0732 S521-1

Nationwide Drive.

Against Law.

Enforcement.

Intelligence.

Operations.

September 18, 1975. 94-1.

ii+40+vi p. Index. $ 0.65.

S/N 052-070-02895-5.

CIS/MF/3 Item 1042.

Y4. J89/2: In 8/19.

MC 02304(76). LC 75-603338.

Hearings before the Subcom on Internal Security to investigte the alleged existence of a nationwide drive against the intelligence operations of local police depts, the FBI, the CIA and other Federal, State, and local enforcement agencies directed against organized crime, civil disorders and national and international terrorism. Appendix (p. 39-40) contains an article.

(CIS)

0733 S521-1. 1: September 18, 1975. p. 3-37.

Witness: McNamara, Frank J., former staff dir, House Un-American Activities Committee; former Exec Sec., Subversive Activities Control Bd. Discussion: Evaluation of domestic terrorist threat and law enforcement counter capacity; relationship between domestic and foreign terrorism; review of national investigative commissions' recommendations for improving intelligence

gathering; criticism of certain efforts to half police intelligence gathering; charged support of terrorist by Communist front groups. Insertions: Court support of police intelligence gathering activities, case summaries (p. 21-27). Collection of court decisions regarding Communist party terrorist activities (p. 28-31). (CIS)

0734 S521-2

Terroristic Activity,
Hostage Defense Measures, Part 5.
July 25, 1975. 94-1.
ii+261-317+v p. il. Index.
$ 0.80 S/N 052-070-03106-9.
CIS/MF/3 . Item 1042.
Y4. J89/2: T27/4/pt. 5.
MC 03308(76) IC 75-600818.

Continuation of hearings before the Subcom on Internal Security on the nature and extent of worldwide terrorist activity. This volume discusses practical defence and survival measures for persons taken hostage by terrorists. Also examines the strategy and tactics of violence practiced by principal terrorist organizations, most notably the Uruguayan National Liberation Movement, known as the Tupamaros, the German Baader-Meinhof gang and the Japanese Red Army (JRA).

Hearing was conducted by subcom staff members in executive session and later authorized for public release. Includes subject index (p. 1-v). (CIS)

0735 S521-2.1:July 25, 1975. p. 261-317.

Witness: McClure, Brooks, Foreign Service Officer, USIA; Spec. Asst for Policy, Plans and Natl Security Council Aff, Intl Security Directorate, DOD.

Statement and Discussion: Characterization of terrorist, their motivations, and modus operandi; guidelines for hostage survival under extreme physical/mental deprivation; assessment of terrorist movements, their origins, financial/ideological backing, news usage and tools of propaganda. (p. 261-285)

Intensification of terrorists' use of violence and relative impotence of present statutory countermeasures; specifics on organization/operations of Tupamaros (charts, photos, p. 295-307), Baader-Meinhof gang, JRA and other subversive groups. (p. 285-317). (CIS)

0736 S521-3

Terrorist Activity:
The Cuban Connection in Puerto Rice; Castro's Hand in Puerto. Rican and U.S. Terrorism, part 6.
July 30, 1975. 94-1.
ii+319-496+xviii p. Index.
$ 1.95 CIS/MF/4.
. Item 1042.
Y4. J89/2:T27/4/pt. 6.

MC 00689(76). LC 75-600818.

Continuation of hearings before the Subcom on Internal Security on the nature and extent of worldwide terrorist activity. This volume examines evidence of Cuban influence over the Puerto Rican pro-communist leftist independece movement and Puerto Rican Socialist Party (PSP) and their political and terrorist tactics. Includes numerous articles and political statements throughout. Appendix (p. 417-496) contains articles, speech and meeting transcript excerpts, reports, and:

(a) Browne, Marjorie A. (CRS), "United Nations Consideration of the Status of Puerto Rico, a Chronology: 1953-1975" Aug. 22, 1975 (p. 418-422).

(b) Roberts, Roslyn D. (CRS), UN special committee on granting independence to colonies membership list, 1962-74 (p. 423-436).

Hearing was held in executive session. Includes subject index (p. i-xviii).

(CIS)

0737 S521-3.1: July 30, 1975. p. 320-365.

Witness: Martinez, Francisco (assumed name), researcher and consultant on PR aff.

Statement and discussion: Chronicle of Communist infiltration of pro-independence groups and PSP and description on infiltrators 'tactics; examination of PSP activities aimed at U.S., including planned Bicentennial celebration disruption; interactions to Puerto Rican radicals with world Communist organizations and with Cuba.

(CIS)

0738 S521-3.2: July 30, 1975. p. 365-415.

Witness: Tarabochia, Alfonso L., Chief Investigator, Sub com Staff.

Statement Discussion: Cuban efforts in UN to detach Puerto Rico from U.S. (correspondence, p. 369-377); evidence of Soviet intelligence involvement in Cuban subversive activities in Latin America; activities of Communist Party, U.S.A., Cuban Directorate of intelligence, PSP and Venceremos brigades in agitation for Puerto Rican detachment; organization, goals (chart, communiques p. 406-409) and identification of terrorists operating in U.S., including connections with Fuerzas Armadas de Liberation National.

Insertion: Bombings in US by Puerto Rican terrorists, 1974-75, list (p. 410-411).

(CIS)

0739 S521-43

West Germany's Political Response to Terrorism.

April 26. 1978. 95-2.

ii+23 p. Index + CIS/MF/3.

. Item 1042.

Y4. J89/2: W52g.

LC 78-602951.

Hearing before the Subcom on Criminal Laws and Procedures to consider West Germany's political response to terrorism since the early 1970s, and ways in which the U.S. might benefit from the German experience. Includes subject index (p. 21-23).

(CIS)

0740 S381-32

Combating International and Domestic Terrorism.
June 8, 1978. 95-2.
iii+119p. + CIS/MF/4.
. Item 1039.
Y4. F76/2: T27/2.
MC 78-24610. LC 78-603137.

Hearings to consider S. 2236 (text p. 2-61), the Act to Combat International Terrorism to strengthen Federal programs and policies for combating international and domestic terrorism. Includes provisions to:

(a) Require Periodic report on acts of international terrorism, nations supporting Terrorism and federal and international capabilities to combat terrorism.

(b) Authorize the President to terminate assistance under the foreign Assistance Act of 1961 and the arms Export control Act to nations which support terrorism.

(c) Amend the Federal Aviation Act of 1958 to require DOT to assess and publicize findings on Security of foreign airports.

(CIS)

0741 S383-12

To Counter International Terrorism.
July 10, 1978. 95-2. 35p.
+CIS/MF/3 .Item 1008-A.
S.Rpt. 95-970.
MC 78-24844.

Recommends passage with amendment of S. 2236, the act to combat international terrorism, to strengthen federal programme and policies for combating international and domestic terrorism. Includes provisions to:

(a) Require periodic report on acts of international terrorism, nations supporting terrorism and Federal and international capabilities to combat terrorism.

(b) Authorise the President to terminate assistance under the Foreign Assistance Act of 1961 and the arms Export Control Act to nations which support terrorism.

(c) Amend the Federal Aviation Act of 1985 to require DOT to assess and publicize findings on Security of Foreign airports.

(d) Require Treasure Dept to establish standards for identification and detection taggants, substances added to an explosive material during manufacturing, which permit identification of manufacturer following detonation, or detection of explosives prior to detonation.

0742 S383-9

Countering International Terrorism.
June 15, 1978. 95-2. Sp.
+CIS/MF/3 .Item 1008-A. S Rpt.
95-936. MC 78-27060.

Recommends passage with amendments of S. Con. Res. 72, to condemn international terrorism as obstacle to peace in the Middle East. Also recommends that President terminate assistance to nations, organizations, groups, or individuals who commit or attempt to commit acts of terrorism.

(CIS)

0743 S383-2

Terrorism in Italy.
May 2-1978. 95-2. 2p+CIS/MF/3.
.Item 1008-A. S.Rpt. 95-774.
MC 78-19418.

Recommends passage of S. Res. 419, to express the sense of the senate to condemn the kidnapping of Aldo Moro and support actions of the Italian government to suppress terrorism and preserve democracy.

(CIS)

0744 S381-12

International Terrorism.
September 14, 1977. 95-1.
iv+90p. il. +CIS/MF/3 .Item 1039
.Y4. F76/2:T27. MC 78-16220.
OC 78-601216.

Hearing before the subcom on Foreign Assistance on available U.S. policy options for combating international terrorism.

Includes State Dept correspondence concerning assistance to terrorists from Libya, Iraq, Somalia and other nations (p. 2-5, 82-87); and additional submitted correspondence (p. 89-90).

(CIS)

0745 S521-31.8: August 15, 1978 p. 92-129.

Witnesses: Mignosa, Sebastian S.,
Chief Domestic Security and Terrorism Section, FBI.

Lawton, Mary C. Dept. Asst Atty Gen., office of Legal Counsel, Justice Dept. Kornblum, Allan N., Chief Atty Investigation Review unit.

Statement and Discussion: Explanation of Justice Dept.,

1976, guidelines for initiations and performance of FBI domestic security investigation primarily involving potential terrorism; description of department Investigation Review unit procedures for oversight and termination of investigations: Clarification of FBI investigatory discretion under guidelines.

(CIS)

0746 S181-15. 14; March 11, 1980 p. 515-602.

Witness: Webster, William H., Dir, FBI. Budget Explanation: FBI request for F481 for law enforcement activities including:

(a) Criminal and Security investigations concentrated on white-collar crime, organized crime, Foreign Counter-intelligence and terrorism.

(b) Investigative support, including FBI agent training and forensic laboratory services.

(c) State and local assistance, including fingerprint identification and criminal justice and statistics' services through uniform crime reporting program and National Crime Information Centre.

(CIS)

0747 S521-62.2: September 12, 1979, p. 38-72.

Witnesses: Ruff, Charles F., Act Dept. Atty Gen,
Justice Dept.
Michel, Paul R., ASSOC Dep Atty Gen. Hotis, John B.

Spec Asst to Dir, FBI.

Mullen, Francis M., Jr., Asst Dir, Criminal Dir, Justice Dept.

Mignosa, Sebastian S., Section Chief, Domestic Terrorism, FBI.

Statement and Discussion: Explanation of FBI investigative inquiries and full investigation guidelines and their viewed consistency with proposed Charter; need for retention of investigative flexibility; role of FBI in monitoring potentially criminal organizations; scope of FBI authority in investigation of terrorist activities; effect of proposed charter provision authorizing FBI investigations of state law violations.

(CIS)

0748 S381-4

International Terrorism. Insurgency and Trafficking: Present Trends in terrorist Activity.

May 13-15, 1985. 99-1.

iv+426p. +CIS/MF/7.

.Item 1039-A; 1039-B.

S. Hrg. 99-372.

Y4. F76/2: Hrg. 99-372.

LC 86-601233.

Joint hearing with the senate Judiciary Committee to examine international terrorism trends and charactristics and review U.S. efforts to combat terrorism. Also examines the relationship between illegal drug trafficking and international terrorism. Supplementary material (p. 90-93, 205-232, 410-426) includes correspondence, witnesses, written replies to committee question and :— Terrorism and violence against civilians and in South Africa and Namibia, govt. repts., with 1976-84 lists (p. 205-232).

(CIS)

0749 S521-40

Supplementary Extradition Treaty between the U.S. and United Kingdom of Great Britain and Northern Ireland.

No. 5, 1985. 99-1 iv+198p. GPO $5.50.

CIS/MF/5.

.Item 1042-A; 1042-B.

S. Hrg. 99-523.

Y4. 89/2; S. hrg. 99-523.

LC 86-60/967.

Committee Serial No. J-99, 71, hearing before the Subcom on the Constitution to examine legal and constitutional aspects of a supplementary extradition treaty between the U.S. and Great Britain and Northern Ireland, signed June 25, 1985, excluding certain terrorist crimes from the scope of the political offense exception to extradition. Supplementary material (p. 3-51, 167-198) includes correspondence and:

(a) "Extradition Treaty between the Government of the U.S. and Government of the U.K. of Great Britain and Northern Ireland" text. June 8, 1972 and Oct. 21, 1976, (p. 3-15).

(b) "Supplementary Extraditions Treaty with the United Kingdom" Press message, text, July 17, 1985, (p. 16-22).

(c) Thompson, Duane K., "Evolution of the Political Offense Exception in an age of Modern Political Violence" Yale J. of world Public order, vol. 9, 1983, (p. 23-49).

(d) Field, Louis G., Jr. "Bringing Terrorist to Justice. The Shifting sands of the Political Offense Exception" International Aspects of Criminal Law (p. 180-198). (CIS)

0750 S181-26.5: March 11, 1985, p. 391-414.

Witness: Borg, Parker W., Act Dir, office. for counter-terrorism and Emergence Planning. State Dept. Budget Explanation: State Dept FY 86 request for anti-terrorism training and assistance programs for foreign government officials.

Insertion:

State Dept, "Report to the Congress on the Anti-terrorism Assistance Program" March 5, 1985 (p. 395-402).

(CIS)

0751 S383-3.

Diplomatic Security and anti-Terrorism Act of 1986.

May 20, 1986. 99-2, 34 p.

+CIS/MF/3.

.Item 1008-C; 1008-D.

S. Rpt. 99-304.

Y1.1/5. 99-304.

Recommends passage with an amendment of H.R. 4154, the Diplomatic Security and Anti-Terrorism Act of 1986 in the following titles:

Title I. through IV, the Diplomatic appropriations for and restructure, state Dept. comprehensive security enhancement program for diplomatic missions and personnel abroad and foreign missions in the U.S.

Title V, to amend the State Department Basic Authorities Act of the 1956 to authorize State Dept FY 86-FY 87 appropriations for rewards for Information regarding international terrorism and major drug trafficking offenses.

Title VI, the Fascell Fellowship Act, to establish a fellowship program to provide scholars, students, and teachers in Russian and East European languages and area studies with temporary positions at diplomatic posts in the Soviet Union and East European countries.

Title VII, to authorize FY 86-FY 87 appropriations for Peace Corps Programs. H.R. 4151 is related to S. 2015, S. 1941, and S. Res. 190.

(CIS)

0752 S181-32

International Terrorism, FY 85. Special Hearing:

Department of State.

Nov. 27, 1984. 98-2.

iii+29 p. +CIS/MF/3.

.Item 1033; 1033-A.

S. Hrg. 98-1269.

Y4. Ap. 6/2: S. hrg. 98-1269.

MC 85-18646 LC 85-602118.

Hearing before the *Subcom on Foreign Operations Appropriations* to review Federal programs for combating international terrorism.

(CIS)

0753 S521-16

*Legislative Initiatives to Curb Domestic and International Terrorism.*
June, 5, 6, 13, 1984. 98-2.
IV+194p. +CIS/MF/4.
.Item 1042-A; 1042-B.
S. Hrg. 98-1078.
Y4-J89/2: S. Hrg. 98-1078.
MC 85-9499: LC 85-601783.

Committee Serial No. J89-123. Hearings before the *Subcom on Security and Terrorism* to consider the following Administration bills to strengthen federal programs for combating international and domestic terrorism.

S.2623 (text, p. 6-15), the Aircraft Sabotage Act, to amend the Federal Aviation Act of 1958 to implement the Montreal Convention (text, Signatures, p. 64-80) strengthening aircraft piracy and sabotage sanctions.

S. 2624 (text, p. 16-20), the Act for the Prevention and Punishment of the crime of Hostage-Taking, to establish Federal Jurisdiction and Penalties in certain hostage taking cases. Bill would implement, and International convention against the taking of hostages.

S. 2625 (text, p. 21-27), the Act for Rewards for Information Concerning Terrorist Acts, to authorize Justice and State Dept. rewards for information regarding terrorist acitivity.

S. 2626 (text, p. 28-36), the Prohibition Against the Training or Support of Terrorist Organisations Act of 1984, to impose criminal penalties on U.S. Citizens or businesses providing military or intelligence assistance to international terrorist groups and governments which support terrorism.

Also considers S. 2470 (text, p. 3-5) the Anti-Nuclear Terrorism Act of 1984, to amend the Atomic Energy Act of 1954 to require nuclear power plant licencses to fingerprint certain employees and to authorize FBI to provide criminal history information to power plant employers.

Includes correspondence and an article.

(CIS)

0754 Vance, Cyrus R. Terrorism : Scope of the Threat and Needs for Effective Legislation. *Department of State Bulletin*, March 1978, pp. 53-55.

The Secretary of State's statement before the Senate Committee on Governmental Affairs, 23 January, 1978.

(N&G)

0755 Valizer, Michael. The New Terrorists. *The New Republic*, 30 August, 1975, pp. 12-17.

Terrorism, which had its origins in the 1869s, has now taken the form of random murder; it disregards the category of innocent people and its goals are repression, and destruction. Terrorism is the ultimate in lawlessness which operates in an atmosphere of permissiveness. The moral ugliness of terrorism

has been revealed, and unless this can be dealt with, the prospects are frightening.

(PRAJ: PRID)

0756 Vychodil, Frantisek. The Concept of the So-called fight against International Terrorism in the Policy of the USA. *International Relations*, (Prague), 1982, pp. 60-76.

The American Policy of state terrorism is based on a preventive strategy according to which military intervention should be made earlier than actual conflicts occur. In particular, national liberation movements are systematically suppressed under the guise of a so-called fight against international terrorism. However, present US policy does not correspond to the objective condition of the 1980s. American imperialism is no longer strong enough to carry out all its threats and demonstrations of force.

(IPSA)

0757 Walker, Clive. *The Prevention of Terrorism in British Law*. Manchester Univ. pr. 1986 (Based on thesis (Ph. D.), Manchester University.)

Focus on the Prevention of Terrorism Act 1984; some comparison with relevant laws in both Irish jurisdictions; suggested reforms.

(PAISB)

0758 Wall, James M. Rescue at Entebbe. *Christian Century*, Volume 93, Number 24, 21-28 July, 1976, p. 651.

The raid on Entebbe was not wanton aggression against Uganda. It was the act of a nation defending its citizens in highly unusual circumstances. These circumstances need correcting, with international agreements which will forestall future hijackings.

(PRAJ: PRID)

0759 Walter, EV. Politiche della violenza: de Montesquieu ai terroristi (The politics of violence from Montesquieu to the terrorists/La politique de la violence: de Montesquieu aux terroristes). *Comunita*, Volume 25, Number 163, 1971, pp. 7-30.

Montesquieu avait oppose la republique, dont le principe etait la vertu, et la dictature, dont le principe etait la terreur. Les terroristes revolutionnaries de 1793, Robespierre et Saint - Just, Concillierent les deux principles dans le gouvernement revolutionnaire, avec cette nuance que, selon Saint Just, la terreur devenait principe republica in lorsque la vertu manquait.

(IPSA)

0760 Walter, EV. Violence and the Process of Terror. *American Sociological Review*, Volume 29, Number 2, April 1964, pp. 248-257.

Since the notion of terrorism is commonly ambiguous, a more precise concept, the process of terror, is defined and illustrated. It is composed of three elements; violence, fear, and reactive behavior, and may be organized in systems. Types of system are clarified and the siege of terror distinguished from the regime of terror. Various social uses of violence are distinguished from violence in the service of power and the latter further distinguished from the use of violence to change the conditions of control. The relation between resistance and violence is explored. Terrorism is distinguished from other social processes,

such as warfare and punishment that resemble it. A typology of power systems based on the use of violence is suggested, and a comparative study of terror regimes' projected.

(PRAJ: PRID)

0761 Walter, Eugene Victor. *Terror and Resistance : A Study of Political Violence*. New York, Oxford University Press, 1969.

Author has attempted to evolve a general theory of terrorism. The objective of the study is to find out why some men, who have authority, choose to rule by violence and fear. Author has studied some primitive African Societies.

0762 Walzer, Michael. *Just and Unjust Wars : A Moral Argument with Historical Illustrations*. New York, Basic Books, 1977.

See esp. 197-206, wherein Walzer argues that the rather precise "political code" which demarcated protected persons from acceptable victims has seen a significant deterioration in the manifestations of contemporary terrorism.

(N&G)

0763 Ward, James J. Terror, Revolution, or Control? The KPD's Secret Apparat during the Weimar Republic. *Terrorism : An International Journal*, Volume 7, Number 3, 1984.

After several unsuccessful attempts to take power by force, the German Communist Party (KPD), from 1923 onwards, concentrated its efforts on electoral politics, trade union activity and the struggle against Social Democratic reformism. However, the Communists had not relinquished their goal of a forcible seizure of power, as shown by the existence throughout the Weimar period of a secret Communist apparatus (Apparat) whose goals were to undermine the German armed services and police, train party cadres for insurrectionary combat, and carry out other subversive activities. Developed with Soviet assistance and headed by German Communists who had been trained in Russia, the Apparat controlled a network of spies, agents and informers that penetrated German army and police units, government office and hostile political organizations. The Apparat also distributed illegal propaganda, furnished "military-political" training and literature to KPD members, performed espionage and counterespionage duties, and made preparations for the party's continued operation whether Communist organizations were to be outlawed. Occasional terrorist acts can be laid to the Apparat, which, although prosecuted vigorously by Weimar authorities, scarcely constituted a serious revolutionary threat. The most important function of the Apparat was to control the communist rank and file itself through surveillance of party members, searches and interrogations, and denunciations and betrayals. Ironically, it was the very existence of the Apparat that provided the Nazis with further corroboration for their claims to have saved Germany from Bolshevism.

(T)

0764 Ward, William J. DMSO (Dimethyl Sulfoxide) : A New Threat in Public Figure Protection. *Assets Protection*, Number 3, 1976, pp. 11-15.

Minimizes the possibility that DMSO may be used in mixtures with poisons as an assassination agent.

(N&G)

0765 Wardlaw, Grant. *Political Terrorism - Theory, Tactics, and Counter Measures*. Cambridge, Cambridge University Press, 1982.

Emphasis is laid on the 'policy issues' which confront a democratic state to combat terrorism and at the same time remain democratic. The various aspects of revolutionary and sub-revolutionary terrorism are discussed. Author warns that to overestimate the threat of terrorism and to overreact, may destroy the democratic society itself.

0766 Warren, J. Korea : The Samurai and the Boeing (In French). *Jeune Afrique*, Number 484, 14 April, 1970, pp. 32-33.

Two weeks ago a Boeing 727 of Japan Airlines was hijacked by nine members of the "Red Army". The latter group is well known in Japan as one of the most violent factions of the extreme left. The nine carried Samurai swords and dynamite. They informed the pilot that they wanted to go to North Korea, which, diplomatically, does not exist for Japan. After a variety of events, the plane did land in North Korea with the nine terrorists, one official-hostage, the vice-Minister of Transport of Japan and three crew members. It now seems possible that North Korea will use the Boeing as a means of forcefully opening a dialogue with Japan.

(PRAJ: PRID)

0767 Waterman, D.A., and Jenkins, Brian M. *Heuristic Modelling Using-Role-Based Computer Systems*. Santa Monica, Calif., Rand Corporation, 1977.

Report of efforts to analyze international terrorist activities through a computer-based program.

(N&G)

0768 Watson, Francis M. *Political Terrorism : The Threat and the Response*. Bridgeport, Luce, 1976.

This work covers a variety of terrorist groups from the "Tupamaros of Uruguay to Patricia Hearst and the Symbionese Liberation Army". Emphasis is placed on the propaganda impact of terrorism, the use of violence on innocent citizens, the goals of alienated groups and the need for close international cooperation to understand and to contain deviant terroristic activity.

(BRD)

0769 Watt, David. Curbing Terrorism - A Global Response? *Atlas*, January 1978, pp. 36-37.
(From *Financial Times of London*, October 21, 1977).

The Obvious moral is that one should never give in to blackmail... the only certain way to stop kidnappings and hijackings is to remove the rewards. But "never" is too strong a word. If the terrorists threaten to blow up a city with a nuclear bomb, what then? If hundreds of passengers are involved, what then? There can be a point where the price is too high. Another theory is that the international community cannot now fail to agree on declaring hijackers, genuine outlaws. But 40 countries have not signed the Hague Convention of 1970 outlawing hijackers and terrorists. The Communist block is selective—some terrorists are considered freedom fighters. And the Western countries do not consider East Europeans who hijack planes to the West as terrorists. Everyone agrees that mercenaries who hijack planes for money are terrorists. But these are very few. How then can the other hijackers be stopped? One answer is a solid front of sovereign states who hold out against the hijackers and the other is a moral

consensus against him. But neither one is very practical. However, there is a growing recognition that some of the more lunatic groups are beyond the pale, such as the Baader-Meinh of gang. But there are going to be capitulations to terrorists for some time. "Caution and cunning, rather than bravado, are the most valuable commodities here and we must foster them as best we can."

(PRAJ: PRID)

0770 Weinberg, Leonard. Patterns of Neo-Fascist Violence in Italin Politics. *Terrorism : An International Journal*, Volume 2, Numbers 3-4, 1979.

This paper explores the characteristics and meaning of Fascist violence in Italy during the two major crisis periods that appear to have stimulated it. The Pattern of Fascist attacks during the post-World War I era is compared to acts of Neo-Fascist violence from the late 1960s through the early 1970s. Substantial differences are disclosed with respect to the targets the Fascists chose to assult in the two eras. Much of the initial wave of Fascist violence was directed against peasants, workers and the employment-related organisations that sought to act on their behalf. Major targets of Neo-Fascist violence, on the other hand, have been university and secondary school students: groups that went totally unscathed in Dopoguerra. The differences and similarities between the two waves of Fascist violence are then used as evidence to speculate about the nature of fascism in Italy.

(T)

0771 Weinberg, Leonard and Eubank, William-Lee. Italian Women Terrorists. *Terrorism : An International Journal*, Volume 9, Number 3, 1987.

This paper seeks to assess the role of women in Italian terrorist groups. It is based on biographical information concerning 451 women who were active in such organizations between 1970 and 1984. The analysists suggest that there were a number of ways in which women terrorists differed from their male counterparts. These differences have to do with the time at which women became involved in terrorist activities/the routes they took prior to entry in the groups, the particular terrorist organisation they joined and the roles they came to play in them.

(T)

0772 Wellmer, Albrecht. Terrorism and Social Criticism. *Telos*, Number 48, Summer 1981, pp. 65-78.

It has become a matter of life and death for the left to develop a clear consciousness not only of the ideological and repressive, but also of the progressive and emancipatory contents of bourgeois democracy. Political concepts cannot be detached from the historico-political contexts in which they originated. The attempt to link social criticism and terrorism actually conceals the interplay of terrorism and reaction. This interconnection has become a matter of life and death for the socialist left.

(IPSA)

0773 Wells, Charles A. Moscow Backfire. *Between the Lines*, April 1, 1966, p. 4.

At the Havana Conference of the "Latin American Solidarity Organization for the Liberalization of the Western Hemisphere", delegates from 20 Communist states heard Moscow promise support of subversive and revolutionary activity in Latin America. But the USSR, which had tried to out do china, soon

had to backtrack, in the face of protests from Latin American capitals and embassies and from native national revolutionary leaders. Similar disclaimers proved necessary in Africa, as an aftermath of the Havana Conference.

(PRAJ: PRID)

0774 West Africa : Rebellion of Angels. *Observer*, (London), 10 January, 1971, p. 4.

"For the first time in Africa, a militant alliance between the R.C. Church and a rebellious guerrilla movement has been disclosed, at two political trials in the West African black state of Cameroun. These ended last week with death sentences for Albert Ndongmo, Bishop of Nkongsamba, and five others." Sketches in the history of political unrest in Cameroun in recent years.

(PRAJ: PRID)

0775 Wilkinson, Paul. *Terrorism and the Liberal State*. New York, John Wiley and Sons, 1977.

A work which borders on the elegant, particularly with Wilkinson's treatment of the foundations of the liberal state. Wilkinson attempts to balance the obligations of the state to the individual, with the doctrines of government, law and authority. Although he is identified with the "law and order" school of thought, Wilkinson concedes that those who are denied the rights of citizenship cannot be morally bound to obey the dictum of the state. Although marred by a few errors, in particular with regard to the Middle East, this work stands far above the typical work in the field.

(N&G)

0776 Wilkinson, Paul. *Political Terrorism*. New York, John Wiley and Sons, 1974.

An exceptional general treatment of political terrorism. Wilkinson has provided an historically informed work, which combines a competent treatment of the 19th century origins, modern terrorism with a discussion of its contemporary manifestations. Wilkinson's succinct analysis of terrorism is complemented with some masterful syntheses of the more important works in the field (and adjacent fields of study). Wilkinson proffers an "elementary typology of political terrorism" which distinguishes between revolutionary, sub-revolutionary and repressive variants; however, he fails to provide a discernible basis for identifying revolutionary vis-a-vis sub-revolutionary terrorism but this is only a minor demerit in an otherwise useful and informative book. A relatively extensive (157 entries) bibliography is provided.

(N&G)

0777 Wilkinson, Paul. Terrorism : The International Response. *World Today*, Volume 34, Number 1, January 1978, pp. 5-13.

As long as there remains a hard core of actively pro-terrorist states, attempts at universal conventions and treaties against terrorism are doomed to fail. Meanwhile the national anti-terrorist measures and a sophisticated intelligence gathering system are vital.

(IPSA)

0778 Wilkinson, Paul. Three Questions on Terrorism. *Govt. and Opposition*, Volume 8, Number 3, Summer 1973, pp. 290-312.

This is a discussion of three major questions which have to be tackled before any full-scale analysis of terrorism is possible : (i) How is terrorism to be defined and what differentiates terrorism from other forms of organized violence? (ii) What are the major forms of terrorism and how are they to be

identified and delineated? (iii) With the aid of comparative analysis and the integrative and historical literature, can any preliminary etiology of terrorism be deduced?

(IPSA)

0779 Wilkinson, Paul. (Ed.). *British Perspectives on Terrorism*. Winchester, Allen and Unwin Ltd., 1981.

Most of the essays in this book are indeed British perspectives and the relevance to broader questions related to terrorism is thus circumscribed. However, two specific chapters on hostage-taking and on kidnapping have international relevance. The four chapters are on IRA terrorism. The book offers fourteen 'ground rules' for dealing with terrorism, including meausres to prevent anti-terrorist forces becoming a danger to their democratic masters.

(BRD)

0780 Willenz, Eric. U.S. Policy on Terrorism in Search of an Answer. *Terrorism : An International Journal*, Volume 9, Number 3, 1987.

This paper explores some of the underlying reasons that have made the United State a primary target of terrorist attacks. Failing to take sufficient account of these factors has promoted U.S. policy makers to overemphasize military solutions in dealing with the highly differentiated and indirect threats which terrorism presents.

(T)

0781 Willrich, Mason. Terrorists Keep out. *Bulletin of the Atomic Scientists*, Number 31, May 1975, pp. 12-16.

An overview of the problem, with commentary on the safeguards against nuclear theft and sabotage taken to date and concluding with recommendations for additional protective measures.

(N&G)

0782 Willrich, Mason. (Ed.). *International Safeguards and Nuclear Industry*. Baltimore, Johns Hopkins University Press, 1973.

The Danger of diversion and the existing safeguards.

(N&G)

0783 Willrich, Mason., and Taylor, Theodore B. *Nuclear Theft : Risks and Safeguards*. Cambridge, Mass., Ballinger Publishing Co., 1974.

The influential Ford Foundation study that sparked much of the concerns for the prospect of the diversion or theft of nuclear materials by terrorists and criminals. Of particular interest is their discussion of the technology and the materials which might enable a few persons ( or even one person) to construct a crude fission bomb or a radiological weapon. Their analysis of the physical security short-comings in the storage and shipment of nuclear materials is also noteworthy: however, a number of the deficiencies noted have since been corrected or ameliorated (in large part as a very result of their book).

(N&G)

0784 Wilson, James O. Talking About Terrorism. *Commentary*, Volume 72, Number 1, July 1981, pp. 34-39.

Terrorism is the deliberate, systematic murder, maiming, and menacing of the innocent to inspire fear in order to gain political ends. This definition distinguishes pure terrorism and guerrilla warfare directed at the political or military arms of unoccupying power. In thinking about terrorism it is sometimes assumed that terrorists are but an extreme expression of underlying social injus-

tices and political tensions and that this symptom cannot be treated without first treating the underlying causes. This is an error. Whatever the root causes of terrorism, the terrorists inevitably develop a stake in opposing solutions to be problems.

(IPSA)

0785 Wilson, Carlos. *Tupamaros : The Unmentionables*. Boston, Branden Press, 1974.

By an insider, who has provided primary materials (communiques, transcripts, etc.) and an apologia for the Tupamaros as well as a diatribe against the U.S. government and its role in Uruguay.

0786 Wilson, RD. *Cordon and Search*. Aldershot, Gale and Polden, 1949.

A British view of terrorism in mandatory Palestine.

(N&G)

0787 Wohlstetter, Roberta. Terror on a Grand Scale. *Survival*, Number 18, May/June, 1976, pp. 98-104.

Much of the commentary and analysis of the nuclear terrorism question is notably historical in emphasis, depending as it does on the vulnerabilities resultant of modern technology. Wohlstetter provides an anecdote to such contributions, by tracing the problem to the earliest days of the nuclear age, and highlighting the development which combine to create the current concern. While she takes a restrained view of the problem, she does find cause for being disquieted, particularly in light of contemporary examples of careless slaughter of innocents by terrorists.

(N&G)

0788 Wolf, John B. Organization and Management Practices of Urban Terrorist Groups. *Terrorism : An International Journal*, 1978, pp. 119-186.

A discussion of the cellular organizational framework utilized by terrorists. Unusually well-informed.

(N&G)

0789 Wolf, John B. Urban Terrorist Operations. *Police Journal*, (England), Number 49, October-December 1976, pp. 277-284.

Wolf cites the Tupamaros as an example of successful urban terrorists.

(N&G)

0790 Wolf, J.B. *Fear of Fear : A Survey of Terrorist Operations and Controls in Open Societies*. New York, Plenum, 1981.

The work focuses on combating terrorism at the operational level. The author describes the nature of terrorist activity, the structures of terrorist organisation, global terrorist coalitions, and the politics of terrorism. In the second part of his study, he considers the means available and appropriate to democratic societies for combating what he considers to be the gravest peril of the 1980s.

(BRD)

0791 Wolf, John B. Controlling Political Terrorism in Free Society. *Orbis*, Winter 1976, pp. 1289-1308.

Wolf has this definition: "Political terrorism may be defined as the threat of

use of deliberate violence, indiscriminately or selectively against either enemies or allies to achieve a political end." In his view, action must be taken against the terrorists, since submission only increases the number and pitch of their demands. He examines various ways of controlling terrorism : revision of the laws and enactment of nationwide penal codes, improved court management, and laws which would make payment of ransoms illegal; establishment of a hostage policy, making the media more responsible so that the terrorists do not have a glamour image; estalishment of a police task force to handle terrorist activities; creation of a Cabinet Committee to consider such activities; formation of a counter-terrorist and response group, liason between federal and local law enforcement agencies.

The danger is not likely to go away. In fact, it is likely to increase. "No doubt some will argue that there is no way to guard against the unknown and unseen and will oppose the expenditure of tax dollars for preventive measures. This sort of fatalism can result in terrorist incidents that might otherwise have been prevented... It would be foolish to pretend that the tide of sabotage, extortion, bombings and hijackings can be totally turned back. But if we are not to surrender to lawlessness, we must expand our present efforts to make terrorism less effective and less attractive as a political weapon."

(PRAJ: PRID)

0792 Wurth-Hough, Sandra. Network News Coverage of Terrorism : The Early Years. *Terrorism : An International Journal*, Volume 6, Number 3, 1982-83.

The electronic media influence public opinion by defining which national and international issues become significant, and shape public debates by the television images conveyed to the American audience. Based upon the Vanderbilt Television News Archieve, this study examines the image projected in reporting of terrorist activities by the three major national networks, the American Broadcasting Company (ABC), the Columbia Broadcasting System (CBS), and the National Broadcasting Company (NBC). The reality presented by the media is explored by comparing variables such as story emphasis and depiction, frequency, length of coverage and location in the newscasts.

(T)

0793 Yoder, Amos. United Nations Resolutions against International Terrorism. *Terrorism : An International Journal*, Volume 6, Number 4, 1982-83.

Nine years after the Munich Massacre of 11 Israeli athletes and after a request by the Secretary-General for the General Assembly to act on the problem, the General Assembly reached a general consensus on a terrorism resolution. The resolution endorses a UN Committee's recommendations to refrain from assisting terrorism in any way and to cooperate in the final elimination of terrorism. Negotiation of the resolution was difficult because third world countries did not want to weaken opposition to "colonial, racist, and alien regimes," and they have held back from approving an international convention that would require trying or extraditing those accused of terrorist crimes. Problems of constitutional protection to individuals in democracies and of political asylum also stand in the way of an overall convention. Nevertheless, the General Assembly resolution has been useful in promoting cooperation among states to eliminate terrorism and in encouraging support for conventions against specific types of terrorism such as hijacking, taking of hostages, attacking diplomatic targets and supporting nuclear terrorism.

(T)

0794 Yodyat, Aryeh. The Soviet Union and the Palestine Guerrillas. *Mizan*, January/February 1969, pp. 8-17.

Good piece, especially on Soviet criticism of the Fedayeen's tactics. "... a paradoxical situation developed : The Soviet Union was supporting a movement and its activities not because it liked them, but because it felt it would gain too much unpopularity by opposing them, whereas support would entitle it to a certain measure of supervision."

(M&G)

0795 Young, Robert. Revolutionary Terrorism, Crime and Morality. *Social Theory and Practice*, Volume 4, Number 3, Fall 1977, pp. 287-302.

In this paper I offer an account of the nature of revolutionary terrorism. I then proceed to offer two defences for certain revolutionary terrorist activities: as a response to state-inspired terrorism and along lines analogous to the circumstances of a just war. It is stressed that revolutionary terrorism may prove more economical in terms of loss of life and destruction than is the case with conventional war, despite the fact that the bestiality of such terrorism in as much emphasized in the media. Finally, I take up questions about indiscriminateness, harm to innocents, what constitutes "success" and the like.

(IPSA)

0796 Young, Rochfort and Adams, John. *Case for Detention*. London, Bow Publications, 1974.

Argues for continuance of detention without trial in Northern Ireland as long as the judicial system continues to be ineffective.

(N&G)

0797 Zabih, Sepehr. Aspects of Terrorism in Iran. *Annals of the American Academy of Political and Social Science*, Number 463, September 1982, pp. 84-94.

Even prior to the Constitutional Revolution of 1905-11, acts of terrorism were a commonly accepted form of political and religious struggle in Iran. Since the 1978-79 turmoil, terrorism has been used frequently by governments in power and has attained a transnational dimension. Beginning in the early 1900s, the composition and ideological orientation of violent groups have changed dramatically from religious fundamentalist in the forties and fifties to Marxist and Marxis Islamic since the mid-sixties. After the 1979 revolution began, there was a significant realignment of all political terrorist forces. In order to overthrow the Shah, these groups joined Khomeini and staged successful insurrection. Two years later, the more secular groups deserted the Islamic Republic in order to wage an armed struggle for its overthrow. The transnational dimension of terrorism in Iran has also changed. Such states or entities as Libya, Lebanon, the Palestine Liberation Organization (PLO) and Shia Lebanese Amal are no longer on the side of either Khomeini or his arch opponents. For the Foreseeable future, political terrorism will continue to be a common feature of the Iranian scene.

(PRAJ: PRID)

# PART – II

# ADDENDA

0798 Anderson, Jack. Terrorism Abetted by Pakistan (in India). *Current*, October 12, 1985, p.4.

The American columnist Jack Anderson accuses Pakistan of supporting Sikh extremists with both arms and training. He is also making a one-hour movie on modern India, where he would try to depict the damage caused by the terrorists in Punjab.

0799 Bochikarvov, V. Backing the Terrorists. *New Times*, Februray 1986, p.8.

Article criticizes President Reagan for supporting Jonas Savimbi, leader of the UNITA terrorists, in his struggles against the Marxist Government in Luanda.

0800 Camper, Frank. China, Pak Aiding Terrorists. *Times of India*, March 17, 1986, p.16.

Frank Camper writes that he was told by Sikhs, who had undergone training in his school, that China and Pakistan were aiding the Sikh terrorists' cause, providing both money and weapons as well as safe areas inside their own borders, for training or hiding. Terrorists had formulated a plan to contaminate food and water sources in India and to destroy India's nuclear reactors. Camper states further that he was keeping an FBI agent informed about his encounters with Sikhs.

0801 Charles, KJ. Terrorism: An Instrument of Oppression. *Patriot*, June 11, 1986, p.4.

Terrorism, according to the author, is the last desperate resort of persecuted groups, for whom all democratic representations are closed down. Author cites the examples of Israel, South Africa and Sri Lanka Governments, who have refused to recognize the desperations of oppressed peoples in territories under their jurisdiction.

0802 Combating Terrorism. *National Herald*, April 11, 1986, p.5.

Article stresses for a comprehensive extradition treaty, between India and England, which would provide an effective deterrent to the activities of Sikh terrorists that are operating in Britain with impunity. It is, however, dismayed over the talks held between British foreign secretary and New Delhi, but hopes that those at the helm of affairs in the United Kingdom would not abdicate their responsibility for the sake of a set of looney gangsters.

0803 Curbing Terrorism. *Hindustan Times*, March 26, 1986, p.6.

Article deals with the cooperation US Government has extended, after initial hesitation, to Indian Government to help in curbing Sikh terrorists in USA and especially in the case of Gurpartab Singh Birk, a Sikh terrorist. Also the US Attorney-General's disclosure that a group of lawyers of the two countries will be constituted to plug the loopholes in the extradition treaty, is welcomed.

0804 Devikar, DK. Soviet Union and Terrorism. *Clarity* (Bombay), May 18, 1986, p.4.

Article emphasizes the role Soviet Union is playing in fighting the menace of international terrorism.

0805 Dr Isidore, International Terrorism. *Daily,* (Bombay), January 28, 1986, p.9.

The international terrorist groups, are aided and abetted by powerful individuals, Government agencies and even Heads of State.

In Punjab, terrorists aim to overthrow the Government to create an independent state, which goes against the canons of the constitution. Author welcomes Akali Dal Government's policies in combating terrorism and advises central government to take severe action against countries which aid and abet terrorism.

0806 Dubey, K.P. Lingering Shadow of Terrorism in India. *Indian Nation*, January 11, 1987.

Terrorism and secessionism in India, particularly in Punjab, Kashmir and some parts of North-Eastern States has taken an acute form, creating terror, affecting the lives of people.

0807 Easier Extradition. *Tribune*, March 11, 1986, p.4.

The article criticizes the passive attitude of British Government, towards other countries' protest, about its indulgent attitude to persons accused of criminal acts on its soil. The Thatcher Government's decision to amend the 116-year old extradition law represents a significant step forward. India should press for a comprehensive treaty on the subject because terrorism in Punjab is largely financed and supported from British soil.

0808 Extremists Abroad. *Deccan Herald,* (Bangalore), January 30, 1986, p.8.

Article deals with the murder of moderate Sikh leader Tersem Singh Toor, in his liquor shop at Southall. The reported assurance of British Home Secretary Douglas Hurds to Indian High Commissioner P.C. Alexander, to bring to book those responsible for Toor's murder is reassuring, but serious thought should be given by British Government to stop and apprehend the terrorist elements from doing such destardly acts.

0809 Maini, Darshan Singh. Dialect of Terrorism I & II. *Tribune*, December 3-4, 1986, p.4.

Author views terrorism as psycho-pathological problem while recognizing

the economic and ideological aspects of terrorism.

0810 Move to Curb Terrorism. *Deccan Chronicle*, February 12, 1986, p.6.

Article discusses the proposed extradition treaties between India and Canada, to curb the Sikh terrorists. The double standards used by certain nations has resulted in the growth of terrorism in some part of the world. Member-States of the UN General Assembly should sign existing global treaties against terrorism and take steps to harmonise domestic legislation with those treaties.

0811 Namboodiri, PKS. Terrorism and Intervention. *Mainstream*, July 6, 1985, p.5.

Author differentiates between war, insurgency, guerrilla warfare and terrorism. He further differentiates between terrorism by individuals/groups and state-sponsored terrorism.

0812 New Legislation to Control Terrorism Urged. *Patriot*, November 6, 1985.

Article discusses a paper presented at the four day All India Police Science Congress, in Shillong on November 5, 1985, which suggests that government enact an emergency legislation to control terrorism.

Paper suggested that police officers should be trained to combat terrorism. The urban terrorists were young, educated, married males, less than 25 years, and belong to middle class families. Paper also suggests a definite link between terrorists and smugglers and that most terrorists had links with international smugglers.

0813 Pak Aid to Terrorists. *Deccan Chronicle*, February 8, 1986, p.6.

Article accuses Pakistan and some other external forces for providing sophisticated arms and training to Sikh extremists and encouraging separatist feelings in Kashmir valley. Also Sikh separatists have bases in Canada and some of them have undergone training in mercenary schools.

0814 Politics of Assassination. *Link*, August 4, 1985, p.1.

Article talks about fresh assassination attempts by Sikh extremists, particularly the murder of Lalit Maken but hopes that country will frustrate their designs, as it has done before. It warns the country about Reagan's double standards in dealing with extremists (particularly Sikh extremists) and advises that the country should deal firmly with extremists.

0815 Protecting Murderers. *Patriot*, January 30, 1986, p.4.

Article accuses British Government for affording refuge to Khalistanis and Kashmiri separatists, thereby encouraging their nefarious deeds. The murder campaign against moderate Sikhs and Indian diplomats in that country, raises serious doubts about British Government's sincerety. Article urges Indian Government to take strong and firm stand with British Government on these issues.

0816 Reagan Terrorism. *New Age*, April 20, 1986, p.2.

Article severely condemns President Ronald Reagan for US bombing raid of Libyan establishments and the brazen manner in which Reagan justified it and even threatened to repeat it again. All major leaders of world, except Margaret Thatcher of Britain, have criticized this move of President Reagan.

0817 Sharma, V. D. Terrorists: Double Faced British Policy. *Patriot*, March 17, 1986, p.4.

Author criticizes the policy of the U.K. Government to control the activities of Sikh extremists in Britain and calls it not only double-faced but also hypocritical and cites concrete examples.

0818 State Terrorism in South Africa. *Deccan Chronicle*, July 23, 1985, p.6.

Article criticizes President P.W. Botha of South Africa for assuming emergency powers to crush (suppress) the majority blacks and warns that it may lead to a blood bath. The transition to majority rule in South Africa he says, is historically inevitable. Article urges the comity of nations to liberate the majority blacks from the racist rule.

0819 State Sponsored Terrorism. *New Wave*, July 7, 1985, p.13.

Article discusses and criticizes the conference of anti-government rebels of Angola, Nicaragua, Afghanistan, and Laos in an Unita Camp on the Angolan territory, organized by CIA, with President Reagan's personal approval.

0820 Subrahmanyam, K. Terrorism: To the Forefront of the Stage. *Strategic Analysis,* (New Delhi), June 1986, pp. 237-248.

Author discusses two categories of terrorism - one which is plain criminal and the other political and both are on increase.

0821 Syria Abetting Terrorism. *Mid-Day,* (New Delhi), January 22, 1987, p.16.

US Defence Secretary Weinberger has charged Syria, Iran and Libya for supporting international terrorism to promote their political goals and stated that United States will still consider military measures as a last resort against states which support terrorism.

0822 Terrorisation. *Patriot*, April 22, 1984, p.4.

Author criticizes Reagan's type of terrorism and argues for a world-wide alert against U.S. terrorism.

0823 Terrorism. *Democratic World*, May 19, 1985, pp. 3-4.

Terrorism is a product of either despotic systems which do not allow the expression of dissent or that of economic reasons when a section of people get no benefit from national growth. Sikh terrorism does not fit into these two categories and is directed from abroad by rich Sikhs. Article does not see any future for Sikh terrorism in India and supports these arguments by analyzing the fate of Naxalites in India.

0824 Terrorism. *National Herald*, June 29, 1985, p.7.

Article welcomes the Canadian Government's declaration that it would not allow terrorists to turn their country into a playground, after the sabotage of the Air India's 747 Boeing and urges different nations especially US, Canada and Britain to collectively evolve steps to meet the grave situation created by International terrorism.

0825 Terrorism – A Global Phenomenon. *Search Light*, (Patna), October 6, 1985, p.5.

Article discusses the role of Libya, South Yemen, Syria and Iran, in supporting the international terrorist organizations with money, massive quantities of arms, as well as in setting up terrorist schools in their countries to impart training to the terrorist groups.

0826 Terrorism Unlimited. *Pioneer*, (Lucknow), April 25, 1986, p.6.

Most of the present day terrorism has its roots in the Arab-Israel unresolved conflict in West Asia. No Western country is free from this menace. Terrorism has to be combated globally, not by repression alone but by removing root causes of this strife. Unfortunately countries like US, Britain, France have used double standards viz Britian, which claims special relations with India, accommodating Sikh terrorists expatriates, US raid on Libya and subsidy to Israel and Pakistan's support to Sikh extremists with US backing.

0827 Varma, Parpuranand. Terrorism: World Wide Phenomenon. *Hindustan Times*, July 19, 1985, p.9.

Nearly all democracies are facing the problem of terrorism, since criminal law and judicial system is based on democratic principles. Now some Democracies have developed systems of secret survelliance of subversive elements with certain checks, to counter the menace. Author cites two judgements of the European Court of Human Rights, which have become a standard for all European courts.

0828 War as Terrorism. *National Herald*, November 9, 1985, p.5.

Article welcomes the Canadian Government move against Sikh extremists. The new regulation issued by the Canadian Government through its order in Council does seek to expand its extradition act to include India. Side by side Britian pledges to evolve a legal machinary to send back to India the extremists based in London, which would help in fighting Sikh terrorism. Similarly Reagan's assurance to Mr. Rajiv Gandhi for his cooperation in fighting the terrorist threat, would help in dealing with this menace, is a welcome sign.

# PART — III
# REFERENCES

0001 A Conspiracy in Islamabad. *Times of India*, 10 February 1971, p. 6.

0002 A Danger in Europe's Terrorism Convention: The End for the Political Refugee. *The Times*, 7 February 1978, p. 14.

0003 A Season of Booms. *Link*, Volume 20, Number 12, 30 October 1977, pp. 27-28.

0004 A Sinister Phase. *Times of India*, 12 May 1985, p. 1.

0005 A Warning. *Times of India*, 2 February 1971, p. 1.

0006 A Welcome Turn. *Tribune*, 26 December 1984, p. 4.

0007 Abdi, S.N.M. Terror in Shangri-La. *Illustrated Wkly India*, Volume 106, Number 11, 1985, pp. 20-23.

0008 Abraham, Abu. Escape from Paradise. *Deccan Herald*, Magazine Section, 10 June 1984, p. 5.

0009 Abraham, A.S. Politics of Violence. *Times of India*, 18 May 1984, p. 6.

0010 Abraham, A.S. Scourge of the Terrorist : A Failure of International Will. *Times of India*, 28 June 1985, p. 8.

0011 Abraham, A.S. Indian Stand on Terrorism : No Need for a Crystal Ball. *Times of India*, 2 May 1986, p. 8.

0012 Abraham, A.S. Pressures on the System : Coping with Trauma of Punjab. *Times of India*, 23 August 1985, p. 8.

0013 Abrahamson, D. Political Terror in U.S. What Next? *U.S. News*, Number 76, 4 March 1974, pp. 15-17.

0014 Abrahamson, David. *The Murdering Mind*. New York, Harper Colophon, 1973.

0015 Abu-Lughad, Ibrahim. Unconventional Violence and International Law. *American Journal of International Law*, Number 67, November 1973, pp. 100-104.

0016 Abu-Shakrah, J. *Israeli Settler Violence in the Occupied Territories 1980-84*. Illinois, Palestinian Human rights Campaign, 1985.

0017 Act of State Terrorism. *Deccan Herald*, 23 September 1985, p. 8.

0018 Act of Vengence. *Times of India*, 5 September 1985, pp. 1-2.

0019 Adamie, Louis. *Dynamite : The Story of Class Violence in America*. New York, Viking Press, 1934.

0020 Adams, James. *The Financing of Terror*. London, New English Library, 1986.

0021 Adams, James Ring. Armenian Terrorism : Lessons and Links of Anti-Turkish terrorism. *Wall St. J*, Volume 202, Number 32, August 1983.

0022 Adams, William C. The Beirut Hostages. *Public Opinion*, Number 8, August/September 1985, pp. 45-48.

0023 Adding up to an Epidemic. *Time*, Volume 106, Number 36, 3 November 1975.

0024 Adelman, Jonathan. R. *Terror And Communist Politics : The Role of Secret Police in Communist State*. Boulder, Westview, 1984.

0025 Adie, W.A.C. China, Israel and the Arabs. *Conflict Studies*, Number 12, May 1971.

0026 Adkins, E.H. Jr. Protection of American Industrial Dignitaries and Facilities Overseas. *Security Management*, Number 18, July 1974, p. 14.

0027 After Hearst Arrest : Drive to Root Out U.S. Terror Gangs.. *U.S. News*, Volume 79, Number 22, 6 October 1975.

0028 After Mountbatten. *Economist*, Number 272, 1 September 1979, pp. 11-12 & pp. 19-20.

0029 Aftermath of the Kidnappings : Relationship of Terrorism and Increased Intelligence Activities. *Nation*, Volume 218, Number 292, 9 March 1974.

0030 After the Hijacking. *Indian Express, Delhi*, 9 July 1984, p. 6.

0031 After the Blasts. *Business Standard*, 24 May 1985, p. 5.

0032 Again, the Palestinians : Fatah Raid on Nahariya and Israeli Retaliation. *Time*, Volume 104, Number 18, 8 July 1974;

0033 Agirre, Julen. *Operation Orgo : The Execution of Admiral Luis Carrero Blanco*. New York, Quadrangle Books, 1975.

0034 Agony in the Air. *Economic Times*, 7 July 1984, p. 5.

0035 Agony in the Arqub : Israeli Assaults. *Time*, Number 104, 30 September 1974, pp. 43-4.

0036 Agrawala, S.K. *Aircraft Hijacking and International Law*. New York, Dobbs Ferry, Oceana, 1973.

0037 Agrov, Shhomo. *An Ambassador Speaks out*. London, Wiedenfled and Nicolson, 1983.

0038 Aguilera Peralta, Gabriel. Terror and Violence as Weapens of Counter-insurgency in Guatemala. *Latin Am Perspectives*, Number 7, Spring/Summer 1980, pp. 91-131.

0039 Ahuja, Charanjit. Punjab : The Unresolved Issues. *Indian Express*, Magazine Section, 8 December 1985, p. 3.

0040 Akali Resolve to Crush Terrorism. *Times of India*, 7 January 1986, p. 1.

0041 Akalis Continue to Provoke. *Madhya Pradesh Chronicle*, 13 June 1985, p. 4.

0042 Al-Ayouty, Yassin. Egypt and the Palestinians. *Current History*, Number 39, January 1973, pp. 5-12.

0043 Al-Ayouty. Palestinians and the Fourth Arab : Israeli War. *Current History*, February 1974, pp. 74-78.

0044 Albright, Joseph. Series of Three Articles on the Security of Nuclear Weapons. *Atlanta Journal Constitution*, 8,15,22 January 1978.

0045 Aleock, N. et al. The Prediction of Civil Violence to the Year 2001. *Journal of Interdisciplinary Cycle Research*, Volume 9, Number 4, 1978, pp. 307-24.

0046 Al Fatah Hijackers. Threaten World Peace. *Organiser*, Volume 24, Number 6, 19 September 1970, p. 6.

0047 Alines, Ronald C. *The Jewish Underground Against the British Mandate in Palestine*. M.A. Thesis, New York Union College, 1973.

0048 Alexander, Yonah. Narco-terrorism : Some Strategic Considerations. *Crossroads*, 20 Number, 1986, pp. 55-71.

0049 Alexander, Yonah. From Terrorism to War : The Anatomy of the Birth of Israel. In Alexander Yonah (Ed.). *International Terrorism : National Regional and Global Perspectives*. New York, Praeger Publishers, 1976.

0050 Alexander, Yonah. Terrorism and the Media in the Middle East. In Alexander, Yonah and Finger, Saymaur, M. (Eds). *Terrorism Interdisciplinary Perspective*. New York, The John Jay Press, 1977.

0051 Alexander, Yonah and Friedlander, Robert. *Self-Determination : National, Regional, and Global Dimension*: Boulder, Colorado, Westview Press, 1979.

0052 Alexander, Yonah and Cline, Ray S. *Terrorism as State Sponsored Covert Warfare*. Democracy L.M. Fairfax, Herobooks, 1984.

0053 Alexander, Yonah. *Communications Aspects of International Terrorists*. Toronto, ont., International Studies Association, February 1976.

0054 Allbach, D.M. Countering Special-Threat Situations. *Military Police Law Enforcement Journal*, Number 2, Summer 1975, pp 34-40.

0055 Allen, Thomas B. The Enemies of all Mankind : Piracy and Terrorism Combine to Create New Dangers for Mariners. *Sea Power*, Volume 38, Number 11, October 1985, pp. 48-52.

0056 Alon, Hanan. *Counting Palestinian Terrorism in Israel : Towards a Policy Analysis of Counter-measures*. Diss, Santa Monica, The Rand Corporation, 1980.

0057 Al-Qasimi, Sultan Muhammad. *The Myth of Arab Piracy in Gulf*. London, Croom Helm Ltd., 1986.

0058 Altheide, David L. Impact of Format and Ideology on TV News Coverage of Iran: Production Formats Compatible with Ideological Statements without Intending to be. *Journalism Q*, Number 62, Summer 1985, pp. 346-51.

0059 Alsina, Geronimo. The War and the Tupamaros. *Bulletin Tricontinental*, August 1972, pp. 29-42.

0060 Alves, M.M. Kidnapped Diplomats : Greek Tragedy on a Latin State. *Commonwealth*, Number 92, 1970, pp. 311-14.

0061 Alves, M.M. *A Grain of Mustard Seed*. Garden city, New York, Doubleday Anchor Press, 1973.

0062 American Reactions are a Little Primitive. *Middle East Rept*. Number 17, January/February, 1987, pp. 39-43.

0063 Anable, D. Tackling the International Problem. *Current*, Number 180, February 1976, pp. 57-60.

0064 Anable, D. Terrorism : Loose Net Links, Diverse Groups no Central Plot; and Terrorism : How a Handful of Radical States Kept it in Business. *Christian Science Monitor*, 14, 15 March 1977, pp. 18 and 19, and 14 and 15 respectively.

0065 Anand, V.K. Governments : The Greatest Terrorists. *U.S.I.J* Volume 113, Number 474, pp. 209-20.

0066 Anand, V.K. *Terrorism and Security*. New Delhi, Deep and Deep Publication, 1984.

0067 Anand, V.K. Propaganda and Terrorism. *The Hindustan Times*, 17 September 1980.

0068 Anand, V.K. Special Police Force. *The Hindustan Times*, 13 November 1980.

0069 Anand, V.K. Terrorism : Planning Safer Human Settlements. *School of Planning and Architecture Journal*, September 1983.

0070 Anand, V.K. Soldiers Role In International Security. *The Times of India*, 13 May 1980.

0071 Anand, V.K. Intelligence for Internal Security. *Suraksha*, July 1981.

0072 Anand, V.K. Governing Disturbed Areas. *Vikrant*, July 1981.

0073 Anand, V.K. Future Terrorism : Threats and Security. *United Services Institution of India Journal*, Volume 115, Number 480, April - June 1985, pp. 115-25.
0074 Anderson, W. *Age of Protest*. Pacific Palisades, Calif, Goodyear Publishing, 1969.
0075 Andics, Hellmut. *Rule of Terror : Russia Under Lenin and Stalin*. New York, Holt, Rinehart & Winston, 1969.
0076 Andreski, Stanislav. *Parasitism and Subversion : The Case of Latin America*. New York, Pantheon, 1967.
0077 Andrews, William R. - *The Village War : Vietnamese Communist Revolutionary Activities in Dinh Tuong Province, 1960-1964*. Missourie, University of Missouri Press, 1973.
0078 Another Hijacking. *Northern India Patrika*, 8 July 1984, p. 4.
0079 Answer to Terrorism. *The Hindustan Times*, 24 August 1985, p. 9.
0080 Antonius, George. *The Arab Awakening*. Beirut, Khayat, 1955.
0081 Arafat, Yasser. Address to the 29th Session of the United Nations General Assembly, 13 November, 1974. *New York Times*, 14 November 1974.
0082 Arendt, Hannah. *On Revolution*. New York, Viking, 1965.
0083 Arendt, Hannah. *On Violence*. London, Penguin, 1970.
0084 Arey, James A. *The Sky Pirates*. New York, Charles Scribner's Sons, 1971.
0085 Around the Globe Outbrakes of Terror. *U.S. News*, Volume 79, Number 76, 29 September 1975.
0086 Arul, F.V. Urban Terrorism. *Indian Journal of Criminology*, (Supplement), Volume 7, Number 2, pp. 167-70.
0087 Arul, F.V. Urban Terrorism. *CBI Bull*, Volume 17, Number 10, October 1983, pp. 1-3.
0088 Aruri, Naseer H. U.S. Policy and Terrorism. *American Arab Affairs*, Number 14, Fall, 1985, pp. 59-70.
0089 Ashwood, Tom. *Terror in the Skies*. New York, Stein and Day, 1986.
0090 Asprey, Robert. *War in the Shadows : The Guerrilla in History*. Two Volumes, New York, Doubleday & Company, 1973.
0091 Aston, Clive C. Political Hostage-taking in Western Europe. *Conflict Studies*, Number 15, 1984, p. 21.
0092 At War with the IRA. *Newsweek*, Volume 84, Number 46, 9 December 1974;
0093 Atla, Charles and Groffier, Ethel. *Terrorism et Guerrilla; La Revolt Armee Devent Les Nations*. Montreal, Lemeak, 1973.

0094 Atwater, James. Time to Get Tough with Terrorists : An Interview with Brain Crozier. *Readers Digest*, April 1973, pp. 89-93.

0095 Aubry, Dixon, et al. *Communist Guerrilla Warfare*. New Delhi, English Book Dept., 1962.

0096 Australia Parliament. *Protective Security Review Reports*, 15 May 1979 unclassified Version Hope, R.M. 1979.

0097 Austria. Federal Chancellery. *The events of September 28 and 29, 1973: A Documentary Report*. Vienna, Idem, 1973.

0098 Avner, Pseud. *Memoirs of an Assassin*. New York, Thomas Yoseloff, 1959.

0099 Azad, Abul Kalam. *India Wins Freedom*. Calcutta, Orient Longmans 1959.

0100 Baffling Ineptitude. *Times of India*, 5 April 1984, p. 8.

0101 Bailey, Martin. Terrorism Reaches New Heights. *Amrit Bazar Patrika*, 15 July 1985, p. 6.

0102 Bailey, Martin. Terrorism Spreads. *Tribune*, 15 July 1985, p. 4.

0103 Bailey, Sydney D. *Prohibitions and Restraints in war*. London, Oxford University Press, 1972.

0104 Bains, Chester A. *Vietnam : The Roots of Conflict*. Englewood Cliffs, New Jersey, Prentice-hall, 1967.

0105 Baldwin, David A. *Bargaining with Airline Hijackers. The 50% Solution : How To Bargain Successfully with Hijackers, Strikers, Rosses, Oil magnates, Arabs, Russians, and other Worldly Opponents in this Modern World*, edited by I. William zartman. Garden City, New York. Anchor Press/Doubleday, 1976.

0106 Bandyopadhyay, Jayanta. Technological Terrorism: *Indian Express*, Delhi, 25 December 1986, p. 6.

0107 Banerjee, Sumanta. Wanted an MP's Watch Dog Panel. *Deccan Herald*, 21 May, 1985, p. 8.

0108 Barber, Noel. *The War of the Running Dogs : The Malayan Emergency, 1948-1960*. London, Collins, 1971.

0109 Barber, Charles T. *Sanctions Against Modern Transnational Crimes*. Paper Presented to the Conference on New Directions in International Relations. Teaching and Research, Bloomington, Indiana, May 1976.

0110 Barder, Liz. Supermarket Killing Jolt, Belgium Back to Reality. *Amrit Bazar Patrika*, 22 November, 1985, p. 6.

0111 Barkey, David W. and D. Stanley Eitzen. Toward an Assessment of Multinational Corporate Social Expenditures in Relation to Political Stability and Terrorist Activity: The Argentine Case (Whether

Particular Activities of Multinationals Encourage or Discourage Terrorist Attacks). *Inte An Econ Affairs*, Number 34, Spring 1981, pp. 77-90.

0112 Barnala Warns Terrorists of Harsh Steps. *Times of India*, 16 February 1986, p. 1.

0113 Barnes, J. War of the Proles. *Newsweek*, Number 81, 19 February 1973, pp. 51-52.

0114 Barrett, R.T. Political Assassination in Japan. *Great Britain and the East*, Number 50, 10 March 1938, p. 260.

0115 Barrie, G.N. Crimes Committed Abroad Air-Craft. *South African Law Journal*, Number 83, 1968, pp. 203-208.

0116 Barron, John. Trained as a Terrorist at Age Nine. *Statesman*, 19 July, 1985, p. 8.

0117 Barron, John. *KGB : the Soviet Work of Soviet Secret Agents*. New York, Bantam, 1974.

0118 Barton, M. International Terrorism. *Review of International Affairs*, Number 23, 20 April 1972, p. 25.

0119 Battling Terrorism. *Hindustan Times*, 3 August 1985, p. 9.

0120 Baryshev, Alexander. El Salvador : Anatomy of Terror. *New Times*, Number 19, May 1981, pp. 23-25.

0121 Bassiouni, M. Cherif. International Control of Terrorism: Some Policy Proposals. *Internat R Criminal Policy*, Number 37, 1981, pp. 44-54.

0122 Baassiouni, M. Cherif. Terrorism and the Media. *Journal of Criminal Law and Criminology*, Number 72, Spring 1981, pp. 7-55.

0123 Bassiouni, M. Cherif. (Ed.). *International Terrorism and Political Crimes*. Springfield, Charles C. Thomas, 1975.

0124 Bassiouni, M. Cherif. The Political Offence Exception in Extradition Law and Practice. In Bassiouni, M. Cherif. (Ed.) - *International Terrorism and Political Crimes*. Springfield, Illionis, Charles C. Thomas, 1975, pp. 398-447.

0125 Bassiouni, M. Cherif. Methodological Options for International Legal Control of Terrorism. In Bassiouni, M. Cherif. (Ed.). *International Terrorism and Political Crimes*. Springfield, Illionis, Charles C. Thomas, 1975, pp. 485-492.

0126 Baudouim, Jean. *Terrorism et Justice Montreal*. New York, Editions du Jour, 1970.

0127 Bauer, Yehuda. - *From Diplomacy to Resistance : A History of Jewish Palestine, 1939-1945*. Philadelphia, Jewish Publication Society, 1970.

128 Baumann, Carol Elder. *The Diplomatic Kidnappings : A Revolutionary Tactics of Urban Terrorism*. The Hague, Nijhoff, 1973.

129 Baxter, R.R. Skeptical Look at the Concept of Terrorism. *Akron Law Review*, Number 7, Spring 1974, pp. 380-87.

130 Beall, Marshall D. Hostage Negotiations. *Military Police Law Enforcement Journal*, Number 111, Fall 1976.

131 Beatings, Filth, Hunger, Isolation-the Ordeal of Captivity of the American Hostage Held by Iran. *U.S. News*, Number 90, 2 February 1981, pp. 32-33.

132 Backett, J.C. Northern Ireland. *Journal of Contemporary History*, Number 6, 1971, pp. 121-134.

133 Beeson, T. British and the IRA. *Christian Century*, Number 93, 28 January 1976, pp. 60-62.

134 Beeman, William O. Terrorism : Community Based or State Supported? *Am-Arab Affairs*, Spring 1986, pp. 29-36.

135 Behind Hijacking Plot. *Link*, Volume 13, Number 26, 7 February 1971, p. 9.

36 Beirut's Order. *Deccan Herald*, 24 May, 1985, p. 8.

37 Bejor, Hector. *Peru 1965 : Notes on A Guerrilla Experience*. New York, Monthly Review, 1970.

38 Bell, J. Bowyer. The Escalation of Insurgency : The Experience of the Provisional IRA (1969-1971). *The Review of Politics*, Number 35, July 1973, pp. 398-411.

39 Bell, J. Bowyer. *The Secret Army : A History of the IRA*. London, Anthony Blond, Cambridge, MIT Press, 1974.

40 Bell, J. Bowyer. Assassination in International Politics : Lord Moyne, Count Bernadotte and the Lehi. *International Studies Quarterly*, Number 16, March 1972, pp. 59-82.

41 Bell, J. Bowyer. *The Long War : Isreal and the Arab Since 1946*. Englewood Cliffs, New Jersey, Prentice-Hall,1969.

2 Bell, J. Bowyer. Arafat's Man in the Mirror : The Myth of the Fedayeen. *New Middle East*, Number 19, April 1970, pp. 19-24.

3 Bell, J. Bowyer. *The Myth of Guerrilla : Revolutionary Theory and Malpractice*. New York, Alfred. A. Knopf, 1971.

4 Bell, J. Bowyer. Strategy, Tactics, and Terror : An Irish Perspective. In Yonah, Alexander (Ed.) *International Terrorism : National Regional and Global Perspectives*. New York, Praeger Publications, 1976, pp. 65-69.

0145 Bell, J. Bowyer. Endemic Insurgency and International Order: The Eritrean Experience. *Orbis*, Number 17, Summer 1974, pp. 427-480.
0146 Bell, J. Bowyer. The Terrorist Threat to United States Businesses Abroad. *Enterprise*. Number 5. August 1981, pp. 2-4.
0147 Bell, J. Bowyer. Transnational Terror and World Order. *South Atlantic Quarterly*, Number 74, Autumn 1975, pp. 404-417.
0148 Bell, J. Bowyer. Contemporary Revolutionary Organizations. In Robert O. Keohane and Joseph S. Nye, Jr., (Eds.). *Transnational Relations and World Politics*. Cambridge. Harvard University Press, 1973, pp. 153-168.
0149 Bell, J. Bowyer. The Chroniclers of Violence in Northern Ireland: The First Wave Interpreted. *The Review of Politics*, Number 34, October 1974, pp. 521-543.
0150 Bell, R. G. The U. S. Response To Terrorism Against International Civil Aviation. *Orbis*, 1976, pp. 1326-43.
0151 Bellinger, J. B. Civilian Role in Anti-Guerrilla Warfare. *Military Review*, September 1961.
0152 Ben-Dak, Joseph D. (Ed.). *The Future of Collective Violence: Societal and International Perspectives*. Lund, Studentilitteratur, 1974.
0153 Bennett, James P. and Saaty, Thomas L. *Terrorism: Patterns for Negotiations, Three Case Studies Through Hierarchies and Holarchies*. The Wharton School, University of Pennsylvania, August 1977.
0154 Bennett, Richard L. *The Blacks and the Trans*. Boston, Houghton Mifflin, 1959.
0155 Bennett, W. T. U. S. Initiatives in the United Nations to Combat International Terrorism. *International Lawyer*, Number 7, 1973, pp. 753-759.
0156 Bennett, W. T. U. S. Outlines Principles for Work of Adhoc Committee on Terrorism, Statement. 24 July, 1973. Jr. *Department State Bulletin*, Number 69, 3 September, 1973, pp. 337-39.
0157 Bennett, W. T. U. S. Votes Against UN General Assembly Resolution Calling for Study of Terrorism. *Department of State Bulletin*, Number 68, 22 January 1973, pp. 81-94.
0158 Benson, Mike. et al. Women as Political Terrorists. In *Research in Law, Deviance and Social Control*, 1982, pp. 121-30.
0159 Berard, Stanley P. Nuclear Terrorism: More Myth Than Reality. *Air Univ R.*, Number 36, July-August 1985, pp. 30-36.

0160 Béres, Louis Rene. The Threat of Palestinian Nuclear Terrorism In the Middle East. *International Problems*, Number 15, Fall 1976, pp. 48-56.

0161 Béres, Louis Réne. Terrorism and the Nuclear Threat in the Middle East. *Current History*, Number 70, January 1976, pp. 27-29.

0162 Béres, Louis Réne. *Apocalypse: Nuclear Catastrophe in World Politics*. Chicago, University of Chicago Press, 1980.

0163 Béres, Louis Réne. Terrorism and International Security: The Nuclear Threat. *Chitty's Law Journal*, Volume 26, Number 3, 1978, pp. 73-90.

0164 Béres, Louis Réne. Guerrillas, Terrorists and Polarity: New Structural Models of World Politics. *The Western Political Quarterly*, Number 27, December 1974, pp. 624-636.

0165 Béres, Louis Réne. The Nuclear Threat of Terrorism. *International Studies Notes* of the International Studies Association, Number 5, Spring 1978, pp. 14-17.

0166 Berger, Elena. Dealing with Libya. *Editorial Research Repts*, 14 March, 1986, pp. 187-204.

0167 Beri, H. M. L. Terrorism in Nepal. *Assam Tribune*, 10 July 1985, p. 4.

0168 Beristain, A. Terrorism and Aircraft Hijackings. *International Journal of Criminology and Penology*, Number 11, 1974, p. 327.

0169 Bhatt, S. C. Extradition: A Weapon against Terrorists. *Madhya Pradesh Chronicle*, 9 November, 1985, p. 4.

0170 Bhatt, S. C. International Terrorism in India. *Assam Tribune*, 13 April 1985, p. 4.

0171 Bhattacherjee, Arun. Curbing Terrorism becomes More Difficult. *Amrit Bazar Patrika*, 22 March 1985, p. 1.

0172 Bidwai, Praful. Murderers by Another Name. *Times of India*, Sunday-Review, 28 July, 1985, p. 1.

0173 Bienen, Henry. *Violence and Social Change: A Review of Current Literature*. Chicago, University of Chicago Press, 1968.

174 Bienen, H. and Gilpen, R. Economic Sanctions as a Response to Terrorism. *The Journal of Strategic Studies*, Volume 3, Number 1, 1980, pp. 89-98.

175 Bilinsky, Yaroslav. The Background of Contemporary Politics. In Arvids Ziedonia, Jr. Rein Taagepara and Mardi Valgemae (Eds.) *Problems of Mininations: Baltic Perspectives*. San Jose, California State University, Association for the Advancement of Baltic Studies, Inc., 1973.

0176 Billington, George R. *Nuclear Terrorism*. Maxwell Air Force Base, Air University, 1975.

0177 Binder, Sepp. *Terrorisms: Heraus for Denung and Antwort.* Bonn, Verlag News Grosellshehaft Geselles Chaft Gmbh, 1978.

0178 Birrell, Derek. Relative Deprivation as a Factor in the Conflict in Northern Ireland. *Sociological Review*, Number 20, August 1972.

0179 Bishop, Joseph W. Jr. Law in the Control of Terrorism and Insurrection: The British Laboratory Experience. *Law and Contemporary Problems*, Number 42, Spring 1978, pp. 140-201.

0180 Bishop, J. W. Jr. Can Democracy Defend itself against Terrorism. *Commentary*, Volume 65, Number 5, 1978, pp. 55-62.

0181 Bite, Vita. International Terrorism. *Library of Congress Congressional Research Service*, 31 October, 1975.

0182 Black, Eduin F. If Terrorism Goes Nuclear. *Washington Report*, May 1976.

0183 Black Friday. *Economic Times*, 13 May 1985, p. 5.

0184 Black September, Somber March, Executions in the Saudi Arabian Embassy – Khartoum. *Newsweek*, 12 March 1973, pp. 18-20.

0185 Blackburn, Robin. (Ed.). *Strategy for Revolution: Essays on Latin America by Regis Debray*. New York, Monthly Review, 1970.

0186 Blacker September; Reactions to Massacre in Khartourm. *Time*, 19 March 1973.

0187 Blackmail in Vienna. *Time*, Volume 102, Number 50, 8 October 1973.

0188 Blacksten, Ric and Engler, Richard. *Hostage Studies*. Artington, VA, Ketron Concept Paper, Ketron, Inc., 1974.

0189 Blacely, Stephen B. Capitol Security Strengthened after Terrorist Bomb Explodes (includes a list of major incidents of violence at the Capitol since 1814). *Cong Q W Rept.*, Number 41, 12 November 1983, pp. 2355-8.

0190 Blasts in Nepal. *Assam Tribune*, 27 June 1985, p. 4. and *Deccan Herald*, 21 June 1985, p. 6.

0191 Blishchenko, Igor Pavlouich. *Terrorism and International Law*. Moscow, Progressive Publishers, 1984.

0192 Blishchenko, I.P. International Violence as a Special Problem of the Fight Against Crime. *International Review of Criminal Policy,* Number 32, 1976, pp. 8-13.

1093 Blood in the Temple. *Indian Express*, Delhi, 28 November 1985, p. 6.

0194 Bloodier Friday in the South: Dublin Bombing. *Time*, Volume 103, Number 32, 27 May 1974.

0195 Bloody Thursday in Birminghum: Bombing of Bars by the IRA. *Time*, Volume 104, Number 58, 2 December 1974.

0196 Bloody Truce. *Time*, Volume 105, Number 37, 28 April 1975.

0197 Bloomfield, Louis M and Fitzgerald, Gesald F. *Crimes Against Internationally Protected Persons: Prevention and Punishment.* An Analysis of the UN Convention. New York, Praeger, 1975.

0198 Blow to Terrorism. *Patriot*, 27 September 1985, p. 4.

0199 Blum, J. The Protection of Persons and Installations at Risk: the German Way (Police Anti-Terrorist Measures). *Police Studies*, Number 1, December 1978, pp. 53-61.

0200 Blum, Yehuda Z. The Gulf of Sidra Incident. *Am. J. Internal Law*, Number 80, July 1986, pp. 668-77.

0201 Bobrow, D. B. Preparing for Unwanted Events. *Terrorism: An International Journal*, Volume 1, Numbers 3/4, 1978, pp. 397-422.

0202 Bocca, Geoffrey. *The Secret Army*. Englewood Cliffs, New Jersey, Prentice-Hall, 1968.

0203 Boire, Martin C. Terrorism Reconsidered as Punishment Toward an Evaluation of the Acceptability of Terrorism as a Method of Societal Change or Maintenance. *Stanford Journal of International Law*, Volume 20, Number 1, Spring 1984, pp. 45-134.

0204 Boiter, Albert. Terrorism and Linkage: Moscow's Reaction. *Pol. Communication And Persuasion*, Number 1, 1981, pp. 301-5.

0205 Boltwood, Charles E.; Cooper, Michael R., Fein, Victoria E. and Washburn, Paul U. Sky-Jacking, Airline Security and Passenger Reactions: Toward a Complex Model for Prediction. *American Psychologist*, Number 27, June 1972, pp. 539-545.

0206 Bomb Scare: Bomb Scare in Sangam Express. *Northern India Patrika*, 2 October 1985, p. 4.

0207 Bombay's Death Comment. *Patriot*, February 1985, p. 4.

0208 Bombs Bullets and Fear: Ulster's Agency Flares Anew. *U. S. News*, Number 76, 22 April, 1974, pp. 61-2.

0209 Bomb-Throwing Terrorists of old Russia. *Sr. School*, Number 105, 7 November 1974, pp. 10-11.

0210 Bombing Near U. S. Embassy Anex in Beirut: Remarks of President Reagan, 20 September 1984 and a Question and Answer Session with Reporters. *W. Comp Press Docs*, Number 20, 24 September 1984, pp. 1317-18.

0211 Bombs Away: Bombing by the Weather Underground. *Newsweek,* Volume 85, Number 20, 10 February 1975.

0212 Bonanate, Luigi. Some Unanticipated Consequences of Terrorism. *J. Peace Research*, Volume 16, Number 3, 1979, pp. 197-211.

0213 Bond, James E. *The Rules of Riot: Internal Conflict and the Law of War*. Princeton, New Jersey, Princeton University Press, 1974.

0214 Booth, John A. Rural Violence in Columbia, 1948-1963. *Western Political Quarterly*, Number 27, December 1974, pp. 657-679.

0215 Borisov, J. *Palestinian Underground: The Story of Resistance*. New York, Judea Publishing Company, 1947.

0216 Borodin, Nikolai. The Palestinian Resistance Movement: A Soviet View. *New Middle East*, December 1972, pp. 27-28.

0217 Bortos, M. International Terrorism. *Review of International Affairs,* Number 23, 20 April 1972, pp. 25-26.

0218 Bossony, Stefan. and others. *International Terrorism: The Communist Connection*. Washington, D. C., 1978.

0219 Boston, Guy D.; Marcus, Maruin and Weaton, Robbert J. *Terrorism - A Selected Bibliography.* Washington, National Institute of Law Enforcement and Criminal Justice. U. S. Dept. of Justice, 1976.

0220 Boulton, David. *The Ulster Volunteer Force, 1966-1973: An Anatomy of Loyalist Rebellion*. Dublin, Gill and Macmillan, Torc Books, 1973.

0221 Bouthoul, Gaston. Le Terrorism. *Etudes Polemogigues*, Number 8, April 1973, p. 37.

0222 Bouza, A. V. *Police Intelligence: The Operations of an Investigative Unit*. New York City, New York, AMS Press, Inc., 1976.

0223 Bowden, Tom. The IRA (Irish Republican Army) And the Changing Tactics of Terrorism. *Political Quarterly*, Number 47, October/December 1976, pp. 425-437.

0224 Bowen, Gordon L. The Political Economy of State Terrorism: Barrier to Human Rights In Guatemala. in Shepherd, George W. Jr. and Ved P. Nanda, (Ed.). - *Human Rights and Third World Development,* 1985, pp. 83-124.

0225 Bowen, D. and Masotti, L.H. *Civil Violence: A Theoretical Overview*. Cleveland, Case Western Reserve Civil Violence Research Centre, 1968.

0226 Boyle, K. and Hillyard, P. *Law and State: The Case of Northern Ireland*. London, Martin Robertson and Company Ltd., 1975.

0227 Boyle, Robert P. International Action to Combat Aircraft Hijacking. *Lawyer of The Americas*, Number 4, ;1972, pp. 460-473.

0228 Brach, Richard S. The Inter-America Convention on the Kidnapping of Diplomats. *Columbia Journal of Transnational Law*, Number 10.1071, pp. 292-412.

0229 Bradford, A. Lee. Legal Ramifications of Hijacking Airplanes. *American Bar Association Journal*, Number 48, November 1962, pp. 1034-1039.

0230 Bradshaw, Jon. The Dream of Terror. *Esquire*, July 18, 1978, pp. 24-50.

0231 Brady, David and Rappoport, Leon. Policy-Capturing in the Field: The Nuclear Safeguards Problem. *Organizational Behaviour and Human Performance*, Number 9, April 1973.

0232 Brandon, Henry. Jordon: The Forgotten Crisis: Were we Masterful... *Foreign Policy*, Number 10, Spring 1973, pp. 158-170.

0233 Bremer, L. Paul III. Practical Measures for Dealing with Terrorism. *Dept. State Bull*, Number 87, March 1987, pp. 1-4.

0234 Brewer, Gary D. *Existing in A World of Institutionalized Danger*. New Haven, Conn., School of Organization and Management, Yale University, Technical Report 102, March 1976.

0235 Breytenbach, B. *The True Confessions of an Albino Terrorist*. New York, McGrew, 1986.

0236 Brodie, Thomas G. *Bombs and Bombings : A Handbook to Detection, Disposal and Investigation for Police and Fire Departments*. Springfield, IL, Charles C. Thomas, 1975.

0237 Brody, Reed. *Contra Terror in Nicaragua: Report of a Fact Finding Mission. September 1984 - January 1985*. South End Pr., 1985.

0238 Brower, Charles N. Department Urges Senate Advice and Consent to Ratification of Montreal Convention on Aviation Sabotage. *Department of State Bulletin*, Number 67, 16 October 1972, pp. 444-448.

0239 Brower, Charles N. Aircraft Hijacking and Sabotage: Initiative or Inertia. *Department of State Bulletin*, Number 68, 18 June 1973, pp. 872-875.

0240 Browne, Jaffrey T. *International Terrorism : The American Response*. Washington, D.C., The American University, School of International Service, December 1973.

0241 Browne, Malcoln. *The New Face of War*. London, Cassell, 1966.

0242 Bruxelles. *Editions De L*. University of Bruxelles, 1974.

0243 Buch, M.N. Ideology Replaced by Population. *Madhya Pradesh Chronicle*, a June 1985, p. 4.

0244 Buck, J. J. Londoners Fight Bombs: Cheery Bravery of Steel Shutters? *Vogue*, Volume 166, Number 80, 1976.

0245 Buckley, E.F. Dance of the Terrorist : Punishment for Terrorist. *National Review*, Volume 26, Number 339, 15 March 1975.

0246 Buckley, William F. Jr. *UN Journal : A Delegate's Odyssey*. New York, G.P. Putnam's Sons, 1974.

0247 Buckelew, Alvin H. *Terrorism and the American Response*. Kottakuppam, Tamil Nadu, Mirza Pubs. 1984.

0248 Bullets, Bombs and a Sign of Hope : Maalot Attack by the Popular Democratic Front for the Liberation of Palestine. *Time*, Number 103, 27 May 1974, pp. 24-6.

0249 Bullets Against Ballot. *Statesman*, Delhi, 6 September 1985, p. 6.

0250 Burgess, William H. Countering Global Terrorism. *Military Review*, Volume 66, Number 6, June 1986, pp. 72-80.

0251 Burki, S.J. Social and Economic Determinants of Political Violence : A Case Study of the Punjab. *Middle East Journal*, Number 25, 1971, pp. 465-480.

0252 Burnett, H.B. Jr. Interview with Sean Mcbride. *Skeptic*, January/February 1974, pp. 8-11 and 54-57.

0253 Burnham, David. Nuclear Facilities told to Sterngthen Antiterrorist Guard. *The New York Times*, 20 February 1977, p. 1.

0254 Burnham, James. Notes on Terrorism. *National Review*, Number 24, 13 October 1972, p. 1116.

0255 Burnham, James. Anti-terror Problems. *National Review*, Volume 26, Number 265, 29 March 1974.

0256 Burnham, James. Entering the Terrorist Age? *National Review*, Volume 26, Number 262, 15 March 1974.

0257 Burnham, James. Roots of Terrorism. *National Review*, Volume 26, 16 March 1974, p. 311.

0258 Burnham, James. The Protracted Conflict. *National Review*, 1, 15 and 29 March 1974.

0259 Burton, Anthony M. *Urban Terrorism : Theory, Practice and Response*. London, Leo Cooper, 1975.

0260 Busuttil, James J. The Bonn Declaration on International Terrorism : A Non-Binding International Agreement on Aircraft Hijacking. *Internat and Comparative Law* (4th Ser), Number 31, July 82, pp. 474-87.

0261 Byron, C. Armagh : This is IRA Territory. *Time*, Volume 107, Number 26, 12 January 1976.

0262 Calculated Affront. *Tribune*, 26 September 1984, p. 4.

0263 Californias Underground. *Time*, Volume 106, Number 25, 6 October 1975.

0264 Callahan, Edward F. Terror in Venezuela. *Military Review*, Number 49, 1969, pp. 49-56.

0265 Calvert, Peter. The Diminishing Returns of Political Violence. *New Middle East*, May 1973, pp. 25-27.

0266 Campbell, John F. Rumblings Along the Red Sea : The Entrean Question. *Foreign Affairs*, Number 48, April 1970, pp. 537-548.

0267 Camper Reveals All. *Statesman*, 15 September 1985, p. 6.

0268 Campion, D.R. Of Many Things. *America 130*. 18 May 1974.

0269 Camus, Albert. *The Rebel : An Essay on Man in Revolt*. Translated by Anthony Bower, New York, Vintage Books, 1956.

0270 Camus, Albert. *Neither Victims Nor Executioners*. Chicago, World Without War. 1968.

0271 Can Airports be Safe from Terror Bombings? *U.S. News*, Volume 80, Number 58, 12 January 1976.

0272 Can U.S. Stem Tide of Revolution at its Doorstep? Washington Urging Moderation: Terrorists Use Gun and Bomb in a Battle to the Death for Power in Troubled Central America. *U.S. News*, Number 89, 3 November 1980, pp. 57-8.

0273 Canadian Council on International Law. *Conference Proceedings on International Terrorism*. Ottawa, October 18-19, 1974.

0274 Centrell, C.L. Political Offense Exemption in International Extradition : A Comparison of the United States, Great Britain and the Republic of Ireland. *Marguette Law Review*, Number 60, 1977, pp. 777-824.

0275 Carlton, David. *Terrorism : Theory and Practice*. Boulder, Colorado, 1979.

0276 Carlton, David and Carlo, Schaerf (Ed.). *Contemporary Terror : Studies in Sub-State Violence*. Macmillan, London, St Martin's 1981 Papers Presented at the Seventh Course of the International School on Disarmament and Research on Conflicts, Ariccia, Italy, 18-27 August 1978.

0277 Carnage At Imphal. *Patriot*, 16 March 1984, p. 4.

0278 Carr, Gordon. *The Angry Brigade : A History of Britain's First Urban Guerilla Group*. London, Gollancz, 1975.

0279 Carroll, R. Terror Incorporated. *Newsweek*, Volume 86, Number 40, 14 July 1975,

0280 Carroll, R. Year of Terror. *Newsweek*, 5 January 1976, pp. 24-6.

0281 Carroll, R. All Roads Lead to Paris. *Newsweek*, 21 July 1975, pp. 23-24.

0282 Carroll, R. All Roads Lead To Paris. *Newsweek*, 14 July 1975, p. 40.

0283 Carroll, R. and others. To Catch a Terrorist : Police Tactics. *Newsweek*, Volume 86, Numbers 36-7, 22 December 1975.

0284 Carroll, R. and Others. Tanzania : Animal Behaviour. *Newsweek*, Volume 85, Number 35, 2 June 1975.

0285 Carron, John and Torento. *Terrorism in Theory and Practice*. N.W. Washington, D.C. The Atlantic Council of Canada, 1978.

0286 Carter, B. and others. Maalot Remembered. *Newsweek*, 14 July 1975, p. 9.

0287 Casert, John S. *The Red Brigades*. Woodhill, 1978.

0288 Catton, W.R. Jr. Militants and the Media: Partners in Terrorism? *Indian Law Journal*, Number 53, 1978, pp. 680-715.

0289 Cause for Alarm. *Times of India*, 26 February 1986, pp. 1-2.

0290 Cause-fire Strains:Fedayeen Attach on Shamir Kibbutz. *Time*, Volume 103, Number 4, 24 June 1974.

0291 Chakhotin, S. *The Rape of The Masses*. New York, Haskell, 1971.

0292 Chakravarti, Nikhil. Raj Vocabulary. *Times of India*, Delhi, Magazine section, 26 May 1985, p.4.

0293 Chakravarti, P.R. Politics and Shandean of Violence. *Madhya Pradesh Chronicle*, 29 December 1983, p.7.

0294 Chaliand, Gerard. *The Palestinian Resistance*. Middlesex, Penguin, 1972.

0295 Chaliand, Gerard. *Revolution in the Third World : Myths and Prospects*. New York, The Viking Press, 1977.

0296 Chaliand, Gerard. *Terrorismes et Guerrillas : Techniques aetuelles de la Vilence*. France, Flammarion, 1985.

0297 Chaliand, Gerard. *Codebook : ITERATE International Terrorism : Attributes of Terrorist Events*. Ann Arbor, University of Michigan, 1976.

0298 Challenge of Terrorism. *Statesman*, 16 May 1985, p.6.

0299 Challenge in Punjab. *Madhya Pradesh Chronicle*, 7 July 1984, p.4.

0300 Cham, B.K. Terrorist Continue to Sneak in from Pak. *Indian Express,* 10 November 1984, p. 5.

0301 Chambard, Claude. *The Marguis: A History of the French Resistance Movement*. Indiana-Polis, Bobbs-Merril, 1976.

0302 Chaplin, David. Peru's Postponed Revolution. *World Politics,* Number 20, April 1968.

0303 Chapman, Robert D. *Crimson Web of Terror*. Boulder, Paladin Pr., 1980.

0304 Chappell, Duncan and Monahan, John, (Eds.). *Violence And Criminal Justice*. Lexington, Mass., Lexington Books, D.C., Heath, 1975.

0305 Charnay, Jean-Paul. Terrorisme et Politique. *Review Politique et Parlementaire,* Number 84, 1982, p. 75.

0306 Charters, David. The Changing Forms of Conflict in Northern Ireland. *Conflict Q*, Number 1, Fall 1980, pp. 32-39.

0307 Charters, David. Swift And Bold: An Appraisal of Hostage Rescue Operations. *Conflict Q*, Number 1, Summer 1980, pp. 26-33.

0308 Chase, L.J. (Ed.). *Bomb Threats, Bombings, and Civil Disturbances: A Guide for Facility Protection*. Corvallis, Oregon, Continuing Education Publications, 1971.

0309 Chatterji, Sunit Kumar. Africanistics and Genocide. *Man in India*, Volume 44, Number 1, January-March 1964, pp. 31-49.

0310 Chawla, N.L. Terrorism, Violence and Media. *Mainstream,* Volume 23, Number 47, 20 July 1985, p. 7.

0311 Chawla, N.L. Terrorism, Violence and Role of Media. *Patriot,* 15 July 1985, p. 4.

0312 Chawla, N.L. Media Is also an Intelligence Agency. *Times of India*, Magazine Section, 9 June 1985, p. 2.

0313 Chaze, William L. We want Justice Done; Capture of the Hijackers in the Latest Terrorist Rampage Still Leaves the World Asking: Where And Who – Next ? *U.S. News,* Number 99, 21 October 1985, pp. 24-7.

0314 Chaze, William L. Terrorism: Russia's Secret Weapon ? *U.S. News,* Number 90, 4 May 1981, pp. 27-29.

0315 Chaze, William L. In War on Terrorists, Some Victories but - It's an Uphill Struggle with a Resilient Enemy: And now the Authorities are Bracing for a Dangerous New Challenge – Again by the PLO (Palaestine Liberation Organization). *U.S. News,* Number 92, 28 July 1982, pp. 27-29.

0316 Cherico, P. Security Requirements and Standards for Nuclear Power Plants. *Security Management,* Number 18, January 1975, pp. 22-24.

0317 Chisholm, Henry J. *The Function of Terror and Violence in Revolution.* Georgetown University, Unpublished Master's Thesis, 1948.

0318 Chopra, Maharaj K. International Terrorism: Idealism, Romance and Menance. *Organizer,* Volume 29, Number 27, 28 November 1977, p. 5.

0319 Chopra, V.D. Design Behind the Ominous Developments. *Patriot,* 20 May 1985, p. 4.

0320 Chowdhury, Neeraja. Andhra Police - Terrorist Encounters. *Statesman*, 4 July 1985, p. 5.

0321 Chowdhury, P. Roy. Manipur: Peace with Vigilance. *Link,* Volume 26, Number 16, 27 November 1983, pp. 15-21.

0322 Civiletti, B.R. Terrorism: The Governments Response Policy. *FBI Law Enforcement Bulletin,* Volume 48, Number 1, 1979, pp. 19-22.

0323 Clark, Michael K. *Algeria in Turmoil*. New York, Praeger, 1959.

0324 Clark, Richard C. *Technological Terrorism.* Greenwich, Deuin, 1980.

0325 Clarke, G. When Terrorists become Respectable. *Time,* Number 104, 25 November 1974, pp. 44-5.

0326 Clawson, Patrick. Why we Need More but Better Coverage of Terrorism. *Orbis*, Number 30, Winter 1987, pp. 701-10.

0327 Clear than ever no Sure Way to Handle Global Terrorist: Who they are what they have done. *U.S. News*, Number 80, January 1976, pp. 27-28.

0328 Clery, Roger. Le Terrorisme, mance de defense. *Defense natilmnall,* Number 41, May 1985, pp. 115-119.

0329 Cline, Ray S. Terrorism: Seedbed for Soviet Influence. *Midstream,* Number 26, May 1980, pp. 5-8.

0330 Cline, Ray S. and Alexander, Yonah. *Terrorism as State Sponsored Covert Warfare.* Democracy in Fairfax, Hero Books, 1986.

0331 Cline, Ray S. and Alexander, Yonah. *Terrorism the Soviet Connection*. New York, Crane Russak and Co., 1984.

0332 Clissold, Stphen. (Ed.). *A Short History of Yugoslavia: From early Times to 1966.* Cambridge. Cambridge University Press, 1966.

0333 Clutterbuck, Richard. Terrorism and the Security Forces in Europe. *Army Quarterly,* Number 111, January 1981, pp. 12-29.

0334 Clutterbuck, Richard. *The Media and Political Violence.* London, Macmillan, 1981.

0335 Clutterbuck, Richard. Terrorist International. *Army Quarterly,* Number 104, January 1974, pp. 154-159.

0336 Clutterbuck, Richard. Intimidation of Witnesses and Juries. *Army Quarterly,* Number 104, April 1974, pp. 285-294.

0337 Clutterbuck, Richard. Police and Urban Terrorism. *Police Journal* (England), Number 48, July-September 1975, pp. 204-214.

0338 Clutterbuck, Richard. Kidnapping. *Army Quarterly,* Number 104, October 1974, pp. 529-534.

0339 Clutterbuck, Richard. (Ed.). *The Future of Political Violence: Destabilization, Disorder and Terrorism.* New York, Macmillan Pvt. Ltd., 1986.

0340 Clutterbuck, Richard. *Britain in Agony: The Growth of Political Violence.* London, Faber and Faber, 1978.

0341 Clutterbuck, Richard. *Living with Terrorism.* London, Faber and Faber, 1975.

0342 Clutterbuck, Richard. The Police and Urban Terrorism. *Police Journal,* Volume 48, Number 3, July-September 1975, pp. 204-14.

0343 Clutterbuck, Richard. *Guerrilla and Terrorists.* Ohio University Press, 1980.

0344 Clutterbuck, Richard. *Protest and The Urban Guerrilla.* London, Abelard-Schuman, 1973.

0345 Clutterbuck, Richard. Terrorism and Urban Violence. *Acad Pol. Science Proc.,* Volume 34, Number 4, 1982, pp. 164-75.

0346 Coad, Malcolm. Murder on the Campus: Kidnappings and Assassinations at San Carlos University in Guatemala. *Index on Censorship,* Number 10, Fall 1981, pp. 48-54.

0347 Cobo, Juan. The Roots of 'Violencia'. *New Times,* 5 August 1970, pp. 25-27.

0348 Cockburn, Alexander. International Terrorism and Double Standards: Reporting and Analysis in the United States of Israeli-Palestinian Incidents. *Wall St. J.,* Volume 199, Number 27, 15 April, 1982.

0349 Cohen, A.S. *Theories of Revolution: An Introduction.* New York, A Halstead Press Book, John Willey and Sons, 1975.

0350 Cohen, Guela. *Women of Violence: Memoirs of A Young Terrorist 1943-1948.* Translated by Hillel Halkin. New York, Holt, Rinehart and Winston, 1966.

0351 Cohen, M.J. British Strategy and the Palestine Question. *Journal of Contemporary History,* Volume 7, Numbers 3-4, July-October 1972.

0352 Coker, Christopher. *Terrorism.* Gloucester, Watts, 1986.

0353 Colebrook, J. Israel with Terrorists. *Commentary,* July 1979, pp. 30-39.

0354 Cole, Richard B. *Executive Security: A Corporate Guide to Effective Response to Abduction and Terrorism.* New York, Wiley, 1980.
0355 Collins, Patrick. *Living in Troubled Lands: The Complete Guide to Personal Security Abroad.* Boulder, Paladin Press, 1981.
0356 Comay, M. Political Terrorism. *Mental Health Society,* 1976, pp. 349-61.
0357 Combating Terrorism: When Solidarity knows no Limits. *Eastern Journal International Law,* Volume 10, Number 3, October 1978, pp. 204-22.
0358 Committee on Internal Security, House of Representatives. *Terrorist.* Part 1-4. Washington, 1974.
0359 Compion, D.R. Of Many Things. *America*, Number 129, 8 September 1973.
0360 Coogan, Tim Pat. *The IRA.* New York, Praeger, 1970.
0361 Cooley, John K. Moscow Faces a Palestinian Dilemma. *Mid East,* Volume 11, 1970, pp. 32-35.
0362 Cooley, John K. China and the Palestinians. *Journal of Palestine Studies,* Volume 1, Number 2, 1972, pp. 19-34.
0363 Conference on the Defence of Democracy Against Terrorism in Europe: Tasks and Problems. *Compendium of Documents*, Strasbourg, 1981.
0364 Conference Board Record. Terrorist Bombings Sputter Back to Normal. *Idem,* Number 10, October 1973, pp. 6-9.
0365 Connolly, Stephen and Druehl, Gregory. The Tupamaros: The New Focus in Latin America. *Journal of Contemporary Revolutions*, Volume 3, Number 3, Summer 1971, pp. 59-68.
0366 Conquest, Robert. *The Great Terror.* New York, Macmillan, 1968.
0367 Containing Fresh Terrorism. *Madhya Pradesh Chronicle*, 1 November 1985, p. 4.
0368 Contrary Approaches to Stemming Violence. *Hindu*, 2 May 1985, p. 8.
0369 Convention to Prevent and Punish the Acts of Terrorism Taking the form of Crimes against Persons and Related Extortion that are of International Significance. *Pan American Union. Seric Sobre Tratades 37*. Washington, D.C., 2 February 1971.
0370 Convention for the Prevention and Punishment of Terrorism. Geneva, 16 November, 1937. *League of Nations Doc. C. 94. M. 47, 1938.* V. pp. 5-17.
0371 Cooper, H.H.A. Whether Now ? Terrorism on Brink. *Chitty's Law Journal,* Volume 25, Number 6, 1977, pp. 181-90.

0372 Cooper, H.H.A. Hostage Rescue Operations. Déouement at Algeria and Mogadishu Compared. *Chitty's Law Journal*, Volume 26, March 1978, pp. 91-104.

0373 Cooper, H.H.A. Terrorist and the Victim. *Victimology,* Number 1, Summer 1976, pp. 229-239.

0374 Cooper, H.H.A. Terrorism the Problems of the Definition. *Chitty's Law Journal*, Volume 26, Number 3, 1978, pp. 105-108.

0375 Cooper, H.H.A. Terrorism and the Intelligence Function. *Chitty's Law Journal*, Volume 24, Number 3, 1976, pp. 13-8.

0376 Cooper, H.H.A. What is a Terrorist: A Psychological Perspective. *Legal Medical Quarterly,* Volume 1, Number 1, 1977, pp. 16-32.

0377 Cooper, Mary H. Dealing with Terrorism: Opening a New Chapter. *Editorial Research Repts,* p. 30, May 1986, pp. 391-408.

0378 Copeland, M. Unmentionable Uses of CIA Counter-terrorist Activity. *National Review*, Number 25, 14 September 1973, pp. 990-7.

0379 Corporation for Public Broadcasting. NOVA: The Plutonium Connection. Transcript in *Congressional Record,* Number 121, March 11, 1975.

0380 Corsi, Jerome R. Terrorism As a Desperate Game: Fear, Bargaining, and Communication in the Terrorist Event. *J. Conflict Resolution*, Number 25, March 1981, pp. 47-85.

0381 Costa-Gavras. and Solinas, Franco. *State of Siege.* New york, Ballantine, 1973.

0382 Costello, Deelan. International Terrorism and the Development of the Principle aut Dedere aut Judicare. *The Journal of International Law and Economics*, Number 10, 1975, p. 483.

0383 Cosyns-Verhalgen, Roger. *Actualite du Terrorisme: Selection Bibliographyque.* Bruxelles, Wavre, 1973.

0384 Courter, Jim. Protecting our Citizens: When to use Force against Terrorists. *Policy R.,* Spring 1986, pp. 10-17.

0385 Cousine, N. Total Power and Total Madness. *Saturday Review*, Volume 3, Number 4, 7 February 1976.

0386 Coyle, Dominick J. *Minorities in Revolt: Political Violence in Ireland, Italy, and Cyprus*. Fairleigh, Dickinson University Press, 1983.

0387 Craig, Alexander. The Urban Guerrilla in Latin America. *Survey*, Number 17, Summer 1971, pp. 112-128.

0388 Crelinsten, R.D. International Political Terrorism: A Challenge for Comparative Research. *International Journal of Comparative and Applied Criminal Justice,* Volume 2, Number 2, 1978, pp. 107-26.

0389 Crelinston, Ronald D. and Laborge-Altmejd, Danielle, (Eds.). *Hostage Taking: Problems of Prevention and Control.* Montreal, International Centre for Comparative Criminology, 1976.

0390 Crenshaw, Martha. The Causes of Terrorism. *Comparative Politics*, Number 13, July 1981, pp. 379-90.

0391 Crenshaw, Martha.; Dvor, Yehezkel and O' Brien, Conor C. (Eds.). *Terrorism, Legitimacy and Power; The Consequences of Political Violence.* Middletown, Wesleyan U Pr., 1982.

0392 Criley, Richard L. The Cult of the Informer Revisited: Anti-Terrorism Policy in the United States. *Crime and Social Justice*, Numbers 21-22, 1984, pp. 183-90.

0393 Crime and the Punishment: Capture of Saudi Arabia Embassy in Paris by Fedayeen. *Time*, 17 September 1973, pp. 39-40.

0394 Crime Does Pay: Political Kidnappings. *Time*, 23 April 1973, pp. 32-3.

0395 Crime Of Crime. *Tribune*, 15 October 1985, p. 4.

0396 Crisis in Sri Lanka. *Hindustan Times*, 1 December 1984, p. 9.

0397 Cross, James E. *Conflict in the Shadows.* New York, Doubleday, 1963.

0398 Crotty, William J. (Ed.). *Assassinations and the Political Order.* New York, Harper S. Row, 1971.

0399 Crowson, Delmar L. *Progress and Prospects for Nuclear Materials Safeguards.* Vienna, International Atomic Energy Agency, SM 133/60, 1970.

0400 Crozier, Brian. (Ed.). *Annual of Power and Conflict 1978-79: A Survey of Political Violence and International Influence.* London, Inst. Study Conflict, 1978.

0401 Crozier, Brian. *South-East Asia in Turmoil.* Baltimore, Penguin, 1965.

0402 Crozier, Brian. (Ed.). *New Dimensions of Security in Europe.* London, Institute for the Study of Conflict, May 1975.

0403 Crozier, Brian. Anatomy of Terrorism. *Nation*, Number 188, 1959, pp. 250-252.

0404 Cult of Violence. *Madhya Pradesh Chronicle*, 2 August 1985, p. 4, *National Herald*, 2 August 1985, p. 7, *Tribune*, 2 August 1985, p. 4.

0405 Commingham, Bill. *On Bended Knees: The Night Rider Story.* Clanahan, Mc Clanahan Pub., 1983.

0406 Cunningham, W.C. and Grass, P.J. *Prevention of Terrorism Security: Guidelines for Business and Other Organizations.* Molean, Virginia, Hallerest Press, 1978.

0407 Curbing Terrorism. *National Herald,* 29 December 1986, p. 7.

0408 Curious Incident. *Times of India*. 13 July 1985, p. 8.

0409 Curtis, Lynn, A. *Violence, Race and Culture*. Lexington, Mass, Lexington Books, 1975.

0410 Cygielman, Victor. Roots Of Jewish Terror. *New Outlook*, Number 27, June-July 1984, pp. 13-15.

0411 Dadrian, V. Factors of Anger and Aggression in Genocide. *Journal of Human Relations*, Number 19, 1971, pp. 394-417.

0412 Dahlgren, Harold E. *Profile of Violence: An Analytical Model.* Washington, D.C., Central Intelligence Agency (PR 76 10025), June 1976.

0413 Dahs, Hans. Das Anti-Terroristen Gesets - Eine Niederlage Des Rechtestoats. *Neue Juristishe Wochensehrift,* Number 29, 1970, p. 2146.

0414 Dalal, Nergis. Hands Up, Hijackers. *Times of India*, Delhi, Magazine Section, 30 September 1984, p. 3.

0415 Dalen, Hendrik Van. Terrorism and Human Nature. *Military Policy Law Enforcement Journal*, Summer 1979, pp. 9-14.

0416 Dallin, Alexander and Breslaunce, George W. *Political Terror in Communist Systems*. Stanford, California, Stanford University Press, 1970.

0417 D'Amore, Louis J and Teresa E. Anuza. International Terrorism: Implications and Challenge for Global Tourism. *Bus Q,* Number 51, November 1986, pp. 20-29.

0418 Dane, Louis. Indian Nationalism: The Emergence of Terrorism. *Advent,* Volume 25, Number 1, February 1968, pp. 13-20.

0419 Dang, Satyapal. War On Terrorists and Communalist. *Secular Democracy*, Volume 19, Number 7, July 1986.

0420 Dang, Satyapal. Punjab: A Battle Not Joined. *Link,* Volume 28, Number 34, 30 March 1986, pp. 22-23.

0421 Dang, Satyapal. Punjab: Grim but not Hopeless. *Mainstream*, Volume 24, Number 44, 5 July 1986, pp. 4-5.

0422 Dang, Satyapal. Such was Amit Ram. *New Age,* Volume 34, Number 28, 13 July 1986, pp. 1-2.

0423 Danger in Punjab. *New Age,* Volume 34, Number 5, 2 February 1986, p. 2.

0424 Danger in Tripura. *Statesman,* Delhi, 1 July 1985, p. 6.

0425 Das Gupta, R.K. Sikh Renaisssance and Indian Nationalism. *Amrita Bazar Patrika,* 22 August 1985, p. 6.

0426 DasGupta, S. Violence - Development and Tensions. *International Journal of Group Tensions,* Number 1, 1971, pp. 114-29.
0427 DasGupta, Punyapriya. Two Steps Bac!: in Nepal. *Deccan Herald,* 4 July 1985, p. 6.
0428 DasGupta, Punyapriya. Counter Productive Terrorism by France. *Deccan Herald,* 11 September 1985, p. 8.
0429 Datta, Surinder K. Why the Terrorists? *Hindustan Times,* 6 July 1984, p. 9.
0430 Datta, Ray and Sunand, K. Battle Against Terror. West May Now Respond to Indian Pleas. *Statesman,* Delhi, 28 June 1985, p. 6.
0431 Davidson, Ian. U.S., E.C. Disagree on How to Deal with Terrorism: Reaction to U.S. Raid on Libya Underscores Difference over the Use of Military Force. *Europe,* May 1986, pp. 16-17.
0432 Daverger, Mavrice. Resistance, Terrorism et droit d asile. *Le Monde,* 9 September 1982, p. 1.
0433 Davies, Donald M. Terrorism: Motives and Means. *Foreign Service Journal,* September 1962, pp. 19-21.
0434 Davidson-Smith, G. A Positive Approach to Terrorism: The Case for an Elite Counter-Force in Canada. *Journal of the Royal United Service Institute for Defence Studies,* Volume 129, Number 3, September 1984, pp. 17-22.
0435 Davis, Jack. *Political Violence in Latin America.* London, International Institute for Strategic Studies, 1972.
0436 D. John and Gibron, Leslie, K. *Contemporary Terrorism.* Gaithersburg, Md. International Association of Chiefs of Police, 1978.
0437 D'oliviera, Col. S.L. Uruguay and the Tupamaro Myth. *Military Review,* Volume 53, Number 4, April 1973.
0438 DeBecker, Gavin. Protecting VIP's Part I. *Counterforce,* Number 1, 2 March 1977, pp. 11-14.
0439 De Boer, C. The Pools: Terrorism and Hijacking. *Public Opinion Quarterly,* Volume 43, Number 3, 1979, pp. 410-18.
0440 De Gramont, Sanche. Moslem Terrorists in a New Job. *New York Herald Tribune,* 9 July 1962, pp. 1-2.
0441 De Leon, Peter.; Jenkins, Brian; Keller, Konrad and Krofcheck. *Attributes of Potential Criminal Adversaries to U.S. Nuclear Programs.* Santa Monia, Calif., Rand Corporation, R-2223-SL, February 1978. Reprinted in: *U.S. Congress, Senate, Committee On Governmental Affairs.* An Act to Combat International Terrorism,

Hearings before the Committee on S. 2236. 95th Con., 2nd sess., 1978, pp. 555-639.

0442 De Recquingny, Colonel. Urban Terrorism. *Military Review*, Number 38, 1969, pp. 93-99.

0443 De Schutter, Bart. La Convention Europeanne Pour La Repression Du Terrorism: Un Faux Pas En Avaint ? *Journal Des Tribunaux*, Number 4991, 1977, p. 217.

0444 De Schutter, Bart. Problems of Jurisdiction in the International Control and Repression of Terrorism. In Bassiouni, M. Cherif, (Ed.). *International Terrorism and Political Crimes*. Springfield, Illinois, Charles Thomas, 1975, pp. 377-390.

0445 Deakin, Thomas J. The Legacy of Carlos Marighella. *FBI Law Enforcement Bulletin*, Volume 43, Number 10, October 1974, pp. 9-15.

0446 Deal Is Possible. *Times of India*, 21 January, 1985, p. 6.

0447 Death in the Afternoon: Zambian Sentries Open Fire on Canadian Tourists. *Newsweek*, Volume 18, Number 50, 28 May 1973.

0448 Death of Dialogue: Statement of N. Hawatmeh and Subsequent attack on Maalot. P. Jacobs. *Progressive*, Number 38, September 1974, pp. 38-42.

0449 Death Penalty for Terrorists ? *Christian Century and Continuing New Christian*, Volume 90, Number 333, 21 March, 1973.

0450 Death Penalty for Terrorism. *Times of India*, 19 May 1985, p. 2.

0451 Death in Rome Abroad Flight 110. *Time*, Volume 102, Number 28, 31 December 1973.

0452 Defeat this Diabolism. *Financial Express*, 13 May 1985, p. 5.

0453 Dekel, Ephraim Pseud. Krasher. *Shai: Historical Exploits of Haganah Intelligence*. New York, Yoseloff, 1959.

0454 Delhi Stands Up. *Times of India*, 28 January 1986, p. 8.

0455 DeNike, Douglas L. Radioactive Malevolence. *Bulletin of the Atomic Scientists*, February 1974, pp. 16-20.

0456 Denton, Jeremiah. International Terrorism: The Nuclear Dimension. *Terrorism: An International Journal*, Volume 9, Number 2, 1987, pp. 113-23.

0457 Deplorable. *Political and Economic Review*, Number 49, 10 February 1971, p. 2.

0458 Derber, M. Terrorism and the Movement. *Monthly Review*, Number 22, February 1971.

0459 Dershowitz, Alan M. Terrorism and Preventive Detention: The Case of Israel. *A Commentary Report*, 1970, pp. 3-4.

0460 Dershowtiz, Alan M. Terrorism and Preventive Detention: The Case of Israel. *Commentary,* Report, December 1976, pp. 6-7.
0461 Details on Rome Terrorism Disclosed. *Aviation Weekly,* Volume 100, Number 26, 28 January 1974.
0462 Devi, M.G. Indira. Terrorist Movement in South India. *Journal Kerala Studies*, Volume 5, Number 1, March 1978, p. 131.
0463 De Wit, J. and Ponsaers, P. On Facts and how to Use Them. *Terrorism: An International Journal,* Volume 1, Number 3, 1978, pp. 363-375.
0464 Dilaura, Arnold E. Preventing Terrorism: An Analysis of National Strategy. *SAIS* (School Advanced Internat Studies), Number 7, Winter/Spring 1987, pp. 27-33.
0465 Dilip, R. Politics of Violence. *Patriot,* 7 October 1984, p. 5.
0466 Dillon, Martin and Lehane, D. *Political Murder in Northern Ireland.* Harmondworth, Penguin, 1973.
0467 Dimitrijevic, Vojin. Terrorism as Internation Provocation. *R Internat Affairs,* Number 36, 20 December 1985, pp. 5-7.
0468 Dimitrijevic, Vojin. The Non-aligned Movements and International Terrorism. *R. Internat Affairs*, Number 38, 5 March 1987, pp. 12-14.
0469 Dinstein, Yoram. Terrorism and War of Liberation: An Israeli Perspective of the Arab Israeli Conflict. In Bassiouni, M. Cherif (Ed.). *International Terrorism and Political Crimes*. Springfield, Illinois, Charles, C. Thomas 1975, pp. 155-172.
0470 Dinstein, Yoram. Terrorism and Wars of Liberation Applied to the Arab-Israeli Conflict: An Israelli Perspective. *Israel Year-Book on Human Rights,* Number 3, 1973, p. 78.
0471 Dinstein, Yoram. Criminal Jurisdiction Over Aircraft Hijacking. *Israel Law Review,* Number 7, 1972, pp. 195-206.
0472 Dire Warning. *Patriot*, 18 January, 1985, p. 4.
0473 Do Not Be Deflected. *Indian Express*, Delhi, 26 March 1985, p. 6.
0474 Dobson, Christopher and Payne Ronald. *War Without End. The Terrorists: An Intelligence Dossier*. London, Harrap, 1986.
0475 Dobson, C and Payne, R. *The Weapons of Terrors: International Terrorism at Work.* London, Macmillan, 1970.
0476 Dobson, Christopher and others. *The Carlos Complex: A Study in Terror*. London, Hedder, 1977,
0477 Dobson, Christopher and Payne, Ronald. *Counterattack: The West's Battle Against the Terrorist.* New York, facts on file 1982.

0478 Dobson, Christopher and Payne, Ronald. *The Terrorists: Their Weapons, Leaders and Tactics*. New York, Facts On File, 1982.

0479 Donne, Michael. Struggle to Curb Air Piracy. *Economic Times*, 8 November 1977, p. 10.

0480 Donnediew de Vabres, H. La Repression International Du Terrorism; Les Conventions Do Geneva. *Review De Droit International et de Legislation Comparce,* Number 19, 1938, pp. 37-74.

0481 Doub, William O. and Duker, Joseph M. Making Nuclear Energy Safe and Secure. *Foreign Affairs*, Number 53 July, 1975, pp. 756-772.

0482 Doumergu, Imil. *Saudi Arabia and the Explosion of Terrorism in The Middle East.* London, Inst. Econ. Pol., 1983.

0483 Doyle, E.J. Propaganda by Deed: The Media Response to Terrorism. *The Police Chief,* Volume 46, Number 6, 1979, pp. 40-41.

0484 Drastic but Unavoidable. *Tribune*, 20 May, 1985, p. 4.

0485 Dror, Yenezkel. *Crazy States: A Counter-conventional Strategic Problem.* Lexington, Mass, Heath Lexington Books, D.C., Heath and Company, 1971.

0486 Dugard, John. International Terrorism: Problems of Definition. *International Affairs*, Number 50, January 1974, pp. 67-81.

0487 Dugard, John. Towards the Definition of International Terrorism. *American Journal of International Law*, Volume 67, Number 5, 1973, pp. 94-100.

0488 Duff, Ernest A. and McCamant, John F. *Violence and Repression in Latin America: A Quantitative and Historical Analysis*. Riversidc, New Jersey, Free Press, 1975.

0489 Duncan, Evan. Terrorist Attacks on U.S. Official Personnel Abroad. *Dept. State Bul.*, Number 81, April 1981, pp. 34-37.

0490 Dunn, Lewis A. Nuclear Gray Marketeering. *International Security,* Number 1, Winter 1977, pp. 107-118.

0491 Dunn, Lewis A.; Bracken, Paul and Smernoff, Barry J. *Routes to Nuclear Weapons: Aspects of Purchase or Theft.* Croton-on-Hudson, New York, Hudson Institute, April 1977.

0492 Dutt, J.K. Terrorism in our Times. *United Services Institution Journal*, Volume 107, Number 453, July-September 1978, pp. 228-34.

0493 Dyson, John. *Sink the Rainbow: An Enquiry Into the Greenpeace Affairs.* Gollancz, England, David and Charles, 1986.

0494 Eave, L. Political Terrorism: Hysteria Of the Left. *New York Times Magazine*, 12 April 1970, pp. 25-27.

0495 Economist. Anarcho-Nihilism. *Idem,* Volume 237, Number 6635, 1970, pp. 2-33.

0496 Ecstein, Harry. *Internal War: Problems And Approaches.* New York, Free Press, Macmillan, 1964.

0497 Edwards, Mecheel. *Red Year: The Indian Rebellian of 1957.* London, Hamish Hamilton, 1973.

0498 *Effects Continue to Check Arab Terrorism.* Washington, D.C., Embassy of Israel, 1973.

0499 Efrat, Edgar S. Terrorism in South Africa. In Yonah, Alexander (Ed.). *International Terrorism, National, Regional and Global Perspectives.* New York, Praeger Publishers, 1976, pp. 194-208.

0500 Eggers, William. *Terrorism: The Slaughter of Innocents.* Chatsworth, Calif, Major Books, 1975.

0501 Eichelman, Burr and Sorkis, David A. (Eds.). *Terrorism: Interdisciplinary Perspectives.* Washington D.C., Am. Psychiatric, 1983.

0502 Fighting Extremism in Tripura. *Hindu,* 18 December, 1984, p. 8.

0503 Einaudi, Luigi R. Latin American Student Radicalism: A Different Type Of Struggle. *The Rand Corporation,* Santa Monica, p. 3897, July 1968, p. 16.

0504 Elad, Shlomi and Merari, Ariel. (Eds.). *The Soviet Bloc & World Terrorism.* Boulder Westview, 1984.

0505 Ellenberg, Edward S. The PLO and its Place in Violence and Terror. In Marius H. Livingston (Ed.): with Kress, Lee B., and Wanek Marie G. *International Terrorism in Contemporary World.* Westports Conn., Greenwood Press, 1978, pp. 165-176.

0506 Elliott, John D. Primers On Terrorism. *Military Review,* October 1976.

0507 Elliot, John D. Transitions Of Contemporary Terrorism. *Military Review,* May 1977, pp. 3-15.

0508 Elliott, John D. Action and Reaction: West Germany and the Baader-Meinhof Guerrillas. *Strategic Review,* Number 4, Winter 1976, pp. 60-67.

0509 Elliott, John D. Writer-Theoreticians of Urban Guerrilla Warfare. *Short Essays in Political Science,* March 1975.

0510 Ellis, Albert and Gullo, John. *Murder and Assassination.* New York, Lyle Stuart, 1971.

0511 Elwin, G. Swedish Anti-Terrorist Legislation. *Contemporary Crisis,* Number 1, July 1977, pp. 289-301.

0512 Emerson, Ryan Quade. *Who's Who in Terrorism, 1984.* United States and International. International Research Centre on Terrorism. Suite A-560, 1926, Hollywood Blvd., Hollywood FL 33020.

0513 Emike, Abel A. The Impact of International Terrorism and Hijacking of Aircraft on States Sovereignty: The Israeli Raid on Entabbe Airport Revisited. *Journal of the Indian Law Institute*, Volume 23, Number 1, January-March 1981, pp. 90-107.

0514 Emshwiller, John R. In Atom-Bomb Scare, Federal NEST Team Tiles to the Rescue, Anti-Terrorism Squad Nuclear Emergency Search Teams. *Wall St J*, Volume 196, Number 1, 21 October 1980.

0515 Ending Global Murder. *Times of India*, 7 January 1986, p. 8.

0516 Ending Terrorism. *National Herald,* 17 October 1985, p. 5.

0517 Entschilessung Zu-dar Europaisehen Konvention Zur Bekamfung Des Terrorismus. *EP-DOK,* Volume 513, Number 76, 13 January 1977, Sitzungs Dokumente 1976-1977. Luxembourg, 1977.

0518 Entschliessung Zu Der Europaischen Konvention Zur bekamfung Des Terrorismus. *Drucksache*, Volume 8, Number 231, 24 March 1977, Deutscher Budestag.

0519 Entworf eines Geretzes Zu Dem Europaischen Uebereinkommen Con 27 January 1977 Zur Bekampfung Des Terrorismus. *Drucksache* 456/1/7, 19 Ocober 1977, Bundesrat.

0520 Epstein, D.G. Combating Campus Terrorism. *Police Chief,* Number 46, 47 and 49, January 1971.

0521 Epstein, William. *The Last Chance: Nuclear Proliferation and Arms Control*. New York, The Free Press, 1976.

0522 Esjon, D.M.R. The Secret Weapon-Terrorism. *Army Quarterly,* Number 78, 1959, pp. 167-180.

0523 Eta Guns for an Army Bullseye. *Economist,* Number 270, 13 January 1979, pp. 41-2.

0524 European Notes. *Econ, and Political Weekly*, Volume 12, Number 40, 1 October 1977, p. 1702.

0525 *European Convention on the Suppression of Terrorism, 23rd and 24th Sittings,* 28th Ordinary Session, 24-28 January 1977, Strasbourg, 1977, pp. 778-798.

0526 Evans, Alona E. *The Realities of Extradition and Prosecution*. A Paper Presented to the Conference on International Terrorism, Ralph Bunche Institute, Graduate School and University Center of CUNY, and the State University College at Oneonta SUNY, 9-11 June, 1976.

0527 Evans, Alona E. and Murphy, John F. (Eds.). *Legal Aspects of International Terrorism*. Lexington, Lexington Bks, 1978.
0528 Evans, Ernest. *Calling A Truce to Terror: The American Response to International Terrorism.* Westport, Greenwood, 1979.
0529 Evans, Ernest. American Policy Response to International Terrorism: Problems of Detterence. In Marius H. Livingston (Ed.). with Kress, Lee B., and Wanek, Marie G. *International Terrorism in Contemporary World.* Westport, Conn., Greenwood Press, 1978, pp. 376-385.
0530 Evans, Robert D. *Brazil, The Road Back from Terrorism*. Montreal, McGill Queen's University Press, 1975.
0531 Executive Protection Programme: A Guideline for Dealing with and Responding to Terrorist Activities Involving Corporate Employees and their Families both in the United States and Overseas. *Personnel J.*, Number 59, November 1980, pp. 915-17.
0532 *Explanatory Rapport on the European Convention on the Supression of Terrorism*. - DPC/CEPC/AV 3, 1977.
0533 Explosions in Nepal. *Amrit Bazar Patrika,* 24 June 1985, p. 6.
0534 Exporting Terrorism. *National Herald*, 22 September 1984, p. 7.
0535 Extremism in Tripura. *Hindu,* 14 January 1985, p. 8.
0536 Faces of Terror. *Northern India Patrika,* 14 August 1985, p. 4.
0537 Facing Terrorism. *Statesman,* Delhi, 21 April 1985, p. 6.
0538 Fairbairn, G. Terrorism and Defence. *World Review*, Volume 18, Number 1, 1979, pp. 48-53.
0539 Fairbairn, G. *Revolutionary Guerilla Warfare : The Countryside Version.* Harmondsworth, England, Penguin Books Ltd., 1974.
0540 Falk, Gerhard. Terror as Politics : The German Case. *International Review Hist. Pol. Sci.*, Volume 20, Number 4, November1983, pp. 22-32.
0541 Falk, Richard A. The Beirut Raid and the International Law of Retaliation. *American Journal of International Law*, Number 63, July 1969, pp. 415-443.
0542 Fallaci, Oriana. A Leader of Fedayeen : We want a War Like the Vietnam War. Interview with George Habash. *Life*, 12 June 1970, pp. 32-34.
0543 Falvey, Anne. Legislative Responses to International Terrorism : International and National Efforts to Deter and Punish Terrorists. *Boston Col. Internat and Comparative Law R.*, Number 9, Summer 1986, pp. 323-59.

0544 Fanon, Franz. *Towards the African Revolution : Political Essays*. New York, Grove, 1967.

0545 Farhangi, Leslie Shirin. Insuring against abuse of Diplomatic Immunity. *Stanford Law R*, Number 38, July 1986, pp. 1517-47.

0546 Farrell, William R. Responding to Terrorism : What, Why and When. *Naval War College Review*, Volume 39, Number 1, January/February 1986, pp. 47-52.

0547 Farrell, William Regis. *The U.S Government Response to Terrorism : In Search of an Effective Strategy*. Westview, 1982.

0548 Fatal Error : Murder of a Bouchiki by Israeli Killers. *Time*, 6 August 1973, pp. 31-2.

0549 Fattah, E.A. Some Reflections on the Victimology of Terrorism. *The International Journal*, Volume 3, Numbers 1-2, 1979, pp. 81-108.

0550 Fawcett, J.E.S. Kidnapping Versus Government Protection. *World Today*, Number 26, 1970, pp. 359-62.

0551 Fay, James R. Terrorism in Turkey : Threat to NATO's Troubled Ally and implications of the Military Coup, September 1980. *Military Review*, Number 61, April 1981, pp. 16-26.

0552 Fearey, R.A. Terrorism : Growing and Increasingly Dangerous. *U.S. News*, Number 79, 29 September 1975, pp. 77-9.

0553 Fearey, Robert A. International Terrorism. An Address Made at Los Angeles on February 19, 1976. Before the Los Angles World Affairs Council of Orange Country. *Department of State Bulletin*, Volume 74, 29 March 1976, pp. 394-403.

0554 Faierabend, IVO, R.L. and Gurr, T.R. *Anger, Violence and Politics: Theories and Research*. Englewood Cliffs, New Jersey, Prentice-Hall, 1972.

0555 Felt, Edward. *Urban Revolt in South Africa 1960-1964: A Case Study*. Eranstori, IL, North Western University Press, 1971.

0556 Felton, John. Reagan Tightens Economic Sanctions on Libya. *Cong Q W Rept.*, Number 44, 11 January 1986.

0557 Felton, John. Reagan, Hill Move to Bolster Embassy Security at United States Embassies Overseas: Some Proposed Anti-terrorism Bill. *Cong Q W Rept*, Number 42, 28 September 1984, pp. 2401-3.

0558 Felton, John. Hostages Return, but Terrorism Problem Lingers. *Cong Q W Rept*, Number 43, 6 July 1985, pp. 1327-9.

0559 Felton, John. Hill Considers Ways to Boost Airport Security : Hijack Crisis Spurs Boycott Proposals. *Cong Q W Report*, Number 43, 29 July 1985, pp. 1252-3.

0560 Fera, Ivan. Battle Cry. *Illustrated Wkly India*, Volume 107, Number 7, 16 February 1986, pp. 32-35.

0561 Fera, Ivan. The Blitzkrieg. *Illustrated Wkly India*, Volume 107, Number 7, 16 February 1986, pp. 26-29.

0562 Fetscher, Iring. *Terrorisms and Reaktoin*. Koln, Europaische Verlagranstalt, 1977.

0563 Fighting Terror. *Times of India*, 22 May 1985, pp. 1-2.

0564 Fighting Terrorism. *Patriot*, 5 August 1985, p. 4, *Tribune*, 14 August 1985, p. 4.

0565 Fighting Terrorism. *Northern India Patrika*, 12 July 1984, p. 4.

0566 Finger, Seymour Maxwell. International Terrorism and the United Nations. In Alexander Yonah (Ed.). *International Terrorism : National, Regional and Global Perspectives,* New York, Praeger Publishers, 1976, pp. 323-348.

0567 Fisher, Catherine Collier. U.S. Legislation to Prosecute Terrorists : Anti-terrorism Or Legalized Kidnapping ? *Vanaderbilt J. Transnation Law*, Number 18, Fall 1985, pp. 915-59.

0568 Fishman, Gideon. Criminological Aspects of International Terrorism : The Dynamics of the Palestinian Movement. In Marc Riedel and Terence P. thornberry, (Eds.). *Crime and Delinquency : Dimensions of Deviance*. New York, Praeger, 1974, pp. 103-113.

0569 Fitzgerald, B.D. The Analytical Foundations of Extortionate Terrorism. *Terrorism : An International Journal*, Volume 1, Numbers 3-4, 1978, pp. 347-62.

0570 Flieger, H. Futility of Terror. *U.S. News*, Number 74, 19 March 1973.

0571 Flight of 006 : And other Terrorism and Anti-terrorism Tactics. *Newsweek*, 20 August 1973, pp. 37-38.

0572 Flores, David A. Export Controls and the U.S. Effort to Combat International Terrorism. *Law and Policy Internat Bus*, Number 13, 2 November 1981, pp. 521-90.

0573 Fogel, Lawrence J. *Predictive Anti-terrorism*. Decision Sciences, Incl, April 1977.

0574 Foley, Charles and Scobie, W.I. *The Struggle for Cyprus*. Stanford, Hoover Institution Press, 1975.

0575 Foley, Tom. International Terrorism : Code Word and Reality. *Pol Affairs*, Number 61, November 1984, pp. 15-21.

0576 Ford, Franklin L. *Political Murder : From Tyrannicide to Terrorism*. Cambridge, Harvard University Press, 1985.

0577 Ford, G.R. and Others. U.S. Deplores Terrorist Incident in Tel Aviv; Statements 6 March 1975. *Department of State Bulletin*, Volume 72, Number 406, 31 March 1975.

0578 Foremost Challenge. *Northern India Patrika*, 6 August 1985, p. 4.

0579 Foreign and Domestic Issues. *W. Comp Pres Docs*, Number 22, 14 April 1986, pp. 451-456.

0580 Forster, A. Violence of the Fanatical Left and Right. *The Annals*, Number 364, 1966, pp. 141-148.

0581 Forum : International Terrorism. *Orbis*, Number 29, Fall 1985, pp. 465-515.

0582 Foul Dead Attempt on the life of Giani Saheb Singh. *Times of India*, Delhi, 28 November 1985, p. 8.

0583 Fowler, William Warner. Terrorism Data Bases : A Comparison of Mission, Methods, and Systems. *Rand Corporations*, 1981.

0584 Francis, Samuel T. Communism, Terrorism and the African National Congress. *J Social Pol and Econ Studies*, Number 11, Spring 1986, pp. 55-71.

0585 Francis, Samuel T. (Ed.). *The Terrorist Underground in United States*. Nathan Hale Institute, 1984. Francis, Samuel T. Terrorist Renaissance : France 1980-1983. *World Affairs*, Number 146, Summer 1983, pp. 54-8.

0586 Franck, Thomas M. International Legal Action Concerning Terrorism. *Terrorism : An International Journal*, Volume 1, 1978, pp. 187-197.

0587 Franck, Thomas M. and Lockwood, Bert B. Jr. Preliminary Thoughts Towards an International Convention on Terrorism. *The American Journal of International Law*, Number 68, January 1974, pp. 69-90.

0588 Franjeck, S. How Revolutionary is the Palestinian Resistance: A Marxist Interpretation. *Journal of Palestine Studies*, Number 1, 1972, pp. 52-60.

0589 Frank, F.R. International Convention Against Nuclear Theft. *Bulletin Atom Scientists*, Volume 31, Number 51, December 1975.

0590 Frank, Gerald. The Moyne Case : A Tragic History. *Commentary*, December 1945, pp. 64-71.

0591 Frankel, William. Victory Against IRA Bombers Claimed. *Statesman*, Delhi, 6 July 1985, p. 6.

0592 Fraysse-Druesne, Chislaine. La Convention Europeane Pour La repression Du Terrorism. *Revue generale de droit international Public*, Volume 82, 1978, p. 969.

0593 Freda, Adler. Newbreed of Terrorists. *Hindu*, 14 July 1985, p. 18.
0594 Freedom to Kill. *Tribune*, 6 February 1984, p. 4.
0595 Freedman, Robert O. Soviet Policy Toward International Terrorism. In Yonah, Alexander (Ed.). *International Terrorism : National and Global Perspective*. New York, Praeger Publishers, 1976, pp. 115-147.
0596 Freeman, Charles. *Terrorism in Today's World*. London, David and Charles, 1980.
0597 Freeman, Charles. *Terrorism*. London, Batsford, 1981.
0598 Freeman, Lawrence. et al. *Terrorism and International Order*. Boston, Routledge, 1986.
0599 Freeman, Lawrence. et al. *Perspectives on Terrorism*. Delhi, Hindustan Publications Corp., 1985.
0600 Fresh Provocation. *Patriot*, 2 October 1985, p. 4.
0601 Freidlander, Robert A. *Terror-Violence : Aspects of Social Control*. New York, Oceana Publication, 1983.
0602 Friedlander, Robert A. Review of International Terrorism and Political Crimes edited by M. Cherif Bassiouni. *Revue Internationale de Droit Penal*, Number 46, 1975, pp. 523-527.
0603 Friedlander, Robert A. Terrorism. *Barrister*, II, Summer 1975, p. 10.
0604 Friedlander, Robert A. Terrorism and International Law : What is being Done ? *Rutgers Camden Law Journal*, Number 8, Spring 1977, pp. 383-392.
0605 Friedlander, Robert A. *Terrorism and the Law*. Research Paper. Copy Gaitherburg International Association of Chiefs of Police.
0606 Friedlander, Robert A. Terrorism and Political Violence : Some Preliminary Observations. *International Studies Notes*, Number 2, Summer 1976, pp. 1-3.
0607 Friedlander, Robert A. Coping with Terrorism : What is to be Done? *Ohio Northern University Law Review*, 1978. pp. 432-443.
0608 Friedlander, Robert A. Reflections on Terrorist Havens. *Naval War College Review*, Number 32, March-April 1979, pp. 59-67.
0609 Friedman, Thomas I. Sources of Terrorism : Links Easy to Establish. *Times of India*, 8 May 1986, pp. 3-5.
0610 From Bombing to Bargaining. *New Republ.*, Number 170, 8 June 1974, pp. 5-6.
0611 Fromkin, D. The Strategy of Terrorism. *Foreign Affairs*, Volume 4, Number 3, July 1975, pp. 683-698.

0612 Frostmann, Harbert M. *International Political Terrorism and the Approaching Emergence of the Authoritarian State*. Alllanquergue, An Classical Coll Pr., 1981.

0613 Fuller, John G. *We Almost Lost Detroit*. Pleasantville, New York, Reader's Digest Press, 1975.

0614 Fuqua, Paul and Wilson, Jerry. *Terrorism : The Executive's Guide to Survival*. Houston, Gulf Publishing Company, 1978.

0615 Furlong, Paul. Political Terrorism in Italy. In, Juliet Lodge (Ed.). *Terrorism : A Challenge to the State*. Oxford, Martin Robertson, 1981, p. 59.

0616 G.M. La Convention Europeene Contre Le Terrorisme Terrorism. *Journal Special Des Tribunaux, Le Contidien Juridique*, Number 137, 1976, p. 2.

0617 Gaddafi's World: Libya's Strongman at Home and Abroad. *World Press R*, Number 33, March 1986, pp. 25-27.

0618 Gaddafi and Terrorism : Sampling Global Opinion on the U.S. Raid and the Future. *World Press R*, Number 33, 6 July 1986. p. 21.

0619 Gadre, Vasant G. Terrorism in Spain. *Hindustan Times*, 15 November 1983, p. 9.

0620 Galor, Noemi. *International Cooperation to Suppress Terrorism*. Croom Helm Ltd., St Martin's, 1985.

0621 Galyean, T.R. Acts of Terrorism and Combat by Irregular Forces - An Insurance War Risk. *California Western International Law Journal*, Number 4, 1974, p. 314.

0622 Gandhi, Rajmohan. Acceptable Terrorism. *Indian Express*, Delhi, 10 September 1985, p. 6.

0623 Garcia-Mora, Manuel R. The Present Status of Political Offenses in the Law of Extradition and Asylum. *University of Pittsburgh Law Review*, Number 14, 1953.

0624 Garcia-More, Manuel R. *International Responsibility for Hostlle Acts of Private Persons Against Foreign States*, The Hague, Martinus Nijhoff, 1962.

0625 Garcia-Mora, Manuel R. The Natural of Political Offenses : A Knotty Problem of Extradition Law. *Virginia Law Review*, Number 48, 1962.

0626 Garcia-Mora, Manuel R. Crimes Against Humanity and the Principle of Non-Extradition of Political Offenses. *Michigan Law Review*, Number 62, 1964.

0627 Garcia-Passalacqua, Juan M. Interwined Futures : Puerto Rico, the United States, the Caribbean Basin, and Central America. *Fletcher Forum*, Number 9, Summer 1985, pp. 269-94.

0628 Gatt, Richard. *Guerrilla Movements In Latin America*. London, Nelson, 1970.

0629 Gaucher, Roland. *The Terrorists*. London, N.P., 1968.

0630 Gellman, Barton. Though Terrorism may be Hard to Define, this Administration Takes it Seriously : Scholars may Debate Terrorism's Meaning and Extent, but the Reagan Administration has Already Decided to turn it as a Weapon Against the Soviets. *Nat J*, Number 13, 12 September 1981, pp. 1631-1635.

0631 Georges-Abeyie, Daniel E. Terrorism and the Liberal State : A Reasonable Response. *Police Studies*, Number 4, Fall 1981, pp. 34-53.

0632 Georges-Abeyie, Daniel E. Toward the Development of a Terrorism Severity. *Police Studies*, Number 6, Winter 1983/1984, pp. 22-29.

0633 Ghastly Murder. *National Herald*, 1 August 1985, p. 7.

0634 Ghosh, Sailendranath. Ideological Setting for Terrorism. *Hindustan Times*, 28 June 1985, p. 9.

0635 Gibson, Richard. *African Liberation Movements : Contemporary Struggles Against White Minority Rule*. New York, Oxford University Press, 1972.

0636 Gilbert, Geoffrey S. Terrorism and the Political Offence Exemption Reappraised. *International and Comparative Law Quarterly*, Volume 34, Number 4, 1985, pp. 695-723.

0637 Gilinsky, Victor. Plutonium, Proliferation and the Price of Reprocessing. *Foreign Affairs,* Number 57, Winter 1978/1979, pp. 374-386.

0638 Gilinsky, Victor. Diversion by National Governments. In Mason Willrich (Ed.). *International Safeuards and Nucleur Industry*. Baltimore, Johns Hopkins University Press, 1973, pp. 159-175.

0639 Gitlin, Jan. *Conquest of Acre Prison*. Tel Aviv, Hardar, 1962.

0640 Glaser, Hermann. The Debate on Terrorism. *Aus Politik And Zeitgeschichte, Beilage Zu Das Parliament*, Number 25, pp. 3-74.

0641 Glaser, S. Terrorism Internation et Sus Divers Aspects. *Reveu International De Droit Compare*, Number 25, 1973, p. 825.

0642 Gleason, J. *Bloody Sunday*. London, Davies, 1962.

0643 Gol, Jean. Aspects Internationaux Du Terrorisme et de sa Repression. *Studia Diplomatica*, Volume 38, Number 4, 1985, pp. 379-389.

0644 Goldie, L.F.E. Combating International Terrorism : The United Nations Developments. *Naval War College Review*, Number 31, Winter 1979, pp. 49-60.

0645 Goodhart, Philip. *The Climate of Collapse : The Terrorist Threat to Britain and her Allies*. Petersham, Surrey, foreign Affairs Publishing Company Ltd., June 1975.

0646 Goodman, R.W. Jr.; Hoffman, J.E., McClanahan, J.R. and Tompkins, T.C. *Compendium of European Theater Terrorist Groups*. Max-well Air Force Base, Ala., Air University, 1976.

0647 Goodman, Walter. Our Terrorists and Theirs (Commenting on United States Foreign Policy). *New Leader*, Number 64, 15 July 1981, pp. 11-13.

0648 Goodsell, James N. Terrorism in Latin America. *Commentator*, March 1966, p. 9.

0649 Gordon, Don. Terrorism : Are we Losing the War. *Journal of Defence and Diplomacy*, Volume 4, Number 3, March 1986, pp. 38-39 and pp. 41-43.

0650 Gott, Richard. *Guerrilla Movements in Latin America*. London, Thomas Nelson and Sons, 1970.

0651 Government not to Yield to Terrorists : PM. *Times of India*, 18 May 1985, p. 1.

0652 Goyal D.R. Paradox of Democracy. Terrorism Private Enterprise. *National Herald*, 10 July 1985, p. 7.

0653 Grachyov, A. Extremism and Terrorism in the Service of World Relation. *Internat Affairs*, July 1981, pp. 7-74.

0654 Grachyov, A. Terrorism as a Method of Imperialist Foreign Policy. Alleged use of Subversive Activities, Military Force, or Threats of Force to Implement United States Policies. *Internat Affairs*, April 1982, pp. 46-55.

0655 Grant, G.M. Physical Protection of Plants and Materials : Physical Protection of Special Nuclear Material in Transit. *Federal Register*, Number 39, 13 November 1974, pp. 40036-40040.

0656 Great Britian. H.M. Stationery Office. *Terrorism in Cyprus : The Captured Documents*. Trans. Extracts Issued by Authority of the Secratary of State for the Colonies, 1956.

0657 Great Britain. *Report of the Commission to Consider Legal Procedures to Deal with Terrorist Activities in Northern Ireland*. London, 1972.

0658 Great Britain. Committee of Privy Counsellors Appointed To Consider Authorized Procedures for the Interrogation of Persons Suspected of Terrorism. *Report London, H.M.S.O.* 1972.

0659 Greaves, A.E. and Pickover, D. Prevention of Terrorism. *Police Review*, 31 August 1979, pp. 1400-1404.

0660 Green, G. *Terrorism : Is it Revolutionary* ? New York, New Outlook Publications, 1970.

0661 Green, L.C. Terrorism and its Responses. *Terrorism : An International Journal,* Volume 8, Number 1, 1985, pp. 33-77.

0662 Green, L.C. International Law and the Suppression of Terrorism. edited by G.W. Bartholomew. *Malaya Law Review Legal Easays*, 1975.

0663 Green, L.C. Double Standards in the United Nations : The Legalization of Terrorism. *Achiv Des Volkerrechts*, Volume 18, 1979.

0664 Green, L.C. *International Terrorism*. Address Delivered to the Edmonton Branch of the Canadian Institute of International Affairs, 20 March 1973.

0665 Green, L.C. *The Nature and Control of International Terrorism*. University of Alberta, Department of Political Science, Occassional Paper. Number 1, 1974.

0666 Greene, R.N. *The Guerrilla And How To Fight Him*. New York, Praeger, 1962.

0667 Greene, T.N. (Ed.) *Guerrilla and how to Fight him*. New York, N.P., 1965.

0668 Greisman, H.C. Social Meaning of Terrorism : Reification, Violence and Social Control. *Contemporary Crisis*, Volume 1, Number 3, 1977, pp. 303-18.

0669 Greisman, H.C. Terrorism and the Closure of Society : A Social Impact Projection. *Technological Foreasting and Social Change*, Volume 14, Number 2, 1979, pp. 135-46.

0670 Grewal, Nahar Singh. Combating Terrorism. *Tribune*, 15 October 1985, p. 4.

0671 Gribble, Leonard. *Hands of Terror : Notable Assassinations of the 20th Century.* London, Frederick Muller Ltd., 1960.

0672 Groom, A.J.R. Coming to Terms with Terrorism. *British Journal of International Studies*, Number 4, 1978, pp. 62-77.

0673 Gross, Bernard, (Eds.).*Le Terrorism*. Paris, Hatier, 1976.

0674 Gross, Feliks. *Violence in Politics : Terror and Political Assassination in Eastern Europe and Russia*. The Hague, Mouton, 1972.

0675 Gross, Feliks. Political Assassination. In Marius H. Livingston (Ed.). With Lee B. Kress; and Marie G. Wanek. *International Terrorism in the Contemporary World*. Westport, Conn., Greenwood Press, 1978, pp. 307-316.

0676 Gross, Leo. International Terrorism and International Criminal Jurisdiction. *American Journal of International Law*, Number 67, 11 July 1973, pp. 506-511.

0677 Grover, Divya. Combating Terrorism. *Northern India Patrika*, 27 October 1985, p. 2.

0678 Growing Menace. *Indian Express*, Delhi, 29 November 1984, p. 6.

0679 Gude, E.W. Dealing with Worldwide Terror. *Society*, Volume 10, Number 9, January 1973.

0680 Gunman Free Five of 156 Hostages. *Times of India*, 30 September 1977, p. 1.

0681 J. Billington. Gun Within. *Newsweek*, Volume 86, Number 13, 6 October 1975.

0682 Gunter, Michael. Contemporary Armenian Terrorism. *Terrorism: An International Journal,* Volume 8, Number 3, 1986, pp. 213-52.

0683 Gunter, Michael M. The Armenian Terrorist Campaign Against Turkey. *Orbis*, Number 27, Summer 1983, pp. 447-77.

0684 Gupta, Anirudha. Acts of State Terrorism. *Deccan Herald,* 10 July 1985, p. 6.

0685 Gupta, Pranay. Cul-de Sac. *Illustrated Wkly India,* Volume 106, Number 18, 8 September 1985, pp. 14-17.

0686 Gupta, Rakesh. Terrorism Of U.S. Radical Right. *Patriot*, 31 July 1985, p. 4.

0687 Gupta, Vinod. Terror Grips a City. *Times of India*, 20 November 1977, p. 2.

0688 Guru Dev, S. Combating Terrorism. *Statesman,* Delhi, 16 July 1984, p. 6.

0689 Hachey, Thomas E. Political Terrorism: The British Experience. In Yonah, Alexander (Ed.). *International Terrorism: National Regional and Global Perspectives*. New York, Praeger Publishers, 1976, pp. 90-104.

0690 Hacker, F.J. *Crusaders, Criminals, Crazies-Terror and Terrorism in our Time*. New York, W.W. North and Company, 1976.

0691 Heager, Robert. In Ulster Violence Turns Hope to Despair. *U.S. News*, Number 90, 2 February 1981, pp. 61-2.

0692 Halt. Who Files There ? Preventing Further Fedayeen Terrorism at European Airports. *Time*, Volume 103, Number 31, 21 January 1974.

0693 Hamilton, C.M.P. Terrorism: Its Ethical Implication for the Future. *The Futurist,* Volume 11, Number 6, 1977, pp. 351-4.

0694 Hamilton, Iain. The Irish Tangle. *Conflict Studies*, Number 6, 1970.

0695 Han, Henry Hyunweek. *Terrorism, Political Violence and World Order*. Lanham, Md., University Press of America, 1984.

0696 Hannay, William A. International Terrorism: the Need for a Fresh Perspective. *International Lawyer,* Volume 8, Number 2, 1974, pp. 268-84.

0697 Harbor No Evil: Israeli Attack on Lebonese Fishing Vessels. *Time*, Volume 104, Number 54, 22 July 1974.

0698 Hardman, J.B.S. *Terrorism - Encyclopedia of The Social Science*, Volume 14, New York, Macmillan, 1937, pp. 575-89.

0699 Harbabi, Y. Fedayeen: Action and Arab Strategy. *Adelphi Paper*, Number 53 December 1968.

0700 Harrick, Philip J. Terrorism: One of the Less Happy Phenomena of our Times: a State Official Outlines Scope of Department Security Operations Internationally, on the Domestic Front and on a Tactical Level: Based on Address. *Dept State News letter*, Fall 1978, pp. 6-9.

0701 Hartle, Anthony E. A Military Ethic in an Age of Terror. *Parameters,* Number 17, Summer 1987, pp. 68-75.

0702 Hassel, Conrad V. The Political Assassin. *Journal of Police Science and Administration*, December 1974.

0703 Havens, Murray C.; Leiden, Carl and Schmitt, Karl M. *The Politics of Assassination*. Engle-wood Cliffs, New Jersey, Prentice-Hall, 1970.

0704 Hayes, B. The Effects of Terrorism in Society: An Analysis, With Particular Reference to the United Kingdom and the European Economic Community. *Police Studies*, Volume 2, Number 3, 1979, pp. 4-10.

0705 Hayes, David. *Terrorists and Freedom Fighters*. Denver, U.K. Wayland, 1980.

0706 Headache for Botha. *Secular Democracy*, 2 December 1986, p-6.

0707 Heikal, Muhammed M. *The Road to Ramadan*. New York, Quadrangle, 1975.

0708 Heims, Andrea R.C. Procedural Democracy and the Terrorist Threat. *Police Studies*, Volume 4, Winter 1982, pp. 23-32.

0709 Heinous Attempt: Assassination Attempt on President Jayewardene. *Amrita Bazar Patrika*, 15 July 1985, p. 6.

0710 Hempstone, I. *Rebels, Mercenaries, and Dividends: The Katauga Story*. New York, Praeger, 1962.

0711 Hennessy, Jessleya. Will Terrorism Become a World Power ? *Eastern Economics*, Volume 64, Number 18, 2 May 1975, pp. 976-78.

0712 Henry, Ernst. The Anatomy of Terrorism. *New Times*, Number 39, September 1981, pp. 28-30 and Number 41, October 1981, pp. 26-28.

0713 Henry, Ernst. *Stop Terrorism*. Moscow, Novesti Press Agency Publication House, 1982.

0714 Henze, Paul B. Coping with Terrorism. *Flatcher Forum*, Volume 9, Number 2, Summer 1985, pp. 307-323.

0715 Heradatviet, Daniel. A Profile of the Palestine Guerrillas. *Cooperation and Conflict*, Number 7, 1972, pp. 13-36.

0716 Heradstveit, David. The Role of International Terrorism in the Middle East Conflict and its Implications for Conflict Resolution. In David Carlton and Carlo Schaerf, (Eds.). *International Terrorism and World Security*. New York, The Halstead Press, 1975, pp. 93-103.

0717 Herman, Edward S. *The Real Terror Network: Terrorism in Fact and Propaganda*. Boston, South End Pr., 1982.

0718 Hidden Hand. *Madhya Pradesh Chronicle*, 28 July 1984, p. 4.

0719 Hijack. *Deccan Herald*, 7 July 1984, p. 6.

0720 Hijack Episode. *Assam Tribune*, 8 July 1984, p. 4.

0721 Hijack Drama. *Times of India*, Delhi, 7 July 1984, p. 6.

0722 Hijacked Plane Leaves Dacca with 24 Hostages. *Times of India*, 3 October 1977, p. 1.

0723 Hijacked Again. *Patriot*, 7 July 1984, p. 4.

0724 Hijackers Release four More Passengers. *Times of India*, 1 October 1977, p. 1.

0725 Hijackers Want $ 6 M dollar Release of 9 Prisoner. *Times of India*, 29 September 1977, p. 1.

0726 Hijacking and After. *Hindu*, 9 July 1984, p. 8.

0727 Hijacking of the Achille Lauro. *W Comp Pres Docs*, Number 21, 14 October 1985, pp. 1234-1237.

0728 Hippchen, L.J. and Yongs, Yim. *Terrorism, International Crime and Arms Control*. Springfield, Thomas Publishers, 1982.

0729 Hirsch, Daniel. Protecting Reactors from Terrorist. *Bulletin of the Atomic Scientists*, Volume 42, Number 3, March 1986, pp. 22-25.

0730 Historical Evaluation and Research Organization. *The Terrorist and Sabotage Threat to U.S. Nuclear Programs: Phase one Final Report*. Dunn Loring, VA, HERO, Auguest 1974.

0731 Hof, Frederic C. The Beirut Bombay of October 1983: An Act of Terrorism. *Parameters*, Number 15, Summer 1985, pp. 69-74.

0732 Hoffacker, Lewis. The Government Response to Terrorism: A Global Approach. *U.S. Department of State Bulletin*, Number 70, 18 March 1974, pp. 274-278.

0733 Hoffman, Bruce. Right-wing Terrorism in Europe Italy, France, and West Germany, Chiefly. *Conflict*, Volume 5, Number 3, 1984, pp. 185-210.

0734 Hoffman, Bruce. Recent Trends in Palestinian Terrorism. *Rand Corporation*, May 1984.

0735 Hoffman, Bruce. The Plight of the Phoenix: the PLO Since Lebanon. *Conflict Q*, Number 5, Spring 1985, pp. 5-17.

0736 Hoffman, Bruce. Left-wing Terrorism in the United States. *Conflict Q*, Number 6, Fall 1986, pp. 5-14.

0737 Holden, David. Which Arafat ? *New York Times Magazine*, 23 March 1975. p. 11.

0738 Holt, Simma. *Terrorism in the Name of God*. New York, Crown Publishers, 1965.

0739 Hope of Mizoram. *Statesman*, Delhi, 24 December 1984, p. 6.

0740 Horchem, Hans J. Right-wing Extremism in Western Germany. *Conflict Studies,* Number 65, 1975.

0741 Horchem, Hans J. *The Urban Guerrilla in West Germany - Origins and Perspectives.* Unpublished Paper Presented at the U.S. Department of State Conference on Terrorism, Washington, D.C., 25-26 March 1976.

0742 Horchen, Hans J. Terrorism in West Germany. *Conflict Studies*, Number 186, May 1986, p. 21.

0743 Horner, C. The Facts About Terrorism. *Commentary*, Volume 69, Number 6, 1980, pp. 40-45.

0744 Horowitz, Irving L. Civil Liberties' Dangers in Anti-Terrorist Policies. *Civil Liberties Review*, March 1977, pp. 25-32.

0745 Horowitz, Irving L. *Toward A Qualitative Micropolitics of Terror.* Delivered at the Conference on International Terrorism. U.S. Department of State, 25-26 March 1976.

0746 Horowitz, Irving L. Political Terrorism and the State. *Journal of Political and Military Sociology*, Volume 1, Number 1, 1973, pp. 147-157.

0747 Horrell, Muriel. *Terrorism in Southern Africa.* Johannesburg, South African Institute of Race Relations, 1968.

0748 Horvitz, J.F. Arab Terrorism and International Aviation: Deterrence Versus the Political Act. *Chitty's Law Journal,* Number 24, May 1976, pp. 145-154.

0749 Hosmer, Stephen T. *Viet Cong Repression and Its Implications for the Future.* Lexington, Mass., Health Lexington Books, 1970.

0750 Hostage Dilemma. *Time,* Volume 105, Number 50, 20 October 1975.

0751 Hostage Incidents: Examples in Modern History. *Dept State Bul,* Number 81, March 1981, pp. 23-28.

0752 How not to Combat Terrorism, Students Kidnapped in Tanzania. *National Review,* Number 27, 12 September 1975, p. 978.

0753 Howard, A.J. Urban Guerrilla Warfare in a Democratic Society. *Medicine, Science and the Law,* Number 12, October 1972, pp. 231-243.

0754 Howe, Irving. Political Terrorism: Hysteria of the Left. *New York Times Magazine,* 12 April 1970, p. 25.

0755 Howley, Dennis C. *The UN and the Palestinians.* New York, Exposition, 1975.

0756 Hudson, Michael C. The Palestinian Arab Resistance Movement: Its Significanace in the Middle East Crisis. *Middle East Journal,* Number 23, 1969, pp. 291-3-1.

0757 Hudson, Michael C. Developments and Setbacks in the Palestinian Resistance Movement. *Journal of Palestine Studies,* Number 1, Spring 1972, pp. 64-84.

0758 Hurewitz, Jacob C. *The Struggle for Palestine.* New York, Greenwood, 1968.

0759 Hurwood, Bernhardt J. *Society and the Assassin: A Background Book on Political Murder.* New York, Parent's Magazine Press, 1970.

0760 Hussain, Mehmood. *The Palestine Liberation Organization: A Study In Ideology and Tactics.* New York, International Publications Service, 1975.

0761 Hutchinson, Martha Crenshaw. *Revolutionary Terrorism: The FLN in Algeria 1954-1962.* Stanford, Hoover Instn Pr., 1978.

0762 Hutchinson, Martha Crenshaw. The Concept of Revolutionary Terrorism. *Journal of Conflict Resolution,* Number 16, September 1972, pp. 383-396.

0763 Hutchinson, Martha Crenshaw. Terrorism and the Diffusion of Nuclear Power. *International Studies Association*, Toronto, 25-29 February. 1976.

0764 Hyams Edward. *Killing No Murder*. New York, Panther, 1970. Original British Edition Published by Nelson in 1969.

0765 Ignatius, David. Tracking Terrorism: Amid Lebanon's Anarchy, its Military Prosecutor Strives to Uncover the Many Sources of Violence. *Wall St J,* Volume 201, Number 60, 11 May 1983.

0766 Ignatius, David. Policy Vacuum: a Clear Plan to Handle Terrorism Still Eludes Divided Reagan Camp; Some Doubt Value of Force; Priority of Saving Lives Leaves U.S. Options. *Wall St J*, Volume 205, Number 14, 20 July 1985.

0767 Ignatius, David. U.S. Readies Anti-Terrorism Policy. *Wall St J.* Volume 203, Number 32, 12 March 1984.

0768 Ikle, Fred C. *The Social Impact of Bomb Destruction*. Norman, Oklahoma, University of Oklahoma Press, 1958.

0769 Ilyin, Boris. After the Terrible Six Months Italy. *New Times*, Number 35, August 1978, pp. 12-14.

0770 Inbari, Pinchas. Underground: Political Background and Psychological Atmosphere Recently discovered Jewish underground movement to drive Arabs from the Israeli-occupied territories. *New Outlook*, Number 27, June-July 1984, pp. 9-12.

0771 Inderjit. Terrorism, Police and God Fathers. *Assam Tribune*, 19 August 1985, p. 4; *Economic Times*, 13 August 1985, p. 5.

0772 India Demands Return of Hijackers. *Times of India*, 6 February 1971, p. 1.

0773 India Firmly Rejects Hijackers' Condition for Return of IA Plane. *Times of India*, 2 February 1971, p. 1.

0774 India on the Map? *Secular Democracy*, 29 November 1984, p. 6.

0775 India Deplores Pak Decision to Free IA Jet Hijackers. *Times of India*, 7 January 1977, p. 1.

0776 Indira Devi, M.G. Terrorist Movement in South India. *Kerala Hist. Soc.*, 1977, p. 103.

0777 Individual's Terrorism. *Assam Tribune*, 18 January 1984, p. 4.

0778 Ingram, Timothy H. Nuclear Hijacking: Now Within the Grasp of Any Bright Lunatic. *Washington Monthly*, January 1973, pp. 20-28.

0779 Institute for Palestine Studies and the Arab Women's Information Committee. *Who Are the Terrorists*? Aspects of Zionist and Israeli Terrorism. 1972.

0780 Institute Strikes Again: Work of Mossad. *Times,* 14 July 1975, pp. 31-32.

0781 Inter-American Judicial Committee. Draft Convention on Terrorism and Kidnapping of Persons for Purposes of Extortion, September 26, 1970. Statement of Reason for the Draft Convention on Terrorist and Kidnapping October 5, 1970. *International Legal Materials,* Number 9, 1970, pp. 1177-82, and 1250-70.

0782 *Interim Report Concerning the Draft European Convention on the Suppression Of Terrorism.* C.M. (76) 137, (DPC) (CEPC) (76) (10), 1976.

0783 Inter Pol. *Northern India Patrika*, 5 November, 1985, p. 4.

0784 *International Terrorism.* 24th Ordinary Session, 17-24 October 1972, 14th and 16th Sittings Strasbourg 1973. pp. 514-535 and 599-605.

0785 International Terrorism. *Orbis,* Volume 29, Number 3, Fall 1985, pp. 465-515.

0786 International Buss Institute. *Terrorism and The Media*. London, 1980.

0787 *International Terrorism*. Proceedings of the Third Annual Conference Of the Canadian Council Of International Law Held At the University Of Ottawa, 18-19 October 1979.

0788 *International Terrorism*. U.S. House Committee on Foreign Affairs, Washington, 1974.

0789 International Terrorism 1977. *Stanford Journal of International Studies*, Volume 12, Spring 1977.

0790 International Terrorism Legislation: Message to the Congress April 26, 1984, Transmitting four Proposed Bills. *W Comp Pres Docs*., Number 20, 30 April 1984, pp. 590-593.

0791 Into Terrorist Hands: Italy and Spain Should Choose their Anti-Terrorist Weapons Carefully. *Economist,* Volume 274, Number 18, 9 February 1980.

0792 IRA. *Handbook for Volunteers of the Irish Republican Army*. Issued by IRA General Headquarters, 1965.

0793 Irish Terror Strikes Abroad. Last Gasp in Fight for Ulster. *U.S. News,* Volume 75, Number 20, 10 September 1973.

0794 Irish Republican Publicity Bureau. *Provisional IRA: Freedom Struggle*. 30 June, 1973.

0795 Is the Terror Tide Rising? *Sr. School*, Number 102, 23 April 1973, pp. 6-8.

0796 Islamic Terrorism. A Growing Peril, What we See now is only the Tip of the Ice-berg. *World Press R*, Volume 34, May 1987, pp. 17-19.

0797 Isolate Terrorism. *Indian Express*, Delhi, 22 April 1985, p. 6.

0798 Israeli Terrorism. *Indian Express*, Delhi, 3 October 1985, p. 6.

0799 Israel's Wagons in a Circle. *Newsweek*, 2 December 1974.

0800 Israel. *Nasser Terror Gangs: The Story of the Fedayeen.* Jerusalem, Ministry of Foreign Affairs, 1956.

0801 Ivienski, Ze'ev. *Individual Terror: Theory and Deed.* Tel Aviv, Hakibbutz Hame'uhad, 1977.

0802 Jabber, Fuad. The Arab Regimes and the Palestinian Revolution, 1967-1971. *Journal of Palestine Studies,* Number 2, 1973, pp. 79-101.

0803 Jack, H.A. Terrorism: Another U.N. Failure. *America*, 20 October 1973, pp. 282-285.

0804 Jack, Ian. Official Terrorism in Sri Lanka. *Times of India*, 4 June 1986, p. 8.

0805 Jacobs, Michael J. Protection of Offshore Assets of the United States from Terrorist Activity. *Natural Resources Lawyer*, Volume 16, Number 4, 1984, pp. 569-595.

0806 Jaehning, W.B. Journalist And Terrorism: Captives Of the Liberatarian Tradition. *Indian Law Journal*, Volume 53, Number 4, 1978, pp. 727-744.

0807 Jain, Girilal. The Exodus Has Begun: Towards a National Disaster. *Times of India*, 28 May 1986, p. 8; 29 May 1986, p. 8.

0808 Jain, Girilal. Failure of Sikh Intellectuals. *Times of India*, 4 July 1984, p. 6.

0809 Jaisingh, Hari. Danger Signals Again. *Indian Express*, 15 May 1985, p. 6.

0810 Janke, Peter. *Guerrilla and Terrorist Organizations: A World Directory and Bibliography*. New York, Macmillan, 1983.

0811 Janke, Peter. Terrorism in Argentina. *R.U.S.I. Journal*, September 1974.

0812 Janke, Peter. The Response to Terrorism. *Royal United Services Institute for Defence Studies,* Ten Years of Terrorism: Collected Views. London, R.U.S.I., 1979, p. 25.

0813 Janke, Peter and Price, D.L. Ulster: Consensus and Coercion. *Conflict Studies*, Number 50, 1975.

0814 Jaura, Ramesh. Creeping Authoritarianism. *Econ. and Political Wkly*, Volume 12, Number 43, 22 October 1977, pp. 1805-1806.

0815 Javits, Senator Jacob K. International Terrorism: Apathy Exacerbates the Problem. *Terrorism: An International Journal*, Volume 1, 1978, pp. 111-117.

0816 Jay, M. Politics of Terror. *Partisan Review*, Number 38, 1971, p. 72.

0817 Jayawardene, C.H.S. and H. Jayewardene. *Tea for Two: Ethnic Violence in Sri Lanka.* Ottawa, Ont., 1984.

0818 Jenkins, Brian M. *Embassies Under Siege: A Review of 48 Embassy Takeovers, 1971-1980.* Santa Monica, Rand Corporation, January 1981.

0819 Jenkins, Brian M. Statements About Terrorism. *Annals of the American Academy of Political and Social Science*, Number 463, September 1982, pp. 11-23.

0820 Jenkins, Brian M. Trends in International Terrorism. *World Affairs J*, Number 3, Spring 1984, pp. 40-48.

0821 Jenkins, Brian Michael. *New Modes of Conflict*. Rand Corporation, June 1983.

0822 Jenkins, B.M. Will Terrorists Go Nuclear. *Rand Report P, 5541*, November 1975, p. 10.

0823 Jenkins, Brian M. *Terrorism and the Nuclear Safeguards Issue*. Santa Monica, Rand Corporation, 1976.

0824 Jenkins, Brian M. *Will Terrorists Go Nuclear?* Discussion Paper No. 64, Santa Monica, Calif., California Seminar on Arms Control and Foreign Policy, October 1975.

0825 Jenkins, Brian M. *Urban Insurgency and Terrorism: an Urban Strategy for Guerrillas and Governments*. Santa Monica, Calif., The Rand Corporation, August 1976.

0826 Jenkins, Brian M. International Terrorism: A Balance Sheet. *Survival*, July/August 1975, pp. 158-164.

0827 Jenkins, Brian M. *High Technology Terrorism and Surrogate War: The Impact of New Technology on Low-Level Violence*. Santa Monica, California, The Rand Corporation Publication, January 1975.

0828 Jenkins, Brian M. *Terrorism Works : Sometimes*. Santa Monica, California, The Rand Corporation Publication, p. 5217, 1974.

0829 Jenkins, B.M. Nuclear Terrorism and its Consequences. *Society*, Volume 17, Number 5, 1980, pp. 5-15.

0830 Jenkins, Brian M. *Terrorism and Kidnapping.* Santa Monica, Calif., Rand Corporation Number p. 5255, June 1974.

0831 Jenkins, B. An Urban Strategy For Guerrillas and Governments. *Rand Abstract P-04670/1*, August 1972, p. 13.

0832 Jenkins, Brian M. (Ed.). *Terrorism And Personal Protection.* Stoncham Butterworth, 1985.

0833 Jenkins, B.M. The Potential for Nuclear Terrorism. *Rand Report P-5876*, May 1977, p. 11.

0834 Jenkins, B.M. The Terrorist Mindset and Terrorist Decision-making: Two Areas of Ignorance. *Rand Report P-6340*, June 1979, p. 6.

0835 Jenkins, B.M. Soldiers Versus Gunmen: The Challenge of Urban Guerrilla Warfare. *Rand Report P-5182,* March 1974, p. 10.

0836 Jenkins, B.M. *Should Corporations be Prevented from Paying Ransom?* Santa Monica, California, The Rand Corporation, Publication P-5291, 1974.

0837 Jenkins, Brian M. International Terrorism: Trends and Potentialities. *Journal of International Affairs*, Number 32, Spring/Summer 1978, pp. 115-123.

0838 Jenkins, Brian M. Upgrading the Fight Against Terrorism. *The Washington Post*, 27 March 1977.

0839 Jenkins, Brian M. Defense Against Terrorism. *Pol. Science*, Volume 101, Number 5, 1986, pp. 773-786.

0840 Jenkins, Brian M. and Wildhorn. *Sorrel Intelligence Constraints of The 1970s & Domestic Terrorism: Executive Summary*. Rand Corporation, 1983.

0841 Jenkins, B.M. and Johnson, J. International Terrorism: A Chronology, 1968-1974. *Rand Report, R-1597-DOS/ARPA*, March 1975, p 58.

0842 Jenkins, Roy. *England Prevention of Terrorism*. London, Her Majesty's Stationary Office, 1974.

0843 Jha, Prem Shankar. Terrorism in Punjab. *Times of India,* 23 April 1984, p. 8, 24 April 1984, p. 8.

0844 Jit, Inder. Terrorism, Police and Godfathers. *Economic Times*, 5 August 1985, p. 5.

0845 Jit, Inder. New Strategy for Punjab Terrorism. *Economic Times*, 5 August 1986, p. 5.

0846 Johnson, Chalmers. *Autopsy on Peoples War*. California, University of California Press, 1973.

0847 Johnson, Francis. *Famous Assassinations of History From Philip of Macedon, 336 B.C. to Alexander of Serbia, A.D. 1903.* Chicago, A.C. Mcclurg and Co., 1903.

0848 Johnson, K. *Guatemala: From Terrorism to Terror.* London, Institute for the Study of Conflict, 1972.

0849 Johnson, P. Age of Terror. *New Statesman*, Number 88, 1974, p. 763.

0850 Joiner, Charles. *The Fedayeen and Arab World Politics*. Morristown, New Jersey, General Learning Press, 1974.

0851 Joint Fight Against Extremists. *Madhya Pradesh Chronicle*, 31 October 1985, p. 4.

0852 Jongmany, Alex P. *Sehmid Amsterdam*. North Holend Publication Company, New Brunsciek, New Jersey, Transaction Books E Distributor, 1985, p. 585.

0853 Joshi, B.K. Terror in the Skies: Dealing with Hijackers. *Times of India*, 12 November 1977, p. 8.

0854 Joshi, B.K. Terrorists Rock West Germany: Shock Wave in Europe. *Times of India*, 23 September 1977, p. 6.

0855 Joshi, B.K. Which Hunt in West Germany: Chancellor's Dilemma. *Times of India*, 17 October 1977, p. 6.

0856 Joshi, H.M. Challenge of Terrorism. *Madhya Pradesh Chronicle*, 8 July 1984, pp. 3-4.

0857 Joshi, H.M. Challenge of Terrorism. *National Herald*, Delhi, 12 July 1984, pp. 7 & 9.

0858 Journalist and Terrorism: Captives of the Liberation Tradition. *Indian Law Journal*, Volume 53, Number 4, 1978, pp. 727-744.

0859 Jovamovic, Milorad. Double Hijacking in the Mediterranian. *Review of International Affairs*, Volume 36, Number 854, 5 November 1985, pp. 23-25.

0860 Joyce, Edward M. Reporting Hostage Crisis: Who's in Charge of Television? *SAIS School Advanced Internat Studies R,* Number 6, Winter/Spring 1986, pp. 169-176.

0861 Kadi, Leila S. (Ed.). *Basic Political Documents of the Armed Palestinian Resistance Movement*. Beirut, Palestine Liberation Organization Research Centre, 1969.

0862 Kahn, E.J., Jr. Profiles: How do we Explain Them ? *The New Yorker*, 12 June 1978, pp. 37-40.

0863 Kaldor, Mary and Anderson, Paul. (Eds.). *Mad Dogs: The US Raids on Libya*. New York, Pluto Pr., 1986.

0864 Kapetanovic, Goran. International Terrorism: Legal and Political Aspects. *R Internat Affairs*, Number 36, 5-20 July, 1985, pp. 8-11.

0865 Kaplan, John. The Assassins. *Stanford Law Review*, Number 5, May 1967, pp. 1110-1151.

0866 Kannabiran, K.G. State of Terrorist. *Indian Express*, Delhi, Magazine Section, 23 June 1985, p. 1.

0867 Karber, Phillip A. Urban Terrorism: Baseline Data and a Conceptual Framework. *Social Science Quarterly*, December 1971, pp. 521-533.

0868 Karkaria, Bachi J. Terror in the Skies. *Illustrated Weekly India*, Volume 98, Number 48, 18 December 1977, pp. 32-34.

0869 Karlekar, Hirammay. The Anatomy of Terrorism. *Indian Express*, Magazine Section, 2 January 1985, p. 1.

0870 Karlekar, Hirammay. Anatomy of Terrorism. *Indian Express*, Delhi, Magazine Section, 2 June 1985, p. 1, p. 6.

0871 Kattary, Sailesh. Target: Rajiv Gandhi. *Illustrated Wkly India*, Volume 106, Number 4, 2 January 1985, pp. 6-11.

0872 Katz, Doris. *The Lady Was a Terrorist: During Israel's War of Liberation*. New York, Shiloni, 1953.

0873 Katz, Samuel. *Days of Fire: The Secret History of the Irgun Zuai Leumi*. Garden City, New York, Doubleday, 1968.

0874 Kautsky, Karl. *Terrorism and Communism: A Contribution to the Natural History of Revolution*. Translated by W.H. Karridge. London, George Allen & Unwin, 1920.

0875 Keeping Terror Alive. *Patriot*, 29 November 1985, p. 4.

0876 Kelly, Joseph B. Assassination in War Time. *Military Law Review*, 30 October 1965, pp. 101-111.

0877 Kelly, Orr. If Terrorists go after U.S. Nuclear Bombs. *U.S. News*, Number 86, 12 March 1978, pp. 43-45.

0878 Kelly, Orr. How U.S. would Deal with Nuclear Terrorists! How the Nuclear Emergency Search Team Handles Threats Involving Nuclear Devices and Material. *U.S. News*, Number 94, 7 February 1983, pp. 49-50.

0879 Kempe, Frederick. Violent Tactics: Terrorist Attacks Grow but Groups are Smaller and of Narrower Focus, They also are More Lethal, as Indicated by Statistics and Explosion in Beirut. *Wall St J*, Volume 201, Number 1, 19 April 1983.

0880 Kempe, Frederick. Violent Tactics: In Europe and Mideast Terrorists Focus on U.S. Installations. *Wall St J*, Volume 201, Number 1, 21 April 1983.

0881 Kennedy, Moorhd. The Root Causes of Terrorism: Terrorism and Retribution will be a Self-perpetuating Phenomenon Unless we Seek to Understand its Sources. *Humanist*, Number 46, September-October 1986, pp. 5-9.

0882 Kerr, Donald. M. Coping with Terrorism. *Terrorism: An International Journal*, Volume 8, Number 2, 1985, pp. 113-126.

0883 Kersteller, W.A. Terrorism and Intelligence. *Terrorism: An International Journal*, Volume 3, Numbers 1-3, 1979, pp. 109-115.

0884 Khaleque, Abdul. *Terrorism Menace: How to Combat it.* Jalpaiguri, a Wadubat Jalpaiguri Kohinoor Prtg. Works, 1932.

0885 Khan, Muhammed Zafrulla. Asylum – Article 14 of the Universal Declaration. *Journal of the International Commission of Jurists*, Number 8, 1967.

0886 Khan, Rahmatullah. Guerrilla Warfare and International Law. *International Studies*, New Delhi, Number 9, October 1967.

0887 Khanduri, P.N. Terrorism. *United Services Institution Journal*, Volume 110, Number 459, January-March 1980, pp. 13-22.

0888 Khanna, K.C. Terrorism and Punjab Poll. *Times of India*, Delhi, 27 August 1985, p. 6.

0889 Khanna, K.C. Still Groping in the Dark: Shadowy World of Terrorists. *Times of India*, 10 January 1986, p. 8.

0890 Khanna, K.C. Akalis and the Terrorists: Cynical Politicking Is not the Way. *Times of India*, 28 May 1985, p. 8.

0891 Khanna, K.C. Security Belt on Border: Many Imaginary Fears. *Times of India*, 19 August 1986, p. 8.

0892 Khanna, H.R. The Killings in Punjab: How Long Must they Go On? *Times of India*, 8 August 1986, p. 8.

0893 Kidnapping in Vienna, Murder in Athens. *Time*, Volume 407, Number 4, 5 January 1976.

0894 Kidwai, Anser. Time to cry Halt. *National Herald*, 5 April 1984, p. 7.

0895 Kiernan, Thomas. *Arafat: The Man and the Myth*. New York, Norton, 1976.

0896 Kimche, Jon. *Israel and the Palestinians In the Arab-Israeli Dispute*. London, Institute for the Study of Conflict, 1971.

0897 Kimche, Jon. Can Israel Contain the Palestine Revolution? *Conflict Studies*, Number 13, June 1971.

0898 Kini, N.G.S. Terrorist World-Outlook in 19th Century Western India. *Political Science Review*, Volume 11, Number 1, January-March 1972, pp. 68-79.

0899 Kirk, Donald. Foiling Kidnappers. *New York Times Magazine*, 19 February 1978, 14 ff.

0900 Kirkham, James F.; Levy, Sheldon G. and Crotty, William J. *Assassination and Political Violence: A Staff Report to the National Commission on the Causes and Prevention of Violence*. New York, Bantam, 1970.

0901 Kirpekar, Subash. Hoshiarpur - a Fanatic Town. *Times of India*, Delhi, 12 June 1985, p. 9.
0902 Kishor, Nand. Violence and Terror, with Special Reference to North East India. *Avadh University Res. J Arts*, Volume 1, Number 1, 1982, pp. 188-94.
0903 Kishwar, Madhu. Journey into Despair. *Illustrated Wkly India*, Volume 107, Number 6, 9 February 1986, pp. 20-23.
0904 Kissinger, Henry A. Hijacking, Terrorism and War. *Department of State Bulletin*, Number 73, 8 September 1975, pp. 360-361.
0905 Kitson, Frank. *Low Intensity Operations: Subversion, Insurgency, and Peacekeeping*. Harrisburg, PA, Stackpole Books, 1971.
0906 Kittrie, N.N. New Look at Political Offenses and Terrorism, in S.F. Landau (Ed.). *Criminology in Perspective: Essays in Honour of Israel Drapkin*, Lexington, MA, Health Lexington Books, 1977.
0907 Knight, R. For Northern Ireland, a Bloody Christmas. *U.S. News*, Number 79, 29 December 1975, pp. 17-18.
0908 Knustor, J.N. The Terrorists' Dilemmas: Some Implicit Rules of the Game. *Terrorism: An International Journal*, Volume 4, 1980, pp. 195-222.
0909 Kobetz, Richard W.K. and Cooper, H.H. *Target Terrorism*. Gaitherburg, Md., International Association of Chiefs of Police, 1978.
0910 Korsch, Karl. *Marxism and Philosophy*. London, NLB, 1970. New York, Monthly Review Press, 1971.
0911 Kottary, Sailesh and others. The Day of Terrorist. *Illustrated Wkly India*, Volume 105, Number 1, 1 April 1984, pp. 19-23.
0912 Kramer, J.J. *Role of Behavioural Science in Physical Security. Proceedings of the Second Annual Symposium, 23-24 March 1977*. Washington, D.C., U.S. Department of Commerce, National Bureau of Standards, 1978.
0913 Krieger, David. When Terrorists go Nuclear. *The Center Report*, June 1974, p. 13.
0914 Krieger, D.M. Terrorists and Nuclear Technology. *Bulletin Atom Science*, Number 31, June 1975, pp. 28-34.
0915 Krosney, H. Israel: Terror and Promise. *Nation*, Number 218, 8 June 1974, pp. 717-719.
0916 Kuhn, Arthur K. The Complaint of Yugoslavia Against Hungary with Reference to the Assassination of King Alexander. *American Journal of International Law*, Number 29, 1935, pp. 87-92.

0917 Kuhne, Robert J. and Schmitt, Robert F. The Terrorist Threat to Corporate Executives. *Bus Horizons*, Number 22, December 1979, pp. 77-82.

0918 Kumar, Prem. New Hope of Goodwill and Peace. *Secular Democracy*, 26 November 1984, p. 6.

0919 Kumar, Surya. Pak Complicity in Sikh Extremism. *Times of India*, Delhi, 20 December 1984, p. 8.

0920 Kumar, S.R. Facing Terrorism. *Search Light*, 7 May 1984, p. 4, p. 5.

0921 Kumar, S.R. Modern Terrorism. *Search Light*, 27 May 1985, p. 4.

0922 Kumar, S.R. Acquaring Up to Terrorism. *Search Light*, 26 August 1985, p. 4, p. 5.

0923 Kupperman, Robert H. and Darrell, M. Trent. The Terrorist International: The Past Is Prologue and America is Vulnerable. *Across the Board*, Number 17, February 1980, pp. 50-68.

0924 Kupperman, Robert H. Countering High Technology Terrorism. *Scandinavian J. Development Alternatives*, Number 3, September 1984, pp. 73-94.

0925 Kupperman, Robert H. Countering Terrorism: Time to Switch Tactics. *Enterprise*, September 1982, pp. 20-22.

0926 Kupperman, R.H. Treating the Symptoms of Terrorism: Some Principles of Good Hygiene. *Terrorism: An International Journal*, Volume 1, 1977, pp. 35-49.

0927 Kuriyama, Y. Terrorism at Tel Aviv Airport and a New Left Group in Japan. *Asian Survey*, Volume 8, Number 3, 1973, pp. 336-346.

0928 Kuroda, Yasumasa. Young Palestinian Commandos in Political Socialization Perspective. *Middle East Journal*, Number 26, Summer 1972, pp. 253-270.

0929 Kutner, Luis. Constructive Notice: a Proposal to End International Terrorism. *New York Law Forum*, Number 19, Fall 1973, pp. 325-350.

0930 Kuwait Hits Back. *Tribune*, 20 July 1985, p. 4.

0931 La Guardia Blast: My God it was Terrible. *Time*, Number 107, 12 January 1976.

0932 Lador-Lederer, J.J. A Legal Approach to International Terrorism. *Israel Law Review*, Number 9, 1974, pp. 194-220.

0933 Lagerwist, Frank A. *Israel and the Politics of Terrorism in the Middle East*. London, Inst Econ Pol., 1981.

0934 Lahore Outrage and after-Pak Rulers' Political Game. *Link*, Volume 13, Number 27, 14 February 1971, pp. 9-10.

0935 Lakos, Amos. *A Bibliography of International Terrorism*. Boulder, Westview, 1986.

0936 Lakshman, Nikhil. Web of Terror. *Illustrated Wkly India,* Volume 106, Number 4, 2 January 1985, pp. 12-15.

0937 Lamrick, H.T. *The Terrorist*. London, Rowman, 1972.

0938 Lang, Daniel. A Reporter at Large: the Bank Drama. *The New Yorker*, Volume 25, 1974, pp. 56-126.

0939 Langeraar, Wijnand. Delimitation of Continental Shelf Areas: A New Approach. *J Maritime Law and Commer,* Number 17, July 1986, pp. 389-406.

0940 Langguth, Gerd. Europe: Spreading Fear of Terrorism, Charting Extremist Organizations and their Aims. *World Press R*, Number 33, November 1986, pp. 19-21.

0941 Lapalmbara, Joseph. The Achille Lauro Affair: a Note on Italy and the United States. *Yale R*, Number 75, October 1986, pp. 542-563.

0942 Lapp, Ralph E. The Ultimate Blackmail. *New York Times Magazine*, 4 February 1973.

0943 Laqueur, Walter. Reflections on Terrorism. *For. Affairs,* Number 65, Fall 1986, pp. 86-100.

0944 Laqueur, Walter. Guerrillas and Terrorists. *Commentary*, October 1974, pp. 40-48.

0945 Lasky, Melvin J. Ulrike and Andreas: The Bonnie and Clyde of West Germany's Radical Subculture may have Failed to Make a Revolution, but They have Bruised the Body Politic. *New York Times Magazine*, 11 May 1975, p. 14.

0946 Lasky, Melvin J. Ulrike Meinhof and the Baader-Meinhof Gang. *Encounter*, Number 44, June 1975, pp. 9-23.

0947 Lasky, M.J. Ulrike and Andreas: Baader-Meinhof Gang. *New York Times Magazine*, 11 May 1975, pp. 14-15.

0948 Laushey, David M. and others. Bengal Terrorism and Marxist Left. *Times of India*, 19 October 1975, p. 8.

0949 Lauterpacht, Hans. Revolutionary Activities by Persons against Foreign States. *American Journal of International Law*, Number 22, 1928, pp. 105-130.

0950 Laxity in Security. *Search Light*, 7 July 1984, p. 4.

0951 Layey, Kathleen A. and Sang, Lewis M. Control of Terrorism Through a Broader Interpretation of Article 3 of the Four Geneva Conventions of 1949. In Cherif M. Bassiouni (Ed.). *International Terrorism and Political Crimes*. Springfield, Illinois, Charles C. Thomas, 1975, pp. 191-200.

0952 Leachman, Robert B. and Althoff, Phillip (Eds.). *Preventing Nuclear Theft: Guidelines for Industry and Government: Security Measures Conference*. New York, Praeger Publishers, 1972.

0953 League of Nations. Draft Convention for the Prevention and Punishment of Terrorism. Draft Convention for the Creation of an International Criminal Court and Observations by Governments. *L.O.N.* 1936, Volume 2, pp. 3-6.

0954 Leaney, B.K. Terrorism - A Sun Marg. *The Australian Police Journal*, Volume 34, Number 2, 1980, pp. 1100-1104.

0955 Lebow, Richard N. The Origins of Sectarian Assassination: The Case of Belfast. *Journal of International Affairs*, Number 32, Spring/Summer 1978, pp. 43-61.

0956 Ledesma, I. Marked for Death. *Newsweek*, Volume 84, Number 53, 4 November 1974.

0957 Lee, Alfred McClung. Terrorism's Social-Historical Contexts in Northern Ireland, in *Research in Social Movements, Conflicts and Change*, 1983, pp. 99-131.

0958 Lee, Alfred McClung. The Dynamics of Terrorism in Northern Ireland, 1968-1980. *Social Research*, New York, Number 48, Spring 1981, pp. 100-134.

0959 Lee, Alfred McClung. *Terrorism in Northern Ireland*. Talonway, New York, Gen Hall, 1983.

0960 Lee, Andrew. International Suppression of Hijacking. in Cherif M. Bassiouni (Ed.). *International Terrorism and Political Crimes*. Springfield, Illinois, Charles C. Thomas, 1975, pp. 248-256.

0961 Lefever, Earnest. A Spectre that Haunts the World. *Indian Review*, Volume 77, Number 12, March 1982, pp. 25-30.

0962 Legerwist, Frank A. *Israel and the Politics of Terrorism in the Middle East*. London, Inst. Econ. Pol., 1981.

0963 Legum, C. How to Curb International Terrorism. *Current*, Number 147, January 1973, pp. 3-9.

0964 Leiden, Carl. Assassination in the Middle East. *Transaction*, May 1969, pp. 20-23.

0965 Lengthening Hands of Terrorists. *Madhya Pradesh Chronicle*, 27 August 1985, p. 4.

0966 Lenz, Robert R. *Explosives and Bomb Disposal Guide*. Springfield, IL, Charles C. Thomas, 1973.

0967 Lerner, Max. Assassination. *Encyclopedia of the Social Sciences*, New York, Macmillan, 1930, pp. 271-275.

0968 Lessons of the Hijack. *National Herald*, Delhi, 7 July 1984, p. 7.

0969 Let CIA, FBI Spy on Americans?. Yes: Interview with Senator John P. East, Republican, of North Carolina; No: Interview with Representative Don Edwards, Democrat, of California Intelligence Gathering on Suspected Terrorists. *U.S. News*, Number 91, 16 November 1981, pp. 33-34.

0970 Leventhal, Paul and Alexander, Yonah. (Ed.). *Preventing Nuclear Terrorism: The Report and Papers of the International Task Force on Prevention of Nuclear Terrorism*. Lexington, Lexington Bks., 1987.

0971 Leventhal, P. and Alexander, F. (Eds.). *Nuclear Terrorism: Defining the Threat*. New York, Pergamon, 1986.

0972 Lewis, Bernard. *The Assassins : A Radical Sect in Islam*. New York, Basic Books, 1968.

0973 Lewis, Bernard. The Palestinians and the PLO: A Historical Approach. *Commentary*, January 1975, pp. 32-48.

0974 Lewis, Flora. Super Power agreement. *Amrita Bazar Patrika*, 9 July 1985.

0975 Liable to Burst. *Hindustan Times*, 29 June 1985, p. 9.

0976 Libyan Raid: Americans Sanction More Raids if Libyan Terrorism Continues. *Gallup Rept.*, April 1986, pp. 2-12.

0977 Lillich, Richard B. (Ed.). *Transnational Terrorism: Conventions and Commentary*. Charlotteswille Michie Co., 1982.

0978 Lillich, R.B. and Carbonneau, T.E. Terrorism Amendment 1976 to the Foreign Assistance Act of 1961. *Journal of International Law and Economics*, Number 2, 1977, pp. 223-236.

0979 Lillich, R.B. and Paxman, J.M. State Responsibility for Injuries Occasioned by Terrorist Activities. *American University Law Review*, Number 26, Winter 1977, pp. 217-313.

0980 Lingering Challenge to Extremists. *Hindu*, 29 November 1985, p. 8.

0981 Lingo, Edward J.Z. Pro-action to the Terrorist Hostage Taking Challenge: A Training Exercise Report on a Simulated Training Incident at Honolulu International Airport. *Police Chief*, Number 49, April 1982, pp. 51-53.

0982 Little, Thomas. New Arab Extremists: A View from the Arab World. *Conflict Studies*, Number 4, May 1970.

0983 Little, Thomas. The Nature of the Palestinian Resistance Movement. *Asian Affairs*, Number 57, 1970, pp. 159-169.

0984 Living in Fear: Executive Kidnapping. *Newsweek*, Number 81, 11 June 1973, pp. 93-94.

0985 Livingston, Neil C. *The War Against Terrorism*. Lexington, Lexington Books, 1982.

0986 Livingston, Neil C. Death Squads (Latin America Chiefly: Implications for United States Policy). *World Affairs*, Number 146, Winter 1983-1984, pp. 239-248.

0987 Livingstone, Neil C. (Ed.). Special Issue: Subnational Conflict, Low-level Conflicts that Include Guerrilla Insurgency, Terrorism, Sabotage, Death squads, and Religious Militias. *World Affairs*, Number 146, Winter 1983/1984, pp. 219-283.

0988 Livingstone, Neil C. (Ed.). Special Issue: Terrorism Comments and Papers by Journalists, Academics, Policy-makers, and Military and Intelligence Specialists Concerned with Terrorism. *World Affairs*, Number 146, Summer 1983.

0989 Livingstone, Neil C. Fighting Terrorism and Dirty Little Wars, some Emphasis on United States Policies in Central America. *Air Univ R*, Number 35, March-April 1984, pp. 4-16.

0990 Lloyd, Richard. *Beyond the CIA: The Frank Terpil Story.* New York, Seaver Books, 1983.

0991 Lockwood, Bert. *The Utility of International Law in Dealing with International Terrorism*. Washington, D.C. Paper Presented to the International Studies Association Convention, 20, February 1975.

0992 London Economic Summit Declaration on Democratic Values, 8 June; London Economic Declaration, Declaration on East-West Relations and Arms Control, Declaration on International Terrorism, 9 June 1984. *W Comp Pres Docs*, Number 20, 18 July 1984, pp. 856-861.

0993 Lopex, George A. *Terrorism, Worldviews and Problems of Policy*. Unpublished Paper, 1982.

0994 Lopex, Vincent C. *What the U.S. Army Should do about Urban Guerrilla Warfare*. Springfield, VA, National Technical Information Center, 1975.

0995 Lorch, Netanel. *The Edge of the Sword : Israel War of Independence 1947-1949*. New York, Putnam, 1961.

0996 Lowry, D. Ill Treatment, Brutality and Torture : Some Thoughts Upon the Treatment of Irish Political Prisoners. *Depaul Law Review*, Number 22, 1973, 553 ff.

0997 Lowry, D.R. Terrorism and Human Rights : Counter - Insurgency and Necessity of Common Law. *Notre Dame Lawyer*, Number 53, 1977, pp. 49-89.

0998 Lubét, Steven. Extradition Reform : Executive Discretion and Judicial Participation in the Extradition of Political Terrorist History, Current Status, and Proposed Reform of the Process Governing the Political Offense Exception in United States Extradition law. *Cornell Internat Law J.*, Number 15, Summer 1982, pp. 247-291.

0999 Lyles, J.C. Unanswered Question for Camilla's Father. *New Christian*, Number 91, 26 June 1974, pp. 659-660.

1000 Lynch, Edward A. International Terrorism : The Search for a Policy. *Terrorism : An International Journal*, Volume 9, Number 1, 1987, pp. 1-85.

1001 Lyons, Martyn. *Revolution in Toulouse : An Essay on Provincial Terrorism*. P Lang Pubs., 1978.

1002 Mebry, R.C. *Nuclear Theft : Real and Imagined Dangers*. Springfield, VA, National Technical Information Service, 1976.

1003 MacDonald, Arthur. Assassins of Rulers. *Journal of the American Institute of Criminal Law and Criminology*, Number 2, November 1911, pp. 505-520.

1004 Mackey, Janet and World without War Council (Eds.). *Terrorism and Political Self-Determination : A Tragic Marriage we could Help Decouple*. Chicago, World Without War, 1980.

1005 Mac, A. Non-Strategy of Urban Guerrilla Warfare, in J. Niezing, (Ed.). *Urban Guerrilla : Studies on the Theory, Strategy, and Practice of Political Violence in Modern Societies*. Rotterdam, Netherlands, Rotterdam University Press, 1974, pp. 22-45.

1006 Mack, A. Terrorism and the Left. *Arena*, Number 51, 1978, pp. 18-31.

1007 Macomber, W.B. Deputy Under Secretary Macomber Discusses Terrorism in Interview on Today Program, Transcript of Interview, 8 March 1973. *Dept State Bulletin*, Number 68, 2 April 1973, pp. 399-402.

1008 Maechling, Charles, Jr. Handcuffing Terrorism : Transnational Law Enforcement, not Politics or Polemics, will Best Protect the West. *For Service J*, Number 64, January 1987, pp. 21-27.

1009 Mahajan, S.K. The Future of Urban Insurgency and Terrorism. *United Services Institution Journal*, Volume 112, Number 470, October-December 1982, pp. 321-331.

1010 Mahendra, Ved. Tackling Terrorism. *Hindustan Times*, 16 July 1984, p. 9.

1011 Mahoney, Harry T. After a Terrorist Attack : Business as Usual. *Security Management*, Number 19, 19 March 1975, pp. 16-19.
1012 Majumdar, Swapna. The Terrorist Strikes Again. *Illustrated Wkly India*, Volume 106, Number 3, 26 May 1985, pp. 14-16.
1013 Makarevich, Lev. Manual for Murder Alleged Connections betwen the U.S. Central Intelligence Agency and various Italian Terrorist Groups. *New Times*, Number 4, January 1979, pp. 28-29.
1014 Malhotra, Avtar Singh. Punjab : Terrorists Desperate as Mass Campaign Picks Up. *New Age*, Volume 34, Number 18, 4 May 1986, p. 15.
1015 Malhotra, Inder. Terror, Crime and State Infrastructure Remains Rusted. *Times of India*, 29 August 1985, p. 6.
1016 Malik, Arshad. Terrorism : International Linkages. *Madhya Pradesh Chronicle*, 16 June 1985, p. 5.
1017 Malik, Harji. A Terrorist Remembered. *Times of India*, Magazine Section, 15 January 1978, p. 11.
1018 Malik, K.N. This is the Politics of Terrorism. *Times of India*, Delhi, (Magazine Section), 8 September 1985, p.5.
1019 Mallin, Jay. *Terror in Vietnam*. Princeton, D. Van Nostrand, 1966.
1020 Mallin, Jay. Terrorism in Revolutionary Warfare. *Strategic Review*, Number 2, Fall 1974, pp. 48-55.
1021 Mallison, W.T., Jr. and Mallison, S.N. The Concept of Public Purpose Terror in International Law. *Howard Law Journal*, Number 18, 1973, pp. 12-28. and *Journal of Palestine Studies*,. Number 4, Winter 1975, pp. 36-51.
1022 Mallison, W.T., Jr., and Mallison, S.N. An International Law Appraisal of the Juridicial Characteristics of the Resistance of the People of Palestine : The Struggle for Human Rights. in Cherif M. Bassiouni (Ed.). *International Terrorism and Political Crimes*. Springfield, Illinois Charles C. Thomas, 1975, pp. 173-190.
1023 Mami, V.S. International Terrorism : Is a Definition Possible ? *Indian Journal International Law*, Volume 18, Number 2, April-January 1978, pp. 206-277.
1024 Mankekar, D.R. Press and Terrorism : Presistent Dilemma. *Mainstream*, Volume 24, Number 3, 21 September 1985, pp.8-10.
1025 Manor, F.S. The New World Disorder : If Terrorism is War by other Means, we aren't even Holding our Position. *Am Spectator*, Number 13, July 1980, pp. 19-21.
1026 Mantell, D.M. The Potential for Violence in Germany. *Journal of Social Issues*, Number 27, 1971, pp. 101-112.

1027 Mardor, Munya. *Haganun*. New York, New American Library, 1966.
1028 Marks, Jim. Terrorism : An International Threat Emphasis on Insurance Aspects of Protecting Executives from Kidnapping and Extortion Attempts. *J Ins.*, Number 41, September-October 1980, pp. 13-18.
1029 Marighella Carlos and Haurahan, Gene Z. (Eds.). *The Terrorist Classic Manual of the Urban Guerrilla*. Chapel Hill, Documentary Pubns., 1985.
1030 Marshall, John. The 20th Century Vehme : Terror by Assassination. *Blackwoods Magazine*, June 1945, pp. 421-425.
1031 Martin, Everett G. Latin America's Terrorist Network. *Wall St J*, Volume 195, Number 24, 15 April 1980.
1032 Martin, L. John. The Media's Role in International Terrorism. *Terrorism : An International Journal*, Volume 8, Number 2, 1985, pp. 127-146.
1033 Masud, Iqbal. Time to Ask Questions. *Indian Express*, Delhi, Magazine Section, 2 June 1985, p. 2.
1034 Mathur, Girish. Barnala's Panthic Rhetoric and Surrender to Terror. *Link*, Volume 28, Number 35, 6 April 1986, pp. 7-9.
1035 Mathur, L.P. *Indian Revolutionary Movement in the United States of America*. Delhi, S. Chand, 1970.
1036 May, W.F. Terrorism as Strategy and Ecstasy. *Social Research*, Number 41, Summer 1974, pp. 277-298.
1037 Mayer, Jane. After the Carnage, Survivors in Beirut are Bitter and Angry : But Marine Officers Express New Resolve in Mission after Terrorist Bombings, October 23 1983. *Wall St J*, Volume 202, Number 1, 24 October 1983.
1038 Mazrui, Ali A. Thoughts on Assassination in Africa. *Political Science Quarterly*, Number 83, March 1968, pp. 40-48.
1039 McAllister, Ian and Richard, Rose. *Can Violent Political Conflict be Resolved by Social Change*. Centre for the Study of Public Policy, University of Stratchclyde, 1982, p. 24.
1040 McCredie, Jeffrey Allan. Contemporary Uses of Force Against Terrorism : The United States Response to Achille Lauro : Questions of Jurisdiction and its Exercise. *Ga J Internat and Comparative Law*, Number 16, Fall 1986, pp. 435-467.
1041 McCormick, R.W. Industrial Security in Europe : A Multinational Concept. *Security Management*, Number 18, July 1974, 8-10 f.

1042 McDowell, Charles P. and Harlan, John P. *Police Response to Political Crises and acts of Terrorism : Some Dimensions for Consideration*. Paper Delivered to the American Society of Criminology Annual Meeting, Toronto, Canada, 30 October, 2 November 1975.

1043 McEwen, Michael T. Psychological Operations Against Terrorism : The Unused Weapon. *Military Review*, Number 66, January 1986, pp. 59-67.

1044 McForan,Desmond. *The World Held Hostage : The War Waged in International Terrorism*. Sandeep, Oak Tree Bks, 1986.

1045 Mc-Gary, E. Coping with Terrorism in Argentina. *Illustration Weekly*, 9 March 1974, p. 40.

1046 McGuire, E.P. The Terrorist and the Corporation. *Across the Board*, Number 14, May 1977, pp. 11-19.

1047 McGuire, E. Patrika. *International Terrorism and Business Security*. Conference bd., 1979.

1048 McGuire, Maria. *To Take Arms : My Years with the IRA Provisionals*. New York, Viking, 1973.

1049 McLellan, Andrew C. Right-wing Terror Paralyzes Guatemalan Labour. AFL-CIO *Free Trade Union News*, Number 35, September 1980, pp. 8-9.

1050 McWhinney, Edward. *Hijacking of Aircraft and International Law*. Hague Racueli, The Hague Academy of International Law, 1973.

1051 McIntyre, Ronald R. The Palestine Liberation Organization : Tactics, Strategies and Options Toward the Geneva Peace Conference. *Journal of Palestine Studies*, Number 4, Summer 1975, pp. 65 89.

1052 Measure of Scepticism. *Times of India*, Delhi, 24 September 1985, p. 8.

1053 *Measures to Prevent International Terrorism*. Study Prepared by the Secretariat in accordance with the decision taken by the Sixth Committee at its 1314th Meeting on 27 September 1972.

1054 MeClung Lee, A. The Dynamics of Terrorism in Northern Ireland, 1960-1980. *Social Research*, Volume 48, Number 1, 1981.

1055 Medzini, Roni. China and the Palestinians. *New Middle East*, Number 32, pp. 34-40.

1056 Melman, Yossi. *The Master of Terrorist : The True Story Behind Abu Nidal*. London, Sicktgwick and Jackson Ltd., 1987.

1057 Melchiori, Barbara A. *Terrorism in the Late Victorian Novel*. London, Croom Helm Ltd., 1985.

1058 Menace of Terrorism. *National Herald*, 22 July 1985, p. 7.

1059 Mengel R.W. The Impact of Nuclear Terrorism on the Military's Role in Society. In Marious H. Livingston (Ed.): With Lee B. Kress and Marie G. Wanek. *International Terrorism in Contemporary World*. Weat Port, Conn., Greenwood Press, 1978, pp. 402-414.

1060 Merari, Ariel. (Ed.). *On Terrorism and Combating Terrorism*. Boston Way, U Pubns Amer, 1985.

1061 Meridor, Yaacov. *Long is the Road to Freedom*. Johannesburg, Newzo Press, 1955.

1062 Merkl, Peter H. (Ed.). *Political Violence and Terror : Motifs and Motivations*. Bukelly, University of California Press, 1986.

1063 Marlean-Ponty, Maurice. *Humanism and Terror : An Essay on the Communist Problem*. Boston, Beacon Press, 1969.

1064 Messmer, Robert F. Safe Houses for Business. *Across the Board*, Number 24, January 1987, pp. 44-51.

1065 Meyer, A.H. Foreign Terrorism Spreading to U.S. ? *U.S. News*, Number 75, 16 July 1973, pp. 37-40.

1066 Meyer, Thomas. *An Ende Der Gwalt ? Der Deutsehe Terrorismus Protokoll Lines Johrzehmts*. Frankfurt/m, Ullstein Gmbh, 1980.

1067 Mickolus, Edward F. Chronology of Transnational Terrorist Attacks Upon American Business People, 1968-1976. *Terrorism: An International Journal*, Volume 1, 1978, p. 217-236.

1068 Mickolus, Edward F. Negotiating for Hostages : A Policy Dilemma. *Orbis*, Number 19, Winter 1976, pp. 1309-1325.

1069 Mickolus, Edward F. Statistical approaches to the Study of Terrorism. In Alexander and Finger (Ed.). *Terrorism : Interdisciplinary Perspectives*. New York, the John Jay Press,1977

1070 Mickolus, Edward F. Comp. *The Literature of Terrorism : A Selectively Annotated Bibliography*. Westport, Greenwood Press,1980.

1071 Mickolus, Edward F. *Transnational Terrorism : A Chronology of Events, 1968-1979*. Westport, Greenwood Press, 1980.

1072 Middlebrook, M. *The Battle of Hamburg*. London, Allen Lane, 1981.

1073 Mideast: Blood and Hope : Maalot. Massacre. *Newsweek*, Number 83, 27 May 1974, pp. 36-40.

1074 Mideast Cross Fire : Fatah attack on Nahariya. *Newsweek*, Number 84, 8 July 1974, pp. 36-37.

1075 Mideast Terror Strikes Americans. *U.S. News*, Number 98, 24 July 1985, pp. 9-12.

1076 Miglani, Surendera. Terrorism's New Frontiers-Letter to the Editor. *Tribune*, 20 May 1985, p. 4.

1077 Miller, Abraham H. (Ed.). *Terrorism, the Media and the Law*. New York, Transnational Pubs., 1982.

1078 Miller, Abraham H. *Terrorism and Hostage Negotiations*. Westview, 1981.

1079 Miller, Abraham H. Terrorism and Government Policy. *Chitty's Law Journal*, Volume 27, Number 2, 1970, pp. 44-49.

1080 Miller, Abraham H. The Evolution of Terrorism. *Conflict Q*, Number 5, Fall 1985, pp. 5-16.

1081 Miller, Abraham H. Negotiations for Hostages : Implications from the Police Experience. *Terrorism : An International Journal*, Volume 1, 1978, pp. 125-146.

1082 Miller, Judith. Bargain with Terrorists ? *New York Times Magazine*, 18 July 1976, 7 ff.

1083 Miller, James A. Political Terrorism and Insurgency : An Interrogative Approach. in Yonah Alexander and Seymour M. Finger (Ed.). *Terrorism : Interdisciplinary Perspectives*. New York, The John Jay Press, 1977, pp. 65-87.

1084 Miller, Martin A. *Kropotkin*. University of Chicago Press, 1976.

1085 Miller, Reuben. Acts of International Terrorism :Governments Responses and Policies. *Comparative Pol Studies*, Number 19, October 1986, pp. 385-414.

1086 Milte, K.L. Terrorism and International Order. *Australian and New Zealand Journal of Criminology*, Number 8, June 1975, pp. 101-111.

1087 Milte, K.L.; Bartholomew, A. A.; O'Hearn, D.J.; and Campbell, A. Terrorism : Political and Psychological Considerations. *Australian and New Zealand Journal of Criminology*, Number 9, June 1976, pp. 89-94.

1088 Mind That Volcano. *Indian Express*, Delhi, 16 May 1985, p. 6.

1089 Mirsky, Zinovy. Terrorism and the Bourgeoisie. *New Times*, Number 34, August 1980, pp. 18-20.

1090 Missile Alert : Preventing Arab attacks at Airports all across western Europe. *Newsweek*, Volume 83, Number 45, 21 January 1974.

1091 Mission Possible. *Time*, Volume 104, Number 40, 30 September 1974,

1092 Mission That Failed : Attacks on Isreal Targets. *Time*, Volume 101, Number 23, 23 April 1973.

1093 Mitchell, Thomas H. Corporate Security in an age of Terrorism : Terrorism, Once Dismissed as an Unlikely Occurence, Now Poses a Threat That More and More Canadian Corporations Must Face At Home and Abroad. *Can Bus R*, Number 11, Spring 1984, pp. 31-36.

1094 Mitchel, T.H. and Mivcheal J. Kelly. Transnational Terrorism and the Western Elite Press. *Political Communication and Persuasion*, Number 1, 1981, pp. 269-296.

1095 Mitie, Midorag. Encore Up Pas Dans La Lutle Contre Le Terrorism. *Revue De Politique International*, 5 January 1977.

1096 MITRE Corporation. *The Threat to Licensed Nuclear Facilities*. McLean, Virginia, September 1975.

1097 Moffett, Matt. Guarding the Gates : Fear of Terrorists Directs New Attention to Illegal Immigrants : Border-tightening Advocates Say Security is at Stake, but Others have Doubts. *Wall St J*, Volume 207, Number 1, 14 May 1986.

1098 Mojekwu, Christopher. From Protest to Terror Violence : The African Experience. in Marius H. Livingston (Ed.). Lee B. Kress, and Marie G. Wanek. *International Terrorism in the Contemporary World*. Westport, Conn., Greenwood Press, 1978, pp. 177-181.

1099 Mommsen, W.J. and Hirschfield, Gerhard. *Social Protest, Violence and Terror in Nineteenth and Twentieth Century Europe*. St. Martin, 1982.

1100 Montana, Patrick J. and Roukis, George S. (Eds.). *Managing Terrorism : Strategies for the Corporate Executive*. Westport, Greenwood, 1983.

1101 Money for Murder. *Tribune*, 19 November 1984, p. 4.

1102 Monkey-Wrench Politics : Why Terrorists Emerge. *Sr School*, Number 105, 7 November 1974, pp. 4-8.

1103 Moodie, Michael. Political Terrorism : A Unique Kind of Tyranny. *Osterrichische Zeitschrift Fur Aussenpolitik*, Number 18, Heft 1, 1978, pp. 27-38.

1104 Moore, Barrington M. Jr. *Terror and Progress in the U.S.S.R.* Cambridge, Mass, Harvard University Press, 1954.

1105 Moore, H.T. Bomb Heard Around the World : Death of H.T. Moorej, Reprint from April 1952 Issue. *Illustration Ebong*, Number 31, November 1975, pp. 63-66.

1106 Moore, J.W. Terrorism and Political Crimes in International Law. *American Journal of International Law*, Number 67, 1973.

1107 Moore, John Norton. Towards Legal Restraints on International Terrorism. *Proceedings of the American Society of International Law*, 1973, pp. 88-94.

1108 Morality of Terrorism. *Newsweek*, Number 83, 25 Februaary 1974, pp. 21-22.

1109 Morello, Ted. Terrorism Back on U.N. Agenda. *Tribune*, 1 August 1985, p. 4.

1110 Morello, Ted. Terrorism and the U.N. *Tribune*, 1 August 1985, p.4.

1111 Morgenthau, Hans J. Remarks. *Terrorism : An International Journal*, Volume 1, Number 1, November 1977.

1112 Morning after a Night of Terror Attacks in Beirut. *Newsweek*, Number 81, 23 April 1973, pp. 35-36.

1113 Morrison, Micah. Prime-time Terror : Double-Dealing in Washington, Dismay in Jerusalem, Business as Usual in Beirut. *Am Spectator*, Number 18, September 1985, pp. 12-14.

1114 Morris, Micheal. *Terrorism*. Cape Town, Howard, 1971.

1115 Morris, R. Patty Hearst and the New Terror. *New Republication*, Number 173, 22 November 1975, pp. 8-10.

1116 Morrison, David C. The Shadow War : The Air Attack on Libya Marks a New Phase in the U.S. Counter-terrorism Struggle, an Era in which the Military will Likely Play a much Greater Role. *Nat J*, Number 18, 10 May 1986, pp. 1100-1105.

1117 Morrison, Perry R. Limits to Technocratic Consciousness : Information Technology and Terrorism as Example. *Science Tech and Human Values*, Number 11, Fall 1986, pp. 1-16.

1118 Moss, Robert. *Urban Guerrillas : The New Face of Political Violence*. London, Temple Smith, 1972.

1119 Moss, Robert. International Terrorism and Western Societies. *International Journal*, Volume 28, Number 3, 1973, pp. 418-430.

1120 Moss, Robert. Urban Guerrilla Warfare. In Jackwell Susman (Ed.). *Crime and Justice, 1971-1972 : An AMS Anthology*. New York, AMS Press, Inc., 1974.

1121 Moss, Robert and Hamilton, Iain. The Spreading Irish Conflict. *Conflict Studies*, Number 17, November 1971.

1122 Mosse, Hilde L. The Media and Terrorism. in Marious H. Livingston (Ed.), with Lee B. Kress., and Marie G. Wane K. *International Terrorism in the Contemporary World*. Westport, Conn., Greenwood Press, 1978, pp. 282-286.

1123 Motivated Violence. *Hindustan Times*, 18 January 1985, p. 9.

1124 Motley, James Berry. Terrorist Warfare : Formidable Challenges. *Fletcher Forum*, Volume 9, Number 2, Summer 1985, pp. 295-306.

1125 Motley, James Berry. Terrorist Warfare : A Reassessment. *Military Review*, Number 65, June 1985, pp. 45-57.

1126 Motley, James Berry. The Case for a Multinational Strike Force. *Journal of Defense and Diplomacy*, Volume 4, Number 3, March 1986, pp. 45-47.

1127 Motley, James Berry. Coping with International Terrorism : The Role of US Intelligence. *Harvard Internat R*, Number 7, May-June 1985, pp. 18-20.

1128 Moughrabi, Fouad. *The Refusal Front : A Study of the High Risk Politics in the Palestine Resistance Movement*. Paper Presented to the International Studies Association Toronto, Canada, 25-29 February, 1976.

1129 Move for Censure of Israel Attack on Lebanon Fails. *U.S. Chronicle*, Number 13, January 1976, pp. 14-18.

1130 Moxon-Browne, E. Terrorism in Northern Ireland : The Case of the Provisional I.R.A. in J. Lodge (Ed.). *Terrorism : A Challenge to the State*, Oxford, 1981, p. 149.

1131 Muakkasah, Sahar and others. Terrorism and Political Destabilistion. Advance Research Enterprise. Book Review, *Indian Express*, Magazine Section, 9 January 1985, p. 5.

1132 Mufson, Steve. Frontier Violence : Despite Mine Attacks South African Whites vow to Stay on Farms; Strategy of Black Nationalists Appears only to Increase Resolve of their Targets. *Wall St J*, Volume 207, Number 1, 31 January 1986.

1133 Mukerjee, Dilip. Reagan, the only Gainer. *Deccan Herald*, 22 October 1985, p. 8.

1134 Murder by Mistake : B. Cabaner Killed by Bomb. *Time*, Volume 105, Number 48, 30 June 1975.

1135 Murder City Gain ? *Hindustan Times*, 21 July 1984, p. 9.

1136 Munger, M.D. *Growing Utility of Political Terrorism*. Springfield, Virginia, National Technical Information Service, 1977.

1137 Murphy, James. The Role of International Law in the Prevention of Terrorist Kidnapping of Diplomatic Personnel. In Cherif M. Bassiouni (Ed.). *International Terrorism and Political Crimes*. Springfield, Illinois, Charles C. Thomas, 1975, pp. 285-313.

1138 Murphy, John F. *Punishing International Terrorists : The Legal Framework for Policy Initiatives*. Teeowa, Rowman and Allanheld, 1985.

1139 Murphy, John F. The Threat and use of Force against International Terrorism : Performance and Prospects. *Illinois Bar Journal*, Number 63, April 1975, pp. 444-452.

1140 Murphy, John F. *The Threat and use of Force against Internationally Protected Persons and Diplomatic Facilities*. Paper Presented to the Conference on International Terrorism, Sponsored by the Ralph Bunche Institute, New York, June 1976.

1141 Murphy, John F. Legal Aspects of International Terrorism : Summary Report of an International Conference, *Am Soc Intl Law*, Number 19, n.d.

1142 Murphy, John F. United Nations Proposals on the Control and Repression of Terrorism. in Cherif M. Bassiouni (Ed.). *International Terrorism and Political Crimes*. Springfield, Illinois, Charles C. Thomas, 1975, pp. 493-506.

1143 Muslih, Muhammad Y. Moderates and Rejectionists within the Palestine Liberation Organization. *Middle East Journal*, Volume 30, Spring 1976, pp. 127-140.

1144 Mystery in Lahore. *Statesman*, Delhi, 10 July 1984, p. 6.

1145 Nair, V. Sankaram. An Episode of Terrorism in South India. *Journal Kerala Studies*, Volume 5, Number 3-4, December 1978, pp. 513-528.

1146 Nairn, Allan. Bank of America Asked to Explain its Support for the Guatemalan Death Squads. *Multinational Moniter*, Number 3, March 1982, pp. 14-15.

1147 Najumddin, Dilshad. Kidnapping of Diplomatic Personnel. *Police Chief*, February 1973, pp. 18-23.

1148 Nakleh, Emile A. The Anatomy of Violence : Theoretical Reflections on Palestinian Resistance. *Middle East Journal*, Number 25, Spring 1971, pp. 180-200.

1149 Nandy, Pritish. The Terror Network. *Illustrated Wkly India*, Volume 106, Number 32, 15 December 1985, pp. 6-17.

1150 Nandy, Pritish. The Killing Fields. *Illustrated Wkly India*, Volume 106, Number 15, 15 December 1985, p. 6-17.

1151 Narayanan, V.N. Terrorism as State Policy. *Tribune*, 17 December 1984, p.4.

1152 Nasution, Abdul Haris. *Fundamentals of Guerrilla Warfare*. New York, Praeger, 1965.

1153 Natanyahu, Benjamin. (Eds.). *International Terrorism : Challenge and Response. Proceedings of the Jerusalem Conference on International Terrorism.* Jerusalem, 1979. New Brunswick, Transaction Books, 1981.

1154 Nath, Trilok. Punjab Scene : Identity of Terrorism. *Patriot*, Magazine Section. 22 July 1986, p. 1.

1155 Nation on Brink of Civil War ? *U.S. News*, Volume 77, Number 43, 28 October 1974.

1156 Nation Sorely Besieged; Betshe'an Raid by the Popular Democratic Front for the Liberation of Palestine. *Time*, Volume 104, 2 December 1974, pp. 43-44.

1157 Nayar, Kuldip. For whom the Bell Tolls. *Tribune*, 17 May 1984, p. 4.

1158 Need for Overhaul. *Amrita Bazar Patrika*, 7 August 1985, p. 6.

1159 Need of National Security. *Madhya Pradesh Chronicle*, 19 July 1985, p. 4.

1160 Nelson, Daniel J. The Problem of Terrorism Against American Forces in Germany. *Atlantic Community Quarterly*, Volume 23, Number 3, Fall 1985, pp. 275-284.

1161 Neo-Fascism on Trial: Italian Social Movement Party and Rightist Terrorism. *Time*, Volume 101, 21 May 1973, pp. 48-50.

1162 Nepal Blasts. *Patriot*, 24 June 1985, p. 4.

1163 News Conference of January 9. *Dept State Bul.*, Number 86, March 1986, pp. 23-26.

1164 New Twists and Turns; Resolution Adopted in Security Council Following the Israeli Raid on Terrorist Headquarters in Beirut. *A Tuckerman Nation*, Volume 216, Number 580, May 1973.

1165 New York State. *Policy Study Group on Terrorism*. Report, of Criminal Justice Services, Executive Park Tower, Stuyvesant Plaza, Albany, New York, November 1985-86.

1166 Neiburg, H.L. *Political Violence : The Behavioral Process*. New York, St. Martins, 1969.

1167 Nijhawan, P.K. No End of Terrorism in Punjab. *Times of India*, Delhi, 22 August 1985, p. 8.

1168 Nixon, R. M. and Others. United State calls for Firm International Stand Against Terrorist Extortion and Blackmail, Statements, March 2, 1973. *Department State Bulletin*, Number 26, March 1973.

1169 No Mercy. *Northern India Patrika*, 19 December 1984, p. 4.

1170 Norden, Eric. The Politics of Death. *Penthouse*, August 1973, 52 ff.

1171 North Atlantic Council Meets in Rome. Secretary of State Haig's Press Conference, Extracts from the Minutes of the Council, the Declaration on Terrorism, and the Final Communique Issued after the Meeting, May 4-5, 1981. *Dept. State Bul.*, Number 81, July 1981, pp. 37-41.

1172 Reed, D. Northern Ireland : The Endless war. *Reader Digest*, Number 107, July 1975, pp. 84-93.

1173 North India Rocked by Bomb Explosions. *Times of India*, 11 May 1985, p. 1.

1174 Not Shop Talk ? *Business Standard*, 18 October 1985, p.5.

1175 Norton, Augustus Richard. Aspects of Terrorism in Lebanon : The Case of the Shi'as. *New Outlook*, Number 27, January 1984, pp. 19-24.

1176 Norton, Augustus R. and Greenberg, Martin H. *International Terrorism : an Annotated Bibliography and Research Guide*. Boulder, Westview, 1979.

1177 Norton, Graham. Tourism and International Terrorism. *World Today*, Number 43, February 1987, pp. 30-33.

1178 Not Yet Out. *Search Light*, 25 November 1985, p. 4.

1179 Oakley, Robert B. Combating International Terrorism. *Department of State Bulletin*, Volume 85, Number 1099, June 1985, pp. 73-78.

1180 Oakley, Robert B. Terrorism : Overview and Developments. *Department of State Bulletin*, Volume 85, Number 2104, November 1985, pp. 61-65.

1181 Oakley, Robert. International Terrorism. *For Affairs*, Number 65, 3 November 1987, pp. 611-29.

1182 Oakley, Robert. Terrorism : The Fight . *Army Q*, Number 115, April 1985, pp. 167-188.

1183 O'Ballance, Edgar. *Language of Violence : The Blood Politics of Terrorism*. PamaronWay, Presdio Pr., 1979.

1184 O'Ballance, Edgar. Some Arab Guerrilla Problems. *Military Review*, Number 52, October 1973, pp. 27-34.

1185 O'Ballance, Edgar. *Terror in Ireland : The Heritage of Hate*. Pamaron Way Novato, Presidio Pr., 1981.

1186 O'Ballance, Edgar. *The Indo-China War, 1945-1954: A Study in Guerrilla Warfare*. London, Faber and Faber, 1964.

1187 O'Ballance, Edgar. *The Red Army of China*. London, Faber and Faber, 1962.

1188 O'Brien, Conor Cruise. The Realities of Terrorism. *Times of India*, 28 March 1984, p. 4.

1189 O'Brien, Conor Cruise. On Violence and Terror. *Dissent*, Number 24, Fall 1977, pp. 433-436.
1190 O'Brien, William V. Counter-terrorism, Lessons from Israel. *Strategic R.*, Number 13, Fall 1985, pp. 32-44.
1191 Ochberg, Frank. (Ed.). *Victims of Terrorism*. Boulder, Westview, 1981.
1192 Ochberg, F. The Victim of Terrorism : Psychiatric Considerations. *Terrorism : An International Journal*, Volume 1, Number 2, 1978, pp. 147-68.
1193 O'Flaherty, Liam. *The Terrorist*. London, E. Archer, 1926.
1194 O'Hefferman, Patrick. *The First Nuclear World War : A Strategy for Preventing Nuclear Wars and the Spread of Nuclear Weapons*. New York, W. Morrow and Co., 1983.
1195 Old Danger Again. *Times of India*. Delhi, 27 March 1985, p. 6.
1196 Ordeal At Sea. *Deccan Herald*, 10 October 1985, p. 8.
1197 O'Neill, Bard E. *Revolutionary Warfare in the Middle East: The Israelis Versus the Fedayeen*. Boulder, Colorado, Paladin, 1974.
1198 O'Neill, Bard E. Towards a Typology of Political Terrorism : The Palestinian Resistance Movement. *Journal of International Affairs*, Number 32, Spring/Summer 1978, pp. 17-42.
1199 O'Neil, Kevin. *How to Protect Your Family from Terrorists*. New York, Crises, Res. Pr., 1979.
1200 On the Brink. *Statesman*, Delhi, 10-13 May 1985, p. 6.
1201 Oppenheimer, Martin. *The Urban Guerrilla*. Chicago, Quadrangle, 1969.
1202 O'Reilly, Brian. Business Copes with Terrorism : U.S. Executives have Learned to Live with the Problem. *Fortune*, Number 113, 6 January 1986, pp. 47-8.
1203 Oseth, John M. Combatting Terrorism : The Dilemmas of a Decent Nation. *Parameters*, Number 15, Spring 1985, pp. 65-76.
1204 O'Sullivan, Edward J. International Terrorism and the Maritime Industry. *Via Port of New York*, Number 38, December 1986, p. 11.
1205 Ottawa Economic Summit Conference : Statement on Terrorism, 20 July 1981. *W Comp Press Docs*, Number 17, 27 July 1981, pp. 780-781.
1206 Outlook in Tripura. *Statesman*, Delhi, 16 December 1984, p. 6.
1207 Outrage Again. *Search Light*, 21 April 1985, p. 4.
1208 Outrageous Crime. *Patriot*, 1 August 1985, p. 4.
1209 Owen, David. State Terrorism, Internationalism and Collective Action. *R. Internat Studies*, Number 13, April 1987, pp. 81-89.

1210 Padgaonkar, Dileep. Fight Against Terrorism : Shades of McCarthyism in Bonn. *Times of India*, 22 October 1977, p. 6.

1211 Padgaonkar, Dileep. Italy Under Siege : No End to Terrorism in Sight. *Times of India*, 18 May 1978, p. 6.

1212 Padover, Saul K. Patterns of Assassination in Occupied Territory. *Public Opinion Quarterly*, Winter 1943, pp. 680-693.

1213 Pak Involvement. *Times of India*, 16 August 1986, p. 8.

1214 Pak-trained Terrorists. *Amrit Bazar Patrika*, 27 August 1985, p. 6.

1215 Pakist Involvement. *Times of India*, 16 September 1985, p. 8.

1216 Pakistani Involvement. *Madhya Pradesh Chronicle*, 13 September 1985, p. 4.

1217 Paine, Lauran. *The Assassin's World*. New York, Taplinger, 1975.

1218 Pal, B.K. Terrorism and Law. *Mainstream*, Volume 24, Number 37, 17 May 1986, pp. 29-30.

1219 Palestine Liberation Organization. *The Activities of the Hagana, Irgan, and Stern Bands*. New York, Idem, N.d.

1220 Palmer, Bruce. Codification of Terrorism as an International Crime. in Cherif M. Bassiouni (Ed.). *International Terrorism and Political Crimes*. Springfield, Illinois, Charles C. Thomas, 1975, pp. 507-518.

1221 Panel on Terrorism and Political Crimes in International Law. *American Journal of International Law*, Volume 67, 1973, p. 87.

1222 Pandey, D.C. Origins of Terrorism : A Socio-Legal Perspective. *Popular Jurist*, Volume 2, Number 4, July- August 1985, pp. 17-19.

1223 Pandit, C.S. Terrorism Rules the World. *Northern India Patrika*, 28 June 1985, p. 4.

1224 Paris, Edmund. *Genocide in Satellite Croatia, 1941-1945. A Record of Racial and Religious Persecutions and Massacres*. Chicago, IL, the American Institute for Balkan Affairs, 1961.

1225 Parry, Albert. *Terrorism : Past, Present, Future*. New York, Vanguard, 1976.

1226 Pasztor, Andy. Renewed Bureau : Under Chief Webster. FBI Takes Bigger Role in Drug and Spy Cases : It also acts against Terrorists and Forges Closer Links with Local Police Units. *Wall St J.*, Volume 208, Number 1, 27 August 1986.

1227 Patra, Saral. Shock in Shangrila and the Region. *Patriot*, 23 July 1985, p. 4.

1228 *Patterns of International Terrorism*. National Foreign Assessment Agency, 1980.

1229 Patterns of Global Terrorism. *Terrorism : An International Journal*, Volume 9, Number 4, 1987, pp. 409-446.

1230 Paul, Leslie. *The Age of Terror*. Boston, the Beacon Press, 1951.

1231 Paust, Jordan J. A Survey of Possible Legal Responses to International Terrorism: Prevention, Punishment and Cooperative Action. *Georgia Journal of International and Comparative Law*, Number 5, 1975.

1232 Paust, Jordan J. Approach to Decision with Regard to Terrorism. *Akron Law Review*, Number 7, Spring 1978, pp. 397-403.

1233 Paust, Jordan J. Terrorism and the International Law of War. *Military Law Review*, Number 64, Spring 1974, pp. 1-36.

1234 Paust, Jordan J. Terrorism and the International Law of War. *Milwaukee Law Review*, Number 64, 1974.

1235 Paust, Jordan J. Selected Terroristic Claims Arising from the Arab-Israeli Conflict. *Akron Law Review*, Number 7. Spring 1978, pp. 404-421.

1236 Paust, Jordan J. Responses to Terrorism : A Prologue to Decision Concerning Measures of Sanction. *Stanford Journal of International Studies*, Number 12, 1977.

1237 Paust, Jordan J. International Law and Control of the Media : Terror, Repression and the Alternatives. *Indiana Law Journal*, Number 53, 1978, pp. 621-77.

1238 Payne, Robert. *Zero : Story of Terrorism*. New York, John Day, 1950.

1239 Payne, Robert. *The Terrorist : The Story of the Forerunners of Stalin*. New York, Funk and Wagnalls, 1957.

1240 Payne, Ronald. Where Oil Barrels become Bombs. *Hindustan Times*, 2 January 1984, p. 9.

1241 Payne, Stanley G. Terrorism and Democratic Stability in Spain. *Current Hist*., Number 77, November 1979, pp. 167-171.

1242 Pedersen, F.C. Controlling International Terrorism : An Analysis of Unilateral Force and Proposals For Multilatteral Co-operation. *Law Review*, Volume 8, Number 1, 1976, pp. 209-250.

1243 Pella, V.V. La Repression du Terrorism Et La Creation D Une Cour International. *Novelle Revue De Droit International Prive*, Number 5, 1938, pp. 785-810, and Number 6, 1936, pp. 120-138.

1244 Pendley, Robert and Scheinman, Lawrence. International Safeguarding as Institutionalized Collective Behaviour. *International Organization*, Number 29, Summer 1975.

1245 Penn, Stanley. Cuban hit Squad : Anti-Castro Omega 7 Evokes Terror in U.S. with Murder Bombs. *Wall St J.*, Volume 198, Number 1, 30 December 1981.

1246 Penn, Stanley. Spreading Fear : New Terrorist Groups are Appearing in U.S., Resembling Old ones; Lawman believe the Cabals Share Havens and Arms, Cooperate in Crimes. *Wall St J.*, Volume 204, Number 1, 26 July 1984.

1247 Peretz, Don. Arab Palestine : Phoenix Or Phantom ? *Foreign Affairs*, Number 48, January 1970, pp. 322-333.

1248 Perez, Frank H. Terrorist Target : The Diplomat. *Dept State Bull.*, Number 82, August 1982, pp. 22-28.

1249 Perez, Marta Brito. Clandestine Tactics and Technology CTT, a Service of the International Association of Chiefs of Police, which Provides Information on Terrorism to Subscribers. *Police Chief*, Number 48, May 1981, pp. 50-51.

1250 Perils of Person. Crackdown on Terrorist Groups. *Time*, Volume 10, Number 51, 4 February 1974.

1251 Perlmutter, P. Israeli: Irish and Arab Terrorism. *Christian Century*, Number 92, 14 May 1975, pp. 486-487.

1252 Petkovic, Ranko. Yugoslavia and International Terrorism. *R. Internat Affairs*, Number 37, 30 January 1986, pp. 1-3.

1253 Picard, Robert G. News Coverage as the Contagion of Terrorism. Dangerous Charges Backed by Dubious Science. *Pol Communication and Persuasion*, Number 3, 4 November 1986, pp. 385-400.

1254 Picard, Robert G. and Rhonda S. Sheets. Terrorism and the News Media : a Research Bibliography. *Pol Communication and Persuasion*, Number 4, 1 November 1987, pp. 65-69.

1255 Pierce, Joe E. *Terrorism; the Middle East and you*. Habi Pr. 1986.

1256 Pike, Douglas. *The Viet-Cong Strategy of Terror*. Saigon, U.S. Mission, 1970.

1257 Pike, Earl A. *Protection against Bombs and Incendiaries : For Business, Industrial and Educational Institutions*. Springfield, IL, Charles C. Thomas, 1973.

1258 Pilot Shot before Landing in Magadishu. *Times of India*, 18 October 1977, p. 1.

1259 Pillay, S. Sivan. Terrorism in West Asia: The Background. *Sarvodaya*, Volume 33, Number 11-12, May-June 1986, pp. 464-470.

1260 Pipes, Daniel. Death to American in Lebanon. Activities of the Radical Fundamentalist Shi'i Muslims: Diplomatic Position of the

U.S. with Iran and Syria. *Middle East Insight*, Number 4, March-April 1985, pp. 3-9.

1261 Pisano, Vittorfranco S. Terrorism in Italy : The Dozier Affair, Abduction of Brigadier General James L. Dozier of the U.S. Army by Italy's Red Brigades, 17 December 1981 and his Subsequent release by a Special Unit of Italy's State Police. *Police Chief*, Number 49, April 1982, pp. 38-41.

1262 Pisano, Vittorfranco S. Terrorism in Italy : From Dozier's Rescue to Hugt's Assassination General James L. Dozier, January 1982, and Leamon R. Hunt, American Diplomat, February 1984. *Police Chief*, Number 51, June 1984, pp. 35-38.

1263 Plantey, Alain. Le Terrorisme Centre Les Droits De I Homme Revue Du Droit Public Et De La Science Politique En France Et A. *1' Etranger*, Volume 101, Number 1, 1985, pp. 5

1264 Plastrick, S. On Terrorism. *Dissent*, Number 21, Spring 1974, p. 143.

1265 PM for Non-Violent Movement in Punjab. *Times of India*, 8 April 1986, p. 9.

1266 PM asks Barnala to Curb Violence. *Times of India*, 24 June 1986, p. 1.

1267 Pluchinsky, Dennis. Middle Eastern Terrorist Activity in Western Europe : A Diagnosis and Prognosis. *Conflict Q.*, Number 6, Summer 1986, pp. 5-25.

1268 Pockrass, Robert M. Terroristic Murder in Northern Ireland : Who is Killed and Why ? *Terrorism : An International Journal*, Volume 9, Number 4, 1987, pp. 341-359.

1269 Pohlmann, Marcus D., and Thomas P. Foley. Terrorism in the 70s : Media's Connection (Pre-emptive Approach to Terrorism Press Coverage). *Nat Forum*, Number 61, Summer 1981, pp. 33-35.

1270 Poirier, Marc. International Terrorism : Extradition. *Harvard International Law Journal*, Number 18, 1977, p. 467.

1271 Policemen in Punjab Demoralised. *Times of India*, 2 February 1986, p. 8.

1272 Political Violence and the Role of the Media : Some Perspectives. Based on Comments at the Jerusalem Conference on International Terrorism, held by the Jonathan Institute, 2-5 July 1979. *Pol Communication and Persuasion*, Number 1, November 1980, pp. 79-99.

1273 *Political Kidnappings*. Committee on International Security House of Representatives, Washington, 1973.

1274 Politics in Uniform. *A Study of the Military in the Arab World and Israel*, Compiled by an-Nahar Arab Report Research Staff, London, Cooperative Printing Company, S.A.L,1972.

1275 Porter, Richard E. Military Hostages : What they Need to know and don't, Code of Conduct for United States Military Personnel who are Victims of Hostile Peacetime Detention, *Air Univ R.*, Number 33, January-February 1982, pp. 94-101.

1276 Portrait of a Terrorist. *Science Digest*, Volume 75, Number 70, June 1974.

1277 Possony, Stefan T. and Bouchey L. Francis. Moscow's Support of International Terrorism. *Ukrainian Q.*, Number 34, Winter 1978, pp. 378-399.

1278 Povlantzas, Nicholas M. Some Problems of International Law Connected with Urban Guerrilla Warfare : The Kidnapping of Members of Diplomatic Missions, Consular Offices and other Foreign Personnel. *Annales D. Etudes Internationales*, Number 3, 1972, pp. 137-167.

1279 Pre-Poll Terrorism. *Madhya Pradesh Chronicle*, 25 September 1985, p. 4.

1280 Pratt, D. Jane. Behaviour and Misbehaviour of Terrorists : Some Cross-National Comparisons, in Allan, M. Fine. *Attributes of Potential Adversaries to U.S. Nuclear Programs in U.S. Department of Commerce; National Bureau of Standards. The Role of Behavioural Science in Physical Security Proceedings of the Second Annual Symposium*, 23-24 March 1977. Washington, 1977, pp. 27-33.

1281 Preserve. *Times of India*. 26 July 1986, p. 8.

1282 Preventing Hijacking. *Times of India*, 14 February 1971, p. 6.

1283 Preston, P. Basque Problem : Guernica Lives. *Nation*, Number 221, 19 July 1975.

1284 Prevention of Terrorism Act 1976. Ibid. Part I, 1976, Ch. 8, pp. 77-94.

1285 Prevention of Terrorism Act 1974. *The Public General Acts and General Synod Measures*. Part II, 1974, Ch. 56, pp. 1823-1836.

1286 Price, H.E. (Jr.). The Strategy and Tactics of Revolutionary Terrorism. *Comparative Studies in Society and History*, Volume 19, Number 1, 1971, p. 54.

1287 Pringle, Peter. Who is Terrorist ? *Amrit Bazar Patrika*, 29 April 1985, p. 6.

1288 Pringle, Peter. If Terrorist go Nuclear. *Tribune*, 5 July 1985, p. 5.

1289 Prohibition Against the Training Or Support of Terrorist. *Organizations Act of 1984.* 2 August 1984, Washington, D.C. V.S.G.P.O. 1984, pp. 1-75.

1290 Prompst Rebuff. *Hindustan Times*, 12 June 1985, p. 9.

1291 Propaganda Abroad. *Northern India Patrika*, 28 August 1985,p. 4.

1292 *Protecting Industrial Business Facilities and Personnel Terrorist Activities*. Raymont, 1977.

1293 Protecting Monuments. *Indian Express*, Delhi, 17 September 1985, p. 6.

1294 Protecting the World from the Terrorist Threat. *Police Chief*, Number 52, April 1986, pp. 28-42.

1295 Pryce-Jones, David. *The Face of Defeat : Palestinian Refugees and Guerrilla*. New York, Holt, Rinehart, and Winston, 1972.

1296 Public Eye Staff NCLC. *La Rouche Cult : Brown Shirts of the Seventies, Fascism in the Eighties*. Rev. ed. Citizens Defence, 1983.

1297 Purnell, Susanna W. and Eleanor S. Wainstein. *The Problems of U.S. Businesses Operating Abroad in Terrorist Environment*. Santa Monica, Rand Corporation, November 1981.

1298 Purohit, Radheshyam. German Terrorism : End of an Era ? *Commerce*, Volume 135, Number 3456, 29 October 1977, pp. 798-800.

1299 Punjab Development BJP Leader Murder. *Deccan Herald*, 27 March 1985, p. 8.

1300 Punjab Fall out on J & K. *Tribune*, 19 May 1984, p. 4.

1301 Pyle, Christopher H. Defining Terrorism. *For Policy*, Fall 1986, pp. 63-78.

1302 Pye, Lucian W. *Guerrilla Communism in Malaya : It's Social and Political Meaning*. Princeton, Princeton University Press, 1956.

1303 Quainton, Anthony C.E. Terrorism: Do Something, but what? *Dept. State Bull.*, Number 79, September 1979, pp. 60-64.

1304 Quainton, Anthony C.E. U.S. Anti-Terrorism Program. *Dept. State Bull.*, Number 80, July 1980, pp. 75-77.

1305 Quainton, Anthony C.E. Combatting Terrorism : A Strategy of Partnership. *Police Chief*, Number 47, May 1980, pp. 22-24.

1306 Quandt, William B.; Jabber, Fuad and Lesch, Ann M. *The Political of Palestinian Nationalism*. Berkeley, University of California Press, 1973.

1307 Quester, George H. Can Proliferation now be Stopped ? *Foreign Affairs*, Number 53, October 1974, pp. 77-97.

1308 Quintero, Morentem Frederico. Terrorism. *Military Review*, December 1965, pp. 55-57.

1309 Quareshi, Saleem. Political Violence in the South Asian Subcontinent. in Yonah, Alexander (Ed.). *International Terrorism : National, Regional, and Global Perspectives*, New York, Praeger Publishers, 1971, pp. 151-193.

1310 Rada, S.E. Transnational Terrorism as Public Relations ? *Public Relations R.*, Number 11, Fall 1985, pp. 26-33.

1311 Radlick, Amy Sands. *Transnational Factors Affecting Quebac Separatist Terrorism*. Toronto, International Studies Association, 25-29 February 1976.

1312 Radovanovic, Ljubomir. The Problem of International Terrorism. *Review of International Affairs*, Number 23, October 1972, pp. 6-8, 5-20.

1313 Raghuvanshi, D.P.S. Terrorism and the Military Response. *United Services Institution of India journal*, Volume 115, Number 482, October-December 1985, pp. 317-324.

1314 Rai, Singh. The Rising Trend of Terrorism. *National Herald*, Delhi, Magazine Section, 30 December 1984, p. 2.

1315 Rama, Swadesh. International Terrorism : A Mode of Combat. *Indian Quart*, Volume 34, Number 4, October-December 1978, pp. 491-502.

1316 Ramachandran, K.S. Bib to Clip Terrorism. *Financial Express*, 21 October 1985, p. 4.

1317 Ramberg, Bennett. Nuclear Plants : Military Hostage ? *Bulletin of the Atomic Scientists*, Volume 42, Number 3, March 1986, pp. 17-21.

1318 Random Killings, Rightist Fears. *Time*, Volume 106, Number 36, 20 October 1975,

1319 Rapoport, David. The Politics of Atrocity. In Yonah, Alexander and Seynour M. Finger (Eds.). *Terrorism : Interdisciplinary Perspectives*, New York, the John Jay Press, 1977, pp. 46-61.

1320 Rapoport, David C. and Alexander Yonah (Eds.). *The Rationalisation of Terrorism*. U Pubns Amer., 1981.

1321 Rapoport, S. E. Between Minimal Courage and Maximum Cowardice : A Legal Analysis of the Release of Abu Daoud. *Brooklyn Journal of International Law*, Number 3, Spring 1977, pp. 195-209.

1322 Rash, W. Psychological Dimensions of Political Terrorism in the Federal Republic of Germany. *International Journal of Law and Psychiatry*, Number 2, 1979, pp. 79-85.

1323 Rattan, H.R. Global Terrorism - Democracy Under Seige. *National Herald*, Magazine Section, 20 June 1985, p. 1.

1324 Rauch, Elmar. The Compatiability of the Detention of Terrorists Order Northern Ireland with the European Convention for the Protection of Human Rights. *New York University Journal of International Law and Politics*, Number 6, 1973, pp. 1-27.

1325 Raufer, Xavier. Euro-terrorism : Comprepour Combate. *Politic International*, Number 30, 1985-1986, pp. 251-263.

1326 Raushenbush, Richard. *The Terrorist War in Guatemala.* Washington, D.C., Coun Inter Ed., 1982.

1327 Rayne, F. Executive Protection and Terrorism. *Top Security*, Number 1, October 1975, pp. 220-225.

1328 Raynor, Thomas P. *Terrorism*. Ann Arbor, Pierian, 1986.

1329 Reagan, Ronald. Prohibiting Trade and Certain Transactions Involving Libya. Executive Order 12543, 7 January 1986. *W Comp Press Doces.*, Number 22, 13 January 1986, pp. 19-20.

1330 Reagan, Ronald. United States Air Strike Against Libya : Address to the Nation, 14 April 1986. *W Comp Press Doces.*, Number 22, 21 April 1986.

1331 Reagan's Hostage Crisis : Revenge or Restrain ? *U.S. News*, Number 99, 1 July 1985, pp. 19-31.

1332 Reed, D. Northern Ireland : The Endless War. *Readers' Digest*, Number 107, July 1975, pp. 84-93.

1333 Reid, Edna. (Ed.). *Terrorism*. Ann Arbor, Pierian, 1986.

1334 Reisman, W.M. Private Armies in a Global War System : Prologue to Decision. *Virginia Journal of International Law*, Number 14, 1973.

1335 Release of Prisoners Sought : Hijackers Threat to Kill Passengers. *Times of India*, 15 October 1977, p. 1.

1336 Relief Planes Unable to Leave : Pak Govt. Delays Visas for Crew. *Times of India*, 1 February 1971, p. 1.

1337 Renegade Terrorism. *Time*, Volume 102, Number 35, 27 August 1973.

1338 Report on Terrorism in Europe. *Doc.*, Number 4258, 5 December 1978.

1339 *Report of the DOD Commission on Beirut International Airport Terrorist Act*, 23 October 1983. Govt. Printing Office, 1984.

1340 Report on International Terrorism Rapporteur : Mr. Czernetz. *Doc.*, Number 3285, 14 May 1973.

1341 Report on the European Convention on the Supression of Terrorism. Rapporteur : Mr. Margue. *Doc.*, Number 3912, 14 January 1977.

1342 Report on International Terrorism Rapporteur : Mr. Blumenfeld. *Doc.*, Number 3201, 18 October 1972.

1343 Report of the *Ad Hoc* Committee on International Terrorism. General Assembly Official Records, 28th Session, Suppl. 28, *UN. DOC.* A/9028.

1344 Report of the *Ad Hoc* Committee on International Terrorism. A/34/37, p. 21.

1345 Report on Legislative Responses to International Terrorism. *Terrorism : An International Journal*, Volume 8, Number 2, 1985, pp. 147-163.

1346 Report on the Conference on Defence of Democracy Agaist Terrorism in Europe. Tasks and Problems Rapporteur : Mr. Calamandrei. *DOC.*, Number 4688, 19 February 1981.

1347 Reshetov, Yuri. International Terrorism : Legal Aspects. *New Times*, Number 15, April 1981, pp. 20-22.

1348 *Responses Au Questionnaire Relatif Aux Apects Juridiques Des Problems Poses Par Le Terrorisme International.* DPC/CEPC (73) 28, Strasbourg, 21 August 1973.

1349 Retaliating with Multiple Terror. *Time*, Volume 104, Number 31, 23 December 1974.

1350 Review of Reviews. Assassine Victims. *Idem*, Number 85, November 1984, pp. 15-17.

1351 Revived Insurgency. *Patriot*, 5 April 1984, p. 4.

1352 Rhan, M.A. *Guerrilla Warfare : Its Past, Present and Future.* Karachi, India, Rangrut, 1960.

1353 Richter, Donald C. *Riotous Victorions.* Ohio-Columbus, Ohio Univ. Pr., 1981.

1354 Right Approach. *Deccan Herald*, 15 May 1985, p. 6.

1355 Rivers, Gayle. *The Specialist : Revelations of a Counter-terrorist.* New York, Stein Day, 1985.

1356 Rivers, Gayle. *War Against Terrorism : How to win it.* New York, Stein Day, 1986.

1357 Robinson, Donald B. *The Dirty Wars.* New York, Dalacarte Press, 1968.

1358 Roberts, Kenneth E. *Terrorism and the Military Response.* Carlisle Barracks, PA, Army War College Strategic Studies Institute, October 1975.

1359 Rocquingny, D.E. Col. Urban Terrorism. *Military Review*, February 1959.

1360 Rogers, C. Pride. Repression and Genocide in Brazil. Christian Century Continuing *New Christian*, Number 91, 15 May 1974, pp. 524-525.

1361 Romaniecki, Leon. The Soviet Union and International Terrorism. *Soviet Studies* (University of Glasgow), Number 24, July 1974, pp. 417-440.

1362 Romaniecki, Leon. *The Arab Terrorists in the Middle East and the Soviet Union*. Jerusalem, Soviet and East European Research Center, Hebrew University of Jerusalem, 1973.

1363 Room At the Top. *Newsweek*, Volume 83, Number 57, 25 March 1974.

1364 Ronchey, Alberto. Guns and Gray Matter : Terrorism in Italy. *Foreign Affairs*, Number 57, Spring 1979, pp. 921-940.

1365 Ronchey, Alberto. Terror in Italy : Between Red and Black. *Dissent*, Spring 1978, pp. 150-156.

1366 Ranchey, Alberto. Guns and Gray Matter : Terrorism in Italy. *Foreign Affairs*, Number 37, Spring 1978, pp. 921-940.

1367 Roots of the Evil. *Tribune*, 1 July 1984, p. 4.

1368 Rosenbaum, David M. Nuclear Terror. *International Security*, Number 1, Winter 1977, pp. 140-161.

1369 Rosenbaum, David M.; Gougin, J.N.; Jeferson, R.M.; Kleitman, D.J. and Sullivan, W.C. *Special Safeguards Study*. Washington, D.C., Atomic Energy Commission, 1974.

1370 Rosenbaum, H. Jon., and Sederberg, Peter C. Vigilantism : An Analysis of Establishment Violence. *Comparative Politics*, Number 6, 1974, pp. 541-570.

1371 Rosenne, Meir. Terrorism : Who is Responsible ? What can be done ? *World Affairs*, Number 148, Winter 1985-1986, pp. 169-172.

1372 Rosie, George. *The Directory of International Terrorism*. Mainstream Pub., 1986.

1373 Rosle, George. *Dictionary of Terrorism*. New York, Paragon Hse, 1986.

1374 Rothstein, Andrew. Terrorism : Some Plain Words. *Labour Monthly*, September 1973, pp. 413-417.

1375 Rothstein, Andrew. Terrorism : Some Plain Words. *Mainstream*, Volume 21, Number 25, 16 February 1974, pp. 21-23.

1376 Roux, J.A. Le Project de Convention International Pour La Repression Des Crimes Presentatnt Un Danger Public. *Revue International De Droit Penal*, Number 12, 1935, pp. 99-130.

1377 Roucek, Joseph S. Sociological Elements of a Theory of Terror and Violence. *American Journal of Economics and Sociology*, Number 21, Spring 1962, pp. 165-172.

1378 Revine, Arthur W. The Contemporary International Legal Attack on Terrorism. *Israel Journal on Human Rights*, Number 3, 1973, pp. 9-38.

1379 Rubin, Alfred P. International Terrorism and International Law. in Yonah, Alexander. and Seymour M. Finger (Eds.). *Terrorism : Interdisciplinary Perspectives*, New York, the John Jay Press, 1977, pp. 121-127.

1380 Rude Reminder. *Northern India Patrika*, 22 November 1984, p. 4.

1381 Rumpf, Helmut. International Legal Problems of Terrorism. *Aussenpolitik : German Foreign Affairs Review*, Volume 36, Number 4, 1985,

1382 Russell, Charles A. Transnational Terrorism. *Air Unversity Review*, Volume 27, Number 2, January-February 1976.

1383 Russell, Charles A.; Banker, Leon J. Jr. and Miller, Bowman M. *Out-Inventing the Terrorist*. Washington, U.S. Air Force Office of Special Investigation, n.d.

1384 Ryans, John K. Jr., and William L. Shanklin. How Managers Cope with Terrorism. *Cal Mgt R.*, Number 23, Winter 1980, pp. 66-72.

1385 Ryter, Stephen L. Terror : A Psychological Weapon. *The Review*, May-June 1966, pp. 145-150.

1386 Sablier, Edouard. La France, Carrefour Du Terrorisme International ? *Politique International*, Number 23, Printemps 1984, pp. 89-95.

1387 Sadhu, Kanwar. New Blood for Terrorist Cause. *Indian Express*, Delhi, 15 May 1985, p. 1 and p. 7.

1388 Safety First : Protecting U.S. Ambassador. *Newsweek*, Volume 87, Number 39, 9 February 1976.

1389 Saha B.P. Terrorism and Public Servants. *Amrita Bazar Patriaka*, 26 July 1984, p. 6.

1390 Sehgal, Nayantara. Dissenters Need not be Enemies. *Indian Express*, Delhi, Magazine Section, 24 November 1985, p. 2.

1391 Saksena, N.S. The Growing Roots of Terrorism. *The Hindustan Times*, 14 December 1979.

1392 Saksena, N.S. Roots of Terrorism in Punjab-I. *Times of India*, 5 December 1983, Roots of Terrorism in Punjab-II. *Times of India*, 6 December 1983.

1393 Saksena, N.S. Foreign Gunman on Indian Social. *Times of India*, Delhi, 2 April 1985, p. 6.

1394 Saksena, N.S. Dangerous Illusions about Terrorism. *Times of India*, Delhi, 10 April 1984, p. 8.

1395 Saksena, N.S. Why Terrorism is so Rampant. *The Times of India*, 5 May 1981.

1396 Saksena, N.S. Terrorism : Present Measures Inadequate. *Times of India*, Delhi, 13 May 1985, p. 8.

1397 Saksena, N.S. Terrorism : Facing the Real Issue. *Times of India*, Delhi, 16 July 1985, p.8.

1398 Salisbury, David F. Terrorists at A-Reactors called a Growing Threat. *Christian Science Monitor*, 20 July 1978, p. 9.

1399 Salisbury, David F. How Modern Science Prevents Nuclear Theft. *Christian Science Monitor*, 14 July 1975, p. 6.

1400 Salmans, S., and Others. Everything Blew, Bombing at la Guardia Airport, New York City. *Newsweek*, Volume 87, Number 31, 12 January 1976.

1401 Salmon, Jean J. A. LA Convention Europeenne Pour La Repression Du Terrorisme : Un Vrai Pas En Arrire. *Journal Des Tribunax*, Number 5007, 1977, p. 497.

1402 Salomone, Franco. Terrorism and the Mass Media. in Cherif M. Bassiouni (Ed.). *International Terrorism and Political Crimes*. Springfield, Illinois, Charles C. Thomas, 1975, pp. 43-46.

1403 Salpeter, Eliahu. Israel's Unsettling Underground : A Time of Soul-searching Arrest of Members of Gush Emunim, the Nationalist Settler Movement, for Alleged Terrorist Attacks Against West Bank Arabs. *New Leader*, Number 67, 28 May 1984, pp. 3-4.

1404 Samber, Bhupinder. Punjab Working Class Against Terrorism. *New Age*, Volume 34, Number 28, 13 July 1986, p. 9.

1405 Sanders, Benjamin. *Safeguards Against Nuclear Proliferation*. Cambridge, Mass., MIT Press, 1975.

1406 Sanders, Sol W. The Sword That is Pointing at Pakistan's Zia Kabul-based Terrorist Organization that Seeks to Overthrow the Regime of President Zia Ul Haq. *Bus Week P.*, Number 60, 9 November 1981.

1407 Santoro, Victor. *Disruptive Terrorism*. UK, Farm Borough, Gordon Pr., 1986.

1408 Santoro, Victor. *Disruptive Terrorism*. Port Townsend, Loompanics, 1984.

1409 Saran, Parmodh. Terrorism. *United Services Institutions of India Journal*, Volume 114, Number 477, July-September 1984, pp. 241-248.

1410 Savinkov, B.V. *Memories of a Terrorist*. New York, Kraus Reprint, 1970.

1411 Sawhney, R.G. Democratic States and the Scourge of Terrorism. *Strategic Analysis*, Volume 10, Number 2, 8 May 1986, pp. 129-39.

1412 Sawhney, R.G. International Terrorism : a One-Sided Debate, *Times of India*, 16 May 1986, p. 8.

1413 Sawhney, R.G. Democratic States and Response to Terrorism. *Strategic Analysis*, Volume 10, Number 4, July 1986, pp. 369-378.

1414 Scali, J.A. U.N. Condemns Acts of Violence in Middle East; Qiryat Shemona Massacre : Statements with Text of Resolution 25 April 1974. *Department State Bulletin*, Number 70, 13 May 1974, pp. 532-534.

1415 Scali, J.A. U.S. Opposes Middle East Violence and Terrorism. Statements, with Text of Resolution Adopted by the Council. 12,17, and 21 April 1973. *Department State Bulletin*, Number 68, 21 May 1973, pp. 656-660.

1416 Schamis, Gerardo J. *War and Terrorism in International Affairs*. Salti Danielle, Tr. From Span., Transaction Books, 1980.

1417 Schelling, Thomas C. Thinking About Nuclear Terrorism. *Internal Security*, Number 6, Spring 1982, pp. 61-77.

1418 Scherer, John L. *Terrorism : An Annual Survey*. J.L. Sherer, 1982.

1419 Schiff, Zeev., and Rothstein, Raphael. *Fedayeen : Guerrillas Against Israel*. New York, Mckay, 1972.

1420 Schiller, David Th. Germany's other Terrorists. *Terrorism : An International Journal*, Volume 9, Number 1, 1987, pp. 87-99.

1421 Schlaefer, Cindy Verne. American Courts and Modern Terrorism : The Politics of Extradition (decisions defining what Constitutes a Political Offence for Purposes of Extradition). *New York Univ J Internat Law and Politics*, Number 13, Winter 1981, pp. 617-643.

1422 Schlesinger, Philip. Terrorism, the Media, and the Liberal-democratic State : a Critique of the Orthodoxy, some Emphasis on British Coverage of events in Northern Ireland. *Social Research*, Number 48, Spring 1981, pp. 74-99.

1423 Schmid, Alex P. and Graaf Janny De. *Violence as Communication : Insurgent Terrorism and the Western News Media*. New York, Sage Pubns., 1982.

1424 Schmid, Alex P. *Political Terrorism : A Research Guide to Concepts, Theories, Data Bases and Literature*. New Brunswick, Transaction Bks, 1984.

1425 Schmid, Alex P. *Political Terrorism : A Research Guide to Concepts, Theories, Data Bases and Literature*. New Brunswick, Transaction Bks, 1986.

1426 Schmidt, Dana A. *Armageddon in the Middle East*. New York, John Jay, 1974.

1427 Schwartz, D. Madison Bombing : Watershed between the Decades. *Nation*, Number 217, 26 November 1973, pp. 554-558.

1428 Schwarzenberger, Georg. Terrorists, Hijackers, Guerrilleros and Mercenaries. *Current Legal Problems*, Number 24, 1971, pp. 257-282.

1429 Scotti. Anthony J. *Executive Safety and International Terrorism : A Guide for Travellers*. P-H, 1986.

1430 Search for a Solution. *Madhya Pradesh Chronicle*, 17 April 1984, p. 4.

1431 Sebastian, P.A. Beware of this Law. *Indian Express*, Delhi, 8 October 1984, p. 6.

1432 Second Coming of Person. *Newsweek*, 2 July 1973, pp. 23-24.

1433 Second Gesture. *Business Standard*, 11 October 1984, p. 5.

1434 Security Council Condemns all Acts of Violence, and Attacks on Lebanon by Israel, Requests Report on Middle East : With texts of Resolutions. *U.N. Monthly Chronicle*, Number 10, May 1973, pp. 33-38.

1435 Security Council Meets on Cuban Complaint. *U.N. Monthly Chronicle*, Number 10, October 1973, pp. 3-7.

1436 Seela, Patrick. Iran Behind Terrorism in Lebanon. *Times of India*, Delhi, 23 October 1985, p. 8.

1437 Segre, D.U., and Adler, J.H. Ecology of Terrorism. *Encounter*, Number 40, February 1973, pp. 17-24.

1438 Seib, Gerald F. Beirut Bloodshed : Reagan Faces Choices in Wake of Massacre of Marines in Lebanon. 23 October 1983. *Wall St J.*., Volume 202, Number 1, 24 October 1983.

1439 Selth, Andrew. International Terrorism and the Hawke Government : A Survey of Foreign Policy Responses. *Australian for. Affairs REC*, Number 57, 14 November 1986, pp. 1007-1014.

1440 Seminario Sobre Terrorismme International 1982 Madrid. *Terrorisme International Dirigido Por Salustionodel Campo-Madrid : Institute De Cuestiones Internationales*, Madrid, 1984.

1441 Sen, Amiaya Kumar. Terrorism in Punjab. *Amrita Bazar Patrika*, 29 April 1985, p. 6.

1442 Sen, Roshni. Great Divide. *Northern India Patrika,* Magazine Section, 4 August 1985.

1443 Sen, Sankar. Challenge of the Terrorists. *Amrita Bazar Patrika*, 4 July 1985, p. 6 and *Northern India Patrika*, 14 July 1985, p. 4.

1444 Sen, Sumanta. Nepal Blasts a Blessing in Disguise. *Times of India*, Delhi, 30 June 1985, P. 1.

1445 Sethi, J.D. India and International Terrorism. *Indian Express*, Delhi, 21 December 1984, p. 6.

1446 Sewell, Alan F. Political Crime : A Psychologist's Perspective. in Cherif M. Bassiouni (Ed.). *International Terrorism and Political Crimes*, Springfield, Illinois, Charles C. Thomas, 1975, pp. 11-26.

1447 Shackleton, Lord. *Review of the Operation of the Prevention of Terrorism Temporary Provisions Acts 1974 and 1976*. London, HMSO, Aug. 1978.

1448 Shadow War : Murder of Y. Alon in Bethesda Md. *Newsweek*, Volume 82, Number 37, 16 July 1973.

1449 Shaffer, Halen B. Political Terrorism. *Editorial Research Reports*, Number 1, 1970, pp. 341-60.

1450 Shahami, R.T. Safety, Security and Men in Power. *Tribune*, 25 July 1984, p. 4.

1451 Sharabi, Misham. *Palestine Guerrillas : Their Credibility and Effectiveness*. Washington, Center for Strategic and International Studies, Georgetown University, 1970.

1452 Shaw, Jennifer and others (Eds.). *Ten Years of Terrorism : Collected Views*. New York, Crane, 1979.

1453 Shearer, I.A. *Extradition in International Law*. Dobbs Ferry, Oceana, Manchester, Manchester University Press, 1971.

1454 Sheets, H. Mass Murder in Uganda. *Readers' Digest*, Number 105, November 1974, pp. 71-72.

1455 Shepard, Ira M. Air Piracy : The Role of the International Federation of Airline Pilots Associations. *Cornell International Law Journal*, Number 3, 1970, pp. 79-91.

1456 Shigenobu, F. Auntie Knows All. *Newsweek*, 30 September 1974.

1457 Shipley, P. *Trotskysim : Entryism and Permanent Revolution*. London, Institute for the Study of Conflict, 1977.

1458 Shiv Kumar, K.P. Indian Youth and Terrorism. *Vivekananda Kendra Patrika*, Volume 14, Number 2, August 1985, pp. 77-81, pp. 241-248.

1459 Shock, Terror and Slender Hopes : Arab Raid on Village of Qiryat Shemona. *Time*, 22 April 1974, pp. 36-37.
1460 Shocking. *Northern India Patrika*, 29 November 1985, p. 4.
1461 Shooting the Moon. *Time*, Volume 103, Number 40, 17 June 1974.
1462 Shrigman, David. The Text Book Approach to Terrorism. *New York Times*, 22 April 1984.
1463 Shultz, George P. Terrorism and the Modern World. *Dept State Bul.*, Number 84, December 1984, pp. 12-17.
1464 Shultz, George P. New Realities and New Ways of Thinking. *Foreign Affairs*, Volume 63, Number 4, Spring 1985, pp. 705-721.
1465 Shultz, George P. Terrorism and the Modern World. *Terrorism : An International Journal*, Volume 7, Number 1, 1985, pp. 431-477.
1466 Shultz, George P. Government and Business : Our Common Defense Against Terrorism. *Dept State Bul.*, Number 85, March 1985, pp. 10-12.
1467 Shultz, R.H. The Limits of Terrorism in Insurgency Warfare : The Case of the Viet Cong. *Political*, Volume 11, Number 1, 1978, pp. 67-91.
1468 Shultz, R.H. Conceptualizing Political Terrorism. *Journal of the International Affairs*, Volume 32, Number 1, 1978, pp. 5-7.
1469 Shultz, R.H. Can Democratic Governments use Military Force in the War against Terrorism ? the U.S. Confrontation with Libya. *World Affairs*, Number 148, Spring 1986, pp. 205-215.
1470 Shutting Freedom House : Schonan Castle. *Newsweek*, Volume 82, Number 55, 8 October 1973.
1471 Siege in Holland : Work of South Moluccan Terrorists. *Time*, Volume 106, Number 32, 22 December 1975.
1472 Signs of Appeasement. *Time of India*, 12 March 1986, p. 8.
1473 Sikhs Speak Up. *Times of India*, 1 April 1986, p. 8.
1474 Silj, Alessandro. *Never Again without a Rifle : The Origins of Italian Terrorism*. New York, Karz, 1979.
1475 Siljander, R.P. *Terrorist Attacks*. Ann Arbon, Thomas Pr., 1980.
1476 Sillenson, K. Teheran Ambush. *Newsweek*, Volume 85, Number 35, 2 June 1975.
1477 Simpson, John and Bennett, Jana. *The Disappeared and the Mothers of the Plaza : The Story of the 11,000 Argentinians who Vanished*. New York, St. Martin, 1985.
1478 Sim, J. and Thomas, P. The Prevention of Terrorism Act : Normalizing the Politics of Repression. *Journal of Law and Society*, Volume 10, Number 1, Summer 1983, pp. 71-84.

1479 Simon, Douglas W. Policy Recommendation Exercises. *International Studies Notes*, Number 2, Spring 1975, pp. 19-21.

1480 Sinclair, Andrew. *Guevera*. London, Fontana/Collins, 1970.

1481 Singh, A.J. Terrorism in Tripura. *Northern India Patrika*, 5 August 1984, p. 4.

1482 Singh, B. Terrorists' Mind. *Patriot*, Magazine, 20 October 1985, p. 1.

1483 Singh, Hardave. Terrorism Strikes Again. *Business Standard*, 25 August 1985,

1484 Singh, J.D. P F L P Guerrillas Hijack B O A C Jet-Flight Since Sunday. *Times of India*, 15 September 1975, p. 4.

1485 Singh, J.D. Terrorism in West Europe, A Growing Menace. *Times of India*, 15 September 1975, p. 4.

1486 Singh, J.D. Piracy in the Air : Search for Preventive Measures. *Times of India*, 18 September 1970, p. 6.

1487 Singh, Khushwant. What Makes a Terrorist ? *Search Light*, 27 May 1985, p. 4.

1488 Singh, Khushwant and Singh, Satinder. *Ghadar 1915: India's First Armed Revolution*. New Delhi, R.K. Publishing House, 1966.

1489 Singh, Rahul. War on the Sikhs. *Indian Express*, Delhi, 21 May 1985, p. 6.

1490 Singh, Rahul. Brutalisation of India. *Indian Express*, Delhi, 11 December 1984, p. 6.

1491 Singh, Rahul. Terrorist Challenge. *Indian Express*, Delhi, 2 April 1985, p. 6.

1492 Singh, Rahul. Punjab: Once Again at Flash-Point. *Indian Express*, Magazine Section, 9 February 1986, p. 1.

1493 Singh, Rahul. Terrorists Trying to put the Clock Back. *Indian Express,* Delhi, 26 March, 1985, p. 1.

1494 Singh, Rai. Ugly Face of Modern Terrorism. *National Herald,* Magazine Section, 21 August 1983, p. 1.

1495 Singh, Shaukin. The Ugly Face of Terrorism. *Link,* Volume 28, Number 18, 8 December 1985, pp. 12-13.

1496 Singh, M.K. Intelligence Not Guns: Only Way of Tackling Terrorism. *Statesman*, Delhi, 2 September 1985, p. 6.

1497 Sinha, Ramesh. India Must Prepare to face more Attacks. *Patriot,* 9 November 1984, p. 4.

1498 Situation in Lebanon. Remarks of President Reagan, 24 October 1983. and a Question and Answer Session with Regional Editors and Broadcasters Chiefly on the Bombing Attack against

American Forces in Beirut, 23 October. *W Comp Pres Docs.*, Number 13, 31 October 1983, pp. 1482-1486.

1499 Sisco, J.J. U.S. Deplores Sudanese Action on Confessed Murderers Statement. *Department State Bulletin*, Volume 7, Number 147, 22 July 1974.

1500 Slaughter in Imphal. *Times of India*, 16 March 1984, p. 8.

1501 Sliwowski, George. Legal Aspects of Terrorism. In David Carlton and Carlo Schaerf (Eds.). *International Terrorism and World Security*. London, Croom Helm, 1975.

1502 Sloan, Stephen. *Simulating Terrorism*. Hagertown, Narman, U of Okla Pr., 1981.

1503 Sloan S. International Terrorism: Academic Quest Operational Art and Policy Implications. *Journal of International Affairs*, Volume 32, Number 1, 1978, pp. 1-5.

1504 Sloan, Stephen. In Search of a Counter Terrorism Doctrine. *Military Review*, Volume 66, Number 1, January 1986, pp. 44-48.

1505 Sloan, Stephen. Simulating Terrorism: From Operational Technique to Questions of Policy. *International Studies' Notes*, Number 5, Winter 1978, pp. 3-8.

1506 Sloan, S. and Kearney, R. Learning About Terrorism: Analysis Simulations and Future Directions. *Terrorism: An International Journal*, Volume 1, Numbers 3-4, 1978, pp. 315-329.

1507 Smart, Ian M.H. The Power of Terror. *International Journal*, Number 30, Spring 1975, pp. 25-33.

1508 Smashing London's Face: IRA Bombing. *Time*, Volume 101, Number 22, 19 March 1973.

1509 Smith, Clifford V. *Safeguarding the Licensed Nuclear Industry*. A Presentation to the October 16-19, 1977, Meeting of the American Nuclear Society Executive Conference on Safeguards.

1510 Smith, D. Scenario Reality: a New Brand of Terrorism. *Nation*, 30 March 1974, pp. 392-394.

1511 Smith, Myron J. Jr. *The Secret Wars: A Guide to Sources in English: Volume 3, International Terrorism, 1968-1980*. Richard D. (Ed.). Santa Barbara, ABC-CLIO, 1980.

1512 Smith, Roger. Processing Plutonium: A Bitter Harvest. *Master in Business Administration*, March 1978, pp. 27-29.

1513 Smith, R.D. and Kobetz, R. *Guidelines for Civil Disorders and Mobilization Planning*. Gaithenburg, Md., International Association of Chiefs of Police, 1968.

1514 Smith, W.H. International Terrorism: a Political Analysis. *The Year Book of World Affairs*, 1977, p. 138.

1515 Sobel, Lester A. (Ed.). *Political Terrorism*. New York, Facts on File, 1975-1978. 2V. V1. V2. 1974-1978.

1516 Sofaer, Abraham D. Terrorism and the Law. *Foreign Affairs*, Volume 64, Number 5, Summer 1985, pp. 901-922.

1517 Sofaer, Abraham D. Fighting Terrorism Through-law. *Department of State Bulletin*, Volume 85, Number 2103, October 1985, pp. 38-42.

1518 Solzhenitsyn, Alexander. *The Gulag Archipelago, I, II, III*. New York, Harper and Row, 1974-1978.

1519 Souchon, Henri. Hostage-Taking: its Evolution and Significance. *International Criminal Police Review*, Number 299, June-July 1976, pp. 168-173.

1520 South African Institute of Race Relations. *Security and Related Trials in South Africa,* July 1976-May 1977. Johannesburg, 1977.

1521 South African Institute of Race Relation. *Administration of Security Legislation, South Africa*, January 1976-March 1977. Johannesburg, 1977.

1522 Soulier, Gerard. Contre Le Terrorism: Quelle Europe Se Dessine? *Le Monde Diplomatique*, November 1976, p. 34.

1523 Sooner or Later All : Attacks on Those in Protestant Catholic Marriages. *Time*, Volume 103, Number 29, 8 April 1974.

1524 Sparrow, Gerald. *The Great Assassins*. New York, Arco, 1969.

1525 Special Report: Terrorism Potential for Terrorist attacks in the United States; Tactics in Thwarting Terrorism in Turkey, West Germany; and Italy; three articles. *U.S. News*, Number 96, 9 January 1984, pp. 24-25.

1526 Special Report: Significant Regional Developments, October-December 1984. *Terrorism: An International Journal*, Volume 8, Number 2, 1985, pp. 165-183.

1527 Spjut, R.J. Review of Counter-Insurgency Theorists. *Political Quarterly*, Number 49, January-March 1978, pp. 54-64.

1528 Sponsler, T.H. International Kidnapping. *International Lawyer*, Number 5, January 1971, pp. 25-52.

1529 Spreading Mideast Terror Traps. *U.S. News*, Volume 74, Number 20, 23 April 1973.

1530 Spreading Political Terrorism in the America. *U.S. News*, Volume 78, Numbers 19-20, 13 January 1975.

1531 Sri Raman J. The Unavailing Anology. *Patriot,* 11 October 1985, p. 4.
1532 St. John, Ronald Bruce. Terrorism and Libyan Foreign Policy, 1981-1986. *World Today*, Number 42, July 1986, pp. 111-115.
1533 St. John, Peter. Analysis and Response of a Decade of Terrorism. *Internat Perspectives*, September-October 1981, pp. 2-5.
1534 Standing up to the Gang Takeover of West Germany Embassy in Stockholm by Supporters of the Baader-Meinhof Gang. *Time,* Volume 105, Number 42, 5 May 1975.
1535 Stafford, David. Anarchists in Britain Today. *Government and Opposition*, Number 6, 1971, pp. 345-353.
1536 Stanley Foundation. The Nuclear Theft and Terrorism Discussion Group Report. *Sixteen Strategy for Peace Conference Report*. Muscatine, Iowa, Idem, 1975.
1537 State of Semi-Siege: Case of J.G. Zuno. *Time*, 16 September 1974, pp. 27-28.
1538 State Terrorism. *Times of India*, 22 May 1985, p. 8.
1539 Statutory Report. *Addendum to the Communication on the Activities of the Committee of Ministers Reply to Recommendation 634, 1972 on International Terrorism*. Doc. 3288 Adendum, 1973.
1540 Stechel, Ira. Terrorist Kidnapping of Diplomatic Personnel. *Cornell International Law Journal*, Number 5, Spring 1972, pp. 189-217.
1541 Steela, R. Massacre At Zion Square. *Newsweek*, 14 July 1975, pp. 34-35.
1542 Steilles, Dennis W. Sovereignty and the New Violence. *Air University Review*, Number 27, July-August 1976, pp. 89-95.
1543 Steinhilper, G. *Violence and Police*. Strasbourg, France, Council of Europe, European Committee on Crime, 1977.
1544 Steinhoff, Patricia. Portrait of a Terrorist: An interview with Kozo Okamoto. *Asian Survey*, Number 16, September 1976, pp. 830-845.
1545 Sterling, Claire. The Red Bridges Have Strange Partners in Crime. *Wall St J*. Volume 200, Number 25, 18 August 1982.
1546 Stetler, Russell. (Ed.). *Palestine: The Arab-Israeli Conflict*. Palo Alto, Calif., Ramparts Press, 1974.
1547 Stevenson, Adlai E. III. Nuclear Reactors: America Must Act. *Foreign Affairs*, Number 53, October 1974, pp. 64-76.
1548 Stevenson, C. Tyranny of Terrorism in the Building Trades. *Readers' Digest*, Number 102, June 1973, pp. 89-94.
1549 Stevenson, C. Yes Construction-Union Terrorism is Real. *Readers' Digest*, Number 103, December 1973, pp. 85-90.

1550 Stewart, Bernard L. State-Sponsored Terrorism, the Threat and Possible Counter measures. *Terrorism: An International Journal*, Volume 8, Number 3, 1986, pp. 253-313.

1551 Still At Large. *Northern India Patrika*, 30 January 1985, p. 4.

1552 Stoffel, John. *Explosives and Homemade Bombs*. Springfield, IL., Charles C. Thomas, 1973.

1553 Stohl, Michael and Lopex, George A. *Government Violence and Repression : An Agenda For Research*. Westport, Greenwood Pr., 1984.

1554 Storr, A. Sadism and Paranoia. In M.H. Livingston (Ed.). *International Terrorism in the Contemporary World*. London, Greenwood Press, 1978.

1555 Story of the Bloodiest Skyjacking, Terrorism in Rome Airport. *U.S. News*, Volume 75, Number 16, 31 December 1973.

1556 Stopping World Terror: Must U.S. Do it Alone? *U.S. News*, Volume 74, 19 March 1973.

1557 Stratton, J.G. Terrorist Act of Hostage-Taking: Considerations for law Enforcement. *Journal of Police Science and Administration*, Number 6, June 1978, pp. 123-134.

1558 Stratton, J.G. Terrorist Act of Hostage-Taking: A View of Violence and the Perpetrators. *Journal of Police Science and Administration*, Number 6, March 1978, pp. 1-9.

1559 Strentz, Thomas. The Terrorist Organizational Profile: A Psychological Evaluation. *In U.S. Congress Senate Committee on Governmental Affairs* an Act to Combat International Terrorism, Hearing before the Committee, 23, 25, 27, 30 January, 22 February, 22 and 23 March 1978. 95th Congress, 2nd Session, 1978, pp. 757-785.

1560 Strother, R.S. Terrorism on the Rampage. *Readers' Digest*, Number 107, November 1975, pp. 73-77.

1561 Styles, George. *Bombs have no Pity: My war against Terrorism*. London, William Luscombe, 1975.

1562 Styles, S.G. The Car Bomb. *Journal of the Forensic Science Society*, Number 15, April 1975, pp. 93-97.

1563 Subrahmanyam, K. Terrorism: to the Forefront of the Stage. *Strategic Analysis*, Volume 10, Number 3, January 1986, pp. 237-248.

1564 Subrahmanyam. K. Terrorism. *Strategic Analysis*, Volume 9, Number 4, July 1985, pp. 14-18.

1565 Subrahmanyam, K. Hijacking of K-421. *Strategic Analysis*, Volume 8, Number 6, September 1984, pp. 479-499.

1566 Sud, K.N. The Cult of Killing. *Patriot*, 24 February 1984, p. 4.

1567 Sudiata, I.K. Integrative and Disintegrative Terror: The Case of Equatorial Guinea. in Marius H. Livingston (Ed.). with Kress, Lee B. and Wanek, Marie G. *International Terrorism in the Contemporary World*, Westport, Conn., Greenwood Press, 1978, pp. 182-194.

1568 Singer, L.W. New Way to Face Terrorists: A Crisis Management System. *Security Management*, Number 21, September 1977, pp. 6-9.

1569 Sundberg, Jacob. The Anti-terrorist Legislation in Sweden. in Marius H. Livingston (Ed.).with Kress, Lee B, and Wanek, Marie G. *International Terrorism in the Temporary World*, Westport, Conn., Greenwood Press, 1978, pp. 111-121.

1570 Sundberg, M. Jacob. Piracy: Sea and Air. International Law Association. *Report of the Fifty-Fourth Conference*. The Hague, 23-29 August 1970. London, 1971, pp. 755-771.

1571 Sunder Ranjan, K.R. Together against Terrorism. *Amrit Bazar Patrika*, 2 October 1985, p. 6.

1572 Supression of Terrorism Act 1978. London, HMSO, 1972, Extract, Ch. 26. Supression of Terrorism Bill Lords. Second Reading Committee. 26 April 1978. London, HMSO, 1978, pp. 1575-1576, 1611-1613.

1573 Suri, Dona. Where Do they Go from Here? *Tribune*, 27 October 1985, p. 1.

1574 Suri, Surinder. Humanism and Nationalism: Answer to Irrational Hatred. *Times of India*, 25 May 1985, p. 8.

1575 Suri, Surinder. Terror Turns Green Revolution Red. *Link*, Volume 28, Number 37, 20 April 1986, pp. 14-16.

1576 Suri, Surinder. At War with Peace. *Times of India* Delhi, Magazine Section, 11 August 1985, p. 1.

1577 Singh, Surjeet, Harkishan. Save Punjab, Save India. *People's Democracy*, Volume 10, Number 14, 6 April 1986, p. 1.

1578 Suter, K. What is Terrorism ? *British Society Review*, December 1977, pp. 66-72.

1579 Swami, Parthasarathi. Terrorism is big Business. *Business Standard*, 30 June 1985, p. 4.

1580 Swarup, Ram. Akali Politics and Terrorism. *Times of India*, Delhi, 30 June 1984, p. 8.

1581 Sweet, William. Anti-Terrorism: New Priority in Foreign Policy (United States). *Editorial Research Reports,* 27 March 1981, pp. 231-248.

1582 Syrkin, Marie. Political Terrorism. *Midstream*, Number 18, 1972, pp. 3-11.

1583 Syrokomsky, V. *International Terrorism and the CIA*. Chicago, Imported Pubns., 1983.

1584 Systematic Fault. *Indian Express*, Delhi, 18 May 1985, p. 6.

1585 Szaz, Z. Michael. Armenian Terrorists and the East-West Conflict. *J Social Pol. and Econ. Studies*, Number 8, Winter 1983, pp. 387-394.

1586 Szumski, Bonnie. (Ed.). *Terrorism: Opposing Viewpoints*. Ser., Shcreview, Park Rod St. Paul, Greenhaven, 1986.

1587 Tackling Terrorism Politically. *Economic and Political Wkly*, Volume 19, Number 38, 22 September 1984, pp. 1650-1652.

1588 Tackling Terrorism. *Hindustan Times*, 9 November 1985, p. 9.

1589 Taking on Terrorism. *Patriot*, 10 September 1985, p. 4.

1590 Take Us Seriously: Murder of Diplomats in Khartaum. *Nation*, Volume 216, Number 356, 19 March 1973.

1591 Tannonbaum, Jeffrey A. The Terrorists. *The Wall Street Journal*, 4 January 1977.

1592 Tarkunde, V.M. The Black Laws. *Sikh Review*, Volume 33, Number 375, March 1985, pp. 35-39.

1593 Tarkunde, V.M. The Anti-terrorist Act and Related laws. *Soc. Action*, Volume 35, Number 4, October-December 1985, pp. 393-401.

1594 Task Force on Kidnapping. *External Affairs*, Number 23, 1971, pp. 6-11.

1595 Taulbee, J.L. Retaliation and Irregular Warfare in Contemporary International Law. *International Lawyer,* Number 7, January 1973, pp. 195-204.

1596 Taylor, Clyde D. Links between International Narcotics Trafficking and Terrorism. *Department of State Bulletin*, Number 85, August 1985, pp. 69-74.

1597 Taylor, D.L. *Terrorism and Criminology: The Application of a Perspective*. West Lafayette, Ind., Purdue University Institute for the Study of Social Change, 1978.

1598 Taylor, Edmond. The Terrorists. *Horizon*, Summer 1973, pp. 58-65.

1599 Taylor, Robert W. and Byong-Suh, Kim. Violence and Change in the Postindustrial Societies: Student Protest in America and Japan in the 1960's. in Marius H. Livingston (Ed.). with Lee B. Kress and

Marie G. Wanek. *International Terrorism in the Contemporary World*. Westport, Coun., Greenwood Press, 1978, pp. 204-219.

1600 Taylor, Theodore B.; Van Cleave, W.R. and Kinderman, T.M. *Preliminary Survey of Non-national Nuclear Threats*. Stanford, Stanford Research Institute Technical Note SSC-TN-5205-83, September 1968.

1601 Taylor, Theodore B. Diversion by Non-Governmental Organisations, in Willrich Baltimore Mason (Ed.). *International Safeguards and Nuclear Industry*. Baltimore (St. Swati), Johns Hopkins University Press, 1973, pp. 176-178.

1602 Teixeira, Bernardo. *The Fabric of Terror: Three Days in Angola*. New York, Dewin-Adair, 1965.

1603 Tension in Nepal. *National Herald*, 24 June 1985, p. 7.

1604 Terekhov, Vladimir. International Fight Against It. *New Times*, Number 11, 1974, pp. 20-22.

1605 Terraine, John. et al. *Ten Years of Terrorism Collected Views*. Jennifer Shaw, etc., 1979.

1606 Terror at the Tower: Explosion in the Tower of London. *Time*, Volume 104, Number 39, 29 July 1974.

1607 Terror Balance. *Patriot*, 21 December 1984, p. 4.

1608 Terror International. *B B C I*, 30 January 1978.

1609 Terror Tactics. *Nation*, Number 218, 1 June 1974, pp. 674-675.

1610 Terry, H.A. Television and Terrorism: Professionalism not Quite the Answer. *Indiana Law Journal*, Volume 53, Number 4, pp. 745-747.

1611 Terrorisation. *Patriot*, 22 April 1984, p. 4.

1612 Terrorism: A Global Phenomenon. *Search Light*, Magazine Section, 6 October 1985, p. 1.

1613 Terrorism: A Nagging Worry for America, Too; All but Gone are the 1960s - Style Radicals, in their Place: Foreign Groups that Sow Turmoil in Many Parts of the U.S. *U.S. News*, Volume 90, Number 30, 1 June 1981.

1614 *Terrorism: A Selected Bibliography, The Pentagon Library.* Washington, D.C., the Library, 1984.

1615 *Terrorism: A Staff Study Prepared by the Committee on Internal Security of the U.S. House of Representatives*. Washington, D.C., U.S. Government Printing Office, 1974.

1616 Terrorism and the U.N. *Tribune*, 24 June 1985, p. 4.

1617 Terrorism Again. *Northern India Patrika*, 22 October 1985, p. 4.

1618 Terrorist Challenge. *Hindustan Times*, 22 April 1985, p. 9.

1619 Terrorism Continues. *Northern India Patrika*, 21 November 1983, p. 4.

1620 Terrorism Complicated a Mission of Peace, Al Fatah Attack on Tel Aviv Hotel. *Time*, Volume 105, 17 March 1975, pp. 31-33.

1621 Terrorism Deadline. *Tribune*, 17 May 1984, p. 4.

1622 *Terror in East Pakistan*. Karachi, Karachi Publications, 1971.

1623 Terrorism: Fire-Fighting Won't Do. *Times of India*, 12 August 1986, p. 1.

1624 *Terrorism and the Media*. London, International Press Institute, 1980.

1625 Terrorism and Marxism. *Monthly Review*, Number 24, November 1972, pp. 1-6.

1626 Terrorism and Political Crimes in International Law. *American Journal of International Law*, Number 67, November 1973, pp. 87-111.

1627 Terrorism. *Dept State Bul.*, Number 82, August 1982, pp. 1-35.

1628 Terrorism. *National Herald*, 29 June 1985, p. 7.

1629 Terrorism in Assam. *Amrita Bazar Patrika*, 7 July 1984, p. 6.

1630 Terrorism. *Madhya Pradesh Chronicle*, 18 July 1985, p. 4.

1631 Terrorism in Latin America. *Atlas*, Number 20, 10 November 1971, pp. 18-21.

1632 *Terrorism in Cyprus. The Captured Document's Transcribed Extract, Issued by Authority of the Secretary of State For the Colonies*. London, H.M. Stationary Office, 1956.

1633 Terrorism in Nepal. *Tribune*, 22 June 1985, p. 4.

1634 Terrorism in Punjab. *Assam Tribune*, 15 May 1984, p. 4.

1635 Terrorism in Punjab. *Deccan Herald*, 30 November 1985, p. 6.

1636 Terrorism in Punjab: Low-Level Pak Involvement. *Times of India*, 16 August 1986, p. 1.

1637 Terrorism in the Skies. *Business Standard*, 25 June 1985, p. 5.

1638 Terrorism in Tripura. *Hindustan Times*, 9 July 1984, p. 9.

1639 Terrorists in Tripura. *Amrita Bazar Patrika*, 19 July 1985, p. 6.

1640 Terrorism is Back. *Deccan Herald*, 15 September 1984, p. 8.

1641 Terrorism on the Home Front: American Managers Should be Aware of this Growing National Problem Interview with Oliver B. Revell, Assistant Director of the Federal Bureau of Investigation; on the Forces that Venerate Domestic Terrorism, the Types of Companies most Likely to Fall Victim, the Bureau's Newest Initiatives against Terrorism, and his views on how Managers should

Judge the Potential for such an Incident. *Personnel Administrator*, Volume 28, Number 21, April 1983.

1642 Terrorism Rides Again. *Statesman* Delhi, 29 November 1985, p. 6.

1643 Terrorism Repressioin du Terrorism Et De La violence an France. *Nr. 44238*, 18 February 1978.

1644 *Terrorism in Europe*. Order No. 376, 31st Ordinary Session, 31st January 1979.

1645 *Terrorism. Staff Study Committee on Internal Security*. House of Representatives, Washington, 1974.

1646 Terrorism Special Issue of Skeptic. *The Forum for Contemporary History*, Santa Barbara, Calif, January-February 1984.

1647 Terrorism to Stall Talks. *Madhya Pradesh Chronicle*, 6 June 1985, p. 4.

1648 Terrorism: The New Global War Emphasis on the M-19 Guerrilla Movement of Colombia and its Seizure of the Dominican Embassy in Bogota, February 1980. *Latin Am. Times*, Number 2, May 1980, pp. 10-15.

1649 Terrorism: What can be Done? *National Review*, Volume 26, Number 303, 15 March 1974.

1650 Terrorists Abroad. *Statesman*, Delhi, 19 October 1985, p. 6.

1651 Terrorists Attacks against U.S. Business. *Terrorism: An International Journal*, Volume 8, Number 2, 1985, pp. 185-204.

1652 Terrorists base Smashed in Raid. *Times of India*, 20 July, 1986, p. 1.

1653 Terrorist gun Down two in Punjab. *Times of India*, 10 April 1986, p. 1.

1654 Terrorist hit List. *Tribune*, 5 September 1985, p. 4.

1655 Terrorist in US Planned to Blow up Strategic Sites. *Times of India*, 15 March 1985, p. 1.

1656 Terrorist Links. *Times of India*, 1 April 1986, p. 8.

1657 Terrorist Mafia. *National Herald*, 26 June 1985, p. 7.

1658 Terrorists Strategy. *Northern India Patrika*, 2 August 1985, p. 4.

1659 Terrorists Strike Again. *Deccan Herald*, 5 September 1985, p. 8. and *Northern India Patrika,* 25 September 1985, p. 4.

1660 Terrorists Wanted to kill Rajiv in France or Algeria. *Times of India*, 17 May 1985, p. 1.

1661 Thadami, Jaya. the Advent of Terrorism. *Tribune*, 20 January 1984, p. 4.

1662 Thapar, Romesh. The Problem of Terrorism. *Econ. and Pol. Wkly*, Volume 20, Number 38, 21 September 1985, p. 1585.

1663 Tharp, Paul A. Jr. The Laws of war as a Potential Legal Regime For the Control of Terrorist Activities. *Journal of International Affairs,* Number 32, Spring/Summer 1978, pp. 91-100.

1664 *The Defence of Democracy Against Terrorism in Europe*. Order No. 396, 32nd Ordinary Session, 26, March 1981.

1665 The Enemy within. *Times of India*, 17 April 1986, p. 8.

1666 The Enemy within. *National Herald*, 4 April 1984, p. 7.

1667 *The ICAU and Arab Terrorist Operations: a Record of Resolutions*. Jerusalem, Ministry of Foreign Affairs, 1973.

1668 *The Law of Limited International Conflict*. Georgetown University, Washington, D.C., Institute of World Policy, April 1965.

1669 The Jonathan Institute. *Abdiction of Responsibility.* Jerusalem, 1979.

1670 The Jonathan Institute. International Terrorism, *Conference News Letter*, 1979.

1671 *The Origins and Fundamental Causes of International Terrorism*,United Nations, General Assembly, DOC. A/C 6/418, 2 November 1972, pp. 6-9.

1672 The Prohibition Against the Training or Support of Terrorist Organizations Act of 1984 Includes Text of the Bell Proposed by the United States Department of State. *J. Palestine Studies*, Number 13, Summer 1984, pp. 134-144.

1673 The Rambo Mood. *Times of India*, 18 July 1985, p. 6.

1674 The Role of International Law in Combating Terrorism. *Current Foreign Policy*, January 1973, pp. 1-7.

1675 The Roots of Terrorism. *Tribune*, 18 September 1985, p. 4.

1676 The Terrorism Act of South Africa. *Bulletin of the International Commission of Jurists,* June 1986, pp. 28-34.

1677 The War Against Terrorism. *Harvard Internat.R.*, Number 7, May-June 1986, pp. 4-23.

1678 Theberge, Leonard and Alexander Yonah (Ed.). *Terrorism and the Media in the 1980.* Conference Report Sponsored Jointly by the Media Institute's Transnational Communications Centre and the Institute for Sudies in International Terrorism, 14 April 1983. *Pol Communication and Persuasion*, Number 2, 3 November 1984, pp. 283-331.

1679 Threat for Bicentennial Year-Terrorists Getting Ready. *U.S. News*, 21 July 1975, pp. 23-25.

1680 Threat fom Terrorists. *Northern India Patrika*, 14 September 1985, p. 4.

1681 Threat from Terrorists. *Northern India Patrika*, 5 November 1985, p. 4.

1682 Threat in Tripura. *Statesman*,Delhi, 26 March 1985, p. 6.

1683 Three Arrested in Raids on Temple Sarais. *Times of India*, 21 April 1985, p. 1.

1684 Thunder in Nepal. *Hindustan Times,* 22 June 1985, p. 9.

1685 Tinker, Jerry M. (Ed.). *Strategics of Revolutionary Warfare*. Philadelphia, Coronet Bks, 1969.

1686 Tinnin, David B. *Hit Team*. Boston, Little, Browns Co., 1976.

1687 Tischendorf, Alfred. The Assassination of Chief Executives in Latin America. *South Atlantic Quarterly*, Number 60, Winter 1961, pp. 80-88.

1688 Todd, William. *Hoskins: The Artist as Terrorist*. Clifton Aves Ehiling, Clifton Bks., 1982.

1689 Together on Terrorism. *Hindustan Times,* 29 October 1985, p. 9.

1690 Toman, Jiri. Terrorism and the Regulation of Armed Conflict. in Cherif M. Bassiouni (Ed.). *International Terrorism and Political Crimes*. Springfield, Illinois, Charles C. Thomas, 1975, pp. 133-154.

1691 Tomasic, Dinko. The Ustasha Movement. *Slavonic Encyclopaedia*, New York, Kennikat Press, 1949, pp. 1337-1341.

1692 Too Early to Judge. *Search Light*, 22 November 1985, p. 4.

1693 Top Targets of Terrorists, U.S. Businessmen on Foreign Assignments. *U.S. News*, Volume 87, Number 61, 26 November, 1979.

1694 Tornoviski; V. *Terrorism in Routina*. London, Geneva, 1980.

1695 Tough Measures to Curb Terrorism. *Hindu*, 22 May 1985, p. 8.

1696 Toward a Grim Millenary. *Time*, 15 April 1974, p. 44.

1697 Trial by Terror: Kidnapping of Foreign Executives. *Time,* 14 January 1974, pp. 24-25.

1698 Training the World in Terrorism. *Hindustan Times*, 30 June 1985, p. 9.

1699 Tragedy in Punjab. *Hindu*, 15 May 1984, p. 8.

1700 Tran, Tam. Terrorism Etle Droit Renal International Contemporain. *Revenue De Droit International De Science Diplomatic Was Et Politiques,* Number 45, 1967, pp. 11-25.

1701 Transistor Bombs Again. *Deccan Herald*, 24 September 1985, p. 6.

1702 Tratsky, L. *The Defence of Terrorism and Communism : A Reply to Karl Kautsky*. 1921.

1703 Trends in International Terrorism, 1982 and 1983. Cordes, Bonnie and Others. *Rand Corp.*, August 1984.

1704 Trent Darrell M. A National Policy to Combat Terrorism. *Policy Review*, Summer 1979, pp. 41-53.

1705 Tripura Storm Signals. *National Herald*, 28 July 1984, p. 7.

1706 Trotsky, Leon. *The Defence of Terrorism*. London, Allen and Unwin, 1921.

1707 Trotsky, Leon. *Against Individual Terrorism*. New York, Path Pr., 1974.

1708 Troubles Spill Over Letterbomb Compaign. *Time*, 10 September 1973, pp. 30-31.

1709 Trouble in Tripura. *Deccan Herald*, 11 July 1984, p. 6.

1710 Trouble in Tripura. *National Herald*, 22 March 1985, p. 7.

1711 Trying Terrorists. *Tribune*, 16 July 1984, p. 4.

1712 Truby, J.D. *How Terrorists Kill*. U.K., Gordon Pr., 1986.

1713 Tuckerman, A. U.N. New Look for 1972 - Debate on Terrorism. *Nation*, 2 October 1972, p. 258.

1714 Tugwell, Maurice. Politics and Propaganda of the Provisional I.R.A. *Terrorism : An International Journal*, Volume 5, 1981, p. 29.

1715 Tugwell, Maurice. Source of Euro-American Discord on Terrorism: Responses Vary Due to Differing Impact, Value Judgements and Terrorism's New form. *Europe Eur Communities*, July-August 1986, pp. 22-23.

1716 Tugwell, Maurice. Terrorism and Propaganda :Problem and Response. *Conflict Q.*, Number 6, Spring 1986, pp. 5-15.

1717 *Two Hundred and Sixtyseven U.S. Lives Were Lost by Terrorism in Lebanon in 1983.* U.S. Dept. of State, September 1984.

1718 Ulansky, A. Middle East; Looking At the TWA Hijack; of Abductors, Hostages and the U.S. Policy of State Terrorism. *New Times*, Number 28, July 1985, pp. 10-11.

1719 Ulster's Civil War: Agony without end; Kill Britons. That's the Battle cry of Terrorists who Assassinated a National Hero; can their New Strategy Drive British out of Northern Ireland? *U.S. News*, Number 87, 10 September 1979, pp. 21-22.

1720 United Kingdom. *Report of the Committeee of Privy Councellors Appointed to Consider Authorized Procedures for the Interrogation of Persons Suspected of Terrorism*. London, 1972.

1721 United Kingdom, Commission on Legal Procedures to Deal with Terrorist Activities in Northern Ireland. *Report to the Commission to Consider Legal Procedures to Deal with Terrorist Activities in Northern Ireland*. HMSO, 1972.

1722 United Kingdom Investigation cite Bomb in Crash of Trans World 707. *Aviation Weekly*, Volume 101, Number 29, 11 November 1974.

1723 United Nations: General Assembly. *Ad Hoc Committee on International Terrorism Report*. New York, United Nations, 1973.

1724 United Nations. *Report of the Ad Hoc Committee on International Terrorism*. New York, United Nations 1977.

1725 United Nations. Terrorist Acts against UN Missions. *UN Monthly Chronicle*, Number 8, November 1971, pp. 61-70.

1726 United States. Terrorism: The Proposed United States Draft Convention. *Georgia Journal of International and Comparative Law*, Number 3, 2 November 1973, pp. 430-447.

1727 United States. Atomic Energy Commission. *Environmental Survey of Transportation of Radioactive Materials to and from Nuclear Power Plants*. Washington, AEC Directorate of Regulatory Standards, December 1972.

1728 United States. *Safeguards Research and Development: Proceedings of a Symposium, 27-29 October 1969*. Springfield, VA, Clearinghouse for Federal Scientific and Technical Information, Wash., 1147, 1970.

1729 United States. *Physical Protection of Classified Matter and Information*. AC Manual Appendix and Revisions 2401. Washington, AEC Division of Security, 26 June 1969.

1730 United States. Advisory Panel on Safeguarding Special Nuclear Masterial. *Report to the AEC*. Washington, Apparently Unpublished, 10 March 1967.

1731 United States. Central Intelligence Agency. Nat. For. Assessment Center. *International Terrorism in 1978*. March 1979. Nat. Tech Info. Service; Subscription Document Expending (DOCEX) Project, Exchange and Gift Division Library of Congress, Washington, DC., 20540.

1732 United States. Central Intelligence Agency. Nat for. Assessment Center. *Patterns of International Terrorism: 1980: June 1981*. Nat Tech Info Service - Photoduplication Service, Library of Congress, Washington DC., 20540.

1733 United States. Chamber of Commerce. *Violence Against Society*. Washington, D.C., Idem, 1971.

1734 United States. Comptroller-General. *Improvements Needed in the Programme for the Protection of Social Nuclear Material: Report to the Congress*. Washington, Government Accounting Office, 7 November 1973.

1735 United States. Congress. *Congressional Record,* 122, Number 113, Staff summary of Government Accounting Office Report. Shortcomings in the Systems Used to Control and Protect Highly Dangerous Nuclear Materials. Energy Research and Development Administration. Staff Summary, 27 July 1976.

1736 United States. Congress House. *Thefts and Losses of Military Weapons and Ammunition, and Explosives, Report of the Subcommittee on Investigation of the Committee on Armed Services.* 94th Congress, 2nd Session, 14 April 1976.

1737 United States Congress. House of Representatives. Committee of the Judiciary. Subcommittee on Crime. *Terrorism Legislation Ninety-Eight Congress.* Second Session on H.R. 5612, H.R. 5690. Terrorism Legislation: 26 September 1984. Washington, D.C., U.S.G.P.O. 1984, III, p. 42, Serial No. 155.

1738 United States. Congress House. International Relations Committee. *Palestinian Issue in Middle East Peace Efforts, Hearings before Special Subcommittee on Investigations,* 30 September 1975. 94th Congress, 1st Session, 1976.

1739 United States. Congress House. Judiciary Committee. *Internationally Protected Persons' Bills: Unsworn Declaration Bills, Hearings 30 June 1976.* 94th Congress, 2nd Session, 1977.

1740 United States. Congress House. Judiciary Committee. *Implementing International Conventions Against Terrorism, House Report 94-1614,* 18 September 1976. 94th Cong., 2nd Sess., 1976.

1741 United States. Congress House. Committee on Foreign Affairs. *International Terrorism, Hearings before the Sub-Committee on the Near East and South Asia.* 93rd Cong., 2nd Sess., 11-24 June 1974.

1742 United States. Congress House. *Political Kidnapping, 1968-1973, a Staff Study Prepared by the Committee on Internal Security.* 95th Congress, 1st Session, 1 August 1973.

1743 United States Congress House of Representatives, Committee on Foreign Affairs Subcommittee on International Operations. *Legislation to Combat International Terrorism 98th Congress Hearing and Markup before the Committee on Foreign Affairs and its Subcommittee on International Security and Scientific Affairs and on International operations.* House of Representatives Ninety Eight Congress On 9 November 1983, 7, 13, 19 June, 26 September 1984. Washington, D.C., U.S.G.P.O. 1984. IV, p. 461.

1744 United States Congress Senate. Committee on Foreign Relations, *Combating International and Domestic Terrorism,* Hearings on S. 2236, 95th Congress, 2nd Sess., 1978.

1745 United States Congress Senate. Foreign Relations Committee. *With Respect to the Release of Aby Daoud, Senate Report 95-1.* 95th Cong., 1st Sess., 1977.

1746 United States Congress Senate. Commission on the Operation of *The Senate. Major U.S. Foreign and Defence Policy Issues.* Committee Print, 95th Cong., 1st Sess., 1977.

1747 United States Congress Senate. Commerce, Science and Transportation Committee. *National Tourism Policy Study,* Hearings, 5 April 1976, 94th Cong., 2nd Sess., 1977.

1748 United States Congress Senate. Judiciary Committee. *Trotskyite Terrorist International, Hearings before the Sub-Committee on Internal Security, 24 July 1975.* 94th Cong., 1st Sess., 1976.

1749 United States Congress Senate. Judiciary Committee. *The Terrorist and His Victim, Hearings July 21, 1977.* 95th Congress, 1st Session, 1977.

1750 United States Congress Senate. Judiciary Committee. *Puerto Rican Workers Organization.* Committee Print, March 1976. 94th Congress, 2nd Session, 1976.

1751 United States Congress Senate. Judiciary Committee. *Terroristic Activity: Terrorist Bombings and Law Enforcement Intelligence, Part 7. Hearings before the Subcommittee on Internal Security,* 23 October 1975. 94th Cong., 1st Sess., 1975.

1752 United States Congress Senate. Judiciary Committee. *Terrorist Activity, Part 3, Hearings before the Sub-Committee on Internal Security.* 93rd Cong., 2nd Sess., 5 July 1974.

1753 United States Congress Senate. Judiciary Committee. *Terroristic Activity, Part 1, Hearings before the Subcommittee on Internal Security.* 93rd Cong., 2nd Sess., 23 September 1974.

1754 United States Congress. Senate. Judiciary Committee. *Panama Canal and the Problem of Security.* Committee Print, 94th Cong., 42nd Sess., October 1976.

1755 United States Congress. Senate. Judiciary Committee. *Implementing International Conventions against Terrorism, Senate Report 94-1273,* 26 September 1976. 94th Cong., 2nd Sess., 1976.

1756 United States Congress. Senate. Judiciary Committee. *Threats to the Peaceful Observance of the Bicentennial, Hearings 18 June 1976.* 94th Cong., 2nd Sess., 1976.

1757 United States Congress. Senate. Foreign Relations Committee. *Terrorist Attack at Istanbul Airport, Senate Report 94-1235*, 16 September 1976. 94th Cong., 2nd Sess., 1976.

1758 United States Congress. Senate. Judiciary Committee. *Terroristic Activity: Interlock between Communism and Terrorism, Part 9, Hearings before the Sub-Committee on Internal Security,* 7 March 1976. 94th Cong., 2nd Sess., 1976.

1759 United States Congress. Senate. Judiciary Committee. *Terroristic Activity, Part 4, International Terrorism, Hearings before the Sub-Committee on Internal Security.* 94th Cong., 1st Sess., 14th May 1975.

1760 United States Congress. Senate. Committee on the Judiciary. *Terroristic Activity: Terrorist Bombings and Law Enforcement Intelligence, Hearings before the Sub-Committee to Investigate the Administration of the Internal Security Act and other Internal Security Laws, Part* 7. 94th Cong., 1st Sess., 23 October 1975.

1761 United States. Senate. Committee on the Judiciary Sub-Committee on Security and Terrorism. *Legislative Initiatives to Curb Domestic and International Terrorism.* Ninety-Eighth Congress Second Session on S. 2470 5,6, and 13 June 1984. Washington, D.C., U.S.G.P.O. 1984, IV p. 194.

1762 United States. Congress Senate. Committee on Governmental Affairs. *An Act to Combat International Terrorism*, Hearings before the Committee, 23, 25, 27, 30 January; 22 February; 22 and 23 March 1978. 95th Cong., 2nd Sess., 1978.

1763 United States Defence Nuclear Agency etal. *New Modes Conflict.* Rand Corp., 1983.

1764 United States. Dept. of Defence. Comm. on *Beirut Internat. Airport Terrorist Act*, 23 October 1983. Report 20 December 1983, 1984, Washington, D.C. 20301.

1765 United States Department of Justice. *Terrorism: Statistics and Techniques.* an FBI Special Study, 12 January 1973.

1766 United State Department. *A Study: Viet Cong Use of Terror.* Saigon, U.S. Mission in Vietnam, 1967.

1767 United States Department of Justice. Law Enforcement Assistance Administration. Private Security Advisory Council. *Prevention of Terroristic Crimes: Security Guidelines For Business, Industry, and other Organizations.*

1768 United States Department of State. *Chronology of Attacks Upon Non-Official American Citizens, 1971-1975.* Washington, D.C., 20 January 1976.

1769 United States Department of Justice. *Terrorism. Its Tactics and Techniques - An FBI Special Study.* Washington D.C. Government Printing Office, 12 January 1973.

1770 United States Department of State. *Chronology of Significant Terrorist Incidents Involving U.S. Diplomatic Official Personnel, 1963-1975.* Washington, D.C., 20 January 1976.

1771 United States Department of State. *Background Documentation Relating to the Assassinations of Ambassador Cleo A. Noel, Jr. and George Curtis Moore.* Washington, Idem, 1973.

1772 United States Department of State. *State Department Conference on Terrorism.* U.S. Department of State External Research Study, XR/RNAS - 21, 29 December 1972.

1773 United States Government Response to Terrorism: A Global Approach. Address 4 January 1975. Hoffacker, L. *Vital Speech,* Number 41, 15 February 1975, pp. 266-68.

1774 United States House. International Relations Committee. *Nuclear Proliferation, Hearings,* 8 June 1976. 94th Cong., 2nd Sess., 1976. Esp. 79-82.

1775 United States House. Small Business Committee. *Problems in the Accounting for and Safeguarding of Special Nuclear Materials, Hearings,* 26 April 1976. 94th Cong., 2nd Sess., 1977. Esp. 111-217.

1776 United States House. Com. on Energy and Commer. Subcom. On Oversight and Investigation. *Nuclear Weapons Facilities: Hearings,* 6 March 1986. on Adequacy of Safeguards and Security at Department of Energy Nuclear Weapons Production Facilities. 1987.

1777 United States House. Com. on the Judiciary. Subcom. on Civil and Constitutional Rights. *Federal Capabilities in Crisis Management and Terrorism: Oversight Hearings,* 5 April 1979, and 19 May 1980, Washington, D.C., 20515.

1778 United States House. Committee on Armed Services. Investigations Subcom. *Adequacy of U.S. Marine Corps Security in Beirut: Summary of Findings and Conclusions, 1983.* 98th Cong., 1st Sess., Washington, D.C., 20515.

1779 United States House Committee on Foreign Affairs. *International Terrorism.* Washington, 1974.

1780 United States House. Committee on Public Works and Transportation. Subcom. on Aviation. *International Terrorism: Hearings,* 18-

25 July 1978. on H.R. 13261, to Amend the Federal Aviation Act of 1958, Relating to Aircraft Piracy to Provide a Method of Combating Terrorism, and for other Purposes. 1978, 95th Cong., 2nd Sess., Washington, D.C., 20215.

1781 United States House. Com. on Internat. Relations. Subcom. on Internat Security and Sci. Affairs. *International Terrorism: Legislative Initiatives: Hearings and Markup,* 12 September- 5 October 1978. 1978, 95th Cong., 2nd Sess., Washington, D.C., 20515.

1782 United States. House. Com. on the Judiciary. Subcom. on Civil and Constitutional Rights. *Federal Capabilities in Crisis Management and Terrorism Hearings, 16 August - 4 October 1978.* 1978, 95th Cong., 2nd Sess., Washington, D.C. 20515.

1783 United States. House Committee on For. Affaris. *International Terrorism, 1985: Hearings and Markup, 5 March-25 June 1985, before the Committee on Foreign Affairs and its Subcommittees on Arms Control, International Security and Science and on International Operations.* on H.R. 2822. 1985, 99th Cong., 2nd Sess., Washington, DC 20515.

1784 United States House. Com. on For. Affairs. Subcom. On Internat. Operations. *Victims of Terrorism Compensation Act: Markup, 8 and 29 October 1985.* 1986, 99th Cong., 1st Sess. Washington, DC. 20515.

1785 United States House Com. on For. Affairs. *Legislation to Combat International Terrorism: 98th Congress: Hearings and Markup, 9 November 1983 - 26 September 1984. Before the Subcommittees on International Security and Scientific Affairs and on International Operations*, on H. Res. 233 and other Bills. 1984, 98th Cong., Washington, DC, 20515.

1786 United States House. *Impact of International Terrorism on Travel: Joint Hearings 19 February - 15 May 1986. Before the Subcommittees on Arms Control. International Security and Science and on International Operations of the Committee on Foreign Affairs and the Subcommittee on Aviation of the Committee on Public Works and Transportation 1986.* 9th Cong., 2nd Sess.

1787 United States House Com. on For. Affairs. Subcom. on Arms Control. *Internat, Security and Science. War Powers, Libya, and State-sponsored Terrorism: Hearings 29 April-15 May 1986.* 1986, 99th Cong., 2nd Sess.

1788 United States House. Com. on Armed Services Investigations Subcom. *Adequacy of U.S. Marine Corps. Security in Beirut: Report,* 19

December 1983, Together with Additional and Dissenting Views. 1983, 98th Cong., 1st Sess., Washington, DC, 20515.

1789 U.S. Israeli Tangle. *Times of India*, 29 January 1985, p. 8.

1790 United States Nat. Defence Univ. *US Strategy to Counter Domestic Political Terrorism*. Motley, James B. 1983.

1791 United States Senate Com. on the Judiciary. Subcom. on Security and Terrorism. *Terrorism in Italy: An Update Report, 1983-1985.* 1985, 99th Cong., 1st Sess., Washington, DC, 20510.

1792 United States. Senate. Com. on Armed Services. *State-Sponsored Terrorism: Hearing,* 28 January 1986. 1986, 99th Con., 2nd Sess.

1793 United States. Senate Com. on the Judiciary Subcom. on Security and Terrorism. *Legislative Initiative to Curb Domestic and International Terrorism: Hearings, 5-13 June 1984, on S, 2470, Anti-Nuclear Terrorism Act of 1984; S. 2623 Aircraft Sabotage Act; S. 2624 Act for the Preventing and Punishment of the Crime of Hostage-taking; S. 2625 Act for Reward for Information Concerning Terrorist Acts; and S. 2626, Prohibition Against the Training Support of Terrorist Organizations Act of 1984.* 1984, 98th Cong., 2nd Sess. Washington, D.C. 20510.

1794 U.S. Senate - Committee on Government Operations. *Peaceful Nuclear Exports and Weapons Proliferation.* 94th Cong., 1st Sess., April 1975.

1795 United States Senate. Committee on the Judiciary. Sumcom. on Security and Terrorism. *Libya-Sponsored Terrorism: A Dilemma for Policymakers, Hearing 19 February 1986, on the Nature and Extent of Libya's Direct Involvement in International Terrorism.* 1986, 99th Cong., 2nd Sess.

1796 United States Senate. Committee on the Judiciary. Subcom. on Security and Terrorism. *Terrorism in the Turkish Experience Hearing,* 25 June 1981. 1981, 97th Cong., 1st Sess., Washington, DC, 20510.

1797 United States. Senate. Committee on the Judiciary. Cubcom. on Security and Terrorism. *Historical Antecedents of Soviet Terrorism: Hearings, 11-12 June 1981.* 1981, 97th Cong., 1st Sess., Washington, DC, 20510.

1798 United States Senate. Committee on the Judiciary, Subcom. on Security and Terrorism. *State-sponsored Terrorism: Report, June 1985*. 1985, 99th Cong., 1st Sess., Washington, DC, 20510.

1799 Use with Care. *Indian Express*, Delhi,, 21 May 1985, p. 6.

1800 Valeriano, Napoleon D. and Bohannon, Charles T.R. *Counterguerrilla Operations: The Phillipine Experience.* New York, Praeger, 1966.

1801 Vallieres, Pierre. *White Niggers of America: The Precocious Autobiography of a Quebac Terrorist.* New York, Monthly Review Press, 1971.

1802 Van, Voris W.H. *Violence in Ulster: an Oral Documentary.* Amherst, University of Massachusetts Press, 1975.

1803 Vance, Cyrus R. Terrorism: Scope of the Threat and Need for Effective Legislation. *Dept. State Bull.*, Number 78, March 1978, pp. 53-55.

1804 Vandalism in Punjab. *Times of India*, 6 December 1983, p. 8.

1805 VanDelen, Hendrik. Terror as a Political Weapon. *Military Police Law Enforcement Journal*, Number 2, Spring 1975, pp. 21-26.

1806 Varma, Paripurnanand. Terrorism-World-Wide Phenomenon. *Hindustan Times*, 19 July 1985, p. 9.

1807 Vas, E.A. Special Units to Deal with Terrorism. *Indian Express*, Delhi, 27 September 1984, p. 6.

1808 Vas, E.A. Punjab - Anatomy of Terrorism. *Hindustan Times*, 15 October 1984, p. 9, p. 11.

1809 Vas, E.A. The Faces of Terrorism. *Monthly Common Indian Economic Conditions*, Volume 26, Number 8, March 1985, pp. 11-12.

1810 Vas. E.A. The Faces of Terrorism. *Seminar*, Number 308, April 1985, pp. 25-29.

1811 Vayrnen, Raimo. Some Aspects of Theory and Strategy of Kidnapping. *Instant Research on Peace and Violence,* Number 1, 1971, pp. 3-21.

1812 Vazeeruddin, Mohammad. Understanding Terrorism. *Tribune,* Magazine Section, 6 January 1986, p. 1.

1813 Venter, Al J. *Africa At War.* Old Greenwich, Conn., Devin-Adair, 1974.

1814 Venter Al J. *The Terror Fighters.* Cape Town and Johannesburg, Purnell, 1969.

1815 Verma, Ravindra. Worse Than Rowlatt Act. *Janata*, Volume 29, Number 21, 20 September 1984, pp. 5-6.

1816 Vernisy, Jacques De. The New International Terrorism: Milliant Regimes Develop a Deadly Alternative to Traditional Diplomacy. *World Press R.*, Number 27, 5 November 1980, pp. 23-25.

1817 Victor, Cacil. International Terrorism: Larger Perspective. *Patriot*, 12 July 1985, p. 4.

1818 Victor, Cacil. Behind International Terrorism. *Mainstream*, Volume 23, Number 47, 20 January 1985, pp. 32-34.

1819 Vidyadharam, Aravind. The Jackal. *Illustrated Wkly. India*, Volume 107, Number 13, 30 March 1986, pp. 28-29.

1820 *Viet Cong Terror Tactics in South Vietnam*. Washington, D.C., Department of State, July 1967.

1821 Violence in Tripura. *National Herald*, 15 April 1985, p. 7.

1822 Viswam, S. Power to use and Misuse. *Deccan Herald*, 24 May 1985, p. 8.

1823 Vital Clues in Blasts Case. *Times of India*, 14 May 1985, p. 1.

1824 Vitiuk, V.V. Toward an Analysis and Evaluation of Terrorism. *Soviet Social*, Number 18, Winter 1979-80, pp. 22-43.

1825 Vitiuk, V.V. *Leftist Terrorism: are the Leftist Terrorists Really Left?* Moscow, Progress Publication, 1985.

1826 Vogler, Theo. Perspectives on Extradition and Terrorism. In Cherif M. Bassiouni (Ed.). *International Terrorism and Political Crimes*. Springfield, Illinois, Charles C. Thomas, 1975.

1827 Valsky, Dmitry. Middle East: The Root Cause. *New Times*, Number 44, October 1985, pp. 14-15.

1828 Vonier, Thomas. Not a Fortress: The New Diplomatic Facilities Meant to Thwart Terrorism Need not be Unattractive nor Interfere with the Mission of the Foreign Service. *For Service J.*, Number 63, July 1986, pp. 22-26.

1829 Voris, W. Van. *Violence in Ulster: an Oral Commentary*, Amherst, 1975.

1830 Wagenlehner, Gunther. Motivation for Political Terrorism in Germany. in Marius H. Livingston (Ed.); with Lee B, Kress; and Marie G. Wanek. *International Terrorism in the Contemporary World*. Westport, Conn., Greenwood Press, 1978, pp. 195-203.

1831 Wagner-Pacifici, Robin E. (Ed.). *The More Morality Play: Terrorism as Social Drama*. Chicago Pr., 1986.

1832 Wahi, Aroon. Combating Trrorism. *Northern India Patrika*, Magazine Section, 20 October 1985, p. 8.

1833 Wahi, Jonathan. Responses to Terrorism : Self-Defense Or Reprisal? *International Problems*, Volume 5, Numbers 1-2, 1973, pp. 28-33.

1834 Walcott, John and Pasztor Andy. Covert Action: Reagan Ruling to Let CIA Kidnap Terrorists Overseas is Disclosed; Decision after

TWA Hijack met Opposition of Aides and Congressional Panels. *Wall St J.*, Volume 209, Number 1, 20 February 1987.

1835 Wallace, Michael. (Ed.). *Terrorism*. Ayer Co. Pubns., 1979.

1836 Walter, Eugene V. *Terror and Resistance: A Study of Political Violence, with Case Studies of some Primitive African Communities.* New York, Oxford University, 1969.

1837 Walter, Eugene V. Violence and the Process of Terror. *American Sociological Review*, 29 April 1964, pp. 248-257.

1838 Waltzer, M. New Terrorists: Random Murder. *New Republic*, 30 August 1975, pp. 12-14.

1839 Walzer, Michael.; Bell, J. Bowyer and Morris, Roger. Terrorism: A Debate. *New Republic*, 27 December 1975. pp. 12-15.

1840 Wannall, W. Raymond. (Ed.). *Who is Tracking the Terrorists?* Nathan Halle Inst., 1984.

1841 War and Terrorism. *National Herald*, 9 November 1985, p. 5.

1842 War Against Terrorism. *Assam Tribune*, 21 October 1985, p. 4.

1843 War of Attrition. *Newsweek*, 1 July 1974, pp. 31-32.

1844 War of Nerves. *Times of India*, 12 September 1985, p. 8.

1845 War on India. *Times of India*, 15 May 1985, p. 8.

1846 Warbrick, Collin. The European Convention on Human Rights and the Prevention of Terrorism. *Internat and Comparative Law Q.*, Number 32, January 1983, pp. 32-119.

1847 Ward, Richard H. The Terrorist Connection: a Pervasive Network. *Police Studies*, Number 8, Winter 1985, pp. 189-197.

1848 Wardlaw, Grant. *Political Terrorism: Theory, Tactics, and Countermeasures.* Cambridge University Press, 1982.

1849 Wardlaw, Grant. Terrorism and Paramilitary Forces. *Pacific Defence Reporter*, Volume 7, Number 1, 1980, pp. 46-51.

1850 Wasmund, Klaus. The Political Socialization of West German Terrorists. in Peter H. Merkl. (Ed.). *Political Violence and Terror.* 1986, pp. 191-228.

1851 Waugh, William L. Jr. The Values in Violence: Organizational and Political Objectives of Terrorist Groups. *Conflict Q.*, Number 3, Summer 1983, pp. 5-19.

1852 Waugh, William L. Jr. *International Terrorism: How Nations Respond to Terrorists*. Chapel Hill, Documentary Pubns., 1983.

1853 Way of Death: Murder of J.A. Swint. *Time,* Volume 102, Number 56, 3 December 1973.

1854 Webb, W. Bomb Squad. *Newsweek,* Volume 84, Number 2, 23 December 1974.

1855 Wechsler, Jill. Terrorism: Business Learns to Cope with Growing Threat. *Assn Mgt.*, Number 30, September 1978, pp. 96-100.
1856 Wedziagoleki, Karol. *Boris Sakinkov: Portrait of a Terrorism*. Suvictochowski, Kingston Pr., 1986.
1857 Weeks, A.L. Terrorism Deadly Tradition. *Freedom at Issue*, Number 46, May-June 1978, pp. 3-11.
1858 Weimann, Gabriel. Media Events: The Case of International Terrorism. *J. Broadcasting and Electronic Media*, Number 31, Winter 1987, pp. 21-39.
1859 Weinberg, Leonard. The Violent Life: An Analysis of Left and Right-wing Terrorism in Italy. in Peter H. Merkl., (Ed.). *Political Violence and Terror.* 1986, pp. 145-167.
1860 Weinberg, Leonard and Eubank William Lee. Italian Women Terrorists. *Terrorism: An International Journal,* Volume 9, Number 3, 1987, pp. 241-262.
1861 Weingarten, Renee. Literary Terrorism. *Commentary*, 1974, pp. 58-65.
1862 Weisband, Edward and Roguly, Damir. Palestinian Terrorism: Violence, Verbal Strategy and Legitimacy. in Yonah, Alexander (Ed.). *International Terrorism: National, Regional, and Global Perspectives*. New York, Praeger Publishers, 1976, pp. 258-319.
1863 Welcome Initiative. *Times of India*, 21 October 1985, p. 8.
1864 Welles, B. IRA Terrorism: No End in Sight. *New Repub.*, Volume 171, Number 17, 7, December 1974.
1865 Wells, Rick. Uganda's Security Nightmare. Alleged Anti-government Rebel Violence. *Africa Rept.*, Number 29, March-April 1984, pp. 24-26.
1866 West Germany and Terrorism. *New Age*, Volume 25, Number 44, 30 October 1977, p. 15.
1867 Westermeyer, J. Assassination in Laos: Its Psychological Dimensions. *Archives of General Psychiatry*, Number 28, May 1974, pp. 740-743.
1868 What Price for Freedom ? Dealing for American Lives. *U.S. News*, Number 99, 8 July 1985, pp. 20-32.
1869 What war on Terrorists is Doing to Life in London. *U.S. News*, Number 77, 23 December 1974.
1870 Whitewash Job. *Times of India*, Delhi, 7 September 1985, p. 8.
1871 Who are the Bomb Throwers? *Society*, Number 11, September 1974, pp. 7-8.

1872 Why Argentina is becoming Land of Vanishing American. *U.S. News*, Number 76, 11 March 1974, pp. 59-60.

1873 Wicker, Tom. Usual Suspects. *Amrita Bazar Patrika*, 5 August 1985, p. 6.

1874 Wiener Library Bulletin. Scope and Limit of a Fedayeen Consensus. *Idem,* 1970-1971, pp. 1-8.

1875 Wilcox, Laird. Master Bibliography on Political Psychology and Propaganda; Espionage and Intelligence Operations; and Terrorism and Assassination. *Editorial Research Service*, 1985.

1876 Wilkinson, Paul. State-Sponsored International Terrorism: The Problems of Response. *The World Today*, Number 40, July 1984, pp. 292-298.

1877 Wilkinson, Paul. Armenian Terrorism Background; Recent Incidents Throughout the World. *The World Today*, Number 39, September 1983, pp. 344-350.

1878 Wilkinson, Paul. Terrorism: International Dimensions, Answering the Challenge. *Conflict Studies*, Number 113, Institute for the Study of Conflict, 1979, p. 8.

1879 Wilkinson, Paul. Terrorism: The International Response. *The World Today*, Number 34, 1978, pp. 5-13.

1880 Wilkinson, Paul. Three Questions on Terrorism. *Government and Opposition,* Volume 8, Number 3, 1973, pp. 290-312.

1881 Wilkinson, Paul. Still Working for the Extinction of Mankind: An Assessment of the Significance of the Resurgence of the Fascist Terrorism in Western Europe. *Across the Board,* Number 18, January 1981, pp. 27-30.

1882 Willenz, Eric. U.S. Policy on Terrorism: Search of an Answer. *Terrorism: An International Journal*, Volume 9, Number 3, 1987, pp. 225-240.

1883 Willey, F and Others. Kuala Lumpur Caper. *Newsweek,* 18 August 1975.

1884 Willey, F. New-look Rogues Gallery. *Newsweek*, 5 January 1976, pp. 27-29.

1885 Williams, Hubert. Terrorism and Local Police. *Terrorism: An International Journal*, Volume 8, Number 1986, pp. 345-350.

1886 Williams, Timothy. The Message of the Bombs: The Resurgence of Political Violence Last Year in Guadeloupe was a Stark Reminder of the Tensions beneath the Affluent surface of France's Carribbean Territories. *Carribbean and West Indies Chronicle*, Number 99, April-May 1984, pp. 6-7.

1887 Willrich, M. Terrorists keep out: Problem of Safeguarding Nuclear Materials. *Bulletin Atom Science*, Number 31, May 1975, pp. 12-16.

1888 Willrich, M. *Civil Nuclear Power and International Security*. New York, Praeger Publishers, 1971.

1889 Wilson, Clifton E. *Diplomatic Privileges and Immunities*. Tucson, Arizona, University of Arizona Press, 1967.

1890 Wilson, Colin and Seaman Donald. *The Encyclopedia of Modern Murder, 1962-1982*. New York, Putnam 1985.

1891 Wilson, Colin. *Order of Assassins : The Psychology of Murder*. London, Rupert Hart Davis, 1972.

1892 Winchester, J.H. Kidnapping Unlimited. *Readers' Digest,* Number 105, July 1974, pp. 70-74.

1893 Winegarten, Renee. Literary Terrorism. *Commentary*, March 1974, pp. 58-65.

1894 Wise, C. and others. Countering Terrorism: The U.S. and Israeli Approach. *Middle East Review,* Volume 9, Number 3, 1977, pp. 55-59.

1895 Wishing Extremists Away. *Search Light*, 4 November 1985, p. 6.

1896 Woetzel, Robert K. The Potential role of an International Criminal Court. *In International Terrorism: Proceedings of an Intensive Panel at the 15th Annual Convention of the International Studies Association*. Institute of World Affairs, University of Wisconsin, Milwaukee, 1974, pp. 73-84.

1897 Wohlstetter, Roberta. Kidnapping to win Friends and Influence People. *Survey,* Number 20, Autumn 1974, pp. 1-40.

1898 Woito, Robert. *To End War - A New Approach to International Conflict*. New York, Pilgrim Press, 1982.

1899 Wolf, John B. Anti-terrorism: Operations and Controls in a Free Society. *Police Studies,* Number 1, September 1978, pp. 35-41.

1900 Wolf, John B. An Analytical Framework for the Study and Control of Agitational Terrorism. *Police Journal,* July-September 1976, pp. 165-171.

1901 Wolf, John B. Controlling Political Terrorism in a Free society. *Orbis,* Number 19, Winter 1976, pp. 1289-1308.

1902 Wolf, John B. Organization and Management Practices of Urban Terrorist Groups. *Terrorism: An International Journal*, Volume 1, Number 2, 1978, pp. 169-86.

1903 Wolf, John B. Prisons, Courts and Terrorism: The American and West German Experience. *Police Journal,* 1977, pp. 221-230.

1904 Wolf, John B. Terrorist Manipulation of the Democratic Process. *Political Journal,* April-June 1975, pp. 102-112.

1905 Wolf, John B. Global Terrorist Coalition: Its Incipient Stage. *Police Journal*, England, October-December 1977, pp. 328-339.

1906 Wolf, John B. Black September: Militant Palestinianism. *Current History,* Numbers 5, 8, 37, 1973.

1907 Wolf, John B. Urban Terrorist Operations. *Police Journal,* England, Number 49, October-December 1976, pp. 277-284.

1908 Wolf, John B. Terrorist Manipulation of the Democratic Process. *Police Journal*, England, April-June 1975, pp. 102-112.

1909 Wolf, John B. British Anti-terrorist Policy in Northern Ireland: Legal Aspects. *Police Chief*, Number 50, April 1983, pp. 36-40.

1910 Wolf, John B. *Fear of Fear: A Survey of Terrorist Operations and Controls in open Societies*. New York, Plenum Pr., 1981.

1911 Wolf, John B. Enforcement Terrorism (use of terrorism by States to Enforce the Status quo). *Police Studies*, Number 3, Winter 1981, pp. 45-54.

1912 Wolfgang, Marain E. (Ed.). *International Terrorism*. Sage, 1982.

1913 Woods, C. Problems of International Terrorism. *Australian Journal of Forensic Sciences*, Volume 12, Numbers 2-3, 1979-1980, pp. 67-74.

1914 Woodward, K. Now the Violent Woman. *Newsweek*, Volume 86, Number 29, 6 October 1975.

1915 World Terrorism Flares Anew Nothing Seems to Stop it. *U.S. News*, Number 78, 17 March 1975, pp. 25-26.

1916 Worse and Worse in Lanka. *Tribune*, 10 December 1984, p. 4.

1917 Wright, Jeffrey W. Terrorism: A Mode of Warfare, Emphasis on the October 1983 Bombing of the Marine Headquarters in Beirut; Implications of International Terrorism for Conventional Military Forces. *Military Review*, Number 64, October 1984, pp. 64-85.

1918 Wright, Robin. *Sacred Rage: The Crusade of Modern Islam*. Simon, 1985.

1919 Wrong Place and Time: Kidnapping of Er. Morgan by Terrorist. *Time*, Volume 106, Number 27, 21 July 1975.

1920 Yahalom, Dan. File on Arab Terrorism. *Journal*, Carts, 1973.

1921 Yalcin, Aydin. Sources of Terrorism in Turkey. *Wall St J.*, Volume 197, Number 20, 22 July 1981.

1922 Year of Terrorist. *National Review*, Number 28, 23 January 1976, pp. 21-22.

1923 You can't Escape. *Newsweek*, Volume 84, Number 42, 30 September 1974.

1924 Young, R. Revolutionary Terrorism, Crime and Morality. *Social Theory and Practice*, Volume 4, Number 3, 1977, pp. 287-302.

1925 Zahn, G.C. Terrorism for Peace and Justice. *Commonwealth*, 23 October 1970, pp. 84-85.

1926 Zawodny, J.K. Infrastructures of Terrorist Organizations. *Conflict Q.*, Number 1, Spring 1981.

1927 Zileri, Enrique. Peru's Internal War: A Latin American Democracy's Struggle Against Terrorism (the Sendero Luminoso Movement). *World Press R.*, Number 31, December 1984, pp. 28-30.

1928 Zilian, Frederick. Jr. The U.S. Raid on Libya and NATO. *Orbis*, Number 30, Fall 1986, pp. 499-524.

1929 Zinam, Oleg. Terrorism and Violence in the Light of a Theory of Discontent and Frustration. in Marius H. Livingstone. (Ed.).; with Lee B. Kress; and Marie G. Wanek. *International Terrorism in the Contemporary World.* Westport, Conn., Greenwood Press, 1978, pp. 240-265.

1930 Zivic, J. The Non-aligned and the Problem of International Terrorism. *Review of International Affairs*, Number 24, 20 January 1973, pp. 6-8.

1931 Zlataric, Bogdan. History of International Terrorism and its Legal Control. In Cherif M. Bassiouni. (Ed.). *International Terrorism and Political Crimes*. Springfield Illinois, Charles C. Thomas, 1975, pp. 474-484.

1932 Zubkowski, L. Kos-Rabcewicz. The Creation of an International Criminal Court. in Cherif M. Bassiouni. (Ed.). *International Terrorism and Political Crimes.* Springfield, Illinois, Charles C. Thomas, 1975, pp. 519-536.

# PART — IV

# FORTHCOMING PUBLICATIONS

01 Anderson, Mary. *Terror Under the Tent*. New York, Dell, November 1987.

02 Ashwood, Tom. *Terror in the Skies*. New York, Stein and Day, March 1987.

03 Ashwood, Tom. *Terror in the Skies*. New York, Stein and Day, 1986.

04 Béres, Louis Réne. *Terrorism and Global Security in the Nuclear Threat.* 2nd Review, Boulder, Westview, March 1987.

05 Bonnie, Szumski. (Ed.). *Terrorism: Opposing View Points.* Shoreview Park Road, Greenhaven, September 1986.

06 Brightfield, Richard. *Terror on Kabran*. New York, Bentam, August 1986.

07 Carlton, Bea. *Terror in the Night*. Denver, Accen Bks., September 1986.

08 Carter, Nick. *Terror Times Two*. New York, Charter Bks., Acc Bks., 1987.

09 Carter, Nick. *Terror Code*. Denver, Acc Bks., April 1987.

10 Chaliand, Gerard. *Terrorism from Popular Struggle to Media Spectable*. U.K. Bks., August 1987.

11 Coker, Christopher. *Terrorism*. New York, Watto, October 1986.

12 Coker, Christopher. *Terrorism and Civil Strife*. New York, Watts, October 1987.

13 Conrad, S. *Terrorism: The Holocaust and the Urgent need for the Establishment of a Palestinian State*. Inst. of Eco. Pol., November 1986.

14 Cross, Gilbert. *Terror Train*. New York, Macmillan, March 1987.

15 Canadian, Darshan S. *Terrorism in Punjab: Selected Articles and Speeches.* Columbia, South Asia Bks., n.d.

16 Edson, J.T. *Terror Valley.* New York, Berkley Pub., February 1987.

17 Frederick, Pohl. *Terror*. New York, Barkley Pub., February 1987.

18 Hanrahan, Gene Z. *Terrorism Two Thousand.* Chapel Hill, Documentary Pubns., Postponed.

19 Horowitz, Irving L. et al. *Terrorism Legitimacy and Power: The Consequences of Political Violence.* Warleyan U. Pr., October 1986.

20 Hyde, Margaret O. and Forsyth, Elizabeth H. *Terrorism: a Special Kind of Violence*. March 1987.

21 Koltz, Tony. *Terror Island*. New York, Bentam, August 1986.

22 Laqueur, Walter and Yonah Alexander. Rev. (Ed.). *Terrorism Reader*. NAL, June 1987.

23 Laqueur, Walter and Yonah Alexander. *Terrorism Reader: A Historical Anthology*. Orig., NAL, March 1987.

24 Lightbody, Andy. *Terrorism Survival Guide: 101 Travel Tips on how to become a Victim*. New York, Dell, April 1987.

25 Michael, Connor. *Terrorism: its Goals, its Targets, its Methods, the Solutions*. Boulder, Paladin Pr., January 1987.

26 Netanyahu, Benjamin. *Terrorism: How the West can Win*. New York, Avon, April 1987.

27 O'Neil, Michael, J. *Terrorist Spectaculars: Should TV Coverage be Curbed*. New York, Priority for Pubns. September 1986.

28 Pierce, Joe E. *Terrorism in the Middle East and You*. Hapi Pr., September 1986.

29 Raynor, Thomas P. *Terrorism: Past, Present, Future*. Watts, March 1987.

30 Seth, McEvoy. *Terror at Play*. Archway, January 1987.

31 *Terror in The Dark*. World Wide Harleuin Bks., n.d.

32 Whitewall, Conrad S. *Terrorism: The Holocaust and the Urgent Need for the Establishment of A Palestinian State*. Inst. Eco. Pol., November 1986.

33 Zimmerman, Dwight J. *Terror for President*. New York, Western Pub., Golden Bks., August 1986.

# Author Index

# Subject Index